ARISTOTLE'S THEORY
OF PRACTICAL COGNITION

81

ae Beitzinger

ARISTOTLE'S THEORY
OF PRACTICAL COGNITION

by

TAKATURA ANDO
Okayama University

THIRD EDITION

THE HAGUE / MARTINUS NIJHOFF / 1971

first edition 1958
second edition 1965
third edition 1971

ISBN 90 247 5027 X

PRINTED IN THE NETHERLANDS

PREFACE

I have much pleasure in writing a preface to Mr. Takatura Ando's book
on Aristotle. Apart from his intrinsic importance, as one of the three or
four greatest of all philosophers, Aristotle is important on having given
for many centuries the greatest influence in moulding the thought of
European countries. The language difficulty has no doubt prevented
him from exercising very much influence on Japanese thought, and I
welcome very warmly to hear that Mr. Ando is about to have his book
printed in Japan. I hope it will be widely circulated, as it must certainly deserve that.

1958   W. D. Ross

AUTHOR'S FOREWORD

In publishing this book, I cannot prohibit myself of reminding the days and nights when it was written. In that era of worldwide madness, Aristotle's philosophy was the only refuge wherein my depressed mind could come to life. It was written bit by bit under all desperate circumstances throughout the war time. My heart was set on the completion of this work while the fate allowed me to live. It was nearly carried out by the end of the war. Having no hope of survival, I buried my manuscript in the earth, without however any expectance of a better lot for it.

The situation grew worse and worse. Towns and cities were burnt and perished day by day. There remained only few of them. In a summer night of 1945, an inauspicious siren blew as if pronouncing our end. I let my wife take refuge with the child, and lay alone on the ground beside the hole in which my manuscript was stored. The blue sky was scattered with twinkling stars, and the buzzying of airplanes came far over from the depth of serene night. I was gazing at the stars with resignation and despise of human nature, but the corps passed over my head without making any attack. A few minutes later, the sky grew red near the horizon, and I found that the victim of that night was the unfortunate neighbour city. After a few days the citizens of Hiroshima and Nagasaki met the utmost misery in history. The war was over, and I survived with my manuscript.

Since that time I tried to publish this manuscript only in vain. At last, I came to the idea to translate it in English and show it to Sir W. D. Ross. When this idea was realized, to my great joy, he gave me a letter full of favour. He acknowledged that he was of the same opinion with regard to many of my arguments, and guaranteed that my treatise would be able to contribute to modern study of Aristotle.

Being much encouraged by this letter and following his advice, I engaged in revising my English with the aid of Dr. S. Nivison of Stanford University. Now, I am firmly convinced of myself being the most fortunate fellow who lived under that starry heaven, not only to enjoy again the Lipton Tea, of which I sadly dreamed in those dreary nights, but also to get the favour of an eminent British scholar, not only to taste again Californian raisins that I vainly desired in those weary days, but also to receive kindness of an excellent American scholar.

I owe my English also to my former colleague Mr. Tyuzo Utidate, who read through my manuscript and gave many advices. My special thanks are due to Prof. John D. Goheen of Stanford University, who paid warm attention to my work and gave me some help. I am grateful to Miss Nobuko Iwai for her assistance. As regards the English rendering of the text, I owe much to Oxford translations and Hick's De Anima.

Kyoto, 1958   T. A.

PREFACE TO THE THIRD EDITION

Owing to the perennial importance of the subject matter, the previous editions of this book succeeded in attracting some attention in spite of its faults both in style and arguments to say nothing of terrible errors of typography. It is partly for this reason that the author ventured to publish the new edition. But in truth, a more important motive lies in the author's desire to recover his self-respect, which was much injured by his immature work. To this purpose, the text was thoroughly re-written, without, however, making any fundamental change as to the main tenet except corrections and additional notes ensued from the reference to some recent works especially of I. J. Walsh and W. F. R. Hardie.

It is an irony of history that the revision was undertaken amid the riot of student power. One quarter of a century has passed since the tragic end of the war. It appears as if the young generation is tired of the peace. They do not demand this kind of work. Perhaps it would be the destiny of the philosopher to think *sub specie aeternitatis*.

Okayama, 1969.   T. A.

TABLE OF CONTENTS

INTRODUCTION

Among the difficulties of Aristotle interpretation, there are two problems of crucial importance, both concerned with the concept of reason, viz., the so-called νοῦς ποιητικός in the *De Anima* and the πρακτικὸς νοῦς in the *Ethica Nicomachea*, though strictly speaking these terms are not found in Aristotle's own statement. νοῦς ποιητικός is opposed to νοῦς παθητικός or νοῦς δυνάμει and forms the core of immortal agent, while πρακτικὸς νοῦς constitutes a part of practical intellect or practical syllogism. These concepts appear in Aristotle's thought independently from different points of view. The νοῦς in the *De Anima* is treated as a substance or an agent of thinking, while in the *Ethica Nicomachea* it is treated as a special function. Whence comes this difference of view points may form an interesting subject of inquiry, which however, we cannot engage in for the moment.

The chief end of this study is to solve the questions concerning practical wisdom, for instance: "What is the function of practical intellect, including of course πρακτικὸς νοῦς in the strict sense?" "What is the construction of practical reasoning?" "How is it distinguished from theoretical reasoning?" "What is the relation between desire, will and intellect with each other?" "In what sense Aristotle admitted moral responsibility and what is the so-called moral weakness?" and so on.

To solve these fundamental questions of Aristotle's ethical theory, this study adopts the wide scope method, and instead of confining itself to a logico-philological investigation in some particular statements in the *Ethica*, it takes a survey of the whole corpus, especially *De Anima* and other biological and physiological books, whereby a special aid is sought in the νοῦς concept in the *De Anima*, which gives a leading principle for the division of the soul, and thus illustrates the interrelation of various mental functions. But apart from this contribution to

the problem of practical intellect, the νοῦς-problem in the *De Anima*
deserves special attention as one of the chief traditional themes of
metaphysica specialis, viz. whether, what part, if any, and in what sense
the soul is immortal.

CHAPTER I

THE STRUCTURE OF THE SOUL

1. Soul and Body

In considering an object, Aristotle always attempts to reduce it to one of his categories. But when he states that the soul is substance, he not only reduces it to the category of substance, but also identifies it with the substance itself.[1] Now the term "substance" has many meanings. Sometimes it means matter, sometimes form, sometimes an individual composed of matter and form. Dealing with the soul, Aristotle at first points out the three meanings of substance,[2] and argues that substance in the proper sense is the body composed of form and matter, especially a natural body or the body which is organized by nature. Of these natural bodies, some have life, and some do not. Hence, a natural body possessed of life must be a substance composed of matter and form. The body which is common to living and lifeless entities being the matter, the formal principle of a living entity must be the soul, which therefore, is said to be substance in the sense of form. It is substance, not in the sense of substratum, but in the sense of a formal principle that gives life to a material body, or rather, it is the life itself.[3]

[1] Strictly speaking, to ask what is the substance, i.e. the essence or definition, of the soul is one thing, to reduce it to the category of substance is another, and to make it the substance of the body is yet another. *De An.* I. 1. 402 a 7: ἐπιζ-ητοῦμεν δὲ θεωρῆσαι καὶ γνῶναι τήν τε φύσιν αὐτῆς καὶ τὴν οὐσίαν, is the first case; *ibid.* 402 a 23: πρῶτον δ'ἴσως ἀναγκαῖον ἐν τίνι τῶν γενῶν καὶ τί ἐστι, λέγω δὲ πότερον τόδε τι καὶ οὐσία ἢ ποιὸν ἢ ποσὸν ἢ καί τις ἄλλη τῶν διαιρεθεισῶν κατηγοριῶν, is the second; and *ibid.* II. 1. 412 a 19: ἀναγκαῖον ἄρα τὴν ψυχὴν οὐσίαν εἶναι ὡς εἶδος σώματος φυσικοῦ δυνάμει ζωὴν ἔχοντος, must be the third. Concerning the difference between the expressions εἶδος τι and εἶδος τινος, which holds also for the case of οὐσία τις and οὐσία τινος, cf. Jaeger, *Aristoteles*, 44, and Nuyens *L'évolution de la psychologie d'Aristote*, 85.

[2] *De An.* II. 1. 412 a 6; 2. 414 a 15; cf. *Met.* VII. 10. 1035 a 2; 15. 1039 b 21; VIII. 2. 1043 a 19; X. 3. 1054 b 4; XII. 3. 1070 a 9, 12; 4. 1070 b 13.

[3] *De An.* II. 2. 414 a 18; *De Juvent.* I. 467 b 14.

Seeing that the animal is a natural being endowed with life, and the principle of life being the soul, the soul seems to be definable as a form of a natural being possessed of life. But this expression appeared for Aristotle not to be strict enough, for the expression "a natural being possessed of life" involves the idea of form, because life is the formal principle of living being, therefore the definition "the form of a natural being possessed of life" would involve the idea of form twice. The substratum, to which form belongs, should be, strictly speaking, "a natural being *potentially* possessed of life." Thus we come to Aristotle's definition of the soul: "substance, in the sense of the form of a natural being, potentially possessed of life."[4]

It is said, on the other hand, that form is the actuality of matter, matter the potentiality of form.[5] It follows therefore that substance in the sense of form is an actuality, and the soul is the actuality of the body.[6] But ἐντελέχεια or actuality has two meanings. It may be explained by the analogy of ἐπιστήμη and θεωρία, i.e. knowledge and contemplation.[7] Compared with ignorance, knowledge has already a form, which however is not completely actual like the act of contemplation. The potentiality of contemplation in a layman is merely passive, and requires studying before it can develop; but the potentiality of an educated man is an active power which can develop by itself into contemplation, and may educate an ignorant man.

δύναμις i.e. potentiality or possibility has also many meanings: most often it is used in a passive sense. As is explained elsewhere,[8] when the

---

[4] *De An.* II. 1. 412 a 19.

[5] *Met.* IX. 8. 1050 b 2; a 16; *De An.* II. 1. 412 a 10; 2. 414 a 17; cf. *Met.* VIII. 2. 1043 a 20; 3. 1043 a 33; b 1; XII. 5. 1071 a 9.

[6] *De An.* II. 1. 412 a 21.

[7] *De An.* II. 1. 412 a 9; *Met.* X. 6. 1048 a 34; *Phys.* VIII. 4. 255 a 33; *De Sensu.* 4. 441 b 22; *Gen. An.* II. 1. 735 a 9; Trendelenburg, *De An.* 314 f.; Boniz, *Met.* II. 394.

[8] *De An.* II. 5. 417 a 21–b 15; cf. Ando, *Aristoteles no Sonzairon* 1958, p. 197 ff. The summary of this inquiry is as follows: – Aristotle admitted two kinds of potentiality: the principle of motion or change in another or in the thing itself *qua* other, and the principle of being moved or changed by another or by the thing itself *qua* other. The one may be called active potentiality or potency, and the other passive potentiality. According to this definition, potentiality belongs to an actual being. On account of this actual basis, this kind of potentiality essentially tends to take a single direction, though this appears to be inconsistent with Aristotle's own statement that every potentiality is "the potentiality of opposites." Potentiality involves in itself motion and rest, or more generally, being and not-being; it may become actual or may not become actual, but in either case it is the cause of motion or being, not the cause of rest or not-being. This fundamental character of potentiality is applicable even to rational poten-

term δύναμις is restricted to the passive sense and signifies the potentiality of thinking in an ignorant man, the active potentiality in an educated man is expressed by the term ἕξις or *habitus*. Compared with the passive potentiality of the material element, it is in a sense a formal principle and an actuality, yet it falls short of the complete actuality and remains in a sense potential. In what sense, then, is the soul said to be actuality? It exists continuously, whether man is awake or asleep. If it ceases to exist when we are asleep and exists again when we are awake, it would by no means be the unity of a person or the living principle of an animal. Now sleeping is related to waking just as knowledge is related to contemplation. The soul, therefore, is the actuality of the body, not like that of contemplation, but like that of knowledge. In other words, the soul is the first actuality of a natural body, potentially possessed of life.[9] Such a natural body being called an organism, the soul may also be called the first actuality of an organic body.[10]

cy, which is considered by Aristotle to be referring to contrary ends. Even passive potentiality, which is *prima facie* quite indefinite and neutral, must have some particular quality as far as it is the principle of motion and reality. The matter of a particular thing must be confined to a particular kind, as Aristotle puts it: *De An.* II. 8. 419 b 14: "It is not concussion of any two things taken at random which constitutes sound." Seeing that even passive potentiality tends to one direction, we must conclude that potentiality as the principle of motion or reality cannot be purely passive and of neutral character.

On the other hand, passive potentiality is assigned to matter as against active potentiality is to form. The pair concepts of matter and form are presumably earlier in his development of thought than those of potentiality and actuality. Aristotle might have constructed his metaphysical theory by elaborating the concepts of matter and form into those of potentiality and actuality. The elaboration was conducted most successfully without however eradicating the fundamental heterogeneity of the two pairs of concepts. Although form corresponds to actuality, and matter to potentiality, neither is form identical with actuality, nor matter with potentiality. The potentiality which goes with matter is only the passive, while the active potentiality is rather homologous with form. It may be said that passive potentiality is the form immanent in matter, or the matter as far as it is considered to be the basis upon which a form is realized, whereas form as such is actuality, but as far as it lacks in and demands matter as its substratum, it is active potentiality.

Active potentiality especially tends to one direction on account of its real foundation. In this point, active potentiality is approximate to ἕξις or habitus. This is one-sided and has real foundation to a larger extent. On the other hand, passive potentiality approaches to ἐνδεχόμενον or possibility. This is two-sided and neutral, being devoid of real foundation, so that it is essentially combined with opposite possibility, and what is possible to be is also possible not to be. The so-called primary matter is most likely in this state. Cf. Hick's note on *De An.* 412 a 27.

[9] *De An.* II. 1. 412 a 27.
[10] *De An.* II. 1. 462 b 5.

This "first" means, however, not "excellent," but rather incomplete
and rudimentally: we might as well say that the soul is the "second
potentiality" of the body, or its ἕξις.

Soul is the substance, in the sense of form, or it may be called the
substance of an organic natural body. It may also be called the λόγος,
the concept, or the essence of such a natural being.[11] For example, if
an axe were a natural body, to be an axe would be its essence or soul.
But, since in fact, the axe is not a natural body, but an artificial tool,
to speak of the "soul" of an axe is nothing more than a metaphor. At
any rate, the cutting function of the axe, seeing of the eye, and the
waking state of the soul, are complete actuality, i.e., actuality in the
second sense.

The soul is the first or incomplete actuality, just like the cutting
faculty of the axe or the seeing faculty of the eye; the body, which is
the substratum of the soul, is lower than that; it is a potentiality to the
soul, just as iron is to the axe, and the pupil is to the eye. As the axe is
an iron possessed of cutting ability, the eye a pupil possessed of sight,
so a living being is a body possessed of soul; it is constituted of soul
and body.[12] As is evident from the above analogy, this constitution is
not a mechanical composition, but an organic unity. Hence it is said
that there is no need to inquire whether soul and body are one, any
more than whether the wax and the imprint are one.[13] Not that body
and soul, existing independently, compose a living being mechanically,
but that soul is the active power in body, body the tool whereby soul
exhibits itself.[14] As far as the soul is the actuality of the body, they are
really inseparable, and can be distinguished only in conception. Aristotle's theory is neither dualism, which composes the thing from presupposed independent elements, nor monism, which deduces many from
the one; it accords more successfully to our present scientific view of
the soul than are some modern metaphysical theories.[15]

Aristotle, of course, does not remain a positivist; his philosophical
interest tends towards metaphysics. As aforesaid, soul and body are

[11] De An. II. 4. 412 a 19; b 16; Met. VII. 10. 1035 b 14; 11. 1037 a 15; Gen.
An. II. 4. 738 b 27; Met. VIII. 3. 1043 b 34; λόγος would be the expression of
εἶδος and τὸ τί ἦν εἶναι is the most special form which determines the being completely.

[12] De An. II. 1. 412 b 19–413 a 3; Met. VII. 11. 1037 a 5.

[13] De An. II. 1. 412 b 6.

[14] De An. II. 4. 415 b 18; cf. Zeller, Ph. d. Gr. II. 2. 486; Baeumker, Das
Problem der Materie in der griechischen Philosophie, 262.

[15] Scheler, Die Stellung des Menschen im Kosmos, V. 1; cf. Nuyens, op. cit.
73–78.

different only in concept, but identical in reality. Yet there is a further question: the soul, in so far as it is the actuality of the body, is really inseparable from it, to be sure, but if there should be another soul which is not the actuality of the body, such a soul will be separable in reality as well.[16] Is there, really, such a transcendent soul, which is quite independent of the body?

For such a question to be possible, some specific difference must be admitted. The fact that there is a difference of degree among living beings, though all have souls, suggests the existence of specific difference in the souls themselves.[17] Against the transmigration theory, which only admits differences as to souls and neglects bodily difference, Aristotle maintains that such an opinion is as absurd as the supposition that the art of building could embody itself in a flute.[18] In the same way, we might say that it is as absurd as to admit only bodily difference without admitting difference of souls. His not mentioning this side of the matter could hardly have been due to carelessness, but was only because this was too evident to be worth mentioning.

Of course, if the differences of the soul are completely parallel to those of the body, there is no room for a transcendent soul to exist. Once the soul is defined as the form of the body, *ex hypothesi*, it is not independent of the body. But is it so self-evident a fact that the soul is not independent of the body? Is it really an *a priori* definition that the soul is the form of the body? Perhaps this is not the case. What we understand under soul is rather something which thinks, perceives, moves and takes nourishment; it is the unity of these functions, or the subject which underlies them. "The form of the body" is an idea, which is arrived at inductively from the empirical observation of these functions. If on the contrary, we simply start from the definition of the soul as the form of the body, and thereby deny the existence of a separable soul, this, without doubt, is a *petitio principii* and nothing else. A true positivist should rather at first observe and compare various forms of soul, and then decide whether there is a transcendent soul or not. This seems to be the way which Aristotle really followed. That the soul is the form of the body is not, for the moment, an ultimate definition, but a mere hypothesis,[19] since it does not decisively rule out the possibility of transcendent soul.

---

[16] *De An.* II. 1. 413 a 4–8; *Gen. An.* II. 3. 736 b 21; *Part. An.* I. 1. 641 b 9 f.

[17] Cf. Brentano, *Die Psychologie des Aristoteles*, 53.

[18] *De An.* II. 2. 414 a 28; I. 3. 407 b 13 ff.

[19] *De An.* II. 2. 413 a 11 ff.; 3. 414 b 20 ff.; 415 a 12. According to Nuyens, this is the final stage of thought which Aristotle attained in his last period. But

To divide the soul into parts and admit a transcendent soul, this is not an attempt original to Aristotle, but a metaphysical heritage from Plato and his predecessors. On the other hand, the souls as the form of the body, even this idea of empirical trend is not entirely original.[20] When Plato says that the soul is the principle of life, whereby one can act as a living body, there is hardly any difference between the two philosophers. The only difference is in to what extent they admitted the separability of the soul. As we shall see later, Aristotle in fact limited the separability more narrowly than Plato, but generally speaking he never denied it completely. In this respect, as in other references, Aristotle was a successor to, no less than an opponent of, his master. He could not avoid to be an opponent in order to be a true successor – this is surely a destined course of every great disciple. To make the soul the form of the body, this, without doubt, is the most suitable view for Aristotle as a great biologist. But the fact that he could not stop there, proves that he was very much a metaphysician[21] in the tradition of Platonism.

It is well known that Plato divided the soul into three parts, the λογιστικόν or the reasoning part, the θυμικόν or the passionate, and the ἐπιθυμητικόν or the appetitive.[22] A pseudo-Aristotelian script, *Magna Moralia* also ascribes to Plato the duopartite theory, which divides the soul into the λόγον ἔχον or the rational, and the ἄλογον or the irratio-

even Nuyens could not deny that Aristotle preserved to the last the transcendent reason which is independent of the body; cf. *op. cit.* 311 ff.

[20] Plato, *Phaedo*, 105 C: "Tell me, then, what is that of which the inherence will render the body alive?" *Crat.* 399 D: "If I am to say what occurs to me at the moment, I should imagine that those who first used the name ψύχη meant to express that the soul when in the body is the source of life, and gives the power of breath and revival, and when this reviving power fails then the body perishes and dies, and this, if I am not mistaken, they called psyche." Corresponding to these passages we find in Aristotle, *De An.* I. 1. 402 a 6: "the soul being virtually the principle of all animal life." *Ibid.* II. 4. 415 b 8: "Now the soul is cause and origin of the living body." *Ibid.* II. 2. 414 a 12: "Now the soul is that whereby primarily we live, perceive, and have understanding": *Part. An.* I. 1. 641 a 18–21: "If now this something that constitutes the form of the living being be the soul, or part of the soul, or something that without the soul cannot exist";

[21] Hence we cannot easily yield to Nuyen's hypothesis, which admits three stages of development in Aristotle's concept of the soul, viz., "the earliest view of mechanism," "the transitional view of instrumentalism," "and the final view of hylemorphism," These three kinds of view are rather juxtaposed with one another and none of which is entirely abandoned. That Aristotle remained a metaphysician till the last period, Nuyens confirms none the less. Cf. *op. cit.* 54.

[22] Plato, *Rep.* 4. 435–442; 6. 504 A. 8. 550 A. 9. 571; 580 E; 581; *Tim.* 69 E–72; 89 E; *Leg.* 9. 863.

nal.[23] As for Plato himself, he mentions the duopartite theory, not however as his own, and Aristotle also treats the two theories distinctively in the *De Anima*.[24] Now that the tripartite theory is proper to Plato, the other must be ascribed to someone else. It may be, as Hicks conjectures, a vulgar opinion before Plato, which provided a basis for his tripartite theory. In his early work, the *Topica*, Aristotle is still following in the main Plato's theory.[25] According to Arnim, this is not a division of the faculties, but of the substantial parts of the soul itself,[26] for functional parts would stand parallel to each other without mutual interference as is seen between βούλησις and ἐπιθυμία in Plato's treatment, the former namely operating in the reasoning part, the latter in the appetitive, thus each part has a special power of reasoning and desiring, and struggles with the other. Nor is such a division, according to Arnim, a difference of viewpoints, just as a sphere appears convex from the outside and concave from the inside; parts thus divided by viewpoints never conflict with each other.

It is true that Plato's tripartite theory is, in the main, a substantial division, and Aristotle may have been following the master's theory in his early period of the *Topica*. But in the middle or later period, as we see his thought in the *De Anima* or in the *Ethica Nicomachea*, the tripartite theory is criticized and there appears a reflection upon the principle of division. Thus, Aristotle asks whether there are various kinds of soul, or is there one soul with several parts, and if the latter is the case, whether these parts are divided conceptually or are they separable τόπῳ i.e. by place.[27] The term τόπῳ is somewhat ambiguous, and is rendered elsewhere by such words as ἀριθμῷ "numerically," κατὰ μέγεθος "by magnitude," or πεφυκότα "naturally," as if Aristotle was embarrassed in finding a suitable expression.[28] At any rate, what

[23] *Mag. Mor.* I. 1. 1182 a 23.
[24] *De An.* III. 9. 432 a 25.
[25] Hick's note on 432 a 26; 411 b 25. Régis assigns this division to Pythagoras; cf. L'opinion selon Aristote, 58.
[26] Arnim, *Das Ethische im Aristotelischen Topik*, 6–12; Strümpel, *Die Geschichte der theoretischen Philosophie*, 324 ff.; Zeller, *Ph. d. Gr.* II. 2. 499 n. 5. The following proposition seems to prove Arnim's opinion. *De An.* III. 9. 432 b 3–7: Then besides these there is appetency, which would seem to be distinct both in concept and in capacity from all the foregoing. And surely it is absurd to split this up. For wish in the rational part corresponds to concupiscence and passion in the irrational.
[27] *De An.* I. 1. 402 b 1; II. 2. 413 b 13; III. 4. 429 a 10; *Eth. Nic.* I .13. 1102 a 28.
[28] Aristotle might have avoided the word οὐσία because it has many meanings, "concept" being only one of these meanings.

is implied by these expressions seems to be something more than a mere difference of concept or a difference due to viewpoints.

There is no doubt, in the first place, that the soul is divisible conceptually.[29] The division of the soul into the vegetable, the animal, and the human, or the division into the nourishing, the sensible, and the reasoning, may be regarded as a conceptual division, the principle of which being the functional differences of the soul.[30] But not all divisions are conceptual, or depend upon functional differences. According to Brentano, Aristotle rather intended to establish a substantial division, and attributed to each part several functions – the principle of this division being a biological classification.[31] Even though this interpretation of Brentano's be admitted, since biological division is dependent upon functional differences, what is most fundamental must be the division by functions. At any rate, Brentano maintains that since there are some genera of animal which exhibit some of these functions together, the soul might be divided into substantial parts which hold these groups of functions. This point will be examined later. What must be inquired first of all is how and in what sense these parts hold their independence against one another, and this is connected with the question whether some function may act apart from the body.[32] If there be such a function, the part which holds this function would be really separable from other parts. If soul and body are quite inseparable, or they are separable *toto caelo*, in both cases it is uncertain whether a part of the soul is really separable from another. But if some parts are separable from the body, while the other parts not, the former would be separable from the latter. Now, without doubt, some part of the soul, e.g., the sensitive, is inseparable from the body. So the key to the question whether the parts of the soul are really separable, will be whether another part, e.g., the reasoning part, may act apart from the body.[33] Is there then, as a matter of fact, such a special part in the soul?

The key to solve this question is found in the beginning of the *De Anima*. Here Aristotle asks whether the πάθη of the soul be peculiar to the soul, i.e., whether they be separate from the body, and answers as follows: "It seems that in most cases it (the soul) neither acts nor is acted upon apart from the

29 *De An.* II. 2. 413 b 29–32.
30 *De An.* II. 3. 414 b 20.
31 Brentano, *Psych. d. Arist.* 57 ff.; cf. *De An.* II. 413 b 32 – 414 a 1.
32 *De An.* I. 1. 403 a 10. II. 1. 413 a 3.
33 *De An.* III. 4. 429 b 5.

body: as e.g., in anger, courage, desire, and sensations in general. Thinking would, most of all, seem to be peculiar to the soul. Yet, if thinking is also a part of imagination, or not independent of imagination, it will follow that even thinking cannot be independent of the body. If, then, there be any of the actions or affections of the soul which are peculiar to it alone, it will be possible for it to be separated from the body: if, on the contrary, there is nothing of the sort peculiar to it, it will not be separable. It will be like what is straight which has many properties – for instance, it touches the brazen sphere at a point – yet the straightness will by no means so touch it if separated (from other concomitants). In fact it is inseparable, since it is always conjoined with body of some sort. So, too, the πάθη of the soul appear to be all conjoined with body: so it is with anger, fear, pity, courage, and also with joy, love and hate; for the body is somehow affected simultaneously with them."[34]

In the foregoing passage, we must first examine the meaning of the term πάθη. The word is derived from πάσχειν, "to suffer," and means a passive state or passivity. It means in the narrow sense, certain mental experiences such as sensation and feeling, in the wide sense, the modes of being in general. If we take it in the wide sense, what is implied in the last sentence is that the soul is quite inseparable from the body. But if we take the word in the narrow sense, it by no means follows that the soul as a whole is inseparable from the body.

Now, the examples of πάθη here mentioned, are anger, courage, desire, and so on, and they appear to be summed up as sensation in general. Of course these activities do not exhaust the functions of the soul. In another place a little distant from the above, we meet a similar enumeration of the πάθη, which are limited to such feelings as "anger," "mildness," "fear," "courage," etc.[35] In addition to this, we notice that ἔργον, "action" is here distinguished from πάθημα, "affection," while in another place,[36] affection and action were exemplified by thinking, sensation, and pleasure. Of these functions, what appears to be qualified for action is only thinking, and all the rest are affections. On these grounds, we may conclude that πάθη here should be taken in the narrow sense, and that there is a room for the soul to be really separable even if all πάθη of the soul are combined with the body, for

---

34 *De An.* I. 1. 403 a 3 ff.
35 *De An.* I. 1. 403 a 16; b 17; *Eth. Nic.* II. 4. 1105 b 20.
36 *De An.* I. 5. 409 b 14–17.

there may be some function of the soul besides what are called affections.

How, then, about the sentence: "If thinking is also a part of imagination or not independent of imagination, it will follow that even thinking cannot be independent of the body"? Does it not amount to saying that the term πάθη includes thinking, and that all functions of the soul are conjoined with the body and inseparable from it? According to Hicks, πάθη should be taken as modes in general, not limited to special passions. Then it will follow that neither the soul is separable from the body, nor the parts of the soul are separable from each other. Moreover, even if the meaning of πάθη be limited to the narrow sense, it is hardly possible that reason should exist separately from the body as far as thinking presupposes imagination as its *sine qua non*. Whether or not thinking is a πάθη of the soul, in as much as it cannot act apart from the body, the soul as a whole must be inseparable from the body, and it would be to no point to argue about the extent of the word πάθη.

A suggestion might be rendered here to the effect that the statement in question, i.e., that reason is a part of imagination or that it is not independent of imagination, may be a hypothetical supposition instead of a categorical assertion. But this suggestion is by no means tenable, since Aristotle really confirms the same thought in many places. He states for example: "The soul does not think without imagination,"[37] At the very time when he is thinking, he must have an image before him,"[38] The reason does not think of outer objects except combined with sensation,"[3], and so on.

If thinking presupposes imagination and imagination depends upon the body, reason as a thinking faculty cannot be separable from the body. If thinking and reason, which are most likely to be separable from the body, should not be so, much less then will the other parts of the soul be so. But Aristotle, thus admitting on the one hand, that the various parts or functions of the soul are inseparable from the body, states on the other hand: "Only reason would seem to be a distinct species of soul, and it alone is capable of separation from the body,"[40] "The reason is doubtless a thing more divine and is impassive,"[41] or "Only the reason comes from outside and is alone divine, for the activi-

---

[37] *De An.* III. 7. 431 a 16; *De Mem.* 1. 449 b 31.
[38] *De An.* III. 8. 432 a 8; a 13.
[39] *De Sensu* 6. 445 b 16.
[40] *De An.* II. 2. 413 b 24.
[41] *De An.* I. 4. 408 b 29; cf. b 24.

ties of the body do not communicate with it,"[42] etc. The cause of reason's being free from such hindrances as beset the sensitive faculty, which cannot feel after too strong a sensation, is that, "The sensitive faculty cannot exist apart from the body, while the reason is separable." Further it is said that the reason is distinguished from other parts of the soul, in that the former is only distinguished conceptually from the body.[43] These and other similar propositions are hardly compatible with the previous view to the effect that reason being a kind of imagination or at least requiring it, forms a unity with and is inseparable from the body.

2. The Problem of Nous Poietikos

Aristotle insists on the one hand upon the combination of soul and body, of reason and imagination, and asserts on the other hand that reason is separable from the body, as if he is going to and fro without decision. Where is the secret of this oscillation and where can we find the key to solve the difficulty? Confronting this question one might be tempted to adopt the philological method and imagine that it may be due to the fact that the books of the De Anima belong to different periods of the author. For splendid indeed have been the contributions of philological studies on the works of Plato and Aristotle. And in fact Jaeger himself refers, though only occasionally, to this point in his notable book on the development of Aristotle's thought. But he does not go beyond indicating that the third book of the De Anima, which involves the problem of reason, is one of the oldest and most durable elements of Aristotle's philosophy, being quite Platonic and not scientific, and that it in this respect forms a contrast with the arguments about soul and sensation in the first two books together with the Parva Naturalia, whose subject and method are consistently biological and psychological.[44] But we can reach no conclusion from these facts alone as to the different periods of the formation of these books. Further, though Jaeger contrasts the whole third book with the other two, seeing that it contains the Platonic view of reason, we must point out that the idea of the separability and immortality of reason is not confined to the third book,[45] and that the first three chapters of the third book,

[42] Gen. An. II. 3. 736 b 27.
[43] De An. III. 4. 429 b 3.
[44] Jaeger, op. cit. 355 ff. Perhaps he considered the theory of reason in De An. II. to be Platonic because of its resemblance to the statement in Met. XII. 9.
[45] De An. I. 4. 408 b 18, 29; II. 2. 413 b 24.

in treating sensation and imagination, continues the arguments of the preceding book, while the reason-theory in question appears only in the fourth chapter. Now there is a radical difference between the arguments in the fourth chapter and those in the fifth chapter, the latter being by no means Platonic. Moreover, as we have seen above, the Platonic tripartite theory as well as the duopartite theory is criticized in the ninth chapter, and various additional parts are enumerated, such as the nutritive, the sensitive, the imaginative, and the desiring; whereas Jaeger himself admits this last to be the true theory of Aristotle in his last period. Thus, if there should be any difference of period in the books of the *De Anima*, it must be found not between the third book and the other two, but within the third book itself. In other words, it would be only the fourth chapter of the third book, that might be conjectured to be earlier. But there is no proof of the early formation of the fourth chapter except the aforesaid difference from the fifth.

A remarkable contribution on this point was made by Nuyence in his monumental study on the evolution of Aristotle's psychology.[46] But since, in the first place, he presupposed the development of the soul-theory as the measure to determine the period of Aristotle's works, and since, in the second place, his investigation has led to the conclusion that the *De Anima* as a whole belonged to the last period, his study, though itself very important, is of no use to solve the difficulty concerning the reason-problem in the *De Anima*. It is true that the thought of separable reason has originated in Plato's theory, and was predominant in Aristotle's early works, but it does not rule out the possibility that this thought was an enduring element of Aristotle's system and required incorporation with later thought of biological trend.

Even if the theory of the separable reason seems to belong to Aristotle's early thought, we should not avoid a philosophical solution of this *difficulty* by resorting to the hypothesis of development. Much more is it the case when philological method does not give us a decisive solution. For this reason, we render a new hypothesis: it may be that we can solve the question by distinguishing within reason what is combined with body and what is not. It seems to be a point in favour of our hypothesis that Aristotle distinguishes active and passive reasons in the fifth chapter, next to the fourth chapter in which the separability of reason was discussed. Thus we are now confronted with the famous

---

[46] Nuyens, *Ontwikkelingsmomenten in de zielkunde van Aristoteles* 1939 French 1948.

picture intellect

problem of νοῦς ποιητικός, which has caused endless discussions in the
history of philosophy. The only source for Aristotle's thought on the
point in question is the following short section.

De An. III. 5. 430 a 10 ff.; ἐπεὶ δ' ὥσπερ ἐν ἀπάσῃ τῇ φύσει ἐστί τι τὸ
μὲν ὕλη ἑκάστῳ γένει (τοῦτο δὲ ὃ πάντα δυνάμει ἐκεῖνα), ἕτερον δὲ τὸ αἴτιον
καὶ ποιητικόν, τῷ ποιεῖν πάντα, οἷον ἡ τέχνη πρὸς τὴν ὕλην πέπονθεν,
ἀνάγκη καὶ ἐν τῇ ψυχῇ ὑπάρχειν ταύτας τὰς διαφοράς. καὶ ἔστιν ὁ μὲν
τοιοῦτος νοῦς τῷ πάντα γίνεσθαι, ὁ δὲ τῷ πάντα ποιεῖν, ὡς ἕξις τις οἷον τὸ
φῶς. τρόπον γάρ τινα καὶ τὸ φῶς ποιεῖ τὰ δυνάμει ὄντα χρώματα ἐνεργείᾳ
χρώματα. καὶ οὗτος ὁ νοῦς χωριστὸς καὶ ἀπαθὴς καὶ ἀμιγής, τῇ οὐσίᾳ ὢν
ἐνέργεια. ἀεὶ γὰρ τιμιώτερον τὸ ποιοῦν τοῦ πάσχοντος καὶ ἡ ἀρχὴ τῆς ὕλης.
τὸ δ' αὐτό ἐστιν ἡ κατ' ἐνέργειαν ἐπιστήμη τῷ πράγματι. ἡ δὲ κατὰ δύναμιν
χρόνῳ προτέρα ἐν τῷ ἑνί, ὅλως δὲ οὐ χρόνῳ·ἀλλ' οὐχ ὁτὲ μὲν νοεῖ ὁτὲ δ'
οὐ νοεῖ. χωρισθεὶς δ' ἐστὶ μόνον τοῦθ' ὅπερ ἐστί, καὶ τοῦτο μόνον ἀθάνατον
καὶ ἀΐδιον. οὐ μνημονεύομεν δέ, ὅτι τοῦτο μὲν ἀπαθές, ὁ δὲ παθητικὸς νοῦς
φθαρτός, καὶ ἄνευ τούτου οὐθὲν νοεῖ.

"But, as in the whole of nature, there is on the one hand something
which serves as matter for each kind (and this matter is potentially all
the members of the kinds), while on the other there is something which
serves as the cause or agent because it makes them all, as e.g. the art is
related to the matter that has been affected. These differences must
exist, therefore, of necessity also in the soul. And so while such a reason
exists because it becomes all things, the other does because it makes
them all, like a certain kind of *habitus* such as light. For light also in a
certain way makes what are potentially colours into actual colours.
And this reason is separable, impassive and unmixed, being in its substance actual. For that which acts is always superior to that which is
acted upon, as principle is to matter. Now actual knowledge is identical
with the object of knowing, but potential knowledge is prior in time in
the individual case, though considered as a whole it is not prior in time.
But it is not at one time thinking and at another not. It is only when
separated that it is just what it is, and this alone is immortal and eternal. But we do not remember, because it is impassive, while the passive
reason is mortal, and one does not think without this."

Anticipating the result of our inquiry, let us paraphrase this passage
as follows: Since every natural being consists of matter and form, soul
and its part, reason, should have matter and form. The material part of
reason is potential, passive and mortal, while its formal part is actual,
active and immortal. It is only the formal part of reason that can continue
existing apart from the body, or holds its proper being in such a separa-

te condition. It is in the state of eternal activity, though lacking in memory. Nevertheless, our act of thinking is possible only through the cooperation of active and passive reasons.

According to our interpretation, Aristotle admitted both separable and inseparable reasons, and there is no incongruity between them. But to maintain this apparently simple interpretation, we must solve many difficulties, for the history of arguments about this problem could sufficiently form a volume in itself. So we shall content ourselves with a short summary, following Brentano.[47]

To begin with, Aristotle's own disciple, Theophrastus,[48] seems to have taken not only the active but also the passive reason as immaterial, and to have made both of them the faculties of the same person.[49] Alexander of Aphrodisias, on the contrary, made the active reason separate from human nature. It was for him a purely spiritual or rational substance, the first ground of things, and the divine intelligence itself,[50] while the passive faculty, i.e., νοῦς ὑλικός[51] was dependent upon a certain mixture of the elements in the human body, both in respect to thinking and to existence; it was perishable with the body.[52] There were, beside Alexander, some who took the νοῦς ποιητικός for God,[53] while others identified it with directly recognized propositions and their consequences.[54]

These two theories of antiquity continued throughout mediaeval and modern ages as the most predominant opposition. Avicenna, an Arabian philosopher, being without doubt under the influence of Alexander, assumed only "the reason that becomes all things" to be human, while "the reason that makes all things" he held to be superhuman. The former, i.e. the *intellectus materialis*,[55] or νοῦς δυνάμει is the

---

[47] Brentano, *op. cit.* 5-36.

[48] Themistius, *Paraph. d. anim.* f. 91.

[49] Brentano contrasted Eudemus to Theophrastus, but since the *Eth. Eud.* was proved by Jaeger to be an early work of Aristotle's, we must naturally omit him.

[50] Alex. Aph. *De An.* I. 139 b; 144 a.

[51] A denomination derived from *De An.*, III. 5. 430 a 10, 19, and continued by Arabian philosophers.

[52] Alex. Aph. *De An.* I. 126, 127.

[53] Themistius, *Paraph. d. An.* 89.

[54] Presumably, their interpretation is founded upon such passages as *An. Post.* II. 19. 100 b 8; *Eth. Nic.* VI. 3. 1139 b 17; 1141 a 5.

[55] In the traditional Latin version, νοῦς δυνάμει is always translated as intellectus, while νοῦς ποιητικός is usually rendered as intelligentia. In the writings translated from the Arabian, the latter means a bodiless spirit. Cf. Thomas Aquinas, *Summ. Th.* I. a 79. 10.

cognitive faculty of man, through which he apprehends rational forms, its subject is the soul, instead of the body. The highest spiritual part of the human soul does not mix with the body[56] and is imperishable[57] in spite of the death of the body. νοῦς δυνάμει recognizes potentially, but in order to accomplish the knowledge, it must be supplied with ideas from a pure spiritual substance outside and independent of human beings.[58] Every rational form exists in advance within pure spirits, the highest[59] of which moves the next and so on until it reaches the active reason, i.e., the *intelligentia agens*, which is called by him the giver of forms. Out of the active reason, rational forms stream into our mind. All that the φαντασία can do, is to make the *intellectus materialis* ready for accepting the emanation.[60] It is none the less a necessary arrangement, in so far as the human soul is bound with the body.[61] The *intellectus materialis* can be illuminated by the *intelligentia agens* and gets a universal knowledge only through individual φαντασία, but those ideas are not kept in the *intellectus materialis*.[62] They must stream into it anew from the *intelligentia agens* whenever we recognize spiritually.[63] Learning is nothing but the acquisition of a complete *habitus*, enabling oneself to combine with the *intelligentia agens* in order to acquire rational forms.

According to Averroes, another representative of Arabian philosophy, not only the active reason, but also the passive reason is pure spiritual substance essentially separate from sensible man. Spiritual

[56] *Lib. Natur.* VI. p. 5. c. 2 princ.
[57] *Ibid.* p. 5. c. 2. This thesis is applied not only to a universal spirit, but also to individual souls; cf. Brentano's note *ad loc.*
[58] *Lib. Natur.* VI. p. 5. c. 5 princ.
[59] This is not God, but the first intelligence that moves the highest sphere; cf. Brentano's note *ad loc.*
[60] *Lib. Natur.* VI. p. 5. c. 5.
[61] *Ibid.*
[62] Sensible forms have their treasure in imagination and memory: imagination being the repository for *sensus communis* or *phantasia*, and memory for estimative or sensible cognition. But there is no treasury of ideas for *intellectus materialis*. For if there were any, it would be a faculty of a bodily organ, since a spiritual being actually knows those things that are involved in it and since to have the forms in itself is the same as to recognize them. But this is impossible, because no form that is involved in a faculty which operates in terms of a bodily organ, is intelligible except potentially. Cf. Brentano, *op. cit.* 12.
[63] *Ibid.* n. 33. *Lib. Natur.* VI. p. 5. c. 6, where among the four alternatives, viz., whether the treasury of intelligible forms is in a bodily organ, or in spiritual part, or there is no such treasury, or *intelligentia agens* acts as a medium that combines the forms with the soul, the last is chosen. In spite of Brentano's opposition, this theory of Avicenna's on νοῦς ποιητικός seems to be fairly probable.

cognition is not innate to man, a child is called spiritual in so far as it
has a rational faculty in potentiality.[64] Man is not different in species
from irrational animals, because the *differentia* of man is not a spiritual,
but a sensitive faculty, which was called by Aristotle νοῦς παθητικός[65]
the *intellectus passibilis*.[66] It is seated in the central cells of the brain,[67]
and through this faculty we can distinguish individual images. But the
animal has, instead of it, only a certain judgement through natural
instinct (*virtus aestimativa naturalis*),[68] in virtue of which the lamb observes the wolf as its enemy. Man is different from other animals in so
far as he has a disposition towards spiritual cognition.[69] He gains habitual knowledge through the combination of the *intellectus passibilis*
with imagination and memory. The subject of this knowledge is not
the spirit, but the *intellectus passibilis*.[70] On the other hand, actual and
spiritual knowledge is found only in a spiritual faculty, to which man
attains through the combination of *intellectus materialis* and *intellectus
agens*. *Intellectus materialis*[71] is called material, because it stands in a
relation of potentiality to intelligible forms,[72] and *intellectus agens* is
called so, because it makes the sensible images in man, which are potentially intelligible, i.e. the φάντασμα, actually intelligible, and thus
moves the material intellect.[73] The *intellectus materialis* receives from
imagination the intelligible forms, which are received by the *intellectus
agens*, while this *intellectus agens* itself does not think them.[74] Each of
these two spiritual beings is one substance and is not divided into many

---

[64] *De An.* III. 1. c. 5. Venet. 1550 f. 164 b.

[65] *De An.* III. 5. 430 a 24.

[66] *De An.* III. 4. c. 20 f. 171 b.

[67] *De An.* III. 5. c. 20 f. 174 b.

[68] Avicenna called the two faculties *virtus cognitiva* and *virtus aestimativa* or
existimativa (*Lib. Natur.* III. p. 1. c. 5). Brentano points out that Averroes, sometimes, e.g. in *De An.* III. 1. c. 20 f. 171 a, says that the *intellectus passibilis* is the
virtus imaginativa, but sometimes identifies it with the *virtus cognitiva*, which is
superior to the imaginative faculty. Hence Brentano takes the former as an indefinite expression for sensible faculty in general. This deserves special attention,
since it is just Brentano himself who identified the νοῦς παθητικός with the
φαντασία. This point will be examined later.

[69] *De An.* III. 1. c. 20. 171 b.

[70] *Ibid.*

[71] The *intellectus materialis* is distinguished from the *intellectus passibilis* in
De An. III. c. 20. 171 a etc. Averroes, nevertheless, declares that the *intellectus
materialis* is also spiritual, e.g. De *An.* I. 1. c. 12; III. 1. c. 4. 160 a 4; c. 20. 171 b.

[72] *De An.* III. 1. c. 5. 160 b.

[73] *De An.* III. 1. c. 5. 165 a; *ibid.* 5 c. 30. 178 b.

[74] *De An.* III. 1. c. 19. 170 a. Not that it thinks nothing, but that its object
belongs to another higher world, viz., the world of spirits.

by the multiplicity of knowing persons.[75] They alone are the eternal in man, while other parts of his that are peculiar to himself perish with his body. Thus at first, the sensitive thinking faculty of the *intellectus passibilis*, combined with imagination and memory, makes the images ready for the act of the *intellectus agens*. When the *intellectus agens*[76] makes the images rational,[77] the *intellectus materialis* receives from them the images, intelligible concepts, or forms of sensible things.[78] Thus the intelligible forms have twofold subjects, viz., images and the *intellectus materialis*.[79] Since these two are united with the same intelligible form, the form of the *intellectus materialis* must also be combined with us through the images. And in as much as each form constitutes a unity with its subject, the *intellectus materialis* itself is also united with us, and we recognize through it as if through an innate faculty of cognition.[80]

As for our union with the *intellectus agens*, it grows gradually with the advance of our knowledge about the corporeal world during our lifetime. The *intellectus materialis* receives the *intellectus agens* together with the truth that was recognized, just as the pupil receives light with actual colour.[81] Thus, when the knowledge of the whole corporeal world is accomplished, the *intellectus agens* is completely united with us, and the whole area of spirit will be revealed, since the *intellectus agens* has at this moment a complete knowledge about all spiritual substances of nature.[82] He who has received the *intellectus agens* most

---

[75] Averroes maintains that the *intellectus materialis* is also indivisible and one in all. *De An.* III. 1. c. 5. 163 b; *ibid.* 164 a; 165 a etc. Brentano ridicules this, but in as much as the *intellectus materialis* is a spiritual faculty and is distinguished from the *intellectus passibilis*, this is not so ridiculous as it might appear.

[76] *De An.* III. 1. 7. 167 b.

[77] The act of the *intellectus agens* must precede that of the *intellectus materialis*. *De An.* III. 1. c. 36. 178 b.

[78] *De An.* III. 3. c. 18. 169 b.

[79] *De An.* III. c. 5. 163 b.

[80] *De An.* III. 1. c. 5. 164 b. Though every one recognizes through one and the same *intellectus materialis*, it does not follow of necessity that we recognize one and the same thing, because we receive the forms from φαντάσματα. These images are not confined to our own, but may be derived from any and every man of the world, so that, we shall never be in need of them in order to think. Knowledge develops or passes away only *per accidens*, i.e. in so far as it is combined with the individual, like Socrates or Plato. Cf. Brentano, *op. cit.* 19, n. 53, 54, 55.

[81] *De An.* III. 5. c. 36. 179 b.

[82] *Ibid.*

completely in his *intellectus materialis*, recognizes[83] what the *intellectus agens* recognizes. This is the highest happiness.[84]

Averroes' theory gained a remarkable acceptance not only in the Islamic world but also in Christian Europe, in spite of the queer mysticism and sophistical expressions he exhibits. As a result, the great scholastics, especially St. Thomas Aquinas, found it necessary to fight against his philosophy with all their strength, condemning the great Arabian as a depraver of Aristotelian philosophy.[85]

The explanation of St. Thomas agrees in the main with the fragments of Theophrastus which are kept in the *paraphrasis* of Themistius. According to St. Thomas, not only the *intellectus agens*, but also what he terms the *intellectus possibilis*[86] is something immaterial, and the latter as well as the former belongs to human nature, they are not pure spiritual substances as Averroes says, but the faculties of the human soul. When Aristotle says that they are separated from the body,[87] he not only means by this that they have no organs like vegetable and sensitive faculties, but find their subject in the soul; human soul has its own faculty, superior to material powers. Both reasons are in their being and function incorporeal and not mixed with matter.[88] The *intellectus possibilis* is the cognitive faculty proper to the spiritual part; all our ideas are found in it, though not actually from the beginning. The *intellectus possibilis* is itself at first merely like a *tabula rasa*; it gains intelligible forms through a kind of passivity. Hence Aristotle[89] says that thinking is a passivity.[90]

Now passivity presupposes an agent; therefore Aristotle says that our knowledge comes from sensation.[91] This agrees with the statement that the soul does not think without images.[92] But as no corporeal thing can give an impression upon an incorporeal thing, a mere faculty of a sensible body is not sufficient to account for our thought; rather, a superior faculty is needed – "The agent is superior to that which is

---

[83] *De An*. III. 5. c. 36. 180 a.
[84] *De An. Beatitud*. c. 4. and 5.
[85] *Opuscul*. XV. De unitate intellectus contra Averroistas.
[86] Thomas called reason that is every thing in potentiality *intellectus possibilis*, instead of *intellectus passibilis* like the Arabians. This denomination is based upon *De An*. III. 4. 429 a 21.
[87] *De An*. III. 4. 429 b 5; *ibid*. 5. 430 a 17.
[88] *Comm. de An*. III. lect. 7.
[89] *De An*. III. 4. 429 a 13.
[90] *Summ. Th*. 1 a 79, 2 corp.
[91] *E.g. An Post*. II. 19. 100 a 10.
[92] *De An*. III. 5. 430 a 18.

acted upon."[93] This superior agent is the so-called *intellectus agens*. The images which have matter are rational only potentially, but the *intellectus agens* abstracts the forms from these images and makes them actually rational. Therefore, the *intellectus agens* is the real agent of spiritual cognition, while the images are only the secondary cause, or so to say, the "matter" of the cause.[94] The *intellectus agens* illuminates the images which are related to reason as colour to sight, and it abstracts from them intelligible forms. Through this illumination and abstraction, we receive in our *intellectus possibilis* the copy of the universal essence of a thing apart from its individual determinations.[95]

This interpretation of St. Thomas' agrees in the main, as we have noticed, with that of Theophrastus', and was greatly esteemed by Brentano. Nevertheless, it has been accused of several difficulties. One of these is that, as Durandus[96] pointed out, though the *intellectus agens* is said to make the images spiritual through bringing something spiritual into them, it would be, in fact, impossible for a sensitive faculty combined with a sense organ to have any spiritual attribute, so that the function which is assigned to the *intellectus agens* should be impossible. Moreover, if the *intellectus agens* makes the images spiritual, they would no longer remain images, whereas Aristotle states on the other hand that we cannot think without having at the same time in us the corresponding images.[97] Consequently, the images would not have been changed into higher intelligibles even at the moment of cognition. Durandus himself denied the *intellectus agens* altogether.

Suarez[98] also tried to reform the theory of St. Thomas, though he himself did not think that he had departed from Thomas' views. According to Suarez, abstraction is not the act of the *intellectus agens* upon sensible images, but is innate to reason, and the presence of sensible images is enough for the act of reason. But sensible images do not act upon reason. Not that reason brings images into the *intellectus possibilis*, but that reason makes in itself a rational image of an object without giving change to sensible images.

Brentano criticizes the theory as follows: Suarez admits the image merely as an assistant cause of spiritual thinking; this may be suitable for Plato, who believed the ideas to be innate to the soul, but not for

[93] *De An.* III. 5. 430 a 18.
[94] *Summ. Th.* 1 a 84. 6 corp.
[95] *Ibid.* 85, 1. ad 4.
[96] *Sent.* 1. dist. 3. q. 5.
[97] *De An.* III. 8. 432 a 8.
[98] *De An.* 1. IV.

Aristotle, who admitted no innate ideas for the spiritual or rational part. Again, it is none the less inappropriate to ascribe an innate idea or thought to the *intellectus agens*. On the other hand, the image, being matter, cannot act upon the spirit, so that there is wanting an active principle which makes the potential thought actual. Even if the *intellectus agens* makes out the idea in the spirit, since the image gives no change to it, the power to engender all ideas must be included in the spirit from the beginning. What reason is there at all for saying that knowledge is impossible without sensation? Why is actual cognition impossible without individual images even after we have aquired knowledge?[99] Moreover, the *intellectus agens* makes no effort, an effort which is necessary to all actions.[100] – As to whether Brentano's criticism is right or not, we shall see later.

Turning to modern interpreters, let us take up at first Trendelenburg.[101] According to him, reason sometimes is combined with the other parts of the soul and cannot exist without them; such a reason is called νοῦς παθητικός.[102] But sometimes it lies beyond the other functions of man, and rules them: in this case, it is called νοῦς ποιητικός. νοῦς παθητικός is that which puts together all the lower faculties that are necessary for the cognition of a thing. It is called νοῦς παθητικός because on the one hand, it is completed by the νοῦς ποιητικός, and on the other hand, it is acted upon by the object of thought.[103] Its function is to acquire a universal concept by means of the comparison of individual sensations with each other.[104]

As for the νοῦς ποιητικός, it is not divine reason itself, but belongs to man,[105] and is not a single entity common for all.[106] Aristotle does not explain the essence and function of this reason.[107] What is evident is only that it comprehends the first and the last principles of knowledge. It is the ultimate witness of truth,[108] without which we have no assurance of anything.[109] Our νοῦς ποιητικός is not the divine reason, yet it is

[99] *De An.* III. 8. 432 a 8.
[100] Brentano, *op. cit.* 28.
[101] Trendelenburg, *Comm. in Arist. de An.*
[102] *Ibid.* 168.
[103] *Ibid.* 493.
[104] *Ibid.* 173.
[106] *Ibid.* 492.
[106] *Ibid*, 493.
[107] *Ibid.* 496.
[108] *Ibid.* 494, 495, 173.
[109] There is no science of principles, for it is impossible to prove the principles. Even the νοῦς παθητικός cannot prove them, for it depends upon the comparison

something godlike, and the divine reason itself is also a νοῦς ποιητικός. Aristotle suggests in a certain place the resemblance of human reason and divine, without defining there or elsewhere in what manner human reason participates in the divine reason.[110] In as much as he has taken it to be something holy, he is led to assume that it does not develop from matter, but comes from outside i.e. is derived from God.[111] Trendelenburg is confident of the conformity of this thought with Aristotle's whole theory of the soul.[112]

Against this interpretation, Brentano points out for the moment one difficulty, viz. that in De An. III. 4, where Aristotle speaks only about the reason which becomes all things, he makes it belong to the ψυχὴ νοητική, unmixed with the body, separated from it, pure, and without matter, and that it is only in the beginning of the fifth chapter, that the νοῦς ποιητικός is introduced.[113]

Brandis also takes the νοῦς ποιητικός as belonging to the individual. It is the cognition of *per se* true and certain principles,[114] while the νοῦς παθητικός is a mediating thought.[115] Human reason is free from matter, but in so far as it derives the material for mediating thinking from sensation, i.e. in so far as it needs images for thinking, or in other words, in so far as it acts as mediating thinking, it is called νοῦς παθητικός, it is neither simple nor eternal. Reason in the strict sense, i.e. the theoretical and actual reason has its true being only when it is separated from the body. Man's proper self is founded upon it. That it acts upon us, means not that it is a manifestation in us of the universal world-spirit, but that it is independent of our body.[116]

Brentano prefers Brandis' theory to Trendelenburg's in that the former admits the reason which becomes all things to be human. But, on the other hand, he points out Brandis's difficulty in explaining why that reason which belongs to the rational part of the human soul should perish with the body, and why active reason should not be a faculty of thinking, if it be not the divine reason but proper to individual souls. To admit that such a reason always thinks would be contrary to ex-

of sensations, and we would have fallen into a vicious circle, if we employed it. Therefore, there remains only the νοῦς ποιητικός which apprehends the first principles by its own faculty. – So argues Trendelenburg, *Comm. in Ar. de An.* 173.

[110] *Met.* XII. 7. 1072 b 18–30.
[111] *Comm. in Ar. de An.* 175.
[112] *Ibid.* 496.
[113] Brentano, *op. cit.* 31 n. 100.
[114] Brandis, *Handbuch.* II. 2. 2. 1177.
[115] *Ibid.* 1178.
[116] Brandis, *Die Entwicklung der griechisch-roemischen Philosophie*, 518.

perience, nor would it agree with Aristotle's theory.[117] It cannot receive a thought anew, either, for such an act will belong rather to the
reason in potentiality, of which it is said not that it becomes a mediating
thought, but that it becomes all things,[118] i.e. all the intelligibles, as
Aristotle explained in the eighth chapter.[119]

Whereas these two interpretations approach that of Theophrastus in
so far as they attribute the νοῦς ποιητικός to the individual, there is in
the modern age another theory which resembles those of Alexander and
Arabian philosophers. According to Ravaisson,[120] man has only passive
reason. This is the universal potentiality in the world of ideas, just as
the first matter is in the world of reality. On the contrary, the νοῦς
ποιητικός is the absolute intelligence, or the creative act which actualizes
all potential forms and brings forth all thoughts. This reminds us of
Avicenna, except that he made all thoughts flow out directly from the
intelligentia agens, while according to Ravaisson, Aristotle admits that
one thought arouses another thought in us, so that here and there only
a higher substance should be thought of as the first mover. This, God
himself, gives the principles directly, and from these principles all
knowledge and all speculative thinking flow out. The divine wisdom
gives also initial light to the distinction of good and bad, and gives to
will the first impulse, so that virtue appears merely as an implement of
absolute thought. In the further determination of the νοῦς, which is all
things in potentiality, Ravaisson agrees almost completely with
Alexander. The sensible principle is, at bottom, identical with the
intellectual and intelligible principles. Hence reason also compares and
distinguishes the abstract form, which is its proper object, with and
from the sensible form. Thus the difference between sensation and
reason is reduced to a distinction between the two sides of one being.
Consequently, reason is bound with the body in its existence, and
nothing that is proper to man is immortal.

Brentano's criticism is as follows: Firstly, as aforesaid, the reason
which becomes all things, i.e. the *intellectus possibilis*, would, in this
theory, be the faculty of a bodily organ, and this is not compatible with
Aristotle's own statements. If such a reason had been found in an
organ, the power of the first mover would have reached this as well as it
does sense. But it can bring nothing spiritual into a power which is

117 *De An.* III. 4. 430 a 5; *An. Post.* II. 19. 99 b 26.
118 *De An.* III. 5. 430 a 14.
119 *Ibid.* 8. 431 b 22; cf. 4. 429 a 17; 429 b 30.
120 Ravaisson, *Essai sur la métaphysique d'Aristote*, I. 586 f.; cf. II. 17, 19.

mixed with matter. Further, if reason should be identical with sense, differing only in state, it cannot be a power without actuality, for when it seizes the first universal presentation, it must be preceded by sensation. If that were the case, Aristotle would have admitted the direct meddling of God in the production of the first sensation rather than in the awakening of universal thought.

Among those who took the νοῦς ποιητικός as the spirit separate from / human nature, Renan noticed a resemblance of this theory to the view of Malebranche,[121] but he could not find the theory compatible with the general tenet of the Peripatetic philosophy, and was compelled to assign it to another thinker. Aristotle might, he thought, have borrowed it from Anaxagoras, taking, however, little care about the incongruity that might result between this theory and that of the *Analytica* or the *De Anima*.

Indeed, there would scarcely be any need for criticism of this interpretation, as Brentano observes. A primitive philosopher or an eclectic might have expressed such a fragmental idea, but we can by no means imagine that Aristotle, a most clearminded and systematic philosopher would have overlooked such an evident contradiction. It is, nevertheless quite another problem to inquire about the origin of the idea of separate reason, or the νοῦς ποιητικός.

Zeller also takes the νοῦς ποιητικός to be the universal spirit, or the / absolute thinking of God. In this respect, he might belong to the tradition of Averroism, as Brentano remarks. It is, however, doubtful whether he is any the more free from the same difficulties. According to Zeller,[122] the νοῦς ποιητικός is the universal spirit and the absolute thought of God; it is quite unique and thinks only itself. The thought of man, in so far as it has not developed from experience, is one and the same with this. Zeller points out, on the other hand, that Aristotle seems to have admitted that the νοῦς ποιητικός belongs also to individual souls;[123] but Brentano opposes him saying that he cannot understand how such a unique and indifferent reason could be the principle of human thinking. According to Brentano, Zeller has no means of explaining the reason that becomes all things or the combination of it with the νοῦς ποιητικός, so that he was compelled to attribute it to the body like a sense;[124] yet being on the other hand unable to deem it

---

[121] Renan, *Averroes et l'Averroisme*, 96.
[122] Zeller, *Ph. d. Gr.* II. 2. 567 ff.
[123] *Ibid.* 441 n. 3.
[124] *Ibid.* 443 n. 4.

something material, and so censures Trendelenburg charging that he altered in this respect the theory of Aristotle.[125] Thus Brentano criticizes Zeller so severely as to judge his interpretation a queer misunderstanding without any merit. But the criticism seems to be somewhat party-spirited and even suspicious of ill feeling. That it is quite unreasonable, we shall explain, examining the difficulties point by point.

3. Against Brentano's Interpretation

To begin with, let us, as a radical opposition to our interpretation, take up and examine Brentano's theory, which is on the traditional line of St. Thomas Aquinas. Brentano distinguishes in Aristotle's passage, three concepts of reason instead of two; viz., νοῦς ποιητικός, νοῦς δυνάμει and νοῦς παθητικός.[126] This does not mean, however, that he recognizes three kinds of reason. Reason in the proper sense, to which human thinking belongs, is restricted to the νοῦς δυνάμει, i.e. potential and receptive reason, its proper function is to receive forms,[127] and the other two are reasons only in an accidental sense. Active reason, being an active principle of thinking, belongs to the human soul, especially to its rational part. Hence it is called reason in an accidental sense.[128] It is identical with receptive reason in respect to existence (*dem Subjekt nach*), but different in respect to essence (*dem Sein nach*).[129] The receptive reason is potential, while the active reason is active;[130] the former thinks, while the latter makes the other think.[131] The active reason acts, at first, upon the sensible part though without consciousness, it makes the rational forms which are immanent to it in the form of φάντασμα or images, actual, and passes them to the receptive reason, thus an actual thought is realized in the receptive reason.[132] In short, the active reason acts directly upon the sensible part, and upon the receptive reason only indirectly. It follows then that not only separability, impassiveness and unmixedness, but also eternity and immortality, which we have considered to be the marks of active reason, are common to

[125] *Ibid.* 442 n. 1.
[126] Brentano, *op. cit.* 143 ff.
[127] *Ibid.* 167, 175.
[128] *Ibid.* 170 ff.
[129] *Ibid.* 167.
[129] *Ibid.* 167. We intentionally avoided literal translation "in respect to subject" and "in respect to being."
[130] *Ibid.* 167, 178.
[131] *Ibid.* 204.
[132] *Ibid.* 147, 173.

human reason as well, and will be attributed primarily to receptive reason.[133]

As for "passive reason" it is different from the receptive and potential reason, and is equal to the φαντασία or imagination,[134] whose function is to be a medium for thinking. The passage "this is perishable," implies the transiency of imagination instead of the mortality of the rational part. There is, according to Brentano, besides the active reason which is immanent in our mind, a divine reason, that thinks throughout eternity,[135] and not "sometimes thinks and sometimes does not." It is only through this divine reason that active reason is combined with the sensitive part.[136]

We never grudge due praise to the profound scholarship of Brentano, to say nothing of his great predecessor, nor can we prohibit ourselves from admiring their thoroughgoing reasoning. It seems to be their Christian prejudice that has led them to this misinterpretation for all their erudition and vigorous thinking. This is after all, too far-fetched an interpretation. To resume, the differences between his theory and ours are as follows: 1) We take the word "reason" throughout in its proper sense, while Brentano takes both the active and the passive reasons to be reason in an accidental sense, so that, according to Brentano, there would, in Aristotle, be no division in the strict sense, of human reason. 2) We admit at least in the passage in Aristotle under discussion, only active reason and passive reason and nothing more. Potential reason is one and the same with passive reason, and active reason is divine as well as human, whereas Brentano distinguishes active reason, potential reason, receptive reason and divine reason as quite different from each other. 3) We confine eternity, immortality and unmixedness to active reason, taking these attributes as tantamount to the separability of the reason from the body. But Brentano attributes them to human reason in general, which is receptive and potential. To us, what is immortal is only active reason, but to Brentano, each individual person is immortal.

Let us then compare and examine two interpretations part for part. "But, as in the whole of nature, there is on the one hand something which serves as matter for each kind (and this matter is potentially all the members of the kinds), while on the other there is something which

---

[133] *Ibid.* 175 ff.
[134] *Ibid.* 208.
[135] *Ibid.* 182.
[136] *Ibid.* 188.

serves as the cause or agent because it makes them all, as e.g. the art is related to the matter which has been affected." In this sentence, in the first place, matter and potentiality, cause and agent, are identified with each other; the former two concepts are opposed to the latter two; while cause and agent are taken, in the main, to be the same as form and actuality.[137] In the second place, this opposition is admitted to be applicable to the whole of nature. Hence we expect firstly that a given natural being should be divided into two parts, form and matter, whereas in fact what we see in the text is the division of the soul, as Aristotle puts it: "These differences must exist, therefore, of necessity also in the soul," and next to this, the division of the reason, viz., "And so, while such a reason exists because it becomes all things, the other does because it makes them all, like a certain kind of *habitus* such as light."

Now, "such a reason," which becomes all things, implies no doubt the reason which was discussed in the previous chapter, viz., that reason which receives the forms. This, even Brentano does not deny. But, thus considered, Aristotle is surely dividing the reason in the proper sense into two parts, unlike Brentano's interpretation in which the active reason is taken to be reason only in an accidental sense. Brentano insists namely that the active reason is not the reason in the proper sense, because it is the principle that makes others think, not the subject that thinks: it is called reason only because it is involved in the rational part of the human soul. But action is the activity of the agent, no less than that of the patient, and thought is the actuality of that which makes one think, no less than that of the thinking subject.[138] If the active principle of thought exists in the human soul, especially in its rational part, why is it impossible for that part to be reason in the proper sense?

To resume, there are both the reason which receives forms and becomes all things, and the reason which makes all things. The one is matter and potential, while the other is cause and agent, and the activi-

---

[137] Form and matter are static concepts, while potentiality and actuality are dynamic, so they do not coincide with each other; form is not always actual, nor is matter always potential. Cf. n. 8.

[138] *Phys.* III. 3. 202 a 13; *De An.* II. 2. 414 a 8, 25; III. 2. 426 a 16; 7. 431 a 1; 431 b 16. In this chapter we often adopt, in place of "agent," the term "subject" as synonymous with "Subjekt" in the German language. This special usage is necessitated to avoid the confusion, since the νοῦς ποιητικός is to be called "the agent" of thinking in a different meaning, i.e., not that which thinks, but that which makes one think.

ty of the latter is explained through the metaphor of light. "For light also in a certain way makes what are potential colours into actual colours."[139] Such being the case, there cannot be any doubt as to the

---

[139] "What are potentially colours" means the sense, not a coloured body in darkness. It is true that a body has an actual colour through being seen, and that light is the principle that makes a body visible. Hence it might appear as if it is the light that makes a body have an actual colour. But this is not really the case, and we must investigate the matter more carefully in accordance with Aristotle's own theory of vision. In *De An.* II. 7. 418 a 26–28, it is said: "The object of sight is the visible and what is visible is colour and something besides which can be described, though it has no name." The primary object of sight is colour, but the secondary object which is said to have no name, means in reality the phosphorescent; cf. 419 a 3. In respect to the activities of them it is said in 418 a 31–b 3: "But colour is universally capable of exciting change in the actually transparent, that is, in light. This being, in fact, the true nature of colour. Hence colour is not visible without light, but the colour of each object is always seen in light." Cf. also *ibid.* 419 a 9–11; 418 b 4–10. Though colour is seen through light, it is not light, but colour, that is active. It is not that colour is illuminated by light (i.e. is passive), and reflects on the eye (i.e. is active), but that colour acts immediately upon a transparent medium, light being its actuality, and through this acts upon the eye. The sequence of the visional sensation is from colour to a transparent medium, i.e. light, and from light to the eye.

Why, then, does it need a transparent medium or light? Aristotle answers as follows. *Ibid.* 419 a 12–21: "If you lay the coloured object upon your eye, you will not see it. On the contrary, what the colour excites is the transparent medium, say, the air, and by this, which is continuous, the sense organ is stimulated. For it was a mistake in Democritus to suppose that if the intervening space become a void, even an ant would be distinctly seen, supposing there were one in the sky. That is impossible. For sight takes place through an affection of the sensitive faculty. Now it cannot be affected by that which is seen, the colour itself: therefore it can only be by the intervening medium: hence the existence of some medium is necessary. But, if the intermediate space become a void, so far from being seen distinctly, an object would not be visible at all."

Colour cannot act directly upon the eye; it acts only indirectly through giving colour to a transparent medium. It is true also with smelling, hearing, and all other sensations whatsoever. Cf. *ibid.* 419 a 25–30; 421 b 17 ff.; 418 b 26–419 a 1. The transparent is the medium between colour and the eye, only when it is actualized into light. Light is the actuality of the substance which is involved in the heavenly bodies or in the air, etc., i.e. the actuality of αἰθῆρ. Cf. *De An.* II. 7. 418 b 9–13; *De Sensu* 4. 439 a 16 ff. It is the colour itself that acts upon the transparent and makes light in a certain sense colour, while that which makes the transparent actually what it is, is not light, but fire. Light is the actuality of the transparent which is actualized by fire. So colour is seen only in light. But, (*ibid.* 419 a 23–25) fire is visible both in light and in darkness: and necessarily so, for it is owing to fire that the transparent becomes transparent.

Such was Aristotle's concept of light, to which the active reason was compared. Active reason was said to "make all things, like a ἕξις such as light." Now ἕξις is an active power which is founded upon an actual thing. Cf. n. 8. As for light, it is the function of a transparent medium. This medium is acted on by fire and colour, and acts upon the eye. Therefore, the active reason which is compared to light would act upon the passive reason rather than upon the object. Brentano

meaning of "this reason" in the following sentence: "And this reason is separable, impassive and unmixed being in its substance actual." In contrast to "such a reason," "this reason" implies of course the active reason which acts as an active principle like light. But it is otherwise with Brentano. Even St. Thomas and Brentano do not deny that "this reason" indicates the active reason, but they read the text somewhat arbitrarily as "even this reason," and allow the characters like separability, impassiveness and unmixedness to the potential reason no less than to the active,[140] the only attribute peculiar to the active reason is restricted to actuality. It is true that in the fourth chapter and elsewhere, these three characters are attributed to reason in general, while reason is simply defined as the faculty of receiving forms. Still, what must be noticed is that Aristotle divides the reason into the active and the passive only in this single place. From the fact that these characters are attributed in other places to reason in general, it does not follow of necessity that they are common both to the active reason and the passive. The attributes which were vaguely assigned to reason in general, when it was taken as a simple entity, might be limited to the active reason when the reason was divided into parts.[141] And this seems in all likelihood to be the case with Aristotle, who, following Plato, at first attributed these characters together with immortality to soul in general, then limited them to reason alone, still obliged to admit that even this reason cannot act without imagination which is combined with the body, could scarcely find the way to avoid contradiction. It seems to support our interpretation that the definite article in "this reason" indicates the active reason in particular; the actuality seems to be the ground of the other attributes than a mere coordinate attribute.[142] Strictly speaking, what is separable, impassive and unmixed should be confined to the active reason. In fact there is a remarkable difference of thought between the fourth and the fifth chapters of the De Anima. On account of an unfortunate attempt of

acknowledged this essential function of light. But in order to insist upon his interpretation to the effect that the active reason acts upon image (φάντασμα) and actualizes the rational forms which are potentially included in it, he emphasizes the word τρόπον τινα and slights the actuality of the active reason. This is a distortion, after all. Cf. Brentano, op. cit. 173.

[140] Brentano, op. cit. 175; De An. III. 4. 429 b 5; a 5, 15, 29, 18, 24. Brentano reads this sentence "Auch dieser Verstand ist frei vom Körper usw."; but in this case, the text should be καὶ οὗτος δὲ ὁ νοῦς χωριστός κτλ. Cf. Zeller, op. cit. 571 n. 2.

[141] Zeller, op. cit. 577 n. 2.

[142] Cf. Hick's note ad loc.

Aristotle's to reconcile the different thoughts, Brentano seems to have failed in catching the real meaning of the fifth chapter.

But suppose we grant Brentano's theory taking the words in the ordinary sense, i.e., separability as "real separability from the body," impassiveness as "not being affected by the body," and unmixedness as "not co-existing with the body," then, it will conflict with the fact that the act of reason is to be related to the body through the medium of imagination. To avoid this difficulty, Brentano is obliged to take the meaning of these attributes quite in a different way, i.e., χωριστός not as "separability from the body," but as "real separateness", ἀπαθές not as "impassive," but as "unchangeable and not losing its essence," ἀμιγής not as "independent of the body," but as "synonymous with separateness," or "not to mix with potential beings." Very ingenious, but none the less too constrained an interpretation,[143] indeed. Taking χωριστός as actual separateness, it is at all events difficult to attribute it to the reason[144] of a living being at least while it is still living, whereas whenever Aristotle uses the term χωριστός with reference to reason, he means thereby almost without exception separability from the body. As far as reason presupposes of necessity imagination, Brentano's interpretation to the effect that the function of reason is not founded upon the body is not admissible from the beginning. Further, if ἀπαθές, following Brentano, means that a thing does not lose its essence through being affected, such an "apathy" will not be confined to the reason, but may be predicated of sense as well,[145] for the eye

143 Brentano, op. cit. 177 f.

144 Since Brentano takes it as actual separation, he feels difficulty in the sentence: χωρισθείς δ' ἐστὶ μόνον ὅπερ ἐστί κτλ. If it were read as separation, it would be incomprehensible that here again the expression "when separated" should appear in a discussion as to the active reason. To avoid this difficulty, Brentano interprets the word χωριστός as "being in its activity independent of the body," with the contention that there is no incongruence in predicating the same attribute to the soul both in lifetime and after death. But it is a redundant, if not a paradox, to say that the soul which is independent of the body in lifetime will be independent of the body after death. χωριστός is rather to be taken as separable or potentially separate.

145 De An. III. 7. 431 a 4 f.: And manifestly the sensible object simply brings the faculty of sense which was potential into actual existence: in this transition, in fact, the sense is not acted upon (οὐ πάσχει) or qualitatively changed. Thus, Brentano's attempt to distinguish ἀπαθές and οὐ πάσχει and to admit the latter to reason, is not tenable. Further in ibid. III. 4. 429 a 29f. it is said: "But that the impassivity (ἀπάθεια) of sense is different from that of intellect is clear if we look at the sense-organs and at sense." Here the impassivity of sense is surely distinguished from that of intellect; sense is impassive none the less. This distinction, however, is not the same as the following one. Ibid. II. 5. 417 b 2–5: "To suffer

does not perish by perceiving light, the ear by hearing a tone. The concept ἀμιγής is, as is well known, borrowed from Anaxagoras, and Aristotle almost always mentions the name of Anaxagoras when he uses this word; therefore, we should take it in the original sense it had in Anaxagoras. In this sense, however, it means the unmixedness of reason with the body and its pure separability from the body.[146] Finally, if we avoid the difficulty by taking these attributes, like Brentano, in the negative sense, we shall be led to an ironical result that there is no real separability among the parts of the soul, for Brentano insists on the one hand, that none of them signifies real separability from the body. This will amount to the absolute denial of the desired conclusion as to the separability of reason.

The above arguments would be enough to prove that "this reason," which is "separable, impassive and unmixed, being in its substance actual," should be restricted to the active reason. But this is confirmed also by the succeeding proposition in the text: "For that which acts is always superior to that which is acted upon, as principle is to matter." We cannot explain why he asserts here the superiority of the agent to the patient, unless we take the subject of the above mentioned attributes to be active reason and makes these words explain the unique status of this reason as against the potential and material reason.[147] We should also notice that the correlative concepts of "patient" and

or be acted upon, is a term of more than one meaning. Sometimes it means a sort of destruction by the contrary, sometimes it is rather a preservation of what is potentially existent by what is actually existent and like it, so far as likeness holds of potentiality when compared with actuality." Both sense and intellect are ἀπαθές in the former sense, as is evident from the statement in 431 a 4, but the intellect is ἀπαθές in its particular sense, viz., not to be mixed with the body, and such an intellect, must be, without doubt, the so-called active reason. Hence Zeller regards this statement to be related to the active reason. Cf. Zeller, *op. cit.* 571. 2. n.

[146] Anaxagoras, *Fr.* 12; cf. *Met.* I. 8. 989 b 15; *Phys.* VIII. 5. 256 b 25; *De An.* I. 2. 405 a 17. None of the proofs that Nuyens presents against this view is persuasive. (*op. cit.* 285) Cf. also *Gen. An.* II. 3. 736 b 28.

[147] According to Brentano, the primacy of active reason is meaningful only if immortality belongs to reason in general; viz., since reason is, as a whole, immortal, it is meaningful to add "much the more is the active reason immortal", whereas if on the contrary one should interpret this to the effect that the passive reason is mortal, while the active reason, being superior to the passive, must also be immortal, it would follow that there is no difference of degree between the mortals. Cf. Brentano, Aristoteles Lehre vom Ursprung des menschlichen Geistes 6 n. But Brentano's inference is not necessary. Whether there be difference of degree beween the mortals, is not the matter of present concern. What is required is to admit that immortality is appropriate to a superior being, even though not every superior being is immortal.

"matter" stand in the same contrast to "agent" and "principle," as do those of "matter" and "potentiality" to "cause" and "agent." So far, our investigation has concerned opposition between the reason which / becomes all things and the reason which makes all things. From the above data, we must conclude that the potential reason is the matter, the patient and the reason which becomes all things, while active reason is the principle, the cause, the agent and the reason which makes all things.

Here we must stop the above line of reasoning, for the next proposition in the text seems to be in all respects an interpolation. In so far as we take the above arguments to have been made about the opposition of the active and the passive reason, it is too abrupt to read: "Now actual knowledge is identical with the object of knowing, but potential knowledge is prior in time in the individual, though considered as a whole, it is not prior in time."[148] This actual knowledge may imply a sort of contemplation which was opposed to knowledge *qua habitus*,[149], whereas the active and the potential reason are the principles of knowledge, but not the knowledge itself. For what purpose is actual knowledge now taken in account? St. Thomas explains that Aristotle, changing his argument at this point, takes both active and potential reason together as potential knowledge, and asks then about actual knowledge.[150] If the text is thus understood, the next statement must be applied exclusively to actual knowledge, and the determination, "It is not at one time thinking and at another not," should be predicated of actual knowledge rather than of active reason. But is it not redundant, if not nonsense, to say that actual knowledge is "not at one time thinking and at another not"? This sentence, therefore must be referred to something other than "actual knowledge." Now, we have learnt from Aristotle, that God is the reason which continues thinking, / in which a human being partakes from time to time.[151] We also notice

148 Themistius substituted ἁπλῶς for ὅλως. This emendation is not necessary, since ὅλως is used synonymously with ἁπλῶς Cf. Hick's note *ad loc.*
149 *De An.* II. 5. 417 a 22–29; cf. *Met. XII.* 9. 1074 b 38 ff.
150 Thomas Aquinas, *De An. Comm.* 740–742.
151 *Met. XII.* 7. 1072 b 14–16; *ibid.* 24–26. 1075 a 7–9: ὥπερ (γὰρ) ὁ ἀνθρώπινος (ἤ) ὅ γε τῶν συνθέτων ἔχει ἔν τινι χρόνῳ οὕτως (δή) ἔχει αὐτὴ αὐτῆς ἡ νόησις τὸν ἅπαντα αἰῶνα, οὐ γὰρ ἔχει τὸ εὖ ἐν τῳδὶ ἢ ἐν τῳδί, ἀλλ' ἐν ὅλῳ τινὶ τὸ ἄριστον, ὂν ἄλλο τι. Ross's emendation marked by brackets is recommendable but we would transpose the passage οὕτως δή ἔχει αὐτῆς ἡ νόησις τὸν ἅπαντα αἰῶνα to the top. This statement is not, as Bonitz and Schwegler suppose, related to discursive thinking and intuition, but to the thinking of the divine and the human reasons. And by our transposition, οὐ γὰρ ... ὂν ἄλλο τι would become the statement about

that this statement as to the temporality of human thinking appears at
the end of the fourth chapter, [152] which precedes immediately the
statement at issue. Consequently, that which is "not at one time
thinking and at another not" must be identified with something beyond
human being; it is, in all probability, the active reason and nothing
else. Only considering thus, we are able to understand the connection
with the next sentence: "It is only when it is separated that it is just
what it is, and this alone is immortal and eternal." But Brentano's
opinion is again opposed to ours. According to him, that which "is not
at one time thinking and at another not," is the divine reason, which,
in its turn, is identical with actual knowledge[153] instead of with active
reason, for the latter cannot be divine, because it is immanent to the
human mind. Thus according to the paraphrasis of St. Thomas and
Brentano, the statement as to divine reason comes to an end. For the
next sentence can by no means be regarded as a statement as to divine
reason, it runs namely: "It is only when it is separated that it is just
what it is, and this alone is immortal and eternal." Thus, St. Thomas
and Brentano distinguish divine reason from active reason in that the
former is transcendent, while the latter is immanent to human being.
The reason which will come to its proper being only when it is separated,
must, until then, be combined with the body. Such a reason, of course,
cannot be divine and absolutely transcendent. St. Thomas and Brentano would not like to take it the active reason, for they attributed
separability, immortality etc. not only to active reason, but also to
reason in general. It follows therefore that the subject of this sentence
must be human reason in general. Thus, according to their interpretation, this chapter treats at first the active and the potential reason
(450a 10–19), then turns to the opposition between actual knowledge
and potential knowledge or human reason (19–22), and finally returns
to the problem of human reason in general. But it is far from being

divine thinking. Thus ἐν τινι χρόνῳ corresponds to ἐν τῳδὶ ἢ ἐν τῳδί, and τὸν
ἅπαντα αἰῶνα to ἐν ὅλῳ τινί. Further, οὐ γὰρ ... ἄλλο τι would correspond to the
sentence in question, viz., De An. III. 5. 430 a 22 f.: ἀλλ' οὐχ μὲν νοεῖ ὁτὲ δ' οὐ
νοεῖ ... καὶ τοῦτο μόνον ἀθάνατον καὶ ἀίδιον. Thus the above quotation would be
translated as follows: "Just as human reason or the reason of a composite being
is in a certain period of time, so is the (divine) self-thought throughout eternity,
for since this (i.e. divine reason) is different from that (i.e. human reason), it
enjoys the good not just in this or in that period, but the best in the whole."

[152] De An. III. 4. 430 a 5.

[153] Brentano, op. cit. 182. De Corte also follows this interpretation. Cf. La
doctrine de l'intelligence chez Aristote 65, 69; cf. also Nuyens's criticism on this
point, op. cit. 33 f.

plausible that Aristotle might deal in such a short course with such manifold themes, without mentioning any notice as to the subject of inquiry. The situation might be somewhat improved if there were any idea of divine reason distinct from active reason, but there is scarcely any hint to this issue. As for Brentano's argument in reference to the distinction between the active reason and the divine is not worth while to be examined. In disproof thereof it would be sufficient if we point out that even human reason is called divine,[154] to say nothing of the active reason. Active reason is not deprived of divinity through being associated with the human soul. It is divine as well as human, human as well as divine,[155] paradoxical as it may sound. Man thinks only through being illuminated by divine reason. Man thinks in God, while God realizes His thought in man. In any case, however, the clause about actual knowledge is an interpolation,[156] after all.

Now we come to the next sentence: "We do not remember, because it is impassive." Since the verb "remember" takes the form of first person plural, "reason" cannot be the grammatical subject. Therefore, former interpreters considered the subject to be ourselves, and argued whether the object should be the eternal action of active reason or its life before birth and after death.[157] Thus understood, that which re-

---

[154] *De An.* I. 4. 408 b 29; *Eth. Nic.* X. 7. 1177 a 15; b 30.

[155] *Eth. Nic.* X. 7. 1177 a 13–17; 1177 b 26–1178 a 3; *Met.* XII. 10. 1075 a 11–15. De Corte argues that as the active reason is said to be in the soul, if it were assumed to be the subject of eternal thinking, there must be human thinking which is eternal and continues without interruption (*op. cit.* 66). We admit that Aristotle's statement at issue implies the immanence of the active reason to the (human) soul. But this does not rule out the possibility for the active reason to be sometimes separate from the human soul. Cf. Nuyens, *op. cit.* 34.

[156] This is not an arbitrary omission. The same sentence is found in ch. 7, 431 a 1, which seems to be its proper position. Kampfe, Kail and Susemihl regard it as an interpolation.

[157] Hicks takes this to mean that we individuals who are born and will die, do not remember the eternal act of active reason, because active reason is impassive and cannot be the object of memory. But this proves nothing, since what makes memory possible is not that the object is passive, but that the mind suffers something. Further, Hicks neglects the temporality of memory, but if memory is synonymous with consciousness and is irrelevant to temporality, even the participation in God's eternal thinking might be counted in the remembering of the active reason.
The following interpretations supplement the first by taking in account the temporality. According to Trendelenburg, what is meant is that man does not remember the thought which the active reason experienced in the previous life. But it is only a matter of course that man does not remember the fact which occurred when he did not exist, and there is no need at all of mentioning in particular that the active reason is impassive. The third interpretation is one held by many commentators from early times, according to which it means that man does not

members is either passive reason or some other part of the soul, e.g.
imagination. In this case however the impassiveness of active reason
cannot be the ground why this reason or another part of the soul
does not remember (the act of reason). Memory is possible for a
subject conjoined with body, no matter whether the object, (i.e. the
active reason) be passive or impassive. Therefore, the real subject
of this memory should be the active reason;[158] it does not remember,
because it is impassive, while memory is possible only when the soul
is acted upon through the body. Thus, both what does not remember and what is impassive are the same active reason. It is not
passive in so far as it is an *active* reason, it is not affected through bodily
changes either, hence it has neither imagination nor memory. Nothing
can be more evident to us than this. But not so for St. Thomas and
Brentano, who considered that reason in general is eternal and immortal, since the reason which is here characterized as impassive must be
the same as this reason. Brentano's interpretation may be expatiated
as follows:[159] It is not reason but concrete individuals that do not
remember. Man is constituted of immortal reason and mortal soul, together with the body which is also perishable. Though the reason in us
is immortal, its eternal life is not remembered by ourselves, because on
the one hand, this reason itself, being impassive, is not the subject of
memory, on the other hand, the part of the soul which holds memory,
is mortal, so that it has no memory of the fact before birth and after
death. This interpretation of Brentano's is supported by the supposition

remember the fact that the active reason would continue to exist after his death.
But as far as memory belongs to a particular person, there cannot be any memory whatever after he passed away, whether the active reason be passive or impassive. Besides, memory about future life is a *contradictio in adjecto*. There is a
fourth theory that explains this as the decline of memory through old age. Cf.
De An. I. 4. 408 b 27. This interpretation was held by Plutarchus and was partly
adopted by Brentano. But it is less plausible, for if this were really the case, what
should be mentioned would be the mortality of the passive reason instead of the
impassiveness of the active reason, not that we do not remember, but that we
forget.

[158] This can be confirmed by other descriptions concerning memory. In *De An.*
I. 4. 408 b 27, it is said that reason does not remember because it is impassive.
In *De Memor.* I. 450 a 12, sense is required for memory, without any determination as to the object. In *De Memor.* I. 450 a 24, it is stated: "And the object of
imagination is *per se* the object of memory, but what is not without imagination
is accidentally the object of imagination." But under this condition, not only the
active reason, but also the passive reason cannot be the object of memory. For
to say that the passive reason does not think without imagination is not the
same as to say that the passive reason itself cannot exist without imagination.

[159] Brentano, *op. cit.* 207–209.

that the reason which is impassive, immortal, and eternal should be
the receptive reason of man, while what is meant by the passive reason
is in fact, imagination or *sensus communis*, quite different from receptive reason.

The assertion that reason in general does not remember, may sound
strange to the ears of those who think consciousness to be essential to
reason, and memory to be essential to consciousness. As far as this
point is concerned, however, Brentano's interpretation is congruent
with Aristotle's thought. According to Aristotle, memory, as well as
love, hatred, and reasoning are not the attributes of reason itself, but
the attributes of the concrete individual, who possesses the reason.[160]
Memory is not concerned with the object of sensation[161] alone, but also
with that of reason, and even in this latter case, it cannot act without
imagination,[162] memory belongs primarily to this faculty,[163] though

[160] *De An.* I. 4. 408 b 25–28.

[161] *De Memor.* I. 450 a 12–16. The immediate object of memory is not concept, but image. Since, however, the soul does not think without an image (*De
Memor.* I. 449 b 30; *De An.* III. 7. 431 a 17), the object of thought may be accidentally the object of memory (*De Memor.* 2. 451 a 28 f.). Image is *per se* the
object of memory, while concept is so only *per accidens.* (*De Memor.* I. 450 a 23).
In other words, memory is concerned directly with image, and only indirectly
with concepts. Concepts are universal and eternal, while memory is a habitual
state of special experience, therefore the apprehension of concepts may be
thought, but it is not memory. (*De Memor.* I. 451 a 1) One and the same instance
of thinking, in so far as it is seen as the receipt of an eternal concept, is contemplation; but in so far as it is seen as the remembrance of a past experience, it is
memory. Cf. *De Memor.* I. 449 b 24 f.; 450 b 24–27; 451 a 26. That which accepts eternal concepts is the passive reason, and that which is concerned with
special and temporal images is the imaginative faculty. The thinking itself may
become the object of memory, but in this respect, it should be regarded as a kind
of image. What one remembers is that he has experienced thinking, not the contents of thought itself; the latter is remembered only accidentally. Cf. *De Memor.*
I. 449 b 18–23.

[162] *De Memor.* I. 450 a 12 f. But to say that memory is impossible without
image is not sufficient to prove that memory is the function of imaginative faculty. The same statement may be applied to thinking as well, and it is actually
stated that thinking is impossible without imagination. Cf. *De Memor.* I. 449 a
31, or *De An.* III. 7. 431 a 17. Thus, if we should assign memory to imaginative
faculty only because memory is impossible without image, from the same ground
we should also assign thinking to imaginative faculty. But in truth, thinking is
the function not of imaginative faculty, but of passive reason. Aristotle does not
explain the difference between thinking and memory. But presumably it is
that while thinking is concerned with the universal, memory is concerned with
special sensible forms. In other words, thinking is concerned with the concept in
terms of an image, while memory is directly concerned with the image and does
not go further. (*De Memor.* I. 450 a 23) The object of thought is the same as the
object of memory only *per accidens.*

[163] Cf. Ch. *II.* 2. Imagination is a habitus acquired from sense impressions or

sometimes it may be attributed accidentally to reason. Hence memory
is not confined to the human being who has opinion and practical wisdom, but also is found in some other animals. If it belonged to the rational part, most animals would have no memory,[164] whereas in fact,

per accidens from thinking as well. (*De An.* III. 3. 428 b 10; *De Somn.* I. 459 a
17). It is, so to say, a weakened sensation (*Rhet.* I. II. 1370 a 28). Sensation is related to an actually existent corporeal substance, or to a being which has matter,
while imagination is something like the remnant of sensation, and can exist without actual object (*De Somn.* 2. 460 b 7), being itself deprived of matter (*De An.*
III. 8. 432 a 9). When this imagination is referred to a past experience, it becomes the object of memory (n. 160, 161). So, imagination presupposes sensation,
but is not identical with it. In as much as imagination is not universal like thought,
it is similar to sensation (*De Somn.* I. 459 a 16). But while a special sense feels
a special sensation with regard to a special object, there is another faculty, which
keeps experience, compares and discriminates them with each other. This is the
so-called *sensus communis* or the first sense, being situated in the heart as the
central organ of the body on account of its uniting function. (*De Juvent.* 3. 469 a
5). Aristotle, feeling a difficulty in the orientation of imagination, assigned it to
sensus communis with some hesitation.

[164] Cf. *De Memor.* I. 450 a 12 ff. There is a question as to whether memory is
not an essential act of the irrational part. In this argument, to deprive reason of
memory and to assign it to a concrete being, memory is ranked with love, hatred
and thought; but thought is obviously an act of reason. Thinking, as well as
memory, cannot act without imagination, to be sure. But if one maintains for
this reason alone, that memory is not a function of the rational part, he must also
admit that thinking likewise is not its proper function. Such a rational part,
which goes beyond memory and thinking, is not human intellect, without doubt.
There is indeed a statement which perhaps proves this. In succession to the observation that if memory were a function of the rational part, most animals
would have no memory, it is said, according to the traditional text, *ibid.* 450 a
18: ἴσως δ' οὐδενὶ τῶν θνητῶν. If memory were a function of the rational part,
how could it be that what is mortal does not have memory at all? Man is mortal,
yet it is endowed with intellect and memory. An act which a mortal being cannot
partake in, is not human without doubt. Aristotle might have implied hereby
that intellectual activity in the strict sense is beyond human intellect, which is
accompanied by the body. But human thinking is, of course, the act of human
intellect. Consequently, the proper act of intellect would be superhuman. Thus
understood, the intellect which does not remember should be a transcendent
pure reason, which is not quite different from divine reason as Brentano maintained. In so far as this premise is concerned, therefore, we may infer without
great difficulty that what does not remember is just this active reason and
nothing else. What must be borne in mind moreover is that Aristotle divided
reason explicitly into the active and the passive only once in *De An.* III. 5.,
while in *De Memor.* reason is taken as a whole to be a divine faculty. It is quite
natural that memory, which was thus excluded from reason, should find no
refuge except in *sensus communis*. But now, when reason is divided into the active
and the passive, the latter being perishable and affected in a manner by the body,
it is doubtful whether memory should be shut out from passive reason. Passive
reason is a mental faculty combined with the body in terms of imagination. It
was the refuge for Thinking, who had been banished with Memory from Reason,
under the same pretext that they had some connection with Imagination. In

most, if not all, of them do remember. Hence it is evident that memory is not appropriate to reason in general, much less to the active reason. In this respect, it might seem to be more faithful to Aristotle's thought to understand the phrase "οὗ μνημονεύομεν δέ" as Brentano actually did, to mean that reason in general does not remember, than to restrict the subject to active reason. But even if active reason does not remember, it does not follow of necessity that passive reason should remember instead. So, our opinion at no point conflicts with Aristotle's general line of thought.

One might, however, raise another objection to it, viz., if memory is not the function of reason in general, it would be redundant to mention in particular that active reason does not remember because it is impassive. To this objection we may answer as follows: What is asked here by Aristotle is not what is the subject of memory, but why in spite of the immortality and eternity of the active reason there is no memory. Therefore, nothing prevents him of saying that the active reason does not remember, even if anything else may not remember. But we will content ourselves with proving that the real subject of the sentence οὗ μνημονεύομεν δέ is active reason, without going so far as to affirm that memory belongs to passive reason.

Hitherto, Brentano's assumption was left untouched, to the effect that the reason which is immortal, imperishable and impassive is the receptive reason, whereas passive reason is another name of imagination quite different from receptive reason. But this assumption of Brentano's is quite inadmissible. According to Brentano, receptive reason accepts from imagination the rational forms, which were contained in it and were realized by active reason, this last mentioned is not, however, a reason in the proper sense. The receptive reason itself is an indefinite faculty of knowledge like the intellect as *tabula rasa* in

that case, Memory, once compelled to lodge in the Imaginative Part, might be accepted in the new home of Passive Reason, who has already become independent of his stern father. Moreover, imagination was divided in the intellectual and the sensible (*De An.* III. 10. 433 b 28), and knowledge is considered to be, in a sense, memory (*De Memor.* 1. 499 b 18). Then, is it not possible that at least such a rational or intellectual memory is a function of the passive reason? But concerning the passive reason, we have no detailed explanation except the statement in question, where it is contrasted with the active reason. Besides, Biehl replaces θνητῶν in the above quotation, with θηρίον. This emendation, which is very plausible, makes our interpretation impossible. So we would not go beyond mere supposition. Speaking more moderately, passive reason would be different from the imaginative faculty in that its objects are universal concepts, while memory, being the reproduction of imagination, belongs to something different from passive reason.

Locke's philosophy; it acts only in terms of imagination, which in its turn, is inseparable from the body. But we wonder, what significance there is in saying that the reason which cannot act without body persists after death in its proper state. To say that such a reason exists separately, would mean that what has no actual form exists by itself. Let Aristotle himself speak: "If it thinks nothing, what is there here of dignity? Such a reason would be just like one who sleeps."[165]

What is then the course of thinking whereby Brentano takes the passive reason for imagination? To us, who understand the reason which is immortal, impassive, and hence does not remember, to be the active reason, the clause "ὁ δὲ παθητικὸς νοῦς φθαρτός" forms a rigid opposition to it. Active reason is impassive and immortal, while passive reason is mortal. Whereas according to Brentano, passive reason is immortal no less than active reason. That it is ἀπαθές means not that it suffers no influence from body, but that it does not lose its essence through being acted upon. Thus understood, the clause "ὁ δὲ παθητικὸς νοῦς φθαρτός" loses its significance; the impassiveness of active reason is diluted, and its rigid opposition to passive reason is corrupted. If reason in general were immortal and impassive, what is mortal and passive can by no means be a real reason, without doubt. Hence St. Thomas distinguishes passive reason from material and potential reason,[166] and assigns the former to the sensible part. On the same ground, Brentano assimilates passive reason with imagination, and gives to it a function of combining active reason with receptive and potential reason.[167] Imagination is called reason because it partakes in the reason, and passive reason is a reason only in an accidental sense. Consequently, that the passive reason is mortal would only mean that imagination perishes with the body, and this mortality does not cover the receptive and potential reason of human being. Human reason, which is receptive and potential, is none the less immortal and imperishable. Thus argues Brentano. But we can hardly repress our interrogation: how is it possible for human reason to be immortal, if it is acted upon and conditioned by imagination; was it not the theory of Aristotle's that human reason is inseparable from the body because it cannot act without imagination? Further, if passive reason is identical with imagination, why should it be discussed in this reference under the accidental denomination of passive reason? According to Brenta-

[165] *Met.* XII. 9. 1074 b 17.
[166] Thomas Aquinas, *De An. Comm.* 745.
[167] Brentano, *Psych. d. Arist.* 208.

no, imagination is here introduced to explain why memory declines and perishes in spite of the eternity of reason.[168] Human reason being impassive – in the special sense which has been stated above – has no memory, but such a reason does not think without imagination. This is just what the clause "ὁ δὲ παθητικὸς νοῦς φθαρτός" really means. Imagination is called passive, because it is acted upon by active reason, which is a special faculty of realizing forms. This imagination acquires the name of reason accidentally, since on the one hand, it is acted upon by the rational part, and on the other, it acts upon the same part. As far as those two kinds of explanation are presented separately, they contain nothing impossible. But, if, in truth, imagination be introduced because human reason or the receptive faculty of thinking cannot think without it, how does this imagination relate to human reason? Is not imagination active, while reason is passive? Was it not said that the receptive reason could not think unless it suffered and received forms from imagination? Now that imagination is considered in such a reference, it ought rather to be active than passive. It was said that imagination was called reason accidentally because it was necessary for the functioning of human reason. Let this supposition be granted for the moment, this does not, however, give a satisfactory illustration as to why imagination should be called passive reason instead of active reason. The term "active reason" was applied already to another faculty, which acts only indirectly upon the receptive reason, through acting at first upon human sensibility. Why then should such a faculty be active, while imagination is passive? Isn't reason in the proper sense, from which these faculties get the name of reason, man's receptive reason? Which of the two acts more directly upon receptive reason? Is it not imagination directly, and active reason only indirectly? Brentano admits that imagination is acted upon by active reason. Then it is evident that active reason is called reason only through being related to human reason, but never until then and by itself. Therefore, imagination would have no ground of being called passive reason, even though active reason acts upon it. Though active reason was attributed in a sense to the rational part of the human soul, Brentano never admits it to be a kind of human reason in the proper sense. If imagination is to be called reason accidentally through being related to man's receptive reason, it might rather form a part of active reason, and receptive reason is more likely to be called passive reason. Moreover, if

[168] Brentano, *op. cit.* 2 09.

imagination is called passive reason, what is truly called reason must
be the active reason, which acts directly upon imagination. While
imagination is thus active upon the receptive reason, why on earth
should one give such a denomination as passive reason? This might
be permissible if there were such usage of terminology. But in fact, this
concept appears only once in all of Aristotle's works. The difficulty increases for an interpreter who regards reason in general to be impassive
and eternal. Brentano maintains that Aristotle called imagination
reason in a certain sense, but none of the evidence that he cites expresses Aristotle's own theory.[169]

After saying that the reason which is immortal, eternal, and does
not remember, is "impassive," Aristotle adds the words, "while
passive reason is mortal." With regard to this statement, it is quite
unnatural to take the former for reason in general, the latter for a
kind of sensibility or imagination. Obviously, "ὁ δὲ παθητικὸς νοῦς
φθαρτός" is opposed to "τοῦτο μόνον ἀθανατόν καὶ ἀμιγής", i.e., the
reason which is referred to by the words, "οὗτος ὁ νοῦς" and which
is called "χωριστὸς καὶ ἀπαθής καὶ ἀμιγής." Thus, both passive reason
and οὗτος ὁ νοῦς must be the kinds of reason. Now that οὗτος ὁ νοῦς is
active reason, passive reason as its opposite must be the potential and
material reason which was regarded previously as contrary to active
reason, the so-called receptive reason by St. Thomas and Brentano.

It is more constrained an interpretation to make both receptive-
potential reason and passive reason stand in opposition to active
reason. In Aristotelian terminology, moreover, the contrary to
ποιητικός is παθητικός rather than δυνάμει, while the contrary to δυνάμει
should be ἐνεργείᾳ, so that again the contrary to active reason should
be passive reason. It might seem then, as if there were potential reason
or active reason besides them. But in fact, active reason is just actual
and passive reason is just potential. To resume our provisional conclusion: "Potential reason is the reason which is material and passive,
and which becomes all things, while on the contrary, active reason is
principle, cause, agent and that which makes all things." What must
be noticed here is the fact that though Aristotle also admits in reason
the opposition of matter or the potential to cause or agent, he never
uses the terms "potential reason" or "active reason" while he does use

---

[169] Brentano, *ibid.* cites *Eth. Nic.* VI. 12. 1143 b 4 as an example of calling
sensation reason; *De An.* III. 3. 427 b 27 as an example of counting the imaginative faculty in reason, and *De An.* III. 10. 433 a 9 etc. of calling it reason or a
kind of thinking. Cf. Zeller's criticism on these points, *op. cit.* 576 n 5.

the term "passive reason."[170] We have used those complex concepts only for convenience' sake or by convention. It may be that he set up in opposition to matter and the potential, not form or the actual, but cause, principle, and agent, because the actuality of reason is the perfection of its activity, and actual reason in the proper sense would coincide with contemplation. Hence the faculty, which is the cause of actual reason or contemplation, and opposed to the material and the passive (reason), might be called "active reason." It is not the complete actuality of thought, but the active principle of contemplation, the reason as a *habitus* (ἕξις) or active potentiality. Thus active reason may sometimes be called actual, but more often is explained as a cause or agent. On the other hand, there is neither ground for distinguishing potential reason from passive reason, nor a real distinction between them. As we have seen above, since the statement preceding the concept of receptive reason has contrasted matter, the potential and the passive with principle, the actual and agent, it would be an extraordinary leap of thought, if this receptive reason should be not the potential reason, but a sort of sensibility which is quite different from that.[171] Besides, it is Aristotle's constant belief and often repeated saying that matter *qua* matter is passive. Hence, it is quite inconsistent with Aristotle's system to distinguish passive reason from potential and material reason.

From all of the foregoing considerations, it seems probable that Aristotle, dividing reason into the active and the passive, took the former as eternal, immortal and separable from the body, and the latter as mortal and inseparable. Receptive reason is mediated by imagination, which, being the function of the sensitive part, is not separable from the body. But active reason is separable from imagination, and so also from the body. Though it may sometimes exist in the soul, in its essence, it is separate from it and transcendent.

Now at last, we come to the incomplete proposition: "καὶ ἄνευ τούτου οὐθὲν νοεῖ." Every possible interpretation has been attempted for this passage. According to Simplicius, it means that active reason never

---

170 The word ποιητικὸς νοῦς might have been avoided lest it should be confused with the productive intellect which is coordinate with πρακτικὸς νοῦς and θεωρητικὸς νοῦς. Cf. Zeller, *op. cit.* 570 n. 4. νοῦς δυνάμει was not appropriate because not only νοῦς παθητικός but also active reason is a kind of δύναμις.

171 *Gen. et Corr.* I. 7. 324 b 18. ἡ ὕλη ἢ ὕλη παθητικός. ibid. I. 4. 320 a 2, 10; 328 b 11; II. 9. 335 b 30; *De An.* II. 2. 414 a 10; *Meteor.* I. 2. 339 a 29; IV. 10. 388 a 21; 11. 389 a 30; *Met.* X. 4. 1055 a 30.

thinks without passive reason. Whether or not passive reason be identical with imagination, this will lead to the same conclusion, that reason cannot exist without body. Zabarella also explains that active reason does not think without passive reason, but he endeavours to keep the separation and transcendency of reason by distinguishing eternal thinking and human thinking and by saying that without passive reason human thinking will perish, but not thinking in general. In modern ages, Zeller is almost of the same opinion as Zabarella.[172] Whereas to St. Thomas, the passage means that reason does not think without passive reason, and though human reason persists after the death of the body, it no longer thinks in the same manner as it now does.[173] To Brentano, who identifies passive reason with imagination, it means that reason does not think without imagination.

Indeed it was Aristotle's own theory, that human reason does not think without imagination. But we can by no means agree with St. Thomas and Brentano, who maintain that human reason persists after the death of the body without thinking and memory.[174] By far the more plausible is the interpretation by Trendelenburg and Hicks to the effect that passive reason does not think without active reason.[175] Thus understood, we can admit without difficulty that active reason is eternal and immortal, while passive reason can think as far as it comes into contact with it; and that this active reason, when separated from the body and from passive reason, neither thinks nor has memory, though it has some sort of reality none the less. What is then this active reason and what is its function? And what kind of thing is this passive reason?

[172] Cf. Hick's note *ad loc.*

[173] Thomas Aquinas, *op. cit.* 745. Cf. Brentano, *op. cit.* 204 ff.

[174] Cf. Brentano, *op. cit.* 128 n 45. Teichmüller, *Studien zur Geschichte der Begriffe.* 434 f.

[175] Zeller's objection to this interpretation is to the effect that the last senstence which begins with οὐ μνημονεύομεν and ends with ἄνευ τούτου οὐθὲν νοεῖ indicates the reason why we do not remember, so that, if ἄνευ τούτου οὐθὲν νοεῖ should mean that the passive reason does not think without the active reason, the subject of the sentence must be the passive reason, but it is only self-evident and there is no need of mentioning in particular that the passive reason does not remember the time when it did not exist. But according to our interpretation, the subject which does not remember is the active reason, and this reason does not remember because it is impassive; ὁ δὲ παηθτικὸς νοῦς φθαρτός constituting another independent sentence. Zeller's reading to combine τοῦτο μέν and ὁ δὲ with ὅτι is grammatically possible. But it is logically preferable to make ὁ δὲ παθητικὸς νοῦς φθαρτός contrast with τοῦτο μόνον ἀθάνατον καὶ ἀΐδιον. Even if Zeller's reading should be adopted, at least it is certain that the real subject of οὐ μνημονεύομεν must be the immortal active reason.

4. Solution of the Problem

As mentioned above, Aristotle's division of reason into the active and the passive appears only once in *De Anima* III. 5., and there is no more description about the essence of these two kinds of reason. The first attempt to be tried, therefore, must be to sift out of the words applied to reason in general, attributes that might be peculiar to each kind of reason. It is said that reason with its separability from the body and transcendent origin, cannot receive the forms of objects without the aid of the body. These two characteristics of reason seem to be quite incompatible. Reason is divine on the one hand, mundane, on the other hand. It is actual, yet potential; immortal, yet mortal. On account of the first characters, reason must be transcendent, but on account of the second characters, it must be conjoined with the body.[176] When divineness, actuality and immortality were monopolised by the active reason, passive reason must remain to be earthly and potential – a faculty of the mortal soul which is combined with the body.

Aristotle seems to have no distinct idea of a bodily organ of thought. He only conjectures that it might be sought either in the heart or in the brain, without deciding which is more probable. But since practical wisdom is assigned to the heart, and the physiological function of the brain is considered to be to cool the blood,[177] and to preserve the whole body,[178] the organ of intellect seems rather to be more appropriate to

[176] Referring to *Met.* XII. 3. 1070 a 21–27, Brentano asserts that Zeller's opinion to make reason precede the body is not conform to Aristotle's theory. (Aristoteles Lehre vom Ursprung des menschlichen Geistes 16 ff). The cited text runs as follows: "The moving causes exist as things preceding the effects, but causes in the sense of definitions are simultaneous with their effects. For when a man is healthy, then health also exists; and the shape of a bronze sphere exists at the same time as the bronze sphere. But we must examine whether any form also survives afterwards. For in some cases there is nothing to prevent this; e.g. the soul may be of this sort – not all soul but the reason; for presumably it is impossible that all soul should survive." But the reason which coexists with the body is nothing but the human intellect which is passive. If the whole reason should coexist with the body, no doubt, it must perish with the body. If the passive reason be like the health of a body or the figure of a bronze cube, the active reason might be compared to medical art as the form of health or to a cubical figure itself. Now it seems to be highly probable that an idea came up to the author to divide reason in two parts and to distribute these opposite characters to each of them.

[177] *Part. An.* II. 7. 652 b 20 ff. Plato was more advanced or at least nearer to the modern theory in making the head the seat of reason. Cf. *Tim.* 44 D; 13 C–D.

[178] *Part. An.* II. 7. 652 b 7.

the heart. At any rate, it is undeniable that Aristotle admitted some material substratum to human thinking.[179]

About passive reason and its physiological basis, we shall inquire afterwards. Our present concern is rather with active reason. The question has been much discussed since ancient times whether active reason is immanent or transcendent, and how it relates to the human reason and to the divine. The point where the interpretations diverge is the problem whether the active reason is a faculty of the human soul or a divine element outside it.[180] But presumably these theories are not really incompatible. Though the active reason may be separable from human being, it is not always separated.

Divinity is not absolutely opposed to humanity.[181] Man is connected with God, through participating in the active reason. But the active reason is not identical with human reason, so that man is a finite being who sometimes thinks and sometimes does not.[182]

There is no absolute diversity between man and God. The active reason is both transcendent and immanent, divine as well as human. But what is the function of this active reason? What sort of activity has this reason upon the passive reason? Reason was divided into the active and the passive, in accordance with the mode of its involvement in the act, and the act of reason is thinking,[183] so that the active reason is the active, and the passive reason is the passive principle of thinking. How then does thinking come into activity? According to Aristotle, human knowledge, thinking as well as sensation, is brought about through the cognitive faculty being acted upon by and receiving the forms from the objects.[184] If the cognitive faculty has any actual form of its own, it cannot reflect the object as it is. Therefore, it has no actual form before cognition, though it has all forms potentially.[185] Sense as a part of the soul has potentially all forms of sensible ob-

---

[179] Cf. *De An.* III. 4. 429 a 25. *In re* Kampe's attempt to admit a material substratum to reason, (*Erkenntnistheorie des Aristoteles* 12–49). Cf. Zeller's criticism in *Ph. d. Gr.* II. 2. 568 n. 3. also *De An.* II. 4. 408 b 5; *Met.* IX. 10. 1035 b 25.

[180] The transcendent theory is supported by Alexander, Avicenna, Averroes, Ravaisson, Zeller etc., while the immanent theory is supported by Theophrastus, Themistius, Thomas Aquinas, Brandis, and Brentano. Trendelenburg, standing in the middle, is most akin to our interpretation. Cf. Ch. II.

[181] *Eth. Nic.* X. 7. 1177 a 13; 1177 b 25.

[182] *De An.* III. 5. 430 a 22; *Met.* XII. 7. 1072 a 16; 1075 a 7; *De An.* III. 4. 430 a 5.

[183] *De An.* I. 3. 407 a 20.

[184] *De An.* III. 2. 427 a 9; 4. 429 a 13–18.

[185] *De An.* III. 4. 429 a 18–24; 429 b 30 f.

jects,[186] and reason is potentially the same as the objects of thought. When a certain sensible object acts upon one of the senses, which has infinite forms in passive potentiality, the special form of this object is actualized in the sense; and this actual form is the sensation of man.[187] In the same way, when an object of thinking gives an actual form to the reason which has infinite forms in passive potentiality, human thinking occurs.[188] What makes the potential sensation in sense actual, is the object of sensation; what realizes the potential thought in reason is the object of thought. No doubt, a concrete object accompanied by matter cannot act upon sense or reason. Though sense and reason may be "the same" as their objects, sensation and thought are not identical with concrete objects, but are the forms of objects without matter.[189] The reception of forms together with matter might well be nutrition, but never sensation. Such a reception is affection in the proper sense, i.e. affection through which the subject changes its character.[190] Sensation receives directly the forms[191] of things, while thinking receives not the forms of things, but the form of forms.[192] Now the thinking of man having such a constitution, its active principle must be the form of forms as its object, while human reason as its subject must be the passive principle which receives the form of forms i.e. Aristotle's "place of forms."[193] But we have previously concluded that the active principle of thinking is the active reason, and that it is of divine essence. Hence it is evident that this divine active reason is nothing but the form of forms as the object of thinking.

What, then, is the form of forms as the active principle of thinking? Seeing that the object of sensation is the form of things, while that of thinking is the form of forms, we might infer, that the object of thought is a higher form which is founded upon sensible objects. And the relation between such a higher form and sensible objects seems to corre-

---

[186] *De An.* III. 8. 431 b 26–432 a 3; cf. *ibid.* II. 5. 416 b 33; 417 a 6; 418 a 2.
[187] *De An.* II. 11. 423 b 31–424 a 2; III. 7. 431 a 4 f.; III. 2. 425 b 26.
[188] *De An.* III. 7. 431 b 16 f.
[189] *De An.* III. 8. 431 b 26; *ibid.* III. 2. 425 b 23 f.; II. 12. 424 a 17–24; III. 4. 430 a 6–9.
[190] *De An.* II. 12. 424 a 32 -b 3.
[191] *De An.* II. 5. 417 b 2–7; III. 7. 431 a 4 f.
[192] *De An.* III. 4. 432 a 2 f.
[193] *De An.* III. 4. 429 a 27–29; Cf. Plato, *Parm.* 132 B, 133 C, 134 A.
The form here meant must be the rational form only, which is distinguished from the others in *De An.* III. 4. 432 a 1. Reason is the place of forms inasmuch as it receives rational forms, it is the form of forms as far as it is potentially identical with the forms it accepts.

spond to the relation of thinking to sensation. Namely, we have seen
above, reason does not think without imagination,[194] and imagination
presupposes sensation.[195] Now, sensation is the form of things, perceived by sense, while image is the same form which is kept in the
soul.[196] To those forms primarily acquired through sensation and
preserved in imagination,[197] reason gives a further formalization, and
produces thought in terms of apprehension and combination of these
higher forms.[198] This supposition may be proved by Aristotle's own
statement: "But, since apart from sensible magnitudes there is nothing,
as it would seem, independently existent, it is in the sensible forms that
the intelligible forms exist, both those which are referred to by abstractions and all the habits and affections of sensible things. And for this
reason, as without sensation a man would not learn or understand
anything, so at the very time when he is actually thinking he must have
an image before him. For images are like sensations except that they
are immaterial."[199] Needless to say, the object of thought is not the
same as the object of sensation, either in the intension or in the extension of these terms. Some things are merely the object of thought
and never of sensation, e.g. God as a pure form.[200] But generally speaking, a thing may be the object of thought as well as of sensation.
Mathematical forms, which are called "abstractions" in the previous
quotation, and the attributes of other, sensible, things are of this
kind.[201] But though both relate to the same object, thinking differs
from sensation in that the former is concerned with the universal, while
the latter is concerned with the individual.[202] In such a case, the universal does not exist apart from the individual, but is immanent to

[194] Plato already admitted the mediating function of imagination for thinking, e.g. in *Phil.* 39 A–C; *Rep.* VI. 510 C.
[195] *De An.* III. 3. 427 b 14–16; 428 b 10–16; 429 a 1–4. Cf. Plato, *Soph.* 264 A.
[196] *De An.* III. 3. 429 a 4–6; 2. 425 b 24; *De Somn.* 2. 460 b 2. 459 a 24. cf.
Plato, *Phil.* 34 A–C.
[197] *De An.* III. 3. 428 a 5–16.
[198] The intuition of forms is conducted by reason, their combination and
separation, by ἐπιστήμη in the strict sense. cf. *An. Post.* III. 23. 85 a 1; 33. 88 b
35; IV. 19. 100 b 22; *Eth. Nic.* VI. 6. 1141 a 7; 1142 a 26; 12. 1143 a 35–b 11.
[199] *De An.* III. 8. 432 a 3.
[200] *De An.* I. 1. 403 b 15.
[201] *De An.* III. 8. 432 a 4–6. Proof of the real agreement of the object of
thought with that of sensation, is the fact that thought presupposes imagination.
[202] *De An.* II. 5. 417 b 22 f; *An. Pr.* III. 18. 81 b 6; 24. 86 a 29; *Phys.* I. 5.
189 a 8; *Eth. Nic.* II. 9. 1109 b 23; VII. 5. 1147 a 26; VI. 9. 1142 a 27; *Met.* III.
6. 1003 a 15; XI. 1. 1059 b 26; VII. 5. 1147 a 26; VI. 9. 1142 a 27; *Met.* III. 6.
1003 a 15; XI. 1. 1059 b 26; 2. 1060 b 20.

it.[203] That which is perceived through sensation and kept and reproduced by imagination is the form of the individual, e.g. the form of a certain triangle or a certain man, Kallias.[204] It is the form, none the less, and does not include the matter itself. Sensation does not involve the matter as such, e.g. the paper it is drawn on or the traces of a pencil it is drawn with or Kallias' body itself. What is perceived by sense is the form of a triangle upon the paper, or the form of Kallias who has a body. What is imagined is also the form of a special triangle and the figure of Kallias. Seeing that sensation and imagination are related to the individual, and that what makes the individual an individual is matter, sensation and imagination must have some bearing on matter. Still they receive the form that is accompanied by matter as materialized form, but not as matter itself. If they receive the matter itself, it would destroy the sense, and the cognition of the object would never be attained. What is then the difference between sensation and imagination? Aristotle says: "Images are like sensations except that they are immaterial."[205] Should we understand this literally to mean that image does not include matter, but sensation does?[206] This would conflict with the above statement that sensation receives the form of object, but does not include matter. Therefore, Aristotle's remark must be understood to imply that sensation receives various accidental forms which accompany the matter, if not matter itself, together with the essential form in question, while imagination, being the act of keeping and reproducing the forms which are abstracted by sensation, does not include such accidental forms of the matter. For instance, on receiving the figure of a triangle drawn on a sheet of paper by a pencil, sensation receives the form of the paper and the traces of the pencil, but the content of imagination is limited to the figure of this triangle, excluding that of the paper and pencil, or abstracting some of the material attributes of the sensation. Both sensation and imagination do not include the matter itself, but imagination lacks the accidental forms of the matter, while sensation has all of them. Such would be the real meaning of this sentence. Next to be noticed is the statement: "The reason which actually thinks is the same as the things which are thought

---

[203] *Met.* VII. 13; VII. 16. 1040 b 26 f.; 1041 a 4; IX. 7. 1049 a 27; X. 2. 1053 b 16; XI. 2. 1060 b 23–28; *An. Post.* I. 24. 85 a 31; *De An.* III. 7. 431 b 12–16; *Met. VII.* 8. 1033 b 20.

[204] Cf. n. 202. also *Eth. Nic.* VII. 5. 1147 b 5.

[205] *De An.* III. 8. 432 a 9.

[206] Cf. n. 189.

of,"207 and the statement: "The actuality of the sensible object is one and the same with that of the sense."208 These statements might also appear to be inconsistent with the previous statement to the effect that sensation abstracts the forms of things excepting matter. But actuality here means not the mode of existence of an individual which has both matter and form,209 but the mode of the form apart from the matter. Sensation is the actuality in the sense that it is identical with the form of a sensible object abstracted from its matter.

Sensation receives the form of a material body, apart from the matter itself, but together with the concomitant attributes which are supported by the matter. For instance, the sensible form of Kallias is perceived in contact with Kallias himself as a concrete individual, and is applicable only to Kallias. But, in imagination, some parts of the accidental attributes are abandoned. In proportion to the degree of this abstraction, imagination is differentiated in order, the most concrete of which is hardly distinguishable from sensation, while the most abstract approaches concept.210 The form of forms, being the object of thinking, is free from all materiality. It is the essence of things, e.g., of triangle or man.211 The form as the active principle of thought is the universal form, or the meaning which is expressed in the form of concept.212 From the psycho-genetic point of view, such a form might seem to be a secondary object derived from concrete individuals. But essentially, a rational form precedes a sensible form, and the object of sensation or thought precedes actual sensation or thinking.213 As for sensation and its object, let them be dismissed for the moment. The active principle of human thinking is the object of thought, and this object, the form of forms, or the conceptual form, is either the same as the active reason, or at least has some essential reference to it. In truth, they are neither quite different nor absolutely identical. Divine reason, active reason, and the form of forms are neither quite different from, nor

207 *De An.* III. 7. 431 b 16.
208 *De An.* III. 2. 425 b 26; 426 a 9; III. 8. 431 b 23; 432 a 2; II. 12. 424 a 18.
209 *Met.* VII. 2. 1042 b 10; 1043 a 6 ff.; 3. 1043 a 30; IX. 8. 1050 a 16; b 2; 1051 b 31; XII. 5. 1071 a 8; 7. 1072 a 25.
210 *De Memor.* 1. 449 b 31 – 450 a 5.
211 *Met.* VII. 7. 1032 b 1 f.; VII. 10. 1035 b 32; 1036 a 1; VII. 8. 1033 b 5; VIII. 4. 1044 a 36; V. 2. 1013 b 23; *Phys.* II. 2.2 194 a 20; II. 3. 194 b 26; *Met.* V. 2. 1013 a 27 f.
212 *Met.* VII. 10. 1035 b 14–16; XIII. 8. 1084 b 10; III. 1. 996 b 8; VII. 10. 1035 a 21; VII. 11. 1036 b 5; VIII. 4. 1044 b 12; XII. 2. 1069 b 34; *Phys.* II. 1. 193 a 31; IV. 1. 209 a 21; *De An.* I. 1. 403 b 1.
213 *Met.* IV. 5. 1010 a 25.

quite the same as, each other.[214] They are all the principles of thought in a wider sense.

[214] In the *De Anima*, there is no special mention on God or the divine reason. Though the active reason is called holy, it is not identical with the divine reason. Our attempt to associate the divine reason in *Met*. XII. with the active reason in the *De Anima*, must confront with a philological challenge. But according to Jaeger, who assigned both of these statements to the early age, there would be no objection in making them associate with each other. For us, however, who regard the notion of active reason to belong to the most advanced stage of Aristotle's thought, and doubt the early formation of the *De Anima* III, there remain only two alternatives: either to deny the early formation of the *Met*. XII, and make it simultaneous with the *De Anima*, or to suppose its early formation and to admit the continuance of its doctrine. The former hypothesis is supported partly by Jaeger's early theory, partly by Nuyens; while the latter hypothesis finds its strong support in the fact that similar thought is found in the *Ethica Nicomachea*, the later formation of which there is no question at all. The soul as the form of the body and the thinking as the reception of conceptual forms with the medium of imagination is, according to Jaeger, characteristic to Aristotle's later age. Though active reason is closely related to the divine reason, it cannot act without passive reason. Hence the *De Anima* III. 5, which contains the theory of active reason must belong to the later period. The same consideration may be applied to *Met*. XII. In 1072 b 20–24, it is stated: "And thought itself thinks itself because it shares the nature of the object of thought; for it becomes an object of thought in coming into contact with and thinking its objects, so that thought and object of thought are the same. For that which is capable of receiving the object of thought, i.e. the essence, is thought. But it is active when it possesses this object. Therefore, the possession rather than the receptivity is the divine element which thought seems to contain, and the act of contemplation is what is most pleasant and best." The last phrase of the above quotation may be rendered either as "the divine belongs to the prime mover rather than to the human mind" or "this (actuality) rather than that (potentiality) is what reason is thought to have of the divine." Cf. Ross's *comm. ad loc.* also *Met*. XII. 9. 1074 b 15–22; 1075 a 5 ff.
All the above statements seem to show that although no technical terms such as νοῦς ποιητικός or νοῦς παθητικός are employed, Aristotle substantially recognized the distinction between the two reasons. This theory, which admits the peculiarity of reason in the soul, and distinguishes the human reason from the reason of God, is fundamentally different from the Platonism in the early period, which assumes soul in general to be immortal and divine. The close relationship of soul and body and the passive character of human reason are peculiar to the later period. This might have conduced as a motivation for the moulding of the concept of active reason.
For the moment we must refrain from deciding the age of *Met*. XII and giving preference to either hypothesis. We would content ourselves with the acknowledgement that it is at least not impossible to explain the active reason in the *De Anima* by making reference to the divine reason in the *Metaphysica*. Not to mention, the active reason is not identical with the reason of God. God is an unmoved mover, not an agent or an efficient cause. This is the most wonderful and the most ingenious idea of God the prime mover, quite unique in the history of human thoughts. Those who deprive God of all influence upon the world are no less deviated from Aristotle's thought than those who regard Him a creator.

It is well known that Aristotle admitted four kinds of cause. They are, *causa materialis*, *causa efficiens*, *causa formalis*, and *causa finalis*.[215] The other causes except *causa materialis* were summarized in the active principle in a wider sense, and were set in opposition to *causa materialis*, the former being referred to form and the latter to matter.[216] Is it then really an adventurous attempt to assign these four causes to those four concepts respectively, viz., to the passive reason, the active reason, the form of forms, and the divine reason? It is rather wonderful why such a natural interpretation should never have been attempted. In the first place, it was already proved by Aristotle's own statement, that passive reason is the material cause from which actual knowledge is formed just as a product is formed from its material. There is also no doubt that active reason, being, as its name shows, the agent, the producer that makes all things, is the efficient cause of thought. As for the formal cause, the object of thought was considered to be the form of forms or the conceptual form, which gives an actual form to passive reason. It was said that reason when it actually thinks is one and the same as the object of thought. What, then, does this mean but that the object of thought is the formal cause of thought? Concerning the object of thought and active reason, there is some difficulty to be examined. Object, as far as it is an object, is beyond dispute objective, while active reason, even though it may be derived from God, as far as it is reason, must be subjective. The argument of those who adopt the immanent theory of active reason is founded upon this. Here, taking into consideration the transcendent theory, we must ask ourselves whether efficient cause may not in some way or other, be an immanent principle. We know that in artificial production, the efficient cause is outside the product but in natural generation,[217] it is immanent to the subject of generation. Now, thinking is neither production nor generation, and its efficient cause may be in some respect external, in some respect immanent to the subject. To explain the matter more fully, let us take up again the metaphor of light and vision. As we have ex-

Cf. *Met.* I. 2. 983 a 8; XI. 7. 1064 a 37; XII. 7. 1072 a 26 ff.; *De Cael.* I. 9. 279 a 32; *Phys.* VIII. 6. 259 a 14, also Brentano, *Arist. Lehre v. Ursp. d. menschl. Geistes* 121–140.

[215] *Phys.* II. 3. 194 b 23–33; *Met.* V. 2. 1013 a 24 ff.; *Phys.* II. 3. 195 a 15; II. 7. 198 a 16; III. 7. 207 b 34; IV. 1. 209 a 20; *De Somn.* 2. 455 b 14; *Gen. An.* I. 1. 715 a 4; V. 1. 778 b 8; *An. Post.* IV. 11. 94 a 21; *Met.* I. 3. 983 a 26.

[216] *Phys.* II. 7. 198 a 24–27; cf. *De An.* II. 4. 415 b 9; *Gen. An.* I. 1. 715 a 6; II. 1. 732 a 4. Zeller, *op. cit.* 328 n. 1.

[217] *Phys.* II. 1. 192 b 21; IV. 4. 254 b 17; *De Cael.* 2. 268 b 16; *Met.* V. 4. 1015 a 14; 1014 b 19.

plained previously, sight results from the action of a coloured object
upon the pupil, through the medium of light. [218] The object gives a
colour to the light which is the actuality of a transparent medium. This
metaphor is quite apt.[219] Let us assign passive reason to the eye,
active reason to the light, and the object of thought to the colour – there
ensues a complete analogy between the two phenomena. The object
of thought is received by passive reason through active reason, and
thereby the form of the object is realized in passive reason. Brentano
also regarded active reason to be a medium like light, but he lost sight
of the completeness of this analogy, and considered that light does not
act upon the object, but on the contrary, being acted upon by the object, acts upon the eye, while active reason acts upon the object.[220]
Thus in Brentano's interpretation the fine analogy has unfortunately
been marred, and the concepts of active and passive reasons have fallen
into absurdity. Now for the first time through our interpretation, the
complete adequacy of this analogy is made clear. The coherency of
Aristotle's theory shines out of the mist of his ambiguous expression.

What, then, does it mean to say that the object of thought is received by passive reason through active reason? What sort of existence
has this active reason, and what is the function of it? The form of
forms, as the object of thought, is in itself transcendent to the subject,
and cannot act directly upon the passive reason. Transcendent meaning is eternal, and independent of human being. In order that a man
may think of something, some one must have thought of it already.

[218] Cf. n. 140.

[219] According to T. Ide, (*Tetugauzassi* No. 622), light is the transparent state
of the medium which exists between the eye and its object, whereas the passive
reason contacts directly with the object. The active reason having nothing to do
but to think himself just as the sun shines by itself. Thus, in spite of his contro-
versy against associating the God of *Met.* XII with that of *De An.* III, he identifies
the active reason with the God, and makes it the third element along with the passive
reason and its object, the intermediary function of the active reason remains
entirely concealed. His misconception due to a false analogy made him remark
that Aristotle's theory of the active reason was a sheer paradox and the false of
transcendent idealism. But this is rather an idle renunciation of understanding
than an interpretation. We believe it is fairly possible to rescue the difficulty by
adopting an appropriate analogy between sight and thinking.

[220] Brentano, *op. cit.* 173. De Corte misunderstands both the act of light and
that of the active reason. He assumes, as it seems, that light acts upon the object and makes it really coloured, and that the active reason also acts upon the
object of intellect instead of upon the passive reason. Cf. *op. cit.* 47. His interpretation, as well as that of Brentano depends upon St. Thomas' Paragr. 730,
though Thomas is not responsible for De Corte's mistake as to the part of light
in vision.

Plato explained human thought to be the immortal soul's reminiscence of knowledge which was acquired in a previous life.[221] Aristotle does not in the last analysis admit the immortality of the individual soul, but requires the immortality of super-individual reason as the active principle of human thought. An individual can only think in a tradition of learning. Though man is by nature able to think, it is only in a similar sense as he is by nature a general.[222] There is in him the possibility of thought only in the first sense of the term δύναμις, viz., in the sense of logical possibility.[223] Man is by nature able to think, in the sense that he belongs to the genus that thinks. This possibility is not δύναμις in the superior sense, but only ἐνδεχόμενον.[224] Such a potentiality cannot become actual by itself, but must at first become a potentiality in the second sense, viz. potency or ἕξις. The development from the first to the second potentiality presupposes an actual being as a medium.[225] The potency that can develop by itself into actual thinking is not such an innate faculty that a man is possessed of in so far as he is a man, but a habitual knowledge which is acquired through learning.

[221] *Meno* 81 ff.; 98 A; *Phil.* 34; *Phaed.* 73 A; *Phaedr.* 275 A.
[222] *De An.* II. 5. 417 b 31.
[223] *De An.* II. 5. 417 a 21–28.
[224] Cf. n. 8.
[225] *De An.* II. 5. 417 a 30–b 2; 417 b 12–16; 417 b 2 ff.; *De An.* I. 5. 430 a 19–21: τὸ δ' αὐτό ἐστιν ἡ ἐνέργειαν ἐπιστήμη τῷ πράγματι· ἡ δὲ κατὰ δύναμιν χρόνῳ προτέρα ἐν τῷ ἑνί, ὅλως δὲ οὐ χρόνῳ· Brentano declares those persons to be quite ignorant of Aristotle's thought, who take this sentence as follows: "Since the human being exists without beginning, an individual may have knowledge potentially before he has it in actuality; yet the actual knowledge is as old as the potential, because another man would have had the knowledge actually before him." (*Arist. Lehre v. Ursp. d. menschl. Geistes* 22 ff.) As the proof for his argument he quotes *Met.* IX. 8. 1049 b 17–25: τῷδὲ χρόνῳ πρότερον ὧδε· τὸ τῷ εἴδει τὸ αὐτὸ ἐνεργοῦν, ἀριθμῷ δ' οὔ. λέγω δὲ τοῦτο ὅτι τοῦδε μὲν τοῦ ἀνθρώπου τοῦ ἤδη ὄντος κατ' ἐνέργειαν καὶ τοῦ σίτου καὶ τοῦ ὁρῶντος πρότερον τῷ χρόνῳ ἡ ὕλη καὶ τὸ σπέρμα καὶ τὸ ὁρατικόν, ἃ δυνάμει μέν ἐστιν ἄνθρωπος καὶ σῖτος καὶ ὁρῶν, ἐνεργείᾳ δ' οὔπω· ἀλλ' τούτων πρότερα τῷ χρόνῳ ἕτερα ὄντα ἐνεργείᾳ ἐξ ὧν ταῦτα ἐγένετο· ἀεὶ γὰρ ἐκ τοῦ δυνάμει ὄντος..." But this is not sufficient evidence for denying the interpretation that a particular knowledge of an individual presupposes a preceding thought. Rather, Brentano forcibly concludes from the above quotation that God as the creator makes potential knowledge actual, by arbitrarily cutting short the statement, whereas what we find in the following is quite a different idea from that of the creative activity of God, it runs namely: ἄνθρωπος ἐξ ἀνθρώπου, ἀεὶ κινοῦντός τινος πρώτου· τὸ δὲ κινοῦν ἐνεργείᾳ ἤδη ἔστιν. It is not the creator, but a man who makes a man; it is not God, but a cultivated man who makes a cultivated man. The phrase, ἀεὶ κινοῦντός τινος πρώτου would mean that there is always a preceding efficient cause which exists in actuality. Even if one understands this to mean that there is an eternal first mover, it does not follow of necessity that God acts as a creator. What the analogy naturally suggests as an efficient cause of thinking is rather a teacher than a creator.

It is developed through education by those who have acquired knowledge by means of actual thinking.[226] Only those who were educated and learned can think by themselves.[227] Even the boy in Plato's *Meno* required the leading of Socrates as the efficient cause to make him think. Consequently, the active reason, that mediates between the passive reason and the transcendent meaning to realize an actual thought, must be a kind of education, wherein the uninscribed reason of a student receives knowledge from the reason of a teacher who already learned. This act of education is the thinking activity of the teacher as well as the realization of the habitual potency of his reason. The active reason in the teacher acts upon the passive reason of the student. This delivery of knowledge between teacher and student may be regarded as the self-preservation of the truth itself. The form of forms is revealed in human thought through the active reason. In education, active reason is presented by the teacher, and acts upon the passive reason of the student; when the student finished learning, he has accomplished the qualification of a teacher, and the two reasons

[226] Similarly with generation. The man in active potentiality exists in the father's seed, while in passive potentiality, it is involved in the mother's menstrual blood. (*Met.* VIII. 4. 1044 a 35) These potentialities are actualized only through the combination of a particular father and a particular mother. (*Pol.* I. 2. 1252 a 26) From a fertilized egg thus generated, comes an embryo, which thenceforth grows through its immanent principle into manhood. (*Met.* IX. 7. 1049 a 14) Now, turning to our question, the mother corresponds to the body, the menstrual blood to the passive reason, and the form of man to the concept as the object of thought. Just as in generation there must be an actual seed or an actual father, so in thinking, there must be an element of knowledge and a teacher. (*Mot. An.* 5. 700 b 2; *Met.* XII. 7. 1073 a 3). The pre- existence of an actual being necessary in spite of Mr. Ide's opposition, and we need not be afraid, like Mr. Ide, that the fallacy of the so-called "third man" which was pointed out by Aristotle in the theory of ideas should be applied to his own theory. It is well known that Aristotle introduced the concept of efficient cause in order to avoid this kind of difficulty.

But there is another question. If the active reason is the knowledge, which is implanted in the soul of a student by a teacher, how is it possible that it is separable from the soul and is immortal? But it seems for us that there is nothing specially difficult, for it is easily explained by the analogy of generation. Just as in generation, what is preserved in eternity is the genus instead of the individual, what is separable and immortal is the thought itself as "an objective mind" instead of a mental activity of a particular person. Cf. *Gen. An.* II. 1. 732 b 32; *De An.* II. 4. 415 a 26; Plato, *Symp.* 206 E; 207 A–D.   Hegel

[227] *De An.* II. 5. 417 b 16–26. The object of thought is sometimes immanent in the soul, and in this respect it may be said that "the passive reason comes into contact immediately with its object." cf. n. 219. But this is a learned state and not innate like the sensitive faculty. Learning requires education by a teacher who introduces transcendent forms into the soul of the student. cf. Plato, *Theaet.* 186 C; *Tim.* 44 A, B.

have come into combination. Since then, he can think independently
of the teacher. Knowledge is conditioned by the object in so far as it is
the cognition of an object, but when it becomes a habit, it is already an
immanent principle. Knowledge mediates the form of forms with
human reason, but once acquired, it acts independently of external
objects. Thus we can solve the antagonism between the transcendent
and the immanent theory of active reason.

Having shown that one can assign the passive reason, the form of
forms, and the active reason, to the material, the formal, and the
efficient cause, respectively, we shall pursue further the analogy of
sight and assign the divine reason to the final cause. Specifically, the
analogy is that between the sun fire, as the origin of light, and the
divine reason as the origin of active reason.[228] The potentially transparent medium becomes actually transparent through the sun fire.
This is light, which mediates between the colour and the eye. In just
the same way is the active reason related to the divine. The divine
reason does not immediately act upon human reason,[229] while the
passive reason is merely potential and uninscribed. The reason *par
excellence* must have an actual form like the divine reason, but in order
to be active (upon the passive reason of man), it must be not only
actual but also itself a kind of potency. Such a potency which is borne
by an actual existence is nothing but the so-called ἕξις or habit. Therefore, the active reason which acts upon the passive reason must be a
ἕξις. And that which makes the active reason what it is, is the divine
reason. On the other hand, that which makes the efficient cause what
it is, is the final cause. Hence the final cause is called the first cause.
But the final cause makes the efficient cause what it is only through
the formal cause. The formal cause is, so to say, the final cause in so
far as it appeared in the particular movement of individuals; in other
words, it is the self-limitation of the latter. In this respect, the efficient
cause precedes the formal cause, and organizes the matter into a
concrete individual. Thus it is the divine reason that makes the form of
forms determine the active reason. God thinks only on himself, just as
the sun shines by itself. Being in this light, everything gives colours to
the light and generates the sight in the eye. Similarly, God is content

---

[228] Cf. *De An.* II. 7. (n. 140); Plato, *Rep.* VI. 507 E-509 A.

[229] However strange it may appear, and in spite of Brentano's opposition, the
final cause or the prime mover is different from the efficient cause or the agent,
as Zeller asserts. Cf. Zeller, *op. cit.* II. 2. 374 n. 2; Brentano, *Arist. Lehre v. Ursp.
d. menschl. Geistes.* 29 ff. *Psychologie des Aristoteles* 235 f.

with His contemplation, while the active reason organizes the form of
forms into the system of human knowledge, and gives it to the reason
of a concrete person; – thus the thought of man is actualized. All these
activities aim at the complete actuality of forms in God. Being illuminated by the divine reason, or aiming at the complete actuality of God,
and stepping into the world of knowledge, our reason participates in
eternity. Man is mortal together with his individual soul, but in so far
as he lives in science, he is immortal.[230] We might rather say that the
immortal reason is science itself. And yet, science becomes rich through
the thinking of man. It is the accumulation of thought or the habitual
contemplation of mankind. The passive reason of man is like the earth,
which receives the seeds, nourishes the trees, and brings forth new
seeds. The passive reason does the same with knowledge. The knowledge of man becomes possible through God, hence man loves Him and
tends towards Him. Aristotle says that man comes to think about
thought itself in accordance with his acquisition of knowledge,[231]
which amounts to saying that in accordance with the act of active
reason, thought becomes its own object. When active reason is thought
of as such, it is the reflection of Divinity in man. God, to Aristotle, is a
pure metaphysical principle which rises above the anthropomorphism
of Greek mythology and is beyond the personality of the Christian
God. He has neither will nor human thinking.[232] Aristotle says that
God is reason or that His act is thinking,[233] to be sure, but since this
reason of God is pure actuality, it is not like human reason which
"sometimes thinks, and sometimes does not," but is an eternal thinking.[234] Such an eternal thinking is not possible for a reason which is
concerned with an object other than thinking itself, because such a
reason is passive and conditioned by an objective form.[235] Consequently, the object of divine reason is nothing but thinking itself, so
that the act of divine reason is νόησις νοησέως.[236] This thinking of

[230] Cf. Plato, *Tim.* 90.
[231] *De An.* III. 4. 429 b 5–10; 430 a 2–4; *Met.* XII. 7. 1072 b 20; cf. Hick's
note *ad loc.*
[232] Plato admitted a Creator God. But Brentano's attempt to interpret
Aristotle's god as an almighty creator cannot stand in the last analysis. Cf.
Psych. Arist. 234 ff.; *Arist. Lehre v. Ursp. d. menschlichen Geistes.*
[233] *Met.* XII. 7. 1072 b 18; 9. 1074 b 21; *Eth. Eud.* VII. 12. 1245 b 17; cf.
Met. I. 2. 983 a 5; (*Mag. Mor.* II. 15. 1212 b 39); *Pol.* III. 16. 1287 a 29; *Top.*
IV. 4. 132 b 11; 6. 136 b 7; *Fr.* 46. 1483 a 27.
[234] *Met.* XII. 7. 1072 b 15 ff.
[235] *Met.* XII. 9. 1074 b 21 ff.
[236] *Met.* XII. 9. 1074 b 33–35. αὐτὸν ἄρα νοεῖ, εἴπερ ἐστὶ τὸ κράτιστον, καὶ ἔστιν ἡ

thinking, corresponds exactly to the form of forms as the object of human reason. We may easily see the relation between them through the following comparison: The meaning means itself; the form of forms is the objective, and the thinking of thinking is the subjective, side of this transcendent meaning. The former is meaning as the object of passive reason, the latter is the same meaning, which, however, is perceived retrospectively by reflective intellect. The world which is governed by God or prevailed over by the divine reason is the world which is organized by meanings, viz. the world of λόγοι or concepts. Thinking of thinking is not only the reflection upon itself of human thinking as it appears to man, but also in its essential being, the act of God who makes man reflect upon himself.

Of course, human reflection, or man's thinking of his own thinking, is the most divine of all human activities. Man does not reflect his own dignity as far as his thinking is concerned with outside objects. In such a condition, he is not yet man *par excellence*. It is only through knowing himself as a man, that he becomes a real man. When he turns his eyes from the object to himself, he finds the _self_ as the subject of thinking. The essence of man is to be a reflecting subject.

5. Comparison with Plato's Thought

We have explained the four concepts of Aristotle, viz., the divine reason, the form of forms, the active reason, and the passive reason, as each being parallel respectively, to the final, the formal, the efficient, and the material cause. We find in Plato analogous concepts in reference to the generation of the world and the formation of knowledge; they are God, the ideas, the good, and the reason or the soul. But how these concepts are related to each other is not evident, because Plato's statement of God and the universe is much more of mythological character, than a strictly scientific theory. Moreover, various myths are told about the creation and government of the universe by God. The most important of them is the variation-story in the *Statesman*,[237] and the creation-story in the *Timaeus*.[238] These two dialogues are both regard-

νόησις νοήσεως νόησις. According to Brentano, *Arist. Lehre v. Ursp. d. menschl. Geistes* 133 ff.) νοεῖν is the act of νοῦς in the strict sense, i.e. intellectual intuition, and as the object of intellectual intuition God has only himself, but other things may be the object of another kind of intellect, e.g. ἐπιστήμη or scientific knowledge. But this argument of Brentano's cannot persuade us.

[237] *Pol.* 269 ff.
[238] *Tim.* 28 ff.

THE STRUCTURE OF THE SOUL

ed as belonging to the later period and though the former probably precedes the latter, there is no great interval between them. From the fact that in such close sequence these quite different stories of creation are told, we may safely guess that these myths are the expressions of phantastic imagination rather than a scientific theory.[239] Of these two stories, no doubt, the latter is by far the more important. In the *Statesman*, the myth is more accidental to the main theme, while in the *Timaeus*, it forms the principal subject, and is far more detailed in its contents. It is in the latter that we find an intimate relation to Aristotle's theory.

Now, according to the myth in the *Timaeus*, the universe is the product of a creation which originates in the beneficence of God.[240] This creation begins at first with the production of the universe, which is itself the created god, a body pervaded by the soul. Then, the universe is divided into heavenly bodies.[241] The created god is trusted by the one Creator to produce the lower beings. He produces mortal bodies and mortal souls, into which the one Creator inspires immortal souls homogeneous with the created god.[242] The creation by God is performed following the model of immortal ideas,[243] and these ideas compose a scale, which is ruled by the idea of the good.[244] How then, should we conceive the relation holding among the Creator, the ideas, and the idea of the good, all of which being the principles of creation? If the idea of the good is the uniting principle of the ideas, while God creates everything through imitating the ideas, are God and the idea of the good the same? If they are different, how do they relate to each other? If the idea of the good is the real principle of unification, God would no longer be the real creator or the ruler. But if on the contrary, God is the real creator, the idea of the good could no longer be an independent principle. Further, if the ideas are the models of creation, yet different from God, then neither could God be the real creator, nor could the idea of the good be the uniting principle of the ideas. It would be inconsistent to say, on the one hand, that God creates ideas, while saying on the other hand, that the creation cannot dispense with models. In consideration of these difficulties, Zeller identified God, the ideas,

---

[239] Cf. Cornford, *Plato's Cosmology* 28 ff.; Taylor, *Comm. on Plato's Tim.* 59.
[240] *Tim.* 29 E.
[241] *Ibid.* 34, 36, 40.
[242] *Tim.* 41. But in *Phil.* 30, the human soul is derived from the soul of the universe.
[243] *Tim.* 27 E.
[244] *Rep.* VI 508 B-C.

and the idea of the good altogether.[245] But if they are perfectly identical, whence comes the conceptual difference? May we not solve these
difficulties by the analogy to our previous interpretation of Aristotle's
concepts? And if we succeed in setting up an analogy between them,
our interpretation of Aristotle's theory would also be confirmed thereby.[246]

For this purpose, let us compare the two theories with each other.
To begin with, in Aristotle, God is an unmoved mover or a final cause,
its essence, pure reason, and its act thinking; compared to visionary
phenomena, it is like the sun as the source of light. But in Plato, there
is not yet the division of cause into kinds. Though Aristotle's criticism
to the effect that Plato acknowledged only formal cause and material
cause cannot be admitted without qualification,[247] at least it is undeniable that there are lacking in Plato any clear-cut concepts of final
cause and efficient cause. He also makes God reason[248] and the cause
of being and cognition,[249] but in what sense He is the cause, is not
distinct enough. He makes the self movent precede the moved
movent,[250] taking it for the essence of life and the first agent.[251] But
the self movent, if not moved by another, has in itself both activity
and passivity, and cannot be eternal or unchangeable as far as it is
movable. That the absolute being should be eternal and unchangeable,
was not sufficiently brought into accordance with the requirement that
it should be the final cause of movement.[252] This was attained for the

---

[245] Zeller, *op. cit.* II. 1. 694–712.

[246] Needless to say, Aristotle admitted no creation whatever. Both the world
and the divine reason are eternal and exist without beginning. What has come
to be, must sometime pass away. Cf. Zeller, *op. cit.* 380 f. It is only what is eternal
that is really immortal. Immortality means for him eternity *a parte ante* as well
as *a parte post.* Cf. Nuyens, *op. cit.* 380 f. But it is doubtful whether Aristotle
deserves a blame on account of his lacking in creation theory, as some Christian
interpreters maintain. (Nuyens, *op. cit.* 318; Joivet, *Essai sur les rapports entre
la pensée grecque et la pensée chrétienne: Aristote et Saint Thomas ou l'idée de créa-
tion* 77). But Aristotle was not ignorant of the creation theory, which manifestly
existed in his predecessors.

[247] *Met.* I. 6. 988 a 8. Against Aristotle's opinion, Ross points out as the expression of Plato's concept of efficient cause: *Phaedr.* 245 C, D; *Legg.* 891–899;
Soph. 265 B-D; *Tim.* 28 C ff.; *Phil.* 23D; 26 E-27. As the suggestion of the final
cause, *Phil.* 20D; 53 E; *Tim.* 19 D ff.; *Legg.* 903 C.

[248] *Phil.* 30, 28.

[249] *Phaed.* 95 E; 100 B.

[250] *Legg.* 894–896.

[251] *Phil.* 26; *Tim.* 46D, E; cf. *Met.* XII. 6. 1072 a 1.

[252] *Zeller,* op. cit. II. 1. 689, 696.

first time when Aristotle admitted the final cause, which moves everything, to be itself unmovable.

Secondly, the idea which is used by the Creator as the model, corresponds to the form of forms or conceptual form in Aristotle. The
Platonic idea is not like the idea in modern philosophy the subjective
image or the content of consciousness, but the objective form or the
noematic object, just as is the form of forms of Aristotle.[253] It is a
transcendent meaning, through participating in which human reason
can think. It is the active principle of human thinking. At the same
time, everything that may become the object of sensation, holds its
existence only through participating in idea; so that idea is the principle of things.[254] The Creator gave forms to indefinite matter by means
of ideas.[255] In these respects, the idea is not different from the conceptual form. One might, on the ground of Aristotle's well known criticism
of the theory of ideas, oppose our explanation which assimilates Aristotle's conceptual forms with Plato's ideas. But, in truth, Aristotle's
criticism was restricted to some unreasonable implications of this
theory, and did not amount to the complete rejection of it. On the
contrary, Aristotle's theory of forms, in its nucleus, is congruent with
Plato's theory of ideas. What Aristotle called the form was a principle
which constitutes the essence of a thing and makes knowledge of that
object possible. In this respect it is similar to Plato's concept of idea.
Hence we may be assured, without violating the history, to compare
Aristotle's form to Plato's idea.

Even if the active principle of human thought be assigned to a transcendent idea or an objective form, it does not deprive the subject of its
activity. The thinking of thinking and the form of forms are two sides
of one divine reason. The relation between God and the idea in Plato is
analogous to this. The thinking of thinking is simple, while the form
of forms contains some plurality. So with God and the idea: God is
simple, but the idea, though it too is simple when compared with
sensible images, is itself coordinated with other ideas. For instance,
man is one compared with Kallias and Socrates, but it is only one
special concept coordinate with horse or colour. It may seem as if this
multiplicity of forms or ideas is quite irrelevant to the simplicity of
God or its activity as thinking of thinking. But just as the thinking of
thinking develops into objective cognition by making itself the form

---

[253] *Phaedr.* 247; Tim. 51; *Phaed.* 100, 102.
[254] *Phaed.* 102; 100 C-E; *Parm.* 130.
[255] Cf. Baeumker, *Das Problem der Materie* 193 ff.

of forms, and then comes back to the absolute self- consciousness through the negation of that objective thinking,[256] so God as a single Creator may create the world only through manifesting Himself as multiple ideas. The idea is not a reality which exists apart from God and precedes His creation as its model, but the other being (*Anderssein*) of the one God. On this account, God remains to be the absolute being, while ideas are what make other things without themselves being made by others.

It is an extremely difficult question, how this simplicity and multiplicity of the absolute being consist at the same time. If there be anything which might mediate between the one absolute Creator and multiple ideas, it must needs be the active reason of Aristotle and the idea of the good in Plato. Both in Aristotle's forms and Plato's ideas, there is some order. The scale of Plato's ideas was less complete, but the idea of the good was no doubt the highest unity of ideas.[257] In Aristotle, conceptual forms are summed up in ten categories, which are practically the fundamental forms of being. The idea of the good in Plato is the principle which mediates the simple consciousness of God with many ideas. Similarly, the active reason of Aristotle may be considered not only as the medium between many conceptual forms and one reason, but also as the principle which differentiates the single consciousness of God into the multitude of forms.[258] The form produces thought in the human soul in terms of active reason, while various forms are derived from the reason of God in so far as God manifests Himself in science. This presumably is the reason why Trendelenburg considered God to be an active reason, even if not every active reason belongs to God. But strictly speaking, the idea of the good in Plato stands not between ideas and the human soul, but between ideas and God, whereas Aristotle's active reason mediates between ideas and passive reason, not between God and forms. This difference is due to the fact that God in Aristotle is what is looked upon and loved from beneath, while God in Plato is a creator and loves others from above. Aristotle, starting from the many, looked for the one, while Plato deduced the many from the one. In Plato, moreover, the soul was not differentiated completely, so that it was combined with the ideas without requiring any medium. In spite of such differences, generally speaking, the divine reason, the active reason, and the form of forms

---

256 Cf. n. 231.
257 *Soph.* 253 D.
258 Cf. Bergson, *L'évolution créatrice* 248.

in Aristotle are analogous to the God as the creator, the idea of the good, and the ideas, in Plato, respectively. They are all in a wider sense the formal principle, and in this respect, they are one and three at the same time.

There remain for us to consider the passive reason of Aristotle and the soul of Plato. These are also in a sense analogous, but not so similar as the other concepts are. In Aristotle, the active reason, being super-individual and immortal, conveys the form of forms or the transcendent meaning to the passive reason. Whereas in Plato, the eternity of ideas directly leads to the immortality of the soul which knows them.[259] The soul is regarded as absolutely simple; such problems as the passivity of human reason and the finiteness of the individual soul are neglected entirely.

The immortal soul was a traditional ideal of the Greek,[260] and formed lifelong belief of Plato, combined with the transmigration theory of the Orphics and Pythagoreans.[261] The belief continued in his thinking until the middle and the late period, represented by the *Republic* and the *Laws*[262] but the most remarkable expression is found in the *Phaedo*. In this early dialogue, Socrates states the hypothesis as follows[263]: The soul cannot attain a complete cognition of truth, because it is bound with the body. Sensation is the obstacle of cognition, rather than its pre-requisite. Eyes and ears are, as Heraclitus said, nothing but evil witnesses. The soul is able to see truth only when it has got rid of the body; this is achieved through death. Hence death is the ideal of the philosopher who loves truth.[264] In this world, however, the soul can neither exist nor think entirely apart from the body. Our thinking in some way depends upon the body; otherwise, the soul would not even be disturbed by the body. Therefore, the soul is *separable* from the body, but is not *separated* from it. The separability of the soul is compatible with the dependence of thought upon physical conditions. The difficulty about the inseparable πάθη of the soul and the separable reason is thus solved. Even when the πάθη of the soul is taken in a wider sense which includes thinking, its inseparability is not of necessity incongruent with the separability of the soul. It is not, however, the whole soul that is separable; it would be absurd to assume

---

[259] *Phaed.* 75 f.; 100; cf. Grote, *Plato* 190 n.
[260] De Coulange, *La cité antique* 7 ff.
[261] Grote, *Plato*, II. 202 n.
[262] *Rep.* 10. 609 ff.; *Tim.* 41, 43, 69; *Legg.* 859 B, 967 E.
[263] *Phaed.* 64. 66 f., 80, 83; cf. *Phaedr.* 245; *Meno* 81, 86.
[264] *Phaed.* 64; *Theat.* 176 A.

that the sensible part is separable from the body. Even in the *Phaedo*, where the separability of soul is affirmed, the function of the separated soul is pure thinking[265] and no other lower consciousness or phenomenon of life. Therefore, if the soul in general means the principle of life, such a separable part of it should be distinguished from the rest by the name of reason. Only the rational part of soul is separable, though in actuality it is combined with the body.[266] Already in the *Timaeus*, Plato divided the soul into immortal reason and other mortal parts. Aristotle's division is simply a natural development of this theory.

But how can it be that, what is separable from the body is bound with it? As far as it is separable, it must essentially be quite independent. How is it possible that such an independent being is apprehended by another? This is a problem which Plato was presumably unable to solve, and it should have been a difficulty even for Aristotle who limited the immortal part of the soul to reason. Perhaps it was as the last attempt to solve this question that he distinguished the active and the passive reason in *De Anima* III. 5. The separability of reason from the body and its dependence upon the body were reconciled by limiting soul to reason, and dividing it into the active and the passive. What is essentially independent is active reason, which is the only divine element. It enters into connection with the human soul by acting upon the passive reason and in this respect only it forms an element of human thinking. Now, the human soul, including passive reason, is by nature the actuality of the body and inseparable from it. So that, strictly speaking, there cannot be any restraint of the soul through the body. At most, the soul is limited by the body only to the extent that man is unable to continue pure scientific contemplation; this limitation is the difference between the man as a rational being and the man as a concrete individual. For Plato, such an explanation was impossible, but even in him, we may find the embryo of an idea which could grow into Aristotle's theory of the reason. Plato distinguished two ways in which the soul is bound with the body. The soul is essentially different from the body; hence the two are in a sense separable. The function most essential to the soul is thinking, but the soul as a whole is not separable from the body, because it is bound with the body, and even

---

[265] *Phaed.* 66–68; cf. Grote, *Plato*, II. 161 n.

[266] *Tim.* 30, 69. This distinction does not imply that Plato abandoned the dualism of soul and body and the immortality of the individual souls. Cf. Nuyens, *op. cit.* 141.

thinking presupposes sensation. Still the way in which the soul is conditioned by the body is not the same in the case of thinking as in the case of sensation. In the case of sensation and desire, the soul is employed by the body, while in the case of thinking, the soul rather employs the body, though it is associated with sensation. In this life, man cannot think apart from the body. But even when he thinks in terms of the body, soul is the master, body the servant.[267] Thinking is the highest activity of the human soul, the most complete of which is found in philosophical contemplation, which is as Socrates put it, the exercise of death in life, or the life most contiguous to death.

Thus Plato admitted that thinking in this life operates in terms of the body. If, then, the soul separated from the body, thinks after death, is this posthumous thinking homogeneous with the thinking in this life? Plato found no essential difference between them, but Aristotle, as we have seen above, refused memory to the active reason separated from the body. He not only divided reason from soul, but also distinguished in reason the active and the passive, and limiting the qualities like immortality, unmixedness, etc. to the former, reconciled the opposite requirements of transcendency and immanency of reason and recognized the essential difference between the thinking which depends upon the body and that which is independent of it. Passive reason thinks through the body, it is conscious and has memory, while active reason is separable from the body and it is not the subject of consciousness, but a kind of objective mind, which conveys transcendent meaning to the passive reason as a personal thinking subject. Such a reason is acting even in our lifetime, for human thinking is impossible without it. Nevertheless, this reason is immortal and separable from the body. Being separable, it will be separated from the body, and once separated, it has no longer memory or consciousness. This actual separateness of active reason seems, in Aristotle, to be confined to the case of death. Thus, the primitive belief in the immortality of the individual soul which has personal memory and consciousness seems to have been abandoned.

As to the nature of this immortal reason, we suggested to interpret it as the system of knowledge or, saying more widely, culture in general, as the expression of transcendent meaning. It is true that active reason is essentially super-individual and divine, even when it makes human thinking act in man's lifetime by giving conceptual forms to passive

---

[267] *Phaed.* 66, 83.

reason. Though we cannot think without the body, as far as we are concerned with forms, we live in the world-mind, or rather the world-mind is living in us.[268]

Aristotle seems to have admitted the separation of active reason only when the body dies. But, speaking more essentially, this separation is not of necessity confined to the moment of death, rather it is always taking place whenever we express our thought, for when the thought makes itself objective and eternal, it is emancipating itself from the body, step by step. And since conscious thinking is done through the passive reason participating in the active reason, the world-mind is returning every moment to its proper independent existence. We are dying in every moment of our life, and we are living in every moment the life of the dead. The death of the body, being the extinction of a subject, in which the development of the world-mind takes place, or the ending of a special unit of this development, has, of course, a great significance. But such an event is taking place, more or less, every moment in our life. Thus considered, Plato's saying, "Philosophy is the study of death," might gain a more profound significance.

We may resume the above arguments as follows: Putting forward later Platonism against the early theory of the immortal soul, Aristotle at first restricted the immortal part to reason. But his positivistic mind compelled him, on the other hand, to admit the fact that reason is combined with the body through imagination and sensation. With this cognition of the fact alone, the immortality and independence of reason would have been endangered. Aristotle seems to have endeavoured to rescue it through dividing reason into the active and the passive, and confining divinity and immortality to the former. But he did not succeed in giving his thought a fully logical and systematic expression, and emphasized sometimes the necessity of imagination in human thinking, sometimes the separability of reason, his reflection about the species of reason, which was intended to unite the two characters, appeared only once in *De Anima* III. 5, and in quite an unsatis-

[268] The active reason had been thinking before a man's birth, it lost its memory at his birth when it united with the body, then it has acquired abstract ideas by means of sensible experiences. This career of the active reason appeared to Brentano to be an uncomprehensible process. (Arist. *Lehre v. Ursp. d. menschl. Geistes* 81). This is because Brentano took the active reason as a more psychological phenomenon. But for us, who are aquainted with Kant's transcendental idealism and Hegel's philosophy of (objective or absolute) mind, it is not so uncomprehensible. This, however, is not an anachronism, because Hegel's philosophy may be regarded in many points a revival of the Greek thoughts.

factory form. This want of clear statement has presented great difficulties to the history of philosophy. We must notice in particular, that
this sequence of Aristotle's thought is not divergent from Platonism,
but rather on the line of Plato's theory of ideas and soul, with thorough
differenciation of the concepts and emendation of theoretical difficulties.

6. *Parts of the Soul*

As is evident from the above investigation, what is really separable
from the body is only reason, especially the active reason, which, in
this respect, is essentially different from the other parts of the soul.
And if active reason is separable from the body in reality, it will be
separable from the other parts of the soul in reality as well. Therefore,
the division of the soul is not to be confined to conceptual division,
but may sometimes mean existential division. It is true that when we
cut certain plants and animals, the parts of their soul are also divided
along with their body, whereas the parts of the soul themselves are not
divided from each other.[269] For instance, when we cut the body of an
earthworm, each part of the body has all of the nutritive, the sensitive,
and the moving faculty, and none of these parts does not exist apart
from other parts. Such a phenomenon, however, is not universal to all
kinds of living being. Besides, comparing one kind to another, if the
one has a function which is wanting in the other, these different parts
may be separable from each other, not only conceptually, but also in
existence, e.g., the nutritive faculty may exist apart from the sensitive,
and sensation apart from reason. Among sensations, a lower faculty
such as touch, may exist apart from a higher faculty such as sight.[270]
Generally speaking, a lower function is separable from a higher, in the
sense that the one may act apart from the other. Is this because each
function has its proper subject, and the real separation of such subjects
makes the separation of these functions possible? But we cannot find
such a real separation except between active reason and the soul which is
bound with the body. For the soul other than active reason is the actuality
of the body, so that its subject must be the body too. If, then, each part
of the soul has its proper subject, these subjects must be different parts
of the body. Is it then the case that to the head belongs its proper part
of the soul, to the heart its proper part, to the limbs their proper

---

[269] *De An.* I. 5. 411 b 19 ff.; 413 b 16.
[270] *De An.* II. 2. 413 a 31 ff.; II. 3; I. 5. 410 b 18.

part, and so on? What is it, then, that unites these parts of soul and body, and makes one living being? According to Aristotle, not that body unifies the parts of the soul, but that soul unifies the parts of the body. The soul being thus the principle of unification, it must needs exist as a whole in an individual; the parts of the soul must not be distributed to each part of the body, but pervade the whole body.[271] This is proved by the fact that when we cut a certain plant or animal, each of the divided parts has various functions in the same manner.[272] Provided that the subject of psychical functions is the body, and that the soul pervades the body, it seems much more probable that the parts of the soul are divided by the functions. But there remains another possibility, viz., if a certain function is always accompanied by another certain one, and *vice versa*, we may assume such a complex of functions to be an independent part. This may be called the second or semi-real separation, as against the first or real separation. No doubt, there is, in such complexes, no longer a division in the sense of separate existence. The only possible division left is mere difference of function, or conceptual distinction, which, however, forms the third kind of division. Which of these three kinds of division does Aristotle really imply when he states about the parts of the soul, this must be examined from his own statements.

Concerning the division of the soul, there was, as aforesaid, already before Plato, the duopartite theory of the rational and the irrational, while Plato himself took the tripartite theory of the reasoning, the passionate, and the appetitive, assuming these parts to be really separable. In his early age, Aristotle followed this tripartite theory, but turned later to criticize it. For instance, in *De Anima* III. 9, renouncing both the duopartite and the tripartite theory as insufficient, he adds other parts to them. Here he offers the principle of functional division and argues that if we adopt this principle, we should add such parts as the nutritive, the sensitive, the imaginative, and the desiring part. Since, however, he does not make clear whether this is the only authorized division, it remains doubtful to what extent he allows independence to these enumerated parts. Besides, the parts of the soul which Aristotle mentions here and there are not definite, both in respect of number and in respect of species. Let us, then, compare the main statements in the *De Anima* on this point.

1) *De An.* I. 5. 411a 26: "Now, cognition belongs to the soul and so do

271 *De An.* I. 5. 411 b 9; II. 4. 416 a 8.
272 *De An.* I. 5. 411 b 24.

sensation, opinion, appetite, wish, and desires in general; locomotion also occurs in living beings through the soul; and likewise growth, maturity, and decay. Does, then, each of these belong to the whole soul, so that we think, perceive, are moved, and in each of the other operations act and are acted upon with the whole soul, or are different operations to be assigned to different parts?"

In this place, Aristotle counts as the functions of the soul, cognition, sensation, desires (including appetite and wish), locomotion, growth, maturity, and decay, which are all somewhat closely related to each other. But there is no account how these parts are related to the soul and its parts.

2) *De An.* II. 2. 413 a 22: "But the term life is used in many ways, and if life is present in but a single one of these senses, we say that this thing is living, e.g., reason, sensation, motion and rest in respect to place, and the motion involved in nutrition, and further decay and growth." This also should be taken as a mere enumeration of functions.

3) *De An.* II. 2. 413 b 11: "For the present, let us say so much that the soul is the principle of these functions above mentioned, and is determined by them, namely, by the nutritive, the sensitive, the intellectual, and the motive. But whether each of these is a soul or a part of a soul, and if a part, whether it is separable only conceptually or also in respect to place, these are questions some of which are not difficult to see, but the others have difficulties." These parts are also explicitly enumerated as mere functions, not as part of the soul.

4) *De An.* II. 3. 414 a 31: "Of the powers of the soul above mentioned, namely, the nutritive, the desiring, the sensitive, the locomotive, and the intellectual." This passage is concerned explicitly with the functions.

5) Also in *De An.* II. 3. 415 a 1, Aristotle enumerates as the functions of the soul such parts as the nutritive, the locomotive, the reasoning or intellectual, and imagination.

6) But in *De An.* III. 9. 432 a 26, Aristotle, renouncing the duopartite and the tripartite theory to be insufficient, continues as follows: "For in respect of the differences by which these parts are separated, there appear also other parts which have among them a greater distance than these, namely the parts which we have just discussed, the nutritive, which belongs also to plants and to all living beings, and the sensitive, which cannot easily be classed either as rational or irrational. Further, the imaginative is in its essence different from them all, while it is very difficult to decide with which of these it is identical

or not identical, if one may assume separate parts in the soul. Then besides these there is the desiring, which would seem to be different both in concept and in capacity from all the foregoing." These parts are enumerated on the assumption that the parts of the soul coincide with its functions; the expression might appear as if the parts added by Aristotle were to constitute the whole together with the three maintained by Plato. But in fact, the three parts of Plato's are not so independent as the additional parts; the passionate and the appetitive part having no clean-cut distinction from each other. Aristotle seems to have intended to reserve only the reasoning part out of Plato's three, and add to it his four parts. This is evident from the next quotation.

7) *De An.* III. 10. 433 b 1: "But those who divide the parts of the soul, if they divide and separate them in respect of powers, will find that such parts tend to become very numerous: the nutritive, the sensitive, the thinking, the deliberative, and the desiring, for these differ more widely from one another than the appetitive does from the passionate."

Though the principles of division in the above quotation are numerous and indefinite, they might be reduced to six:

the nutritive (nutrition, growth, decay)
the sensitive
the imaginative
the desiring (appetite, wish)
the motive
the intellectual (reason or rational intuition, opinion, deliberation, reasoning)

Of these six kinds, imagination or the imaginative part appears only once in 6) and besides, its independency is doubtful. Desire is lacking in 1), 2), 3), and 5); motion in 6), and 7). No quotation comprises all these six. This makes us suspect that Aristotle did not intend a complete division of the soul or at least did not attach much importance to it. What is found everywhere is nutrition, sensation, and intellect. Hence we might guess that desire, imagination, and motion have comparatively less importance or have no distinct status. There is intimate connection between imagination and sensation, as well as between desire and motion. The reason why imagination was in most cases omitted would be that it may be reduced to sensation in a wider sense, and further that it is sometimes counted in the modes of intellect. As for desire and motion, an indication of their incomplete separation is the fact that they are never omitted at the same time, though either of the two may drop. According to Brentano,[273] Aristotle may not have enumerated all the parts partly because one may easily supply the rest if one knows the principle involved, partly because he intended to reduce these parts into the three main parts of nutritive, sensitive, and intellectual. For Brentano's assumption to stand, there must be at least a single place in which only the so-called three main parts are enumerated. But in fact, there are always more than four, and besides, they are not definite in kind.

Brentano denies the correspondence between the faculties or functions and the parts of the soul. Different faculties, he thinks, may belong to the same part just as sensation and sensitive desire, being different functions, belong to the same part of the soul. The parts of the soul, then, correspond not to different functions, but to functional complexes. He assumes also that Aristotle admitted firstly the part which accounts for nutrition, reproduction, and lower sensation such as taste or touch, secondly, the part which accounts for such higher sensation as sight or hearing, together with locomotion, thirdly, the part which accounts for intellectual thinking; and that those parts were regarded as the parts of the soul, because they are found separately in different genera of living beings. If, however, Aristotle really divided these three parts, he would have given names to each of them; but it is not really the case, and moreover, these parts do not agree in their contents, with the three parts mentioned by Brentano viz., the nutritive, the sensitive, and the intellectual: for sensation extends both over the first and the second, and desire both over the sensitive and the intellectual part.

Brentano attributed many functions to each of the three parts: to the nutritive part only unconscious assimilation of nourishment, but to both the sensitive and the intellectual part perception in a wider sense, desire, and behavior; and of behavior, some is conscious and some unconscious, so that these parts would possess three or four faculties.[274] It is because he deprived the desiring part of independency that he was obliged to attribute desire and other faculties to the sensitive and the intellectual part.[275] This is pointed out by Aristotle himself as the inconsistency that may result unless we admit independency to the desiring part. In truth, appetite is not the act of the sensitive

[273] Brentano, *Psych. d. Arist.*. 59.
[274] *Ibid.* 61–69.
[275] *De An.* III. 9. 432 b 3–7.

part alone, it is the act of the desiring part as being accompanied by sensation. Similarly, wish is not the act of the intellectual part alone, but the act of the desiring part accompanied by knowledge.

Generally speaking, it is far more natural to identify the parts of the soul with its functions, than to attribute many functions to limited parts assuming some community between the functions which belong to different parts. That the parts are related to one another is compatible with dividing the soul into parts, but the division of the soul would have no significance unless the functions were divided distinctly. Moreover, Aristotle never distinguished the parts from the functions, and mentioned as the parts of the soul sometimes the rational and the irrational, sometimes the so-called functions such as the nutritive, the sensitive, the desiring, the motive etc.

According to Brentano, the soul is divided into parts either from a physical or from a logical point of view. The physical division is the separation of faculties through being distributed to the parts of a substance; such, for example, is the division of the immortal from the mortal part of man. And the logical division is the separation of powers, such that all living beings do not partake both of this and of that power; in this respect the vegetative faculty is divided from sensation, lower sensations from higher ones, higher sensations from locomotion, and further, locomotion from intellectual faculties. And this logical division is, according to Brentano, what Aristotle adopted in most cases.[276] But, as aforesaid, we take this kind of division rather to be a distinction of functions, while the division which Brentano identifies with the logical one is situated in fact between the physical division and the functional one. It is the division which operates as the principle of classification of living beings, and may be called biological division. The authenticity of this division is beyond doubt, but it is only one kind of division made by Aristotle. Unlike our predecessors, we would rather adopt all of the three points of view without limiting ourselves to any one single point. Aristotle would have divided the soul sometimes physically or rather metaphysically, into the rational and the irrational, or more minutely, into active reason and other parts comprising passive reason; sometimes biologically, into the mainly nutritive, the mainly sensitive, and the mainly intellectual complexes of functions – the view Brentano adopted; and sometimes logically, into an indefinite multitude of parts. In short, the division by Aristotle

---

[276] Brentano, *Psych. d. Arist.* 57.

was most likely made from several points of view: sometimes logical, sometimes biological, sometimes physico-metaphysical and so forth.

This would explain the fact that Aristotle, who seems to have presented in the *De Anima* the multipartite theory in place of the traditional duopartite theory, restores the latter and tries to arbitrate both theories in the *Nicomachean Ethics*. He has admitted from the outset that the soul is divisible in many ways from different points of view. Only he asserts that it should be divided into more parts than two or three if we choose a division according to faculties. Thus the duopartite theory and the multipartite theory are compatible without any contradiction.

The synthesis which was tried in the *Nicomachean Ethics*, is as follows: The soul is, at first, divided into the rational and the irrational part. Within the latter, there is the vegetative part, which accounts for assimilation and growth. This is possessed by all living beings, having no reference to reason. Similarly with sensation. There is, in the second place, another part of the irrational soul, which sometimes obeys and sometimes disobeys reason, namely, the desiring part. In accordance with the subdivision of the irrational part, the rational part is also divided into two, the one which has reason in itself, and the other, which obeys the other just as a son obeys his father.[277]

The rational part in the latter sense, however, is not different from the irrational part in the second sense. They are practically the same desiring part, only distinguished through viewpoints. In so far as it has not reason in itself, it is irrational, but in so far as it may obey reason, it is rational. The duopartite theory which divides the soul into the rational and the irrational, originates from the metaphysical point of view, but in the *Ethics*, it lost its metaphysical sense and acquires a practical meaning. Here the division is made in view of the proper virtues and how to rear them. The virtues of the irrational part are called ethical, their essence consists in moderation; whereas the virtues of the rational part are intellectual, which, having in themselves reason and measure, have no need of further determination by reason. They are not characterized by moderation and are developed by teaching. With this qualification, the duopartite theory of the soul seems to have acquired a new significance from the ethical point of view. Unless we admit the multiplicity of dividing principles, it might appear strange that the duopartite theory in the *De Anima*, should appear again in the later

---

[277] *Eth. Nic.* I. 13. 1102 b 28 ff.; cf. *ibid.* I. 7. 1098 a 3.

work of *Ethica Nicomachea*. Hence appears quite naturally the theory
which maintains that the *Nicomachean Ethics* is founded upon the old
duopartite theory. For instance, Jaeger considers[278] that the (*Nicomachean*) *Ethics* is founded upon the primitive view of the soul which
admits only rational and irrational parts. He does not, however, conclude from this that the *Ethics* was formed earlier than the *De Anima*.
He explains instead that though Aristotle reached, in the psychological study, an extremely advanced scientific view by the aid of his
biological study, could not apply this new knowledge to the region of
practical philosophy, and remained in the Platonic tradition. This,
according to Jaeger, is the result of Aristotle's intention to simplify
the problem, as Aristotle put it in the *Nicomachean Ethics*: "the moral
philosophers should have knowledge about the soul only in order to
understand the fundamental phenomena of the objects of his inquiry
and in so far as it is needed for those objects; any further precision
should be more than his purposes call for." Hence Jaeger conjectures
that Aristotle avoided to complicate the problem by introducing the
new idea of soul attained in the *De Anima*. But this hypothesis amounts
to assuming that in the *Nicomachean Ethics*, Aristotle failed to master
thoroughly the theory of the *De Anima*.

Y. Huzii advances Jaeger's theory and assumes the formation of the
Nicomachean Ethics to be prior to that of the *De Anima*. In his study
of Aristotle he states: "We may infer with sufficient reason that
Ethica Nicomachea IV must have been composed remarkably earlier
that these parts of the *De Anima*; its fundamental thought places it in
the age of the *Ethica Eudemia*. For the fundamental concepts in the
(*Nicomachean*) *Ethics* are founded upon the Platonic scheme, which
was abandoned as incomplete already in the *De Anima*, viz., the
scheme which divides the soul into two parts, the rational and the
irrational, without referring to the parts posited later, viz., the
θρεπτικόν, αἰσθητικόν, διανοητικόν, and the concept of the soul as the
first ἐντελέχεια of the organism.[279] This assumption apparently refers
only to the date of the three books V, VI, and VII, especially of book
VI, and Huzii differs from Jaeger only in not admitting book VI to
belong originally to the *Nicomachean Ethics*. He is hesitating to decide
this point, with the conjecture that either the book might originally
have belonged to the *Eudemian Ethics* except for the revision of the
definition of φρόνησις or that the three books, V, VI, and VII of the

---

[278] Jaeger, *Aristoteles* 355 ff.
[279] Y. Huzii, *Aristoteles Kenkyu* (A study of Aristotle) 186.

Nicomachean Ethics might have been composed earlier than the rest of this book.[280] But in the footnote[281] to his proposition to the effect that the concepts in the *Ethics* are founded upon the early thought of the duopartite theory, this interpreter asks us to compare *De An.* III. 9. 432 a 24–7 not with *Eth. Nic.* VI, but with *Eth. Nic.* I. 13. 1102 a 26–1103 a 10. Besides, the fundamental concepts of the intellectual and the ethical virtues are founded upon this duopartite theory, not merely in book VI, but also in the whole *Nicomachean Ethics*. Consequently, if he wishes to set the date of *Eth. Nic.* VI, "remarkably earlier than the *De Anima*," on account of the duopartite theory in book VI, he should rather infer that the whole *Nicomachean Ethics*, was formed remarkably earlier than the *De Anima*. And this, in fact, was his last conclusion: "That Aristotle did not, in this place, have in mind the definition of the soul in the *De Anima*, is evident from the fact that he followed Plato's thought, which strictly distinguished the soul from the body, without taking the soul as the ἐνέργεια of the body. So that it is at least a more natural interpretation to infer that the *Nicomachean Ethics* has been formed earlier than any part of the *De Anima*."[282]

We can, however, by no means agree with this interpretation. For in *Eth. Nic.* I and II, which Huzii recommends us to compare with *De Anima*, we find, along with the two parts, other parts such as the nutritive, the desiring, the appetitive, the intellectual and the sensitive. This shows that Aristotle established in the *Nicomachean Ethics* the concepts of virtues upon the duopartite theory, not because he did not think of the stricter concepts in the *De Anima*. It is true that in book VI, we can find no other parts except the rational and the irrational. From this fact we might assume that book VI is earlier than the *De Anima*. But it is too hasty to conclude that it was formed in the period of the *Eudemian Ethics*, or is borrowed from that work, for we find even in the *Eudemian Ethics* the concepts of the nutritive, the sensitive, and the desiring, evidently enumerated as parts of the soul.[283] If we admit Huzii's reasoning, we shall reach the conclusion that book

---

280 *Ibid.* 184.
281 *Ibid.* 188, n. 2.
282 *Ibid.* 188 n. 3. Nuyens actually reached this conclusion, cf. *op. cit.* 193. His argument, though very ingenious, does not persuade us completely.
283 *Eth. Eud.* II. 1. 1219 b 20–32. Jaeger is not right in saying that Aristotle yet followed Plato completely in *Eth. Eud.* II. 1. 1219 b 28. It is evident from the context that this is not a case of following Plato's scheme as Jaeger interprets, to say nothing of the fact that even the duopartite theory does not belong primarily to Plato. Cf. also *ibid.* 36–1220 a 2 ff.

VI of the *Nicomachean Ethics* must have been formed at least remarkably earlier than *Eth. Nic.* II. 1. – a conclusion which even this interpreter would not venture to assert.

We have seen that in *Eth. Nic.* I various functions proper to the *De Anima*, were enumerated along with the two parts. These heterogeneous groups of concepts are not employed unsystematically, but are coordinated rather well. In *Eth. Nic.* VI, especially, the intellectual part is divided into the scientific and the reasoning, the former being called absolutely rational, and the latter epitactic-rational. This subdivision of the intellectual part gives evidence, no doubt, of the mature reflection of Aristotle's later period; other functions or parts are not enumerated only because the problem at present is confined to the intellectual virtues and there is no need of referring to them. The sensitive part is reduced to the irrational part, because it is common to animals, as is the nutritive part. Elaboration is lacking, because the matter is almost irrelevant to the problem of virtue. The functional division in the *De Anima*, being made mainly from the psychological point of view, has not so much significance as the biological division through functional complexes. What is important for ethics, is the practical value, rather than the real classification, of psychical functions. Nor has the definition of the souls as the first actuality of the body so much importance for ethics, as it has for metaphysics. In short, the synthetic theory of the *Nicomachean Ethics* shows a mature thought of Aristotle than would the absolute renunciation of duopartite theory.

But, as much as we can find this plan of synthesis in the *Eudemian Ethics*, we would not venture to conclude from this, that the *Nicomachean Ethics* is posterior to the *De Anima*, any more than we would conclude that the *Eudemian Ethics* itself is posterior to the *De Anima*. Such a philological presumption is far from our intention, as we believe that the duopartite theory is maintained even in the *De Anima*. We only presume that Aristotle, who presented in the *De Anima* the multipartite theory from the theoretical point of view, was obliged and endeavoured in both *Ethics* to synthesize the two kinds of classification from the practical point of view. The periods of the formation of these three works, therefore, cannot be determined through these considerations.

The second argument which Huzii employs to prove the earlier formation of the *Nicomachean Ethics* as compared to the *De Anima* is more persuasive. It points out the predominance in the *Eth. Nic.* of

the Platonic view, in which the soul is contrasted with the body,
against the new theory of the *De Anima*, which defines the soul as the
actuality of the body. This neglect of the relation between soul and
body surely results in a defect in ethical theory, especially in the
argument concerning ethical virtues. For all that, it would be a too
hasty conclusion to decide from this the period of these works. For, we
find this very thought in *Met.* VIII. 3. 1043 a 34 as well; so that,
according to Huzii's way of argument, *Met.* VIII. together with the
De Anima should be regarded to be later than the *Nicomachean
Ethics*. Taken independently, this hypothesis contains no difficulty,
but it would be beyond the powers of philological inference to presume
a remarkable development[284] of thought without sufficient reason. At
least it seems to be far more probable that Aristotle had divided the
soul in many ways, from such various points of view as the logical-
psychological, the biological, the metaphysical-physical, and the
ethical.

[284] Cf. n. 8.

CHAPTER II

THE FUNCTIONS OF THE SOUL

1. The Development of Functions

We have concluded, in the previous chapter, that the division of the soul was made from various points of view. Many of these schemes of division may have been derived from the predecessors, to which Aristotle added an original division by functions. But without insisting upon a single scheme Aristotle seems to have synthesized them, assigning each one its proper significance. The attempt to prove a transition in his thought by means of philological study has not in so far succeeded.[1] Excessive devotion to philological method will throw the system into poverty. So, it would be a wiser procedure to look for a logical sequence in different elements, unless there be philological reasons for proceeding otherwise, for the thought of an excellent philosopher is neither an incoherent chaos "like an unskilful tragedy,"[2] nor a formula like the works of primitives, it is rather a process of presenting abundant difficulties and solving the questions from a more comprehensive and penetrating viewpoint. This is the most remarkable merit of Aristotle's way of thinking. Even if philological research attained the highest success, and remarkable evidence of transition might be found, it can by no means be concluded that Aristotle altered the thought without any attempt of synthesis. Aristotle was not merely a unique scholar who ranks with Plato and other philosophers in the Academy, but the very man who brought Greek philosophy to perfection. To be an opponent of Plato was one of his aspects, to be a successor to Plato was another. In truth, he was not a mere successor or a mere opponent, but successor and opponent at the same time. We should not suppose him a pure original thinker in his later period, by re-

[1] Cf. Ch. I. n. 46.
[2] *Met.* XIV. 3. 1090 b 19.

garding all Platonic or traditional elements in him as belonging to his
early period. The later Aristotle should be rather regarded as the
systematizer of a most comprehensive and synthetic philosophy.

Now the soul is divided into rational and irrational parts, either
from a metaphysical or from an ethical point of view. Metaphysically,
it is divided according as the parts possess substantial independency
and eternity, while ethically, practical interest how the virtues of each
part of the soul are engendered, gives another meaning to this division.
There are also many other kinds of division, the most important of
which being the biological-psychological one, which is peculiar to
Aristotle. But all these divisions were synthesized in the *Ethica Nicomachea*.[3] It is evident, in the first place, that the nutritive part in the
psycho-biological division is irrational, while the intellectual part is
verbatim rational. The other four parts, the sensitive, the imaginative,
the appetitive and the motive are in one sense irrational, but in another rational. To subsume these intermediate parts under the terms
rational and irrational, Aristotle distinguishes two different meanings for
each of these terms. Thus, just as there are rational parts in the primary
and the secondary senses, so are there irrational parts in both senses.

The irrational part in the primary sense acts quite independently of
reason; to it belongs the so-called vegetative soul[4] that operates purely
physiological and unconscious functions such as nutrition, growth and
reproduction. Whereas the irrational part in the secondary sense is
that which obeys or resists the commands and prohibitions of reason,
just as a man obeys or resists his father's words.[5] The function of this
intermediate part is here represented by desire,[6] but more exactly, it
contains also sensation, imagination and movement. All these functions
are intimately combined as nutrition is with growth and reproduction.
Hence they are treated by the practical interest of ethics almost as a
single part, and are attributed to all or most animals,[7] though sensation
and imagination may also form the principle of cognition.[8] Those ani-

---

[3] *Eth. Nic.* I. 13. 1102 a 26.
[4] *Eth. Nic.* I. 13. 1102 a 32; *De An.* II. 2. 413 b 8.
[5] *Eth. Nic.* I. 13. 1102 b 13.
[6] *Eth. Nic.* I. 13. 1102 b 30; cf. *Pol.* III. 4. 1277 a 6.
[7] *Part. An.* III. 4. 666 a 34; II. 1. 647 a 21; 10. 656 a 3; IV. 5. 681 a 19; *Gen.
An.* I. 23. 731 a 33; b 4; II. 1. 732 a 13; 5. 741 a 9; III. 7. 757 b 16; VI. 1.
778 b 32; *De An.* II. 2. 413 b 1; *De Sensu* 1. 436 b 11; V. 1. 467 b 24; *Met.* I. 1.
980 a 26.
[8] Sensation is a kind of cognition (*Gen. An.* I. 23. 731 a 33). It is discriminating,
like intellect (*Motu An.* 6. 700 b 20; *An. Post.* II. 19. 99 b 35; *De An.* III. 9.
432 a 16; *Top.* II. 4. 111 a 19; cf. *De An.* III. 2. 426 b 10; III. 3. 427 a 16), and

mals move on the occasion of sensation or imagination,[9] while the immediate efficient cause of their locomotion is desire.[10] Hence this part
is sometimes characterized by sensation, instead of desire. It is also on
this account,[11] that Brentano divided the soul into the nutritive, the
sensitive and the rational. In short, the irrational part in the secondary
sense is the conscious soul of animals which is engaged in sensation,
imagination and movement.[12] Because of its practical importance,
ethics emphasizes desire, regarding the other functions as something
preliminary or auxiliary to the activity of this function. Since such a
part of the soul may be, again, regarded rational in so far as it shares
in reason, Aristotle calls it the rational part in the secondary sense,[13]
while the rational part in the superior sense is the thinking part which
involves reason in itself. But in this point, we might rather divide,
more strictly and consistently,[14] the rational part into theoretical intellect, and the practical intellect, the one thinks independently, the other
guides the irrational part in the secondary sense just as a father guides
his son. The rational part in the secondary sense corresponds to the
irrational part in the secondary sense; they are, so to say, the two sides
of one and the same thing, but themselves not quite identical. For to
order is one thing, to obey is another: the former is essentially rational,
while the latter is essentially irrational. It is only accidentally that
the former is irrational and the latter rational. Aristotle himself was
aware of this distinction.[15] The two species of rational parts in the first
division are διανοητικόν and ἠθικόν, while those of the second division
are θεωρητικόν and πρακτικόν.

analogous to simple assertion or thinking (De Ann. III. 7. 431 a 8). In so far as
it is discriminating it is the beginning of induction or the principle of knowledge
(An. Post. I. 18. 81 b 8; Top. 1. 12. 105 a 18) It is not per se a practical principle
(Eth. Nic. V. 2. 1139 a 20; De An. III. 9. 432 b 19). Sometimes the animal soul
is divided into a locomotive faculty and a cognitive faculty, the latter containing
sensation and intellect. (De An. III. 9. 432 a 15; III. 3. 427 a 17). But this is a
distinction from the viewpoint of whether a soul is active or passive against the
object, not a comprehensive classification of sensation. From one point of view,
sensation is a principle of theoretical knowledge, but from another point of view,
it is without doubt practical as serving preservation of life. It is not an immediate agent like desire, but in as much as desire presupposes sensation, it may be
the principle of practice at least indirectly.
   [9] Motu An. 6. 701 a 5.
   [10] De An. III. 10. 433 b 16; Motu An. 6. 701 a 5.
   [11] Brentano, Psych. d. Arist. 58–60.
   [12] Ibid.
   [13] Eth. Nic. I. 13. 1103 a 1 ff.
   [14] Ch. I. 6.
   [15] Eth. Nic. VI. 2. 1138 b 35 ff.

By the combination of the functional division with the traditional duopartite division, Aristotle gave a practical meaning to the former, which was originally of theoretical nature, only the synthesis of these heterogeneous divisions was not complete, as far as the *Nicomachean Ethics* is concerned. Jaeger's criticism[16] to the effect that in the ethics the duopartite theory is dominant, while the functional division which was worked out in psychology is neglected, is right to some extent. But, it is neither because, as Jaeger thinks, Aristotle's ethical thought was disturbed by Platonic theory, nor as Huzii conjectures, is it because ethical theory was formed before psychological theory; rather it is mainly due to the difference of viewpoints. Psychology as a part of natural science, though not in modern sense, is theoretical, whereas ethics, being a kind of practical science, is governed by practical interests. The division and investigation of virtues are not the matters of theoretical knowledge, but the ways of conducting human affairs. Excellence in nutrition, sight or imagination was set aside, because it has no importance for practice. The leading interest of ethical writings is to clarify the virtues[17] in order to contribute to human welfare. To demand ethical theory to be established upon psychology is not so self-evident as it might appear to modern thinkers.[18] No doubt, it is desirable to study the relations between the psychological functions more fully. This will contribute much to our understanding of conduct and virtue. But, for this purpose, investigation must be extended all over the *corpus Aristotelicum* beyond the limit of psychology.

Now the soul was defined as the form of a natural body having in it the capacity of life.[19] It is by nature the activity of the body and the very principle which makes it a living being. The body lives because of the soul, without which it is only a material object.[20] Consequently, the primitive functions of life, such as nutrition or reproduction, are not simply the functions of the body as a mere material object, but in fact those of the soul as the principle of life.[21] Since such is the relation

[16] Jaeger, *Aristoteles* 355 ff.
[17] *Eth. Nic.* I. 13. 1102 a 18–25.
[18] *Met.* IV. 4. 1006 a 6 ff.; *Eth. Nic.* II. 1094 b 19–1095 a 2.
[19] *De An.* II. 1. 429 a 19; Ch. II. 1.
[20] *De An.* I. 5. 411 b 8–10.
[21] *De An.* I. 4. 416 a 18 f; 416 b 9–11; *De An.* III. 12. 434 a 22, 26; II. 4. 415 a 23; *Gen. An.* II. 7. 745 b 24; III. 7. 757 b 16; II. 3. 736 a 35; 4. 740 b 36; 740 b 29; *De Juvent.* 2. 468 b 2; *De Resp.* 8. 474 a 31; 18. 479 a 30. Nutrition as the lowest and the most common function of the soul belongs also to plants. *De An.* II. 2. 314 b 7; 4. 415 a 23; III. 9. 432 a 29; 12. 434 a 22. 26.

of soul and body, there would be no function of the soul which is independent of the body; what we call a function of the body is in fact an act of the soul in the body, and an act of the soul is nothing but a function of the body that operates as the soul. A true physicist who wants a complete apprehension of a psychological phenomenon, should not content himself with observing a mental phenomenon, but also ought to explain its physiological basis.[22] But a possible distinction to be made is that in the case of a lower mental phenomenon, it depends directly upon the body, while in the case of a higher one, it is mediated by lower mental functions. Thus nutrition or reproduction appears as if it were a bodily function, while thinking appears to be independent of the body, though strictly speaking, no function of the soul is possible without the body. The active reason, which appears to be the only exception, is not, as we have seen, a part of the soul, but so to say an objective mind which gives forms to the passive reason.

Body and soul are not related to each other as two heterogeneous principles, but are conjoined as matter and form, the central organ of the body is at the same time the place of the soul and the condition of its unity.[23] Such a central organ of the body, and consequently also of the soul, is the heart,[24] for it is at the same time the starting point and the end of blood vessels,[25] the distributing center of blood,[26] the origin of heat[27] which is necessary for life;[28] once the movement of the heart has stopped, the temperature cools, the circulation of blood ceases, and the

---

22 *De An.* I. 1. 409 b 11 f.

23 *De Juvent.* 1. 467 b 14–17. According to Nuyens, the localization of the soul is peculiar to Aristotle's transitional period, to which belong the *De Partibus Animalium*, the *Juventute et Senectute*, as well as the *De Respiratione*. But we do not find it so incompatible as he says, to assume on the one hand that the soul is the form of the whole body, and on the other hand that its central organ is the heart. Cf. *op. cit.* 164, together with Rolfes's note on this point. Besides, Nuyens finds it difficult to prove the antecedence of the *De Respiratione* to the *De Anima*, because of the reference of the former to the latter in 474 b 11; cf. *op. cit.* 168 f.

24 *De Resp.* 17. 479 a 1; *De Juvent.* 4. 469 a 28; *De Somno.* 2. 456 a 6; *Part. An.* III. 3. 665 a 12; 4. 666 b 14; *Met.* VI. 10. 1035 b 26.

25 *Part. An.* II. 1. 647 b 4; 9. 654 b 11; 665 b 15; 17. 666 a 8, 31; 5. 667 a 16; *Gen. An.* II. 4. 740 a 22, 28; 6. 744 a 5; 6. 743 a 1; IV. 8. 776 b 12; V. 7. 787 b 28; *De Somno.* 3. 456 b 1; *De Juvent.* 3. 468 b 32; *De Memor.* I. 450 a 29; *De Resp.* 8. 474 n 7; *Hist. An.* III. 3. 513 a 22; 4. 514 b 22.

26 *Part. An.* III. 3. 665 a 11, 18; 665 b 20; 666 a 15; *De Resp.* 17. 478 b 35; *De Juvent.* 4. 469 a 33; 1. 468 a 1; 2. 468 a 21.

27 *De Juvent.* 6. 470 a 19; 4. 469 b 8; 5. 470 a 6; *Part. An.* II. 3. 650; a 5.

28 *De Juvent.* 14. 469 b 9–20. *De Resp.* 17. 478 a 24; 478 b 32. *Part. An.* II. 7. 652; b 27; III. 7. 670 a 24; II. 7. 653 b 5; IV. 13. 696 b 17; *Gen. An.* II. 6. 743 b 28.

death of the animal ensues.[29] Thus the heart is the first in generation,[30] and is the central organ of nutrition in sanguine animals,[31] the blood that circulates through it supplies nutriment to the whole body.[32] Food is first taken through the mouth, then digested by the stomach and excreted at the end of the body, but what presides over the whole nutritive process is the heart, the other parts being only ancillary to it.[33]

Strictly speaking, the uniting principle of an animal is not the body, but the soul.[34] But, as far as the soul is the form and actuality of the body, the correlation of psychical functions must correspond to that of bodily organs. The heart is not only the center of nutrition, but also that of sensation,[35], imagination,[36] feeling,[37] desire,[38] motion[39] and even of practical wisdom.[40] The differentiation and development of psychical functions correspond to those of bodily parts, and both of them are proportionate to the complexity of life.[41] But the differentiation and development are so continuous as each term is hardly discernible.[42] The continuity holds throughout between living beings and lifeless things,[43] between soul and body, as well as among the functions of the soul. This is the predominant characteristic of Aristotle's metaphysical principle of matter and form, in contrast to the heterogeneous principles

[29] *De Juvent.* 4. 469 b 13 13–20.
[30] *De Juvent.* 3. 468 b 28; 469 b 30; *Gen. An.* II. 4. 740 a 8, 13; 740 b 3; 5. 741 b 16; 1. 735 a 24; 4. 738 b 16; 740 a 17; II. 6. 43 b 26; III. 2. 753 b 19; *Motu An.* III. 4. 666 a 10, 21; cf. *Gen. An.* IV. 1. 766 b 2; *Met.* V. 1. 1013 a 5; *Part. An.* 4. 665 a 33; 665 b 1; 666 a 20; II. 6. 742 b 36.
[31] *De Juvent.* 3. 469 a 5; *Part. An.* II. 1. 647 a 25.
[32] *De Juvent.* 3. 469 a 2; *Part. An.* II. 3. 650 b 12; 651 a 15; 10; III. 5. 668 a 20.
[33] *De Juvent.* 3. 469 a 2; 469 b 11.
[34] *De An.* I. 5. 411 b 5; *Part. An.* I. 1. 641 a 17–21.
[35] *De Juvent.* 3. 469 a 5, 10; 1. 467 b 28; *Part. An.* II. 1. 647 a 25; III. 3. 665 a 12, 17; 4. 666 b 14; II. 10. 656 a 28; IV. 5. 681 b 15, 32; *Motu An.* II. 702 b 24; *Gen. An.* II. 6. 743 b 25.
[36] *Motu An.* 6. 700 b 19.
[37] *Part. An.* III. 4. 666 a 12.
[38] *De An.* I. 1. 403 a 31; III. 9. 433 a 1; cf. *Motu An.* 7. 701 b 1–8; 702 a 20.
[39] *Part. An.* II. 1. 647 a 25; III. 3. 665 a 12, 17; 4. 666 b 14; *De Somno.* 2. 456 b 4.
[40] *Part. An.* II. 2. 648 a 3 ff.; *Gen. An.* II. 6. 744 a 27; cf. Teichmüller, *Neue Studien zur Geschichte der Begriffe* III. 133–145.
[41] *Part. An.* II. 10. 656 a 1–8; *Gen. An.* VIII. 1. 588 b 4–589 a 2; *De Cael.* II. 12. 292 b 7 ff.
[42] *Hist. An.* VIII. 1. 588 b 4–13; *Part. An.* IV. 5. 681 a 12; 10. 686 b 20 ff.
[43] *Hist. An.* VIII. 1. 588 b 6.

of matter and spirit employed by Descartes or Spinoza. Not only form is accompanied by matter as substratum, but also they are related to each other as potentiality to actuality. The body is the substratum of the soul, but the former is related to the latter as potentiality is related to actuality. The world is constituted of matter and form and forms a continuous development from the corporeal to the spiritual, the lowest limit is *prima materia* and the highest limit God.[44] Thus, the discrete opposition of soul and body was transformed into a system of continuous development full of life.[45] Even the movement of an inorganic body was assimilated to the movement of living being. The movements of earth, water, fire and air are analogous to the movements of animals. They all move according to nature, and if there be any difference, it is only the difference of degree in complexity,[46] and every complexity is due to the complexity of the organs.[47] Every psychical phenomenon is a complex activity of the elements which constitute the organs. Thus, when the term "life" is applied beyond its usual limit to a divine being, some sort of material is assigned to such a being on the analogy of an organism. Where all the matter of an organism is formalized, and there remains only the potentiality of locomotion, such beings, viz., the heavenly bodies, are considered to be the bodies of super-organic souls.[48] Beyond them, there is only a pure form without matter, a

[44] Cf. Zeller, *op. cit.* 505 n. 1. Zeller regards the meridian of the development of nature to be mankind, but according to Aristotle, man is neither the highest being nor even the highest animal. Heavenly bodies and gods are also regarded as living beings, e.g. *Met.* XII. 7. 1072 b 29; *Top.* V. 1. 128 b 19; V. 6. 136 b 7; *De Cael.* II. 2. 295 a 28. 3. 286 a 9; cf. II. 12; II. 2. 284 b 32; *Part. An.* I. 1 641 b 15 ff. This is admitted by Zeller himself in *op. cit.* 467. On the other hand, life is attributed to the elements as well. *Gen. An.* III. 11. 762 a 18–26.

[45] Life is attributed even to air and wind in *Gen. An.* IV. 10. 778 a 2, to the sea in *Meteor.* II. 2. 355 b 4 ff.; 356 a 33 ff. Further, inorganic natural phenomena are explained by analogy with organism. Cf. Zeller, *op. cit.* 506 f.

[46] Aristotle rejects the theories of natural philosophers who explained the soul by supposing it to be constituted of such a simple element as earth, water, fire or air. (*De An.* I. 2). But as the soul is the form of the body, and the body is an organism which is constituted of these elements, the functions of the soul must be, in the last analysis, the complex function of these elements.

[47] Cf. n. 41.

[48] *De Cael.* II. 12. 292 a 18 ff.; II. 2. 285 a 25; 284 b 32; *Part. An.* I. 1. 641 b 15; *Eth. Nic.* VI. 7. 1141 a 35; cf. *Met.* XII. 8. 1073 a 26. The organs and functions of lower animals are simple, but the higher the animals, the more complex the functions. According to this rule, the living functions of heavenly bodies which are superior to mankind would be more complex. But Aristotle in fact did not think so. According to him, lower creatures require only simple functions, because their life is also simple, but man requires far more complex functions in order to share in higher values. Whereas heavenly bodies and gods may be

spirit in complete actuality, i.e. God.[49] All beings and all phenomena
in the universe compose such a complete system of continuous development.[50] The government[51] of God is not His voluntary practice or
production.[52] Practice and production are acts or movements from
desire,[53] whereas desire and movement are peculiar to incomplete
beings.[54] God as a complete being, must be absolutely unmovable,[55]
the contemplation of Himself being His only activity.[56] All living and
lifeless things are moved by Him, through loving and longing for this
supreme Being,[57] who moves others without Himself being moved.
Every activity of all creatures is thus sanctified.[58] What is called
providence is nothing but the power of nature.[59] We may call it pan-
theism in the highest sense, and find in it the archetype of Leibniz's
monadology.

With this magnificient view of the universe before us, let us return
to the present question as to the relations of psychical functions. Of
course, the fundamental principles of Aristotle's metaphysics, matter
and form as well as potential and actual, are applicable to everything.
They are applicable to the relation between the parts of the soul as
well as to the relation of the soul to the body. A living being is constituted of body and soul, as matter and form, and body develops into

simple in another sense, owing to their independent existence and self-sufficient
life (De Cael. II. 12). This is an ingenious thought indeed, but it is not free from
various difficulties that follow from regarding heavenly bodies as animals.

[49] Met. II. 6. 1071 b 21; 8. 1072 a 26, 35; 1074 a 35; De Cael. I. 9. 279 a 16,
cf. Met. V. 7. 1072 b 29; Top. V. 1. 128 b 19.

[50] Cf. n. 42.

[51] Met. XII. 7. 1072 b 7; 8. 1078 b 7 ff; XII. 10. De Cael. I. 9. 279 a 16; Met.
XII. 7. 1072 b 7.

[52] Eth. Nic. X. 8. 1178 b 20; cf. 1178 a 9; 1178 b 5; VIII. 1. 1145 a 25;
Zeller, op. cit. 368 n. 1; Brentano, Psych. d. Arist. 238 ff.

[53] Eth. Nic. VI. 2. 1139 a 17 ff.; 30 ff.

[54] Eth. Eud. VII. 12. 1244 b 8; 15. 1249 b 16; (Mag. Mor. II. 15. 1212 b 35).

[55] Met. XI. 7. 1064 a 37; XII. 7. 1072 a 26; De Cael. I. 9. 279 a 32; II. 12.
292 a 18; 292 b 5; Phys. VIII. 5. 250 b 20; De An. III. 10. 433 b 13.

[56] Met. XII. 7. 1072 b 18; 9. 1074 b 21; Eth. Eud. VII. 12. 1245 b 17.

[57] Pol. III. 16. 1287 a 29; Top. V. 4. 132 b 3; Gen. et Corr. I. 6. 323 a 12.

[58] De Cael. I. 4. 271 a 33; Gen. et Corr. II. 10. 336 b 27 ff.; Pol. VII. 4. 1326 a
32; Eth. Nic. X. 10. 1179 b 21; VII. 14. 1153 b 32.

[59] In Part. An. II. 10. 656 a 7, IV. 10. 686 a 27. Eth. Nic. X. 7. 1177 a 13 etc.,
only reason is assumed to be θεῖον while in De Divin. 463 b 12, other natural
powers are said to be δαιμόνια, cf. Zeller, op. cit. 387 f. It is evident through
comparison with the preceding note, that this difference too cannot be explained
away as a development of Aristotle's thought. It is none the less possible that
Aristotle was led to this distinction through an effort at strictness. What is
δαιμόνιον may be θεῖον in a wider sense.

soul from potentiality to actuality. In the same way, the lower part of
the soul is related to the higher part as matter to form, and the former
develops into the latter as from potentiality to actuality. This differentiation and development of psychical functions illustrates in itself
the scale of biological evolution. The higher function presupposes the
lower, and cannot exist without it, while the lower function does not
necessarily require the higher, and may exist without it.[60] The lowest
functions are nutrition, growth and generation;[61] the part of the soul
which is engaged in these functions is called the nutritive part[62] or
nutritive soul.[63] This function is most necessary and fundamental for
life, and can exist without the others, while the latter cannot exist
without the former.[64] The living beings which have only this lowest
type of soul are plants.[65]

Now, higher functions of life develop in accord with the modes of
nutrition.[66] Living beings that eat other living beings are possessed of
sensation. This is a function of leading nutrition and is characteristic
to all animals as Aristotle puts it:[67] "But the animal must of necessity
possess sensation, if nature makes nothing in vain: for everything in
nature subserves an end, or else will be an accessory of things which
subserve an end. Now every living body having the power of progression
and yet lacking sensation would be destroyed and never reach full
development, which is its natural function. For how in such a case is it
to obtain nutriment? Motionless animals, it is true, have for nutriment
that from which they have been developed. But a body, not stationary,
but produced by generation, cannot possibly have a soul and an intelligence capable of judging without also having sensation." This is

[60] *De An.* II. 2. 413 b 7; 414 a 33; 415 a 23; III. 9. 432 a 29; 12. 434 a 22, 26;
De An. II. 3. 414 b 28–415 a 11.
[61] Nutrition and growth are attributed to the same part. *De An.* II. 2. 413 a
25; 4. 416 b 12; III 12. 434 a 24; *Eth. Nic.* I. 6. 1098 a 1. So with nutrition and
reproduction. *De An.* II. 4. 416 a 19; *Gen. An. II.* 4. 740 b 36.
[62] *De An.* II. 2. 413 a 31; 413 b 5, 7, 12; 3.414 a 31; 414 b 31; III. 9. 432 a 29;
De Somno 1. 454 a 13; *De Juvent.* 2. 468 a 28; *Eth. Nic.* I. 13. 1102 b 11; VI. 13.
1144 a 10.
[63] *De An.* II. 4. 415 a 23; III. 12. 434 a 22; *De Juvent.* 2. 468 b 2; *De Resp.* 8.
474 a 31; 18. 479 a 30; *Gen. An.* II. 3. 736 a 35; 4. 740 b 36.
[64] *De An.* II. 2. 413 a 31; 413 b 5; 3. 414 b 31; *De Somno* 1. 454 a 13; *De Resp.*
8. 474 b 11.
[65] *De An.* II. 2. 413 b 7; 4. 415 a 23; III. 9. 432 a 29; 12. 434 a 22, 26.
[66] *De Juvent.* 1. 468 a 9–12. Plants take nourishment from the earth, while
animals nourish themselves through eating other living beings. *Hist. An.* VIII.
1. 588 a 16–33.
[67] *De An.* III. 12. 434 a 30– b4; *De Sensu* 1. 436 b 12– 437 a 1.

obviously the most explicit manifestation of teleology, – a teleology without, however, any supposition of a creator or a world designer. Though Aristotle was not an atheist, his theory was pantheistic rather than theistic.[68] The evolution of life is neither due to the mechanical activity of elements nor to the regulation of a personal god; rather it is a natural generation from the creative principle immanent to life.[69] Therefore, nothing is more pointless to oppose pragmatism to Aristotle's intellectualism. Aristotle, on the contrary, was a forerunner of pragmatism in finding the origin and essence of sensation and intellect in the necessity of life.[70] It is true that Aristotle sometimes treated sensation as a pure discriminating faculty. But these two aspects are not incompatible with each other. Taken *in abstracto*, sensation is a faculty of discrimination, but *in concreto*, it depends upon the nutrition and conditions desire and conduct through the medium of emotion. It may be said that sensation is pragmatic in its generation, but intellectual in its end. The mere fact that sensation is common to all animals is sufficient to prove the pragmatism.[71] Sensation, in its primitive form, is a practical function that serves directly for the preservation and development of life, i.e., for nutriment and generation.[72] The very center of sensation is found in the heart,[73] which is also the central organ of nutrition. Nevertheless, taken *in abstracto*, sensation is a faculty to receive the forms of the objects and to provide them to theoretical knowledge.

Just as sensation is founded upon nutrition, there is an hierarchical order among sensations. Touch and taste are the lowest of all,[74] and in addition, taste is considered to be a kind of touch, because it feels through directly touching food.[75] Next to taste and touch, come smell, hearing and sight, in ascending order. The general rule of progressive development is applicable also to this case. The lower sensation may

[68] Zeller, *op. cit.* 381.

[69] *Part. An.* I. 1. 641 b 12–26; *Phys.* II. 8. 199 b 26–33; *Met.* XII. 8. 1065 a 26 f.

[70] Cf. Bergson, *L'évolution créatrice* 115 ff. ✓

[71] *Eth. Nic.* VII. 6. 1149 a 10; *Part. An.* I. 5. 651 b 5; III. 4. 666 a 34; II. 1. 647 a 21; 10. 656 a 3; IV. 5. 681 a 19; *Gen. An.* I. 23. 731 a 33; 731 b 4; II. 1. 732 a 12; II. 5. 741 a 9; III. 7. 757 b 16; V. 1. 778 b 32; *De An.* II. 2. 413 b 1; *De Sensu* 436 b 11; *De Juvent.* 1. 467 b 24; *Met.* I. 1. 980 a 28; *Eth. Nic.* IX. 9. 1170 a 16; VI. 2. 1139 a 20.

[72] *Hist. An.* VIII. 1. 589 a 2–5.

[73] *De Juvent.* 3. 469 a 5–8; *Part. An.* IV. 4. 678 b 1–4.

[74] *De An.* II. 2. 413 b 4–7; 414 a 2–4; 3. 414 b 3; *Hist. An.* I. 3. 489 a 17; *Part. An.* II. 8. 653 b 23; *De Sensu* 1. 436 b 13; *De Somno* 2. 455 a 7.

[75] *De An.* II. 9. 421 a 18; III. 12. 434 b 18; *De Sensu* 4. 441 a 3; *Part. An.* II. 17. 660 a 21.

function by itself, but the higher presupposes the lower.[76] Touch and taste act by direct contact with objects, but smell and other higher senses perceive objects through media.[77] What relates directly to nutrition is of course touch and taste, or touch in a wider sense which includes taste. Animals cannot live without this sensation.[78] Generation being a primitive function inseparable from nutrition,[79] is also mediated by touch as the lowest sensation, as Aristotle puts it: "These two senses (i.e. taste and touch), then, are necessary to the animal, and it is plain that without touch no animal can exist. But the other senses are means to well-being, and are necessary not to any and every species of animal, but only to certain species, as for example, those capable of locomotion. For if the animal capable of locomotion is to survive, it must have sensation, not only when in contact with anything, but also at a distance from it."[80] "Thus the animal has sight to see with, because it lives in air or water or speaking generally, in a transparent medium ... It has hearing in order that information may be conveyed to it."[81] Higher sensations are also natural to life, but they are not simply needed for mere existence, but are useful for a better life, for to that end the animal needs a perception of distant objects. Sight and hearing are higher than taste, because they give a knowledge about distant objects and a wider perspective to life. "The senses which operate through external media, viz., smelling, hearing, and seeing, are found in all animals which possess the faculty of locomotion. To all that possess them they are a means of preservation; their final cause being that such creatures may, guided by antecedent perception, both pursue their food, and shun things that are bad or destructive."[82]

The distance of space between object and subject is proportional to the interval of time between sensation and enjoyment, and this distance or interval corresponds to the grade of sensation. A higher sensation allows us a wider observation and earlier foreknowledge of the objects distant in time and space. The same principle is also applicable to the relation of sensation to intellect.[83]

The higher sensations not only guide nutrition and generation more

[76] De An. III. 12. 435 a 12–14.
[77] De An. III. 12. 435 a 14–19.
[78] De An. III. 12. 434 b 10–24; De An. II. 3. 414 b 6–9.
[79] De An. II. 4. 415 a 23; 416 b 24.
[80] De An. III. 12. 434 b 22.
[81] Ibid. 13. 435 b 19.
[82] De Sensu, 1 436 b 18.
[83] Cf. De An. III. 10. 433 b 5 ff.

effectively than the lower in terms of far reaching perception, but also
prepare for higher mental activities. Among the three kinds of sensation smell is the lowest, but in the case of the human being, this has the
function of promoting or inhibiting health besides being immediately
concerned with nutrition. An example of this is the smelling of the
perfume of flowers.[84] Hearing and sight are not irrelevant to nutrition,
but they guide it indirectly.[85] But these higher sensations are already
freeing themselves of the immediate necessity of life, as Aristotle puts
it: "Such sensations are a means of preservation to all that possess
them ... But in animals which have also intelligence they serve for the
attainment of a higher perfection. They bring in tidings of many
distinctive qualities of things, from which the knowledge of truth,
speculative and practical, is generated in the soul. Of the two last
mentioned, seeing, regarded as being supplied for the primary wants
of life and considered in its direct effects, is the superior sense; but for
developing of intelligence, and in its indirect consequences, hearing
takes the precedence. The faculty of seeing, thanks to the fact that all
bodies are coloured, brings tidings of multitudes of distinctive qualities
of all sorts; ... while hearing announces only the distinctive qualities
of sound, and to some few animals, those also of voice. Indirectly, however, it is hearing that contributes most to the growth of intelligence.
For rational discourse is a cause of instruction in virtue of its being
audible."[86] The same thought is found at the beginning of *Metaphysics:*
"All men by nature desire to know. An indication of this is the delight
we take in our senses; for even apart from their usefulness they are
loved for themselves; and above all others the sense of sight. For not
only with a view to action, but even when we are not going to do anything, we prefer seeing (one might say) to everything else. The reason
is that this, most of all the senses, makes us know and brings to light
many differences between things."

Whether hearing or sight be superior, in stating that these higher
sensations act for the sake of higher life, Aristotle often repeats that
they make us discriminate the qualities of many things. Though every
sensation is the discrimination of some differences, these higher sensations are more profitable for the progress of reason. For a mere natural

[84] *De An.* II. 3. 414 b 10 f.; *De Sensu* 5. 443 b 16–30; 444 a 14 f.; 445 a 1–4;
ibid. 27–b 1; *Eth. Nic.* III. 13. 1118 a 16.

[85] *Eth. Nic.* III. 13. 1118 a 16–22.

[86] *De Sensu* 1. 437 a 1 ff. φρόνησις is used here in the wide sense, and means
knowledge in general comprising both practical and theoretical knowledge.

existence it is not necessary to discriminate many differences. Hence the sensations of lower animals are comparatively simple and discriminate only what is necessary for a bare existence.[87] For the sake of well-being, however, one requires more distinct discrimination of minute differences. Concurrent with the expansion of environment, higher sensations gradually develop in order to discriminate many objects, and in further dependance on these intellect grows. Inasmuch as these sensations are necessary for the growth of intellect, the loss of any sense entails a defect in the corresponding portion of knowledge.[88] Sensation and intellect are by no means heterogeneous functions which oppose each other, on the contrary, they are the same function of life on different stages. It is fundamental to the thought of Plato,[89] and here he is followed by Aristotle, to make the object of sensation individual and accidental, and that of knowledge universal and necessary.[90] On the other hand, sensation, being a kind of cognition, is regarded to be homogeneous with intellect.[91] Just as sensation originates itself from the necessity of nutrition, and differentiates itself in accordance with the modes of the latter, intellect is also regarded as an instrument for a more complicated life,[92] and presupposes sensation as its foundation.[93] The knowledge of cause and principle proper to intellect enables us to perceive objects distant in time and space, which might be perceived through sensation if we were present there at that moment.[94] Sensation, on the one side, tending in its pure activity towards intellectual cognition, is regarded as a kind of theoretical knowledge; but intellect, on the other side, presupposes sensation as its *sine qua non* and is continuous with it. In the analysis of rational cognition we find at the top a concept of active reason or divine reason, but at the bottom a sensitive element common to animals. In Aristotle's thought, man is an intermediate being between God and animals; he is

---

[87] Cf. n. 41, n. 48.

[88] *An. Post.* I. 18. 81 a 38–b9.

[89] *Theaet.* 160, 151 ff., 163 ff., 165, 179, 187, 192 ff.

[90] *De An.* II. 5. 417 b 22; *An. Post.* I. 18. 81 b 6; 24. 86 a 29; *Phys.* I. 5. 189 a 7; *Eth. Nic.* II. 9. 1109 b 23; V. 5. 1147 a 26; VI. 9. 1142 a 27; cf. *De Juvent.* 2. 468 a 22; *Met.* I. 5. 986 a 32; V. 11. 1018 b 32; *Gen. An.* I. 2. 716 a 19; *Gen. et Corr.* I. 3. 318 b 29; *Eth. Nic.* IX. 1. 1172 a 36; (*De Spirit.* 4. 482 b 19, 21) etc.

[91] *Motu* An. 6. 700 b 20; *An. Post.* II. 19. 99 b 35; *De An.* III. 9. 432 a 16; *Gen. An.* I. 23. 731 a 33–b2.

[92] *Probl.* XI (XXX) 5. 955 b 23–28. In spite of the spuriousness of this book, the thought is no doubt in accordance with Aristotle's tenet. Cf. Part. *An. IV.* 10. 687 a 7–23; Hick's note on 432 a 2; *Rhet.* I. 6. 1362 a 21–24.

[93] *De An.* III. 3. 432 a 3–8; 427 b 15 f.; 12. 434 b 3–8.

[94] *An. Post.* II. 2. 90 a 24–30.

rather a higher animal which has acquired intellect out of sensibility,   *N B.*
than a mixture of intellect and sensibility.

Generally speaking, those who make sensation an element of intellectual knowledge are called rationalists, while those who make the
former the cause of the latter are called empiricists. Though the two
theories oppose each other in modern times, there is no real antagonism between them. According to Aristotle, sensation is not only an
element of intellectual knowledge, but also the cause of intellect. In   *N. A*
spite of his rationalistic ideal of knowledge, he adopts the empirical
explanation of its growth. Here is also a specimen of a fine harmony
of his metaphysics and positive science.

Since sensation is the origin of intellect, and the ideal of intellectual
activity is pure theoretical knowledge, our mind never leaps immediately from sensation to contemplation. We start from sensation and
first form a memory out of sense impression, then construct an experience from memory and through finding out the universal principle
accomplish an art. That which organizes and employs the art thus
acquired is practical wisdom, the accomplishment of which are ethics
and politics. Absolutely free contemplation is only possible for individuals and societies governed by such a practical intellect.[95]

2. The Reference of Functions

The foregoing considerations have been restricted to the accumulative
progress of psychical functions. Our next problem must be the difference and relation among various functions. To begin with, imagination is next to sensation and stands between sensation and intellect;
sensation is distinguished from imagination in that sensation catches
the form together with the matter, while imagination excludes the
matter.[96] But on the other hand, the exclusion of the matter was
regarded as the mark of sensation, through which it was distinguished
from nutrition. The same differentia cannot be applied twice, therefore
we are obliged to avoid a literal interpretation and consider that sensation unlike imagination receives accidental forms together with the
essential form.[97]

[95] *Met.* I. 1. 980 a 27–b12; 981 b 13–25; *An. Post.* II. 19. 100 a 3 ff., *Eth. Nic.*
I. 1. 1094 a 18–b11.
[96] *De An.* III. 8. 432 a 9.
[97] Cf. Ch. I. 3. Most scholars find no difficulty in the sentence just quoted.
They usually take it to mean that the object of sensation has matter. But this
explains nothing, because Aristotle distinguishes herewith not αἰσθητά and

The act that accepts an external object together with the matter, is nutrition,[98] while sensation receives only the form.[99] This makes us remind of Bergson's theory[100] of sensation to the effect that the sensation consists in the diminution that the imagination suffers from the encounter with an automatic object. This somewhat novel expression is practically the same as Aristotle's theory. When Aristotle states that sensation receives the form of an object without its matter, the abstraction or the exclusion of the matter is nothing but the so-called diminution of Bergson's. Sensation is not an addition of something to the object, but a diminution of something from it, the diminution which is more than a mere limitation, and the active preparation to manage the object.

That sensation receives the form of a body without the matter, implies that sensation consists in abstraction. But to take sensation as a kind of abstraction is not to have an abstract view of sensation. This is by no means a paradox; I only would like to vindicate Aristotle's theory against a superficial attack of *Lebensphilosophen* whose ideal is the concrete cognition. To abstract the form and leave the matter is of course an operation of mind upon an object. It is nothing more and nothing less. Nothing more, because we (with Aristotle) do not presuppose matter and form as independent elements and then construct reality from them. Nothing less, because cognition always requires some active operation upon the object, and where there is no abstraction, there cannot be any cognition whatever. A concrete cognition, in the literal sense, is a *contradictio in adjecto*; a concrete thing does exist, and might be experienced, but can never be recognized. For to experience is one thing, to recognize, another. In truth, even experience, in so far as it is human, is impossible without presupposing some cognition, and consequently, some abstraction too. Therefore, if the expression "concrete cognition" is to have any meaning at all, it can only

---

φαντάσματα, viz. the objects of sensation and the contents of imagination, but αἰσθήματα and φαντάσματα viz. the contents of sensation and those of imagination. One might alter αἰσθήματα to αἰσθητά, but then, the contrast of αἰσθήματα and φαντάσματα would be lost. Whereas what Aristotle here wishes to prove is that intellectual knowledge is impossible without sensation (*De An.* III. 8. 432 a 9). For that purpose, he might have wanted to say that intellect does not think without sensation; but as this is against the fact, he chose to say that intellect thinks with image, since φάντασμα is essentially the same as αἴσθημα. Cf. *De Memor.* 1. 450 a 30.

98 *De An.* II. 1. 424 a 32.
99 *De An.* III. 8. 431 b 26; III. 2. 425 b 23; II. 12. 424 a 17.
100 Bergson, *Matière et mémoire* 25.

mean the ideal of synthesis in terms of abstraction. In other words, it is the end of the efforts to comprehend reality by means of a minute analysis and an exhaustive synthesis.

Though Aristotle regards sensation as a kind of passivity;[101] he never identifies it with the state of pure inertia. He argues that sensation, though concerned with individuals, does not accept the individuals themselves, but perceives a primitive universal therein.[102] The act of sensation that abstracts the form from a concrete thing, is a kind of preparation for managing a body. When something changes into something, matter remains the same notwithstanding the alteration of forms; it is the constant substratum that underlies various forms being neither created, nor destroyed. Matter is something we have nothing to do with, and may be called the obstacle to the will.[103] Yet the will never opposes matter as such. The opposition to the will must be some form or the composite of matter and form. Matter is *per se* indefinite,[104] it is the uninscribed material on which some form is pressed, by nature or by mind; mind in its turn may receive a form from a concrete being. And since form is a definite and eternal being,[105] all mind can do is to deprive something of its form, and transmit it to another thing.[106] The first stage of this act is cognition, and the second, production. To abstract a form from a thing means to catch the essence of it, or to submit oneself to the negation that the thing exerts over the mind. Form is the principle that makes a thing what it is, but whenever a thing is perceived by sense or intellect, it is in a sense transferred to the mind and gives to it the faculty of ruling the thing.[107]

---

[101] *De An.* II. 11. 423 b 31.

[102] *An. Post.* II. 19. 100 a 15– b 1; 31. 87 b 28–31.

[103] Cf. Baeumker, *Problem der Materie* 280 f.; Dilthey, *Beiträge zur Lösung der Frage vom Ursprung unseres Glaubens an der Realität der Aussenwelt* (Gesamm. Schr. V) 104 ff.

[104] *Phys.* IV. 2. 209 b 9; *Met.* IV. 4. 1007 b 28; VII. 11. 1037 a 27; IX. 7. 1049 b 1; *Met.* XII. 10. 1087 a 16; cf. *Met.* VII. 3. 1029 a 20; *De An.* II. 1. 412 a 7; *Met.* VII. 1. 1042 a 27.

[105] *Met.* VII. 8. 1033 b 17; 9. 1034 b 8, 13; VIII. 3. 1043 b 17; 5. 1044 b 2; XII. 3. 1069 b 35; 1070 a 15; *Phys.* V. 1. 224 b 5, 11; *Met.* XI. 11. 1067 b 9.

[106] Generally speaking, there is neither absolute generation nor passing away: the generation of one thing is the passing away of another, and *vice versa*. Cf. *Gen. et Corr.* I. 3; Zeller, *op. cit.* 391. Production is a kind of qualitative change, and the form which constitutes the essence of art derives itself from the productive exercise which precedes the mastery. Just as a man is begot ten of a man, so a house comes out of a house, i.e., we learn the art of building by building a house. Art and producer are the holders or transporters of this form. Cf. *Eth. Nic.* II. 1. 1103 a 33; 1103 b 11; *Met.* IX. 1. 1048 a 26; VI. 7. 1032 a 32; 1032 b 21.

[107] *De An.* III. 8. 432 a 1–3.

We may act upon a thing only through knowing it, that is to say, through depriving a thing of its actual form and replacing that form with another, which the mind has acquired elsewhere and kept in itself. This is the very essence of art, of which we shall state later.[108]

Sensation is the lowest form of cognition, and the minimum requisite of art, so the soul that lacks even sensation cannot produce anything. Nutrition accepts both matter and form of a thing and is quite passive, whereas sensation is active in so far as it makes abstraction. Sensation, imagination, and intellect are all discriminating and descriptive activities, they all apprehend the form of an object and distinguish it from the other. This is possible through abstracting the form from a concrete thing. Consequently, we have here two kinds of discrimination: the one is the discrimination of a form from the matter, the other, that of a form from another form.

Strictly speaking, even nutrition is not purely passive, in so far as it is a kind of living activity. When a living being takes food, matter and form together, the object changes its form or it loses its original form, viz., food is digested and nourishes the living body or becomes the body itself.[109] But, while the form-giving activity of nutrition is performed without consciousness, the separating act of sensation is accompanied by consciousness. In nutrition, the object is at first received as a whole, and then is separated in two elements, form and matter, but in sensation, the object remains as it is, independently, while the two elements are separated in the mind. In the former, transformation is direct and actual, but in the latter, indirect and potential. In other words, nutrition performs passion and reaction at a stroke, but sensation reserves reaction for the future. This is fundamentally identical with Bergson's[110] explanation of sensation as the scheme of potential acts. But the expression of Bergson is less accurate, while Aristotle, who is more analytical and clear-minded, scrutinizes more minutely the functions of the mind. He distinguishes receptions of abstract forms, their synthesis, preservation, modification and realization, calling them, sensation, *sensus communis*, memory, imagination and desire, respectively. Before taking food, animals perceive what and how the objects are, whether or not they are eatable. The difference

---

108 *Met.* VI. 9. 1034 a 23f.; 7. 1032 a 32 f.; 1032 b 13f.; XII. 3. 1070 a 15, 3 0; 4. 1070 b 33; *Gen. An.* II. 1. 735 a 2; II. 4. 740 b 28; *Part. An.* I. 1. 640 a 31 f.; 639 b 15; cf. *Gen. An.* II. 1. 734 b 21; 734 a 31.

109 *De An.* II. 4. 416 a 34–b 1; 416 b 3, 12, 20; III. 12. 434 b 19.

110 Bergson, *Matière et mémoire* 48.

between nutrition and sensation, therefore, is a difference between direct and indirect reactions, between actuality and potentiality, and a difference of temporal and spacial distance between object and agent. The same relation is found among sensation, imagination and intellect as well as among the objects of these functions. For instance, the thinking faculty is found only in an animal which has sensation and imagination, and one cannot think without an image.[111] This implies on the one hand, that the thinking faculty, being developed from imagination and sensation, is a more excellent instrument of life, and on the other hand, that concept is homogeneous with image and sensation, though more general and formal. Nevertheless, the very fact that human thinking cannot operate without images suggests that even theoretical thinking is reversible to practical reality. Imagination is as much the middle term in the descent from intellect to conduct, as it is in the ascent from sense impression to concept. A sense impression being received from a present object,[112] remains in the soul after the real object has passed away,[113] in the form of experience, and develops in art and science.[114] On account of this intermediate character, imagination is sometimes regarded as a mere residue of sensation or inert sensation,[115] sometimes as not only attendant to conceptual thinking, but also *per se* a kind of thinking.[116] It is also said that of instances of imagination, some come from sensation and some from intellect,[117] the former sort being sensitive imagination, the latter called deliberative, reasoning or intellectual imagination,[118] which is of course confined to human being. Further, these kinds of imagination are all accompanied by pleasure and pain, whereby they arouse desire as the motive of conduct. In short, imagination is on the one hand the process through which sensation proceeds towards contemplation, and on the other hand the medium through which intellect guides conduct.

Though sensation and imagination are different functions, they belong to a single part of the soul.[119] Imagination is the fundamental

---

[111] *De An.* III. 7. 431 a 17; 8. 432 a 8, 13; *De Memor.* 1. 449 b 31; *De Sensu* 6. 445 b 16; cf. *Ch.* II. 1.

[112] *De Memor.* 1. 449 b 14.

[113] *De Memor.* 1. 449 b 24 f.

[114] *An. Post.* II. 19. 100 a 3–14; *Met.* I. 1. 980 a 28 ff.

[115] *De An.* III. 3. 429 a 1; *De Somno.* 1. 456 a 17; *Rhet.* I. 11. 1370 a 28.

[116] *De An.* III. 3. 427 b 27–29; 428 a 2–5; *De An.* I. 1. 403 a 8., III. 3. 437 b 28; 10. 433 a 10; cf. *Motu An.* 6. 700 b 17; 7. 701 a 30, 26; b 25; 11. 703 b 18.

[117] *Motu An.* 8. 702 a 19.

[118] *De An.* III. 10. 433 b 29; 11. 434 a 6.

[119] *De Somniis* 3. 462 a 8–12; 459 a 16; 458 b 30.

function common to memory, dreaming, and fantasy,[120] – these are distinguished from one another through the mode of time – and belongs to the part of the soul which manages the so-called *sensus communis*.[121] This *sensus communis* holds a unique status among other sensations. Special sensations act in terms of special organs such as the eye, the ear, the nose etc., while *sensus communis* has no special organ,[122] and belongs to the heart[123] as the central organ common to all special sensations. It is also called the first sense[124] or the origin of sensations;[125] it compares,[126] discriminates,[127] makes unity of special sensations,[128] and perceives or imagines general forms such as motion, rest, figure, magnitude (extension), number, unity[129] and time.[130]

Special sensation is a momentary phenomenon which takes place between an actual object and a certain sense;[131] it is elementary and independent, it disappears as soon as the object disappears, or as the sense ceases to contact the object, whereas perception is a synthetic unity of elemental impressions; for instance, this substance is at once red, hard, wet, spherical, small, and resting etc. A special sense does not afford us the perception of a concrete object. It is the function of *sensus communis* that makes unification out of these qualities. *Sensus communis* is, [132] therefore, an intermediary between special sensation and conceptual thinking.[133]

[120] *De Memor.* 1. 450 a 22–25; 12; *De Somniis* 1. 459 a 21 f.
[121] *De Memor.* 1. 450 a 10 f.
[122] *De An.* III. 1. 425 a 13.
[123] *De Somno* 2. 456 a 6; *De Juvent.* 1. 467 b 28–30; 469 a 20; 3. 469 a 10–12; *Part. An.* II. 10. 656 a 28; 656 b 25; III. 3. 665 a 12; 4. 666 a 11–20, 33; *Part. An.* II. 1. 647 a 23–31; III. 10. 672 b 16; IV. 5. 678 b 2; *Gen. An.* II. 6. 743 b 26; VI. 2. 781 a 21.
[124] *De Memor.* 1. 450 a 10; *De Somniis* 3. 641 a 6; b 4.
[125] *De Somno.* 2. 455 a 15–20; *De An.* III. 2. 426 b 14; 425 b 12–25; *Eth. Nic.* IX. 7. 1170 a 31; *Eth. Eud.* V. 12. 1244 b 26.
[126] *De Somno* 2. 455 a 15 ff.
[127] *De An.* III. 2. 426 b 8 ff.
[128] *De An.* III. 1. 425 b 1.
[129] *De An.* III. 1. 425 a 14; 425 b 4; *De Somniis* 1. 458 b 5; *De Sensu* 4. 442 b 4; *Eth. Nic.* VI. 9. 1142 a 27.
[130] *De Memor.* 1. 450 a 9–23.
[131] *De Memor.* 1. 449 b 14.
[132] *De An.* III. 1. 425 30–b3.
[133] The concept *sensus communis* originates in Aristotle. Plato, in his early period, regarded sensation as a function of the body, while the act of synthesis or apperception was assumed to be intellect (*Phaed.* 65). In his later period, he considered sensation to be a function of the soul which operates in terms of the body, and the unification of impressions was attributed to the soul (*Theaet.* 186 D; 184 D). But there was not yet the concept of *sensus communis*.

Further, in order to unite impression A with impression B, one must hold A till B happens. This is the function of memory. Hence *sensus communis* must be engaged in the perception of time and space, as the framework of the sense composite. And when it comes to form an image independent of the external world, it is called phantasy.

Compared with Kant's pure intuition of time and space, *sensus communis* is more concrete a faculty and is more akin to the so-called transcendental imagination. For Kant, elemental sensations are opposed to pure intuition as matter to form, whereas in Aristotle, there is no such opposition between sensation and *sensus communis*; they are rather continuous and homogeneous. This relation becomes more evident when we compare Aristotle's *sensus communis* and imagination with Kant's *Einbildungskraft*. According to Aristotle an image persists somehow independently of actual perception, and reappears in dream or memory, but sensation cannot persist. Perception is also conditioned by present objects, though it presupposes the synthetic function of *sensus communis*. In sensation and perception the soul is directly in contact with the object, while in imagination it is more remote from the object. By this wider distance, the soul is afforded greater range of freedom. Now turning to Kant, *Einbildungskraft* was divided into the productive and the reproductive;[134] *sensus communis* resembles

---

[134] Kant, *K.d.r.* V.II. 1. 2. *Cass.* III. 126. Kant defines the imaginative faculty as follows: *"Einbildungskraft ist das Vermögen, einen Gegenstand auch ohne dessen Gegenwart in der Anschauung vorzustellen."* He further explains: *"Da nun dessen Gegenwart in der Anschauung sinnlich ist, so gehört die Einbildungskraft der subjektiven Bedingung wegen, unter der sie allein den Verstandesbegriffen eine korrespondierende Anschauung geben kann, zur Sinnlichkeit; sofern aber doch ihre Synthesis eine Ausübung der Spontaneität ist, welche bestimmend und nicht, wie der Sinn, bloss bestimmbar ist, mithin a priori den Sinn seiner Form nach der Einheit der Apperzeption gemäss bestimmen kann, so ist die Einbildungskraft sofern ein Vermögen, die Sinnlichkeit a priori zu bestimmen, und ihre Synthesis der Anschauungen den Kategorien gemäss muss die transzendentale Synthesis der Einbildungskraft sein, welches eine Wirkung des Verstandes auf die Sinnlichkeit und die erste Anwendung desselben, (zugleich der Grund aller übrigen), auf Gegenstände der uns möglichen Anschauung ist. Sie ist als figürlich von der intellektuellen Synthesis (ohne alle Einbildungskraft, bloss durch den Verstand) unterschieden."* Next comes the distinction in question: *"Sofern die Einbildungskraft nun Spontaneität ist, nenne ich auch bisweilen die produktive Einbildungskraft und unterscheide sie dadurch von der reproduktiven, deren Synthesis lediglich empirischen Gesetzen, nämlich denen der Assoziation, unterworfen ist, und welche daher zur Erklärung der Möglichkeit der Erkenntnis a priori nichts beiträgt und um deswillen nicht in die Transzendentalphilosophie, sondern in die Psychologie gehört."* In the first paragraph, Kant attributed *Einbildungskraft* to *Sinnlichkeit*, and in the second paragraph, he makes it *"eine Wirkung des Verstandes,"* and *"die erste Anwendung desselben (d.h. des Verstandes)".* Similarly, *ibid.* 164: *"Nun ist das, was das*

the former, imagination the latter,[135] though the analogy is not complete. *Sensus communis* is the faculty of perception,[136] while imagination is a remnant of actual perception. Hence it might appear as if
sensus communis is more distant from imagination than it is from
special sensations, still they are not so heterogeneous as two kinds of
Einbildungskräfte are with each other. They are, in the last analysis,
the aspects of one faculty.

Imagination, being the faculty of *sensus communis*, is homogeneous
with sensation, though they are different in species. Sometimes, it is

---

*Mannigfaltige der sinnlichen Anschauung verknüpft, Einbildungskraft, die vom
Verstande der Einheit ihrer intellektuellen Synthesis und von der Sinnlichkeit der
Mannigfaltigkeit der Apprehension nach abhängt.*" If this be literally taken, it
would be a paradox to assign *Einbildungskraft* both to *Verstand* and *Sinnlichkeit*.
This seeming paradox comes from the ambiguity of *Einbildungskraft*. In other
words, it is due to the excessively narrow determination to the effect that what
is *a priori* is intellectual and what is intuitive is sensible. *Einbildungskraft* may
be at the same time *a priori* and intuitive. Kant neglected the study of *reproduktive Einbildungskraft*, but it would contribute a great deal in explaining the mediating function of imagination between sensibility and intellect.

   [135] Nisitani assigns memory to the *reproduktive*, and dreaming to the *produktive Einbildungskraft*. Cf. *Aristoteles Ronko.*

   [136] Kant, *K.d.r.V.* I ed. 120: "*Das erste, was uns gegeben wird, ist Erscheinung,
welche, wenn sie mit Bewusstsein verbunden ist, Wahrnehmung heisst,* ... *Weil
aber jede Erscheinung ein Mannigfaltiges enthält, mithin verschiedene Wahrnehmungen im Gemüte an sich zerstreut und einzeln angetroffen werden, so ist eine
Verbindung derselben nötig, welche sie in den Sinnen selbst nicht haben können. Es
ist also in uns ein tätiges Vermögen der Synthesis dieses Mannigfaltigen, welches
wir Einbildungskraft nennen und deren unmittelbar an den Wahrnehmungen aus-
geübte Handlung ich Apprehension nenne. Die Einbildungskraft soll nämlich das
Mannigfaltige der Anschauung in ein Bild bringen; vorher muss sie also die Eindrücke in ihre Tätigkeit aufnehmen, d.i. apprehendieren.*" Ibid. 123: "*Die Einbildungskraft ist also auch ein Vermögen einer Synthesis a priori, weswegen wir ihr
den Namen der produktiven Einbildungskraft geben; und sofern sie in Ansehung
alles Mannigfaltigen der Erscheinung nichts weiter als die notwendige Einheit in
der Synthesis derselben zu ihrer Absicht hat, kann diese die transzendentale Funk-
tion der Einbildungskraft genannt werden.*" Kant is proud of his discovery of this
synthetic action, *ibid.* 120 n. But as mentioned above, nothing is farther from the
truth than to say that no psychologist has ever thought that imagination is the
necessary ingredient of perception. This is just what Aristotle, the founder of
psychology, quite clearly stated. On the other hand, *sensus communis*, which is a
function of imagination homogeneous with memory, dream and phantasy, was,
according to Aristotle, considered to be the faculty of giving unity to special
sensations, and making a uniform perception out of them. Aristotle never limited
it to a mere reproductive faculty. He believed in a certain sense that "*die Sinne
liefern uns nicht allein Eindrücke, sondern setzen solche auch sogar zusammen und
brächten Bilder der Gegenstände zu Wege.*" But he attributed this faculty not to
an elemental and special sensation, but to the faculty of synthetic perception
called *sensus communis.*

limited to higher animals,[137] but sometimes it is attributed even to lower animals, as when Aristotle mentions that when we cut the body of an insect, sensation, movement, imagination, and desire are all found in each part alike.[138] It is somewhat extravagant to admit imagination and desire to each divided part of an insect; but the divergent attribution of imagination may be explained by introducing the measure of degree, for instance, in one place, Aristotle actually allows imagination even to the lowest animals which have only the sense of touch, but with the qualification that such animals have imagination "in an indefinite manner."[139]

Since *sensus communis* is in a sense necessary for every kind of perception, it must be common to all animals in a certain degree.[140] Imagination too, being the faculty of *sensus communis*, belonging to the same organ, the heart, and being something like a remnant of sensation, must needs be attributed to all animals. But as there are various kinds of imagination, not every imagination is common to all animals. Memory, for instance, being a kind of imagination, is confined to those animals which have time perception;[141] not only to man, but also to higher animals. Similarly with the imagination of number.

The reason why Aristotle admits indefinite imagination to lower animals, is, according to his own statement, that such animals also feel pleasure and pain, and consequently have appetites. Hence we learn in what relation appetite or desire in general stands to sensation and imagination. Sensation and desire are so closely connected, that whenever one exists, the other must also exist and the one cannot exist apart from the other.[142] Neither does he who has no sensation have

---

[137] *De An.* III. 3. 428 a 8–11; cf. Hick's note *ad loc. ibid.* 3. 415 a 10 f.; III 3. 428 a 21 f.

[138] *De An.* II. 2. 413 b 16.

[139] *De An.* III. 11. 434 a 4.

[140] *De Somno* 2. 455 a 22–24.

[141] *De Memor.* 1. 449 b 28–30; 2. 453 a 6—9; *Hist. An.* I. 1. 488 b 24–26. Zeller points out Aristotle's inconsistency in sometimes confining memory to rational being, sometimes also granting it to other animals. (*Ph. d. Gr.* II. 2. 401 n. 4) He quotes as an example of the former, *De An.* III. 10. 433 b 5–7: "Now desires arise which are contrary to one another, and this occurs whenever reason and the appetites are opposed, that is, in those animals which have a perception of time. But we can easily perceive that this sentence means only that the conflict among desires, or the antagonism between reason and appetite, occurs only in an animal who has time-perception, and it does not follow of necessity that the converse is also right. It is possible that an animal who has time-perception has no reason and follows only imagination. It should also be noticed that here are used the words "perception of time."

[142] *De An.* II. 3. 414 b 4–6; III. 7. 431 a 13 f.

desire, nor does he who has no desire have sensation. They are related to each other, not as the sensitive part is to the nutritive, but as nutrition is to reproduction.[143] They are not in a subordinate, but in a coordinate relation, so that the sensitive part and the desiring part may have different functions, conceptually or psychologically, but they can never be the classificatory principles of living beings. The so-called conceptual or psychological difference is that, while sensation is the faculty of receiving forms,[144] desire is that of realizing[145] them, viz., passivity *versus* activity. Therefore, though they are accompanied by each other, the relation is not convertible. On the one hand, sensation presupposes desire as its final cause: the animal has sensation in order to desire something. On the other hand, desire presupposes sensation, as its efficient cause:[146] the animal desires only through sensation.

Thus sensation is given to animals to perceive the forms of objects in order to act through desire. Sensation may be an element of theoretical knowledge, but when it is accompanied by pleasure and pain, it becomes the efficient cause of desire and conduct. A pleasant image naturally calls the desire for it, and a painful image calls avoidance of it.[147] Pleasure and pain are originally combined with sensation. Sensation without emotion, or strictly speaking, sensation with minimum feeling is an exceptional phenomenon peculiar to man.

Now, feeling appears to be experienced sometimes with sensation, sometimes with imagination.[148] But considering more carefully, it is doubtful whether a desire is possible when feeling is directly combined with sensation. In such a case, namely there may be an impulsive and reflexive pursuit or avoidance, but no conscious desire or evasion. A lower animal would at once stretch its tentacle, whenever it touches any food, but would not have a conscious desire. A conscious desire or evasion presupposes an image rather than a sensation, as Aristotle himself puts it: there must be an image in order that a desire may exist.[149] Is it not, then, spurious that there is a desire whenever there is a sensation? Should we not rather infer that mere sensation is not sufficient for the existence of desire?

[143] *De An.* II. 4. 416 a 19.
[144] *De An.* II. 5. 416 b 33 f.; I. 4. 408 b 16; II. 4. 415 b 24; *De Somniis* 2. 459 b 5; *Phys.* V. 2. 244 b 11, 25; *Met.* IV. 5. 1009 b 13; *De An.* II. 12. 424 a 18 f.; III. 8. 431 b 23; 432 a 2.
[145] *Motu An.* 6. 701 a 1; 10. 703 a 5; *De An.* III. 10.
[146] *Motu An.* 8. 701 a 35.
[147] *De An.* III. 7. 431 a 8–12.
[148] *De An.* III. 7. 431 b 6–10.
[149] *De An.* III. 7. 431 a 14–17; III. 10. 433 b 28.

THE FUNCTIONS OF THE SOUL

The feelings of pleasure and pain presuppose some distance between stimulus and reaction, so that lower animals scarcely have any conscious sensation. Thus, sensation consists in the distance between stimulus and reaction, feeling being its concomitant. There is feeling of pleasure or pain, whenever there is sensation, and there is desire, whenever there is the feeling of pleasure or pain. But, evidently imagination is more independent of the object than sensation is, and the more complex the manner of acting becomes, the more the importance of imagination increases.

It may be said that there is desire, whenever there is *independent* sensation. But since sensation is in fact dependent upon actual objects, it must be raised to imagination in order to bring the desire in full activity. Consequently, there is no disjunctive question, whether sensation or imagination is the real cause of desire, for the one develops gradually into the other. An animal reacts against the stimulus from outside, sensation is the passive side of this experience, and imagination the active side, they are mediated by the feelings of pleasure and pain; when united with the feeling, imagination becomes a desire.[150] Thus considered, Aristotle's statement that sensation produces desire, is not incompatible with the statement that imagination is the *sine qua non* of desire. Since sensation and imagination are continuous and cannot be divided distinctly, Aristotle sometimes admits imagination to all animals, sometimes confines it to higher ones. That lower animals have imagination and desire "in an indefinite manner," means that their sole sensation, i.e. touch, involves the minimum potentiality of these faculties. Imagination is at a minimum when sensation immediately causes an act, but at a maximum, when desire is accompanied by practical reasoning.

Strictly speaking, every desire presupposes imagination, even when it appears to follow sensation immediately. Though rational imagination is peculiar to man, there is also sensible imagination which is common to man and animals. Since sensation and imagination are common to all animals, and desire always accompanies them, desire

---

[150] *Motu An.* 8. 702 a 17–19: "The organic parts are suitably prepared by the affections, these again by desire, and desire by imagination. Imagination in its turn depends either upon conception or sense-perception. Here the conditional sequence would be, sensation or thinking – imagination – desire – affect – organ. This appears to be different from our interpretation to the effect that affect is placed between desire and the motion of the organ, instead of between imagination and desire. But in truth, affect prevails throughout the whole series.

[151] *De An.* III. 10. 433 b 29 f.; II. 11. 434 a 5–7.

is also common to all animals, though they are differentiated in accordance with the sort of corresponding sensation or in proportion to its dependence upon sensation. Sensations themselves are differentiated through the relation between object and agent; the more closely they are connected, the lower is the sensation. Lower sensations are indispensable for life, while higher ones are useful for a higher and richer life, though less necessary. Every sensation causes action, itself being caused by present objects, but when an animal desires thereupon, it must needs predict some future states that are to be realized. This predictive function is no longer of a sensation, but of an imagination.[152] When the reaction is contiguous to the stimulus, and the act is so simple that one proceeds to enjoy the object at once, the perception of the present object and the imagination of future conduct are so close together that in some extreme cases we can hardly discriminate them from each other. On the contrary, when the end is realized through a complicated procedure, imagination takes place between sensation and desire.

Imagination may be regarded to be a primitive form of thought in so far as it perceives an abstract form. As Aristotle puts it: "But to the thinking soul images serve as sense impressions and when it affirms or denies good or evil, it avoids or pursues."[153] That "the soul never thinks without an image"[154] also suggests that the reason guides the action. Such a reason is united itself with imagination, and determines desires. It differs from sensitive desire or appetite in that "the reason bids us resist because of the future, while appetite regards only the immediate present."[155] The theoretical reason or theoretical intellect is the state where the object is most remote from the agent, so that imagination is not accompanied by a strong emotion that might evoke a desire. Aristotle seems to be aquainted with this real genealogy of intellect, when he set sensation, experience, art, and practical wisdom in an accumulative order and set theoretical intellect on the summit as an uninterested act afforded by leisure.[156]

The so-called indefinite imagination of lower animals is continuous to and hardly distinguishable from sensation. As to rational imagina-

---

[152] *De Memor.* 1. 449 b 27 f. No detail is given about expectation; but as imagination produces in consciousness the image of an object without this object being present, expectation as well as memory must be regarded as a mode of imagination. Cf. *De An.* III. 3. 428 a 7, 16; 2. 435 b 25.

[153] *De An.* III. 7. 431 a 15.

[154] *De An.* III. 7. 431 a 17; 8. 432 a 9; *De Memor.* 1. 449 b 31.

[155] *De An.* III. 10. 433 b 7.

[156] *Met.* I. 1, 2; cf. *Eth. Nic.* X. 7.

tion on the other hand, Aristotle states as follows:[157] "The sensitive imagination, then as we have said, is found in the other animals also but the deliberative one only in the rational animals. For to decide whether to do this or that is already the task of reasoning. And one must measure through a single standard, for one pursues the greater good. Hence one can form a single image out of many images."[158] From what has been said, it is evident that a special image is chosen out of many possible images through deliberation,[159] this is just what

[157] *De An.* III 10. 433 a 10. Calculation or reasoning is opposed to imagination. In such a context, imagination should be restricted to sensible imagination. But the concept "rational imagination" does not demolish the distinction between calculation and imagination. Rational imagination means the imagination which results from reasoning rather than the imagination that reasons.

[158] *De An.* III. 11. 434 a 5–10.

[159] The ἕν in the sentence ὥστε δύναται ἕν ἐκ πλειόνων φαντασμάτων ποιεῖν, is usually taken as meaning an image. But K. Nisitani making it identical with the πρῶτα νοήτα in *De An.* III. 8. 432 a 12 and the πρῶτον καθόλου in *An. Post.* II. 19. 100 a 16, explains it to be the first step in which general concept is formed from accidental images (*Aristoteles Ronko*). But in truth, Aristotle's statement is concerned with practical deliberation and the adjudication of desires, not with the subsumption of images into a general concept. Even if the ἕν might be taken as an image, it is by no means general concept that subsumes special images, but a special image resulted from calculation. Nisitani admits that this statement is concerned with the relation of imagination and desire. He insists nevertheless upon his former interpretation, saying that the same thing could be applied to the theoretical as well as to the practical. In proof thereof he quotes *De An.* III. 7. 431 b 10–12: καὶ τὸ ἄνευ δὲ πράξεως, τὸ ἀληθὲς καὶ τὸ ψεῦδος, ἐν τῷ αὐτῷ γένει ἐστὶ τῷ ἀγαθῷ καὶ κακῷ· ἀλλὰ τῷ γε ἁπλῶς διαφέρει καὶ τινί. Hence he conclude that the truth, being a kind of good, is an object of desire. But the text in question proves only that reason employs images as its medium in practice as well as in cognition; we cannot infer from this that what is derived from such an image must be a general concept. Much less does it imply, as Nisitani maintains, that "the truth, being a kind of the good, becomes the object of desire." The object of desire is the good, not the truth. What the last quotation really means is that just as true and false are the measures of theoretical thinking, so good and bad are the measures of practical thinking, the difference between the two pairs of concepts lies in that the one is applied generally, while the other is peculiar to the individual, just as sensation desires what is more pleasant, so practical intellect desires what appears to be the best. Deliberating imagination must be either imagination founded upon deliberation or imagination that deliberates something. Whereas deliberation (βούλευσις) is concerned in the first place with the affairs that are in our own power and can be otherwise, and in the second place with the means rather than the end, and constitutes προαίρεσις or will. Cf. *Eth. Nic.* III. 5. 1112 a 30; 1112 b 11; VI. 2. 1139 a 13; *Mag. Mor.* I. 35. 1196 b 29; *Rhet.* I. 2. 1357 a 4; 6. 1362 a 18; II. 5. 1383 a 7. So προαίρεσις is said to be βουλευτικὴ ὄρεξις Cf. *Eth. Nic.* III. 5. 1113 a 11; VI. 2. 1139 a 23; *Eth. Eud.* II. 10. 1226 b 17; *Mag. Mor.* I. 17. 1189 a 31. We shall analyse the structure of βούλευσις more fully later on. To sum up, it is a practical reasoning which searches

is called deliberative image. Aristotle continues stating: "And the
reason why the lower animals are thought not to have opinion is that
they do not possess that form of imagination which comes from syllogism, while the latter (i.e., deliberative imagination) implies the former
(i.e., opinion). Hence desire contains no deliberative faculty."[160] The
sentence is very suggestive, it implies in the first place, that deliberation takes the form of syllogism; in the second, that opinion presupposes deliberation or practical syllogism. Let these points be considered later. What is most remarkable is that, in the third place, the
imagination peculiar to man is deliberative, i.e., the imagination inferred from (practical) syllogism, or a special image chosen out of
many possible images.

As desire presupposes imagination, and imagination is divided into
the rational and the irrational, so there must be rational desire as well
as irrational desire. Appetite and passion are irrational desires, wish, a
rational desire which pursues the good.[161] Aristotle even substitutes
for "wish" the term λογισμός which may be rendered as "calculation"
or "reasoning." But there is another concept of προαίρεσις or will,
which is paraphrased by the words βουλευτικὴ ὄρεξις, deliberative
desire" or "desire determined through deliberation." These two concepts, viz., βούλησις and προαίρεσις must be carefully distinguished from
each other; will is constituted of desire and reason,[162] while wish is

for a concrete means to an end, and in its completion forms a syllogism. Now,
συλλογισμός is opposed to ἐπαγωγή; the former proceeds from the general to the
particular, the latter from the particular to the general. Cf. *Eth. Nic.* VI. 3.
1139 b 29; *An. Pr.* I. 24. 43 a 3; *An. Post.* I. 1. 71 a 5; *Top.* I. 12. VIII. 2. 157
a 18. The example of practical reasoning which follows the above quotation is
also such a reductive inference. cf. *De An.* III. 11. 434 a 15 ff.

Thus, we cannot agree with Nisitani, who maintains that deliberative imagination (an imagination formed from deliberation), which, when it acts in practice, makes a universal image of a greater and better thing out of other apparent
goods, has an analogous part when it acts in pure contemplation. We admit
without hesitation that the contemplation is accompanied by images, and there
are different kinds of image. But the text in question is irrelevant to such a thing.
The expression φαντασία corresponds to βουλευτικὴ ὄρεξις which is the paraphrase
of προαίρεσις. But βουλευτικὴ ὄρεξις implies an ὄρεξις which follows from deliberation rather than an ὄρεξις which deliberates. Analogically, the so-called
φαντασία βουλευτική should mean the φαντασία which follows from βούλησις. St.
Thomas takes the ἕν as the third image which forms the standard of estimation.
But in truth, this is rather an image chosen in accordance with a standard.

[160] *De An.* III. 11. 434 a 10.
[161] *Rhet.* I. 10. 1368 b 36–1369 a 7.
[162] *Eth. Nic.* III. 5. 1113 a 9–12; VI. 2. 1139 a 23; *Eth. Eud.* II. 10. 1226 b
17; (*Mag. Mor.* I. 17. 1189 a 3); *Eth. Nic.* VI. 2. 1139 b f 4; 1139 a 31–33. We
translate προαίρεσις as will instead of choice, because the προ in προαίρεσις implies

merely a kind of desire.[163] In the *Ethica Nicomachea*, they are distinguished in such a way that while wish is related to the end, will is to
the means, and that the former is related also to impossibles, while the
latter only to possibles.[164] It follows therefore, that wish, unlike will,
which is already determined by deliberation, is a direct indefinite desire
that might be further determined by deliberation.

There are some controversies about the rationality of wish. According to J. Walter, wish must be irrational, since it is a kind of desire.
Aristotle's real meaning in saying[165] wish belongs to the reasonable
soul, is, he thinks, that it depends upon the possessor of reason, rather
than that it is itself a mode of reason or that its content is conceptual.[166] Against this interpretation of Walter's, Teichmüller maintains
that wish must be rational, because the reason which corresponds to
wish is rational (λογιστικόν).[167] The solution of these opposite interpretations may be found in Aristotle's own statements. Criticizing the
duopartite theory that divides the soul into the rational and the irrational, and the tripartite theory that divides it into the cognitive, the
passionate, and the appetitive, Aristotle states: "Then besides these
there is the desiring, which would seem to be different both in concept
and in capacity from all the others. And surely it is absurd to split this
up. For wish takes place in the rational part, while appetite and passion
occur in the irrational part. And, if the soul is three, desire would take
place in each of these parts."[168] This is a criticism made from the
standpoint of one who divides the soul into many parts according to
its functions. But, as we have seen above, this multipartite theory was
synthesized with the duopartite theory, and the desiring part was reduced to the irrational part. This would be impossible as far as the
purely functional division is maintained. An irrational part which
subsumes the desiring part is a metaphysical and ethical concept
rather than a psychological one. Since wish is a kind of desire, there is
no doubt that it should belong to the desiring part. But inasmuch as

not the estimating preference, but temporal antecedence, as is evident from
Eth. Nic. III. 5. 1113 a 11. *Eth.* III. 4. 1112 a 15; cf. Joachim's note *ad loc.*

[163] *De An.* III. 10. 433 a 23; *Motu An.* 6. 700 b 22.

[164] *Eth. Nic.* III. 4. 1111b 19–30; 5. 1112 b 11; 1113 a 2; (*Mag. Mor.* I. 17. 1189 a 7); *Eth. Eud.* II. 10. 1226 b 9.

[165] *Top.* IV. 5. 126 a 12; *De An.* III. 9. 432 b 5.

[166] Walter, *Die Lehre von der praktischen Vernunft in der griechischen Philosophie* 204 f.

[167] Teichmüller, *Neue Studien zur Geschichte der Begriffe* III: *Die praktische
Vernunft bei Aristoteles* 93 n. 2.

[168] *De An.* III. 9. 432 b 2–5.

the desiring part sometimes cooperates with the rational part, which, however, is the case with the wish *qua* rational desire, wish may rightly be called rational, though *per accidens*. Walter maintains that intellect does not determine the desire itself, but only brings the object to the desire,[169] in such a way that the image or representation that accompanies the intellectual conception begets the desire in terms of pleasure and pain. But once it is admitted that intellect begets a desire in terms of an image, how is it possible to suspect the rationality of this desire? It is true that desire in general is sometimes opposed to will and that the latter is defined as deliberate desire. Walter seems to stick to this point and confined the rationality in practice to this kind of deliberation. But, in our opinion, this does not rule out the possibility that there is another kind of rationality pertaining to wish.

It is evident from the paraphrase "deliberate desire," that will is composed of deliberation and desire. What sort of desire is this, then? Desire was divided into wish, passion and appetite. May all of these three equally constitute will? If practical intellect in general makes will out of any desire, even appetite may become will when it is accompanied by deliberation.[170] And this is really the case, for in the character of a temperate man, appetite obeys reason and desires in accordance with it. But on the other hand, it is said that courage consists in obeying reason,[171] instead of being driven by passion. And this seems to make passion run counter to will as deliberate desire, whereas passion and appetite were defined as irrational desires from the outset.[172] Thence Walter argues that wish must be more intimate to will than the other desires, but without rejecting appetite and passion completely, he admits them to constitute will as far as they cooperate with reason.[173]

This, however, is a very ambiguous and unsatisfactory solution. With all the arguments of Walter's it must be admitted that wish is rational in some sense. What sort of rationality is it then? Is it that wish is in harmony with deliberation?[174] But as far as deliberation presupposes an end and relates only to the means to realize that end, it will lead to a vicious circle. Teichmüller's theory seems to be more consistent. He refuses rationality to desire itself and maintains that

[169] Walter, *op. cit.* 198 f.
[170] *Eth. Nic.* III. 15. 1119 b 11 ff.
[171] *Eth. Nic.* III. 11. 1116 b 23–1117 a 7; cf. *ibid.* 10. 1115 b 11 ff.; 17 ff.
[172] *Rhet.* I. 10. 1369 a 4.
[173] Walter, *op. cit.* 214.
[174] Walter, *op. cit.* 254, 496; *Eth. Nic.* VI. 2. 1139 a 26 ff.

every desire may become a will, if it be accompanied by deliberation as to means.[175] In fact, it is stated by Aristotle that a wicked man follows an appetite with his own will, e.g., an indulgent man pursues an excessive pleasure with will and deliberation, making it his maxim to seek bodily pleasure. Does this imply that deliberation is thinking as to means to realize any casual desire, without having any special intimacy with wish? Surely this is not the case, because, as we have seen above, a wish is said to be a desire based upon *deliberative* or *rational* image. Still, if this deliberation is also related to the means, wish cannot be distinguished from will after all. The only alternative to make the distinction possible is to differentiate "deliberation" and "reasoning." It may be that the deliberation, the reasoning, and the practical syllogism that constitute the wish are different from those that constitute the will, the former being the estimation of the end itself, while the latter the search for the means to realize an end. In fact, with regard to the image or the reason which forms the wish, Aristotle always explains that it teaches us the good and bad of the end,[176] while with regard to the deliberation which forms the will, he makes it the search for the means.[177]

Thus two meanings were distinguished for deliberation or reasoning: on the one hand, it is the estimation of the end; on the other, the search for the means. In the former sense, wish presupposes deliberation, but in the latter sense, deliberation presupposes wish, and through the combination with this wish, it results in the will, which is called a deliberate desire. Will and wish are rational in different senses. Since the deliberation presupposed by the wish is merely the estimation of the end, it may also be related to an impossible thing. For instance, the immortality of an individual life being impossible, it cannot become an object of will when one considers the means of its realization, though it may be the object of wish none the less.

---

[175] Teichmüller, *op. cit.* 94. By the way, Joachim is not right in excluding βούλησις from the ὄρεξις that forms προαίρεσις (cf. p. 104).

[176] *De An.* III. 7. 431 a 14; 432 b 6. In *Eth. Nic.* III. 7. 1114 a 31, it is stated that images lead us to a good or to a bad end, while we are ourselves the cause of these images, and responsible for what kind of image we have. This implies that the image which precedes a desire is the estimation of an end. Cf. *ibid.* III. 6. 1113 a 23 f; 1113 a 29–33; VIII. 2. 1155 b 23–27.

[177] *Eth. Nic.* III. 5. 112 b 11–24; *Rhet.* I. 6. 1362 a 18–20.

3. Desire and Pleasure

Desire follows sensation or imagination, and is divided into the rational and the irrational, in accordance with the division of images into those direct sensitive and those indirect intelligible. The rationality of desire *per se* is not due to the cognition of the means, but to the estimation of the end. Such a rational desire is called βούλησις or wish, another kind of desire, θυμός or passion, is in a sense rational, in another, irrational. It is compared to a hasty servant who runs off before hearing out the matter and mistakes the order, or to a dog, that barks at a familiar visitor as soon as it hears a knock. It listens to an argument to some extent, but mishears it.[178] The place it occupies in desire is analogous to the place that desire in general occupies in the whole soul. The most irrational desire of all desires is appetite: yet even this has some connection with reason in so far as it obeys the orders of reason.[179]

These three kinds of desire all tend to action through being prompted by sensation or imagination, so that they are passive as compared with the latter. In the relation of the animal to its environment, the passive side is sensation and imagination,[180] the active side, desire. The animal is acted upon by the environment, feels sensation and imagination accompanied by emotion and desire to do something, thus it is led to an action, which is a kind of locomotion. Thus, desire is the principle of animal locomotion, therefore, what cannot change its place has no desire.[181] The plant takes nourishment, but never desires; and the animal that does not move has only a germ of desire. Desire is the potentiality of locomotion, while sensation or imagination is the potentiality of desire. Thence it may appear that sensation or imagination is related to desire as form to matter. But strictly speaking, it is the faculty of desire rather than an actual desire that is really a material principle. For desire already contains in itself a sensible or an imaginative form.

Sensation, imagination, desire and act form a group in the order from potentiality to actuality. This whole group forms the irrational part in the secondary sense, and is contiguous on its lower limit with the irrational part in the primary sense, viz., the part which manages nutrition and reproduction; on its upper limit, it is contiguous with

[178] *Eth. Nic.* VIII. 7. 1149 a 24; 1149 b 1, 6.
[179] *Eth. Nic.* III. 15. 1119 b 11–17.
[180] *Motu An.* 7. 701 a 29–b 1.
[181] *De An.* III. 10. 433 b 27 f.; 11. 433 b 31–434 a 5; *De An.* III. 9. 432 b 15–17.

the rational part in the secondary sense, the part which orders and leads the others like a father. So, generally speaking, this part presupposes on the one hand, the nutritive part as its matter or substratum, and on the other hand, requires the rational part as its form or substance in the sense of essence. Thus, desire comes into being to subserve the preservation of life, and its ideal is realized in ethical virtues.

As is well known, not only to Aristotle but also to the Greeks in general, virtue means the excellence of any function whatever.[182] There are virtues of axe and knife as well as virtues of dogs, horses and men.[183] Since the soul is the essence of man, the virtue of man in the superior sense, is the excellence of the soul. Now, in the human soul there are vegetative functions, such as nutrition, growth, and reproduction; animalistic functions, such as sensation, imagination, desire and movement; and besides them there are also pure human or superbiological functions of thinking. But the human soul was divided from the metaphysical and ethical point of view into double irrational and double rational parts. Consequently, the virtues of man should be divided into two kinds of irrational and two kinds of rational virtue, or speaking more minutely, each function of the soul should have its corresponding virtue. But as we have stated in reference to Jaeger's theory, the virtues in Aristotle's ethics do not exactly correspond to psychological functions, and this is neither due to the fact that his ethics has failed to make use of the results of his psychology, nor is it due to the early formation of his ethical books, but chiefly due to the difference of viewpoints. Ethics asks for virtues mainly for the sake of practice, being itself the very development of practical intellect. Therefore, what is irrelevant to human welfare is dismissed altogether from ethical investigation. This is indeed the reason why, e.g., the virtues of the irrational part in the primary sense are not discussed at all, and only those of the irrational part in the secondary sense are admitted as human virtues.[184] Not that the irrational part in the primary sense has no virtue, but that the essence of the human soul was found in rationality. The irrational virtues belong to man only in so far as he is an animal, and not in so far as he is a rational being. The distinctively human virtues are restricted to the functions that partake somehow of reason, even if they should fundamentally belong to the irrational

---

[182] *Eth. Nic.* II. 5. 1106 a 15–19.
[183] *Eth. Nic.* I. 13. 1102 a 16; *Pol.* I. 2. 1253 a 36.
[184] *Eth. Nic.* I. 13. 1102 b 11 f.

part.[185] The irrational functions dominated by reason are esteemed as particularly human, because just those actions constitute the realm of human freedom, while excellence of nutritive function is nothing but natural endowment, with which we have ethically nothing to do. We can manage only those activities of life that are mediated by desire. Consequently, the virtues lower than those of the irrational part in the secondary sense are not worthy of investigation for ethics which aims at practical effects. The virtue of the desiring part is that state of desire in which it tends to realize various effects through being managed by reason. This is the practical reason, the virtue of which is called φρόνησις or practical wisdom. Practical wisdom accompanies of necessity ethical virtues, or we might rather say, that it is the formal principle of ethical virtues.[186]

The essence of ethical virtue is the control of desire or the obedience of the irrational soul to practical intellect. Any kind of desire may be the substratum of such virtues, and there is no discrepancy between Aristotle's psychology and his ethics in this respect. In the psychology the subject of inquiry is restricted to the natural functions of the human soul, while in the ethics their realization in society was considered. What seems to be a discrepancy between these works is in truth merely an appearance due to the complexity of the latter subject.

The ends of desires extend to a wide realm covering all kinds of value, material, vital and spiritual. The nutritive and sexual appetites are founded upon touch and taste, and the virtue of these desires is temperance, the vice, self-indulgence; continence and incontinence are similar characters of lower grade.[187] The vegetative soul as such falls short of having human virtue, but it may develop in ethical virtue as far as it is regulated by intellect. Temperance consists in the moderation of appetite both nutritive and sexual, self-indulgence is its contrary opposition, i.e., excessive appetite or its enjoyment. There may be a character which is lacking in appetite, but it has no ethical significance. Continence and incontinence resemble the above two characters, only in this case excessive desires are present and struggle with reason. But on this point, there would be no need of entering into details. In these lowest desires, what is necessary is to maintain moder-

---

[185] διανοητική ἀρετή being the virtue of the rational part in the proper sense, ἠθική ἀρετή that of the rational part in the secondary sense. cf. 1.

[186] *Eth. Nic.* VI. 13, 1144 b 17-32; cf, Trendelenburg, op. cit. II. 384 ff.

[187] *Eth. Nic.* III. 13. 1118 a 23-26; VII. 6. 1147 b 26-31; 1148 a 4-10; cf. Stewart's note *ad loc.*; *Eth. Nic.* VII. 1. 1145 a 35-b2; 1145 a 16-18; VII. 6. 1148 a 4 ff.; III. 13. 1117 b 23 f.

ation in order to conserve and promote the activity of life. Just as in the case of touch, an excessive stimulus destroys the organ and endangers life,[188] while in higher sensations, there is but little danger of such a kind, so that the moderation of these lower desires is the most fundamental of all ethical virtues, and the *sine qua non* of a good life. For the same reason, Plato regarded temperance to be the fundamental virtue of all citizens, while courage and practical wisdom to be appropriate to higher classes.[189] Among special sensations, smell, hearing and sight are more refined and originally arose for the sake of preservation and reproduction, but with the expansion of their environment they developed to serve pure cognition. The desires which are accompanied by these sensations also require moderation, but they are not indispensable to the preservation of life. Temperance and self-indulgence, as well as continence and incontinence, are found only conditionally in such regions. For instance, those who love the smell of an apple, of roast meat or of cosmetic matter, love in fact the lower pleasures which are associated with these sensations,[190] rather than the enjoyment of these smells themselves. Similarly with hearing and sight. Of these higher sensations, temperance and other kindred characters are found only accidentally.[191]

Desires accompanied by higher sensations aim at higher values beyond the immediate needs of nutrition and reproduction. Even taste, when it wants not much wine or food, but delights in deliciousness, is not of necessity to be blamed as self-indulgence or incontinence.[192] As for smell, man is alone able to enjoy it for its own sake, unlike animals, which enjoy it only for the sake of expected food.[193] The delight in music or play may be in a sense the enjoyment of hearing and sight,[194] but just as these higher sensations are the beginning of intellectual cognition, their objects involve more or less a spiritual meaning, and tend towards some spiritual values.

Generally speaking, desire is the efficient cause of act, and is divided into appetite, passion and wish.[195] The division is no doubt derived

---

[188] *De An.* III. 13. 435 b 15–19.
[189] *Rep.* 432 A.
[190] *Eth. Nic.* X. 13. 1118 a 1–13.
[191] *Eth. Nic.* VII. 6. 1148 b 2–9.
[192] *Eth. Nic.* III. 13. 1118 a 26–32.
[193] *Eth. Nic.* III. 13. 1118 a 16.
[194] *Eth. Nic.* III. 13. 1118 a 6.
[195] *De An.* II. 3. 414 b 2; III. 10. 433 a 23. *Motu An.* 6. 700 b 19, 22; 7. 701 b 1; *Eth. Eud.* II. 7. 1223 a 26; (*Mag. Mor.* I. 12. 1187 b 37)

from Plato's tripartite theory of the soul. Appetite in the strict sense is the sensitive desire which longs for bodily pleasure, especially for the natural and necessary pleasures of eating, drinking and sexual activity.[196] But in its wider sense, it extends to the region of higher values such as property or honour.[197] Aristotle's concept of ἐπιθυμία κατὰ λόγον, i.e. "appetite with reason," probably means such a desire.[198] Both property and honour are more or less indirect values: they have utility rather than value itself,[199] and may lead to vulgar enjoyment no less than spiritual satisfaction. But more properly speaking, these higher values should be regarded as the objects of passion or wish rather than of appetite.[200]

The measure of moderation is applicable also to these desires of higher values. Moderation concerning the desire for property is liberality and magnificence, the corresponding vice of excess being prodigality and vulgarity, the vice of deficiency meanness and niggardliness respectively.[201] The virtue relevant to honour is pride, and the corresponding vices are vanity and humility,[202] to which are analogous ambition and unambitiousness.[203] The emotion against libel is anger. This is a negative passion, and with regard to which there are the virtues of good temper, the vices of irascibility and excessive meek-

[196] ἐπιθυμία is defined as τοῦ ἡδέος ὄρεξις. Top. VI. 3. 140 b 27; De An. II. 3. II. 3. 414 b 5; III. 10. 433 a 25; Part. An. II. 17. 661 a 8; Rhet. II. 11. 1370 a 17; Eth. Nic. III. 3. 1111 a 32; 4. 1111 b 16; VII. 10. 1151 b 11; Eth. Eud. II. 7. 1223 a 34; VII. 2. 1235 b 22. The concept τὸ ἡδύ has also two meanings. In the narrow and more usual sense, it is a lower sensible pleasure. A desire in an animal or a child is always called ἐπιθυμία. cf. Eth. Nic. III 13. 1118 b 8; 15. 1119 b 5; Pol. VII. 15. 1334 b 23; III. 16. 1287 a 31; De An. III. 10. 433 b 6; 433 a 3. It is essentially an irrational desire. cf. Rhet. II. 19. 1393 a 2; 10. 1369 a 4.

[197] Eth. Nic. VII. 6. 1148 a 22, 27.

[198] Rhet. I. 11. 1370 a 17–27.

[199] Eth. Nic. I. 3. 1095 b 26–28; 1096 a 6 f. Honour is the highest of external goods; it is the merit for virtues; Eth. Nic. IV. 7. 1123 b 35; 20; V. 10. 1134 b 7; VIII. 16. 1163 b 4. The distribution of it is the chief problem of politics: Pol. II. 8. 1268 a 21; III. 5. 1278 a 20; IV. 4. 1290 b 12; 13. 1297 b 7; V. 6. 1305 b 4; 8. 1303 b 13. Wealth is obviously of such a nature: Eth. Nic. V. 5. 1130 b 30–32.

[200] Though θυμός is considered to be a kind of ὄρεξις it has no verbal form. We can easily perceive from Aristotle's discussion of the dispositions μεγαλοψυχία and φιλοτιμία that honour is the object of θυμός, but owing to the lack of verbal form of this word, one ought to say ὀρεγεῖν ἐφίεσθαι or φιλεῖν τὴν τιμίαν. Such a disposition is also said to "wish" (βούλεσθαι) for honour (Eth. Nic. VIII. 9. 1159 a 12). The expression θυμός mainly takes the negative form of anger. So it is sometimes omitted from the enumeration of the kinds of desire.

[201] Eth. Nic. II. 7. 1107 b16; IV. 1–6.

[202] Eth. Nic. II 7. 1107 b 21; IV. 7–9.

[203] Eth. Nic. II. 7. 1107 b 25; IV. 10.

ness.[204] Among other ethical virtues, the most predominant are courage and justice. They are also founded upon vital and material values. Courage is not concerned directly with vegetative functions such as nutrition or reproduction, but is grounded more profoundly upon the desire for existence. Of course courage is something more than a vital force; it is the virtue of not fearing death especially in war for the sake of one's own state.[205] But the service for the state does not of necessity require the death in war. What is more essential to courage is the subjugation of the fear of death; the death in war cannot be the matter of virtue, unless life itself is something good and desirable.[206] Yet, through death in war, we get a higher life, in other words, the animalistic life is thereby elevated to human life. Courage is the virtue how to use the life. Just as moderate enjoyment of appetites, being the positive expression of vegetative life, forms the virtue of temperance, so the moderation of fear, the negative expression of the same vegetative life, forms the virtue of courage.

As for justice, though it is a virtue of crucial importance, its basis is nothing but the pursuit of external good such as property or honour.[207] The distribution of property among nations or in a state should be proportionate to the merits of person, e.g., virtue or birth: the appropriate distribution is justice. Generosity and magnificence are similar virtues concerning the wealth, only in a more private reference [208] of expenditure. Let this be sufficient for the explanation how ethical virtues are related to desires.

Ethical virtues are the right states of desires which pursue the value of life, property, honour etc. and are dominated by practical intellect. Honour and property are themselves something good[209], and nutrition and reproduction are necessary for human existence.[210] The asceticism is far from the intention of Aristotle, who esteems reproduction as a

[204] *Eth. Nic.* II. 7. 1108 a 4; IV.11.
[205] *Eth. Nic.* III. 9. 1115 a 35. Häcker, in *Das Eintheilungs- und Anordnungsprincip der moralischen Tugendlehre in der nicomachischen Ethik*, tried to divide the Aristotelian virtues according to the functions of life. He ranked courage in the first class with temperance, the former being the virtue of θυμός the, latter that of ἐπιθυμία. Zeller was opposed to this theory (*Ph. d. Gr.* II. 2. 634 n. 1), and emphasized the social character of this virtue.
[206] Cf. N. Hartmann, *Ethik II.* 3.
[207] *Eth. Nic.* VI. 5. 1130 b 26; 1130 b 3.
[208] *Eth. Nic.* V. 4. 1130 b 1.
[209] *Eth. Nic.* VII. 6. 1146 b 23–29; 1148 a 22–28.
[210] *Eth. Nic.* III. 14. 1119 a 5; VII. 6. 1148 b 15.

holy act through which all living creatures partake in eternity.[211] But desires may be either good or bad, in accordance with their modes of appearance. When desires are regulated by reason, they are moderate and may constitute ethical virtue.[212] Temperance, for instance, is the moderation of desires in nutritive and sexual affairs, good temper, in that of passion and anger. It may appear therefore, that moderation or right reason makes the desire itself rational, and since rational desire is wish, while irrational desire is passion and appetite, it may follow that a good man has only wish and is free from passion and appetite of any kind. This is true to some extent. Instinctive expression of bare appetite and passion is brutal and falls short of virtuous conduct, ethical virtue must be a habit reared by reason.[213] In virtuous character, desire itself must be in a sense rational, whereas rational desire is either wish or will. Now rationality of will is concerned exclusively with the means to an end, while the estimation of an end is allowed only to wish. It follows therefore that the ultimate principle of ethical virtue must be the wish. This does not mean, however, that appetite and passion should be rejected altogether; on the contrary, they must be acknowledged by wish and so to say, converted to it. The matter of ethical virtue is desire in general, only that it must be regulated by and assimilated to wish.[214] On the other hand, wish is not always good, we do not wish something unless we take it to be good,[215] but not all that seems to be good is really good. It is possible to wish something bad or disgraceful, mistaking it for a good thing, e.g., in the case of a self-indulgent person: his act is not only opposed to right reason, but also led by a wrong opinion,[216] and being thus founded upon such a vicious principle, his character itself becomes positively vicious. Such a bad desire convinced of its rightness would be a wish, rather than an appetite or a passion. It may presuppose an appetite, but not that a strong appetite supersedes the reason, but that one wishes an excessive pleasure and pursues it with convinced calculation, even though the appe-

---

[211] *De An.* II. 4. 415 a 28–b7; *Eth. Nic.* VII. 14. 1153 b 32; Plato, *Symp.* 206 E; 2 07 A; *Legg.* IV. 721 B, C; Teichmüller, *Stud. z. Gesch. d. Begr.* 351.

[212] *Eth. Nic.* II. 5. 1106 a 26–32; 1106 b 18–28; 6. 1106 b 36–1107 a 2; II. 9. 1109 a 20; III. 8. 1114 b 27; IV. 13. 1127 a 16; *Eth. Eud.* II. 3. 1220 b 35; 5. 1222 a 11, 13; *Pol.* IV. 11. 1295 a 37; *Eth. Nic.* II. 2. 1104 a 26; VI. 13. 1144 b 26 f.

[213] *Eth. Nic.* II. 1. 1103 a 23–26.

[214] *Eth. Nic.* III. 15. I 119 b 11 ff; 6. 1113 b 1; 14. 1119 a 11.

[215] *Eth. Nic.* VI. 11. 1136 b 7 f.; *Eth. Eud.* II. 7. 1223 b 6 f.; *Eth. Nic.* III. 6.

[216] *Eth. Nic.* VII. 4. 1146 b 22 22 f.; VII. 9. 1151 a 11–14; VII. 8. 1150 a 19; 3. 1146 a 31.

tite may be comparatively weak.[217] Ethical virtue is not the character determined by any random wish. Right reason does not always agree with wish, for not all that one believes to be good, is really so. In his early works, such as *Metaphysica* XII or the *Ethica Eudemia*, Aristotle referred appetite and passion to the apparent good, and wish to the absolute good,[218] but in the *Ethica Nicomachea*, he divided wish itself into what is ideal and what is actual, and assumed that every one wishes what appears good to his image or opinion.[219]

Just as every desire expects pleasure and pain in the future, so the satisfaction or the lack of satisfaction of desire is followed by pleasure or pain. Desire itself being in a state of need, is accompanied by pain.[220] It is pleasant[221] only accidentally in virtue of its expected enjoyment.

[217] *Eth. Nic.* VIII. 6. 1148 a 17–22.

[218] *Met.* XII. 7. 1072 a 27 f.; *Eth. Eud.* VII. 2. 1235 b 21–23.

[219] In *Eth. Nic.* III. 6. 1113 a 15–b 2, Aristotle distinguishes an absolute good and an object of wish, the one as real good, the other as apparent good. In *Eth. Eud.* VII. 2. 1235 b 26–29, imagination and opinion are distinguished from each other, the one gives the apparent good, the other the real good. But this thought was abandoned later. Both imagination and opinion are subjective and finite. In *Eth. Nic.* VIII, 2, 1155 b 21–26, we find a similar distinction as to the object of love. The object of desire is not the same as the object of love, for desire is not the same as love, but the attempt to divide the object of love into what is absolutely lovable and what is really loved as relatively good is analogous to the case of desire, cf. *Top.* VI. 8. 147 a 1 ff. Here there is no detailed treatment of pleasure, but it seems to be implied that the same kind of division is applicable to pleasure as well. As to how these two meanings of good and the pleasant are related to each other, cf. *Eth. Eud.* VII. 2. 1236 a 9, where it is stated that the absolute good is identified with the absolutely pleasant, and the relative good with the relatively pleasant. It seems to be discordant to the distinction between the good and the apparent good, that at the end of the statement in *Eth. Nic.* above referred to, the author denies the difference of the lovable and the apparently lovable. But there is no real inconsistency between the two statements. The good is objective, and may subsist whether a man admits it or not, even if it may appear manifold. The object of love, on the contrary, has no significance apart from affection. Desire and pleasure being essentially subjective feelings, we cannot distinguish τὸ βουλητόν from τὸ φαινομένον βουλητόν or τὸ ἡδύ from τὸ φαινομένον ἡδύ as we may distinguish τὸ ἀγαθόν and τὸ φαινομένον ἀγαθόν. Therefore, the division of the object of desire in *Mag. Mor.* II. 11. 1208 b 37 seems to be unsuitable to Aristotle's thought. About the absolute and the relative good, cf. *Eth. Nic.* VII. 13. 1152 b 26.

Next to be noticed is the statement that the pleasant is mistaken to be good. This statement proves our interpretation to the effect that βούλησις being itself a rational desire, may be sometimes concerned with the object of sensible pleasure. In other words, wish may be indirectly related to lower appetites, as far as we desire something not as pleasant, but as good. The above quotation shows that βούλησις does not always imply a true estimation.

[220] *Eth. Nic.* III. 14. 1119 a 4; VII. 13. 1153 a 31 f. VIII. 15. 1154 a 25–29.

[221] *Eth. Nic.* IX. 1. 1164 a 13 ff.; X. 7. 1177 a 25. In the former, the expecta-

The types of pleasure and pain correspond to the types of desire and its object. Aristotle uses the word pleasure in two meanings, it means in the first place lower feeling of sensual satisfaction,[222] but in the second place it means the feeling that accompanies undisturbed activity of every kind.[223] Appetite pursues pleasure in the former sense, while wish aims at a more noble end.[224] In general, pleasure is divided into the corporeal and the mental.[225] However, body as such cannot feel any pleasure:[226] what is implied by bodily pleasure is the feeling in which bodily affection is predominant. There is the pleasure that accompanies the satisfaction of nutritive or sexual appetite, i.e., the pleasure of touch and taste. Nutrition and reproduction being the most fundamental and indispensable functions of life, the satisfaction of the appetites of which they are the ends is also the most natural and necessary pleasure of living beings.[227] Such pleasure presupposes bodily needs which make us uneasy and unpleasant. The fulfilment of sensitive desire is the process in which bodily needs are satisfied and what is incomplete becomes complete. It is when one takes notice of these natural and necessary appetites, that one takes pleasure to be a kind of motion or generation.[228]

In its wider sense, as aforesaid, pleasure is not limited to the satisfaction of such a necessary desire, but may as well be the pleasure that accompanies a higher sensation or even rational activity. Such pleasure is not the result of any need or want, but of undisturbed exercise of one's proper function, and consequently consists not in motion, but in action.[229] Aristotle even goes so far as to say that just such pleasure is pleasure *par excellence*, whereas the before described necessary pleasure is an accidental one, for the essence of pleasure is the activity of nature, and necessary pleasure is in fact the concomitant experience in the healthy part of the soul when it recovers its injured nature.[230] To re-

tion of profit, in the latter, the love of knowledge is said to be pleasure, cf. *Eth. Eud.* II. 8. 1124 b 16; *Rhet.* I. 11. 1370 b 10, 30; II. 2. 1378 b 7.

[222] *Eth. Nic.* I. 2. 1095 a 22 f.; 3. 1095 b 16 ff.; *Eth. Eud.* VII. 2. 1235 b 22; *Eth. Nic.* II. 7. 1107 b 7.

[223] *Eth. Nic.* VII. 13. 1153 a 12.

[224] *Rhet.* I. 10. 1369 a 3; *Eth. Nic.* VIII. 9. 1159 a 12; V. 11. 1136 b 7; *Eth. Eud.* II. 7. 1223 b 6; cf. *Eth. Nic.* III. 13. 1118 a 1–13.

[225] *Eth. Nic.* III. 13. 1117 b 28 f.

[226] *Eth. Nic.* X. 2. 1173 b 11.

[227] *Eth. Nic.* VII. 6. 1147 b 23–31; VII. 8. 1150 a 16–18.

[228] *Eth. Nic.* VII. 12. 1152 b 12–14; (*Mag. Mor.* II. 7. 1204 a 33).

[229] *Eth. Nic.* VII. 13. 1153 a 7–15; X. 2. 1173 b 7–20.

[230] *Eth. Nic.* VII. 15. 1154 b 15–20.

gard the satisfaction of sensitive desire to be pleasure is the view of
common people, while to take spiritual satisfaction as the real pleasure
is that of a philosopher.

The very best of all ideal pleasures is that of pure contemplation,[231]
which is the most self-sufficient and complete activity of reason.[232]
But in human being, even cognition or contemplation may be regarded
as a kind of satisfaction of desire. For man is not a pure reason, but is
emotional as well as intellectual, and corporeal as well as spiritual.[233]
Such a being does desire to know,[234] and the desire to know is a wish
without doubt.[235] Therefore every kind of human activity is followed
by pleasure and if we refuse the pleasure entirely, it will lead to the
complete denial of human activity.[236] Of course, even if the satisfaction of a desire is pleasure, it does not amount to saying that every
desire is the pursuit of pleasure. Desire aims at an end other than
pleasure, pleasure being mere concomitant of its attainment.[237] To
desire pleasure as such is not honourable, but the pleasure that
follows the satisfaction of desire may vary in value,[238] because pleasure
is correlative to desire; a dog has his pleasure, a horse his, and so has
man his own pleasure.[239]

Now, man is on the one hand a rational being and resembles God,
but on the other hand, he is a kind of animal and living being. His
desires and actions range from the vegetative to the divine, and his
pleasure are also various in proportion to them.[240] Pleasures are differ-

---

[231] *Eth. Nic.* X. 7. 1177 a 22–25.

[232] *Eth. Nic.* X. 7. 1177 a 27; b 1.

[233] *Eth. Nic.* VII. 13. 1152 b 36–1153 a 2. The "naturally pleasant" is considered to be a spiritual and higher pleasure, not the satisfaction of a natural
desire. cf. *ibid.* III. 13. 1118 b 19; *Part. An.* I. 5. 645 a 8; *Met.* XII. 7. 1072 b 14–16;
Eth. Nic. X. 7. 1177 b 26–29; *Met.* I. 1. 980 a 20 f.

[234] *Met.* I. 1. 980 a 22.

[235] *Eth. Nic.* X. 7. 1177 a 25–27.

[236] *Eth. Nic.* II. 2. 1104 b 13–16; *ibid.* 34–1105 a 1; 1105 a 4 f.; VII. 14. 1153 b
30; VIII. 4. 1156 b 16 f.

[237] *Eth. Nic.* VIII. 14. 1153 b 29–32; *Pol.* VIII. 5. 1339 b 31–38; II. 9. 1271
b 7–10; cf. Trendelenburg, *Beiträge zur Philosophie* III. 185, 205, 211; Scheler,
Der Formalismus in der Ethik und die materiale Wertethik 94 f.

[238] *Eth. Eud.* VII. 2. 1235 b 21–23. Besides sensual pleasures which are the
objects of lower desires, there are higher pleasures that accompany more noble
acts. To aim at pleasure itself is an inferior desire, but even a noble act may be
accompanied by some kind of pleasure as a result. cf. *Rhet.* II. 4. 1381 a 6–8;
Eth. Nic. VII. 6. 1148 a 22–26; V. 10. 1151 b 19; VII. 14. 1153 b 7–13; X. 2.
1173 b 20–23; 28–31; 5. 1175 b 24–27; *ibid.* 36–1176 a 3.

[239] *Eth. Nic.* X. 5. 1176 a 3.

[240] *Eth. Nic.* I. 6. 1097 b 32; 1098 a 12.

ent in accordance with man's way of living. The most human mode of living is spiritual or rational activity,[241] viz., contemplation and moral conduct. Of the two, the former is essentially divine, and man can only occasionally partake in it. It is rather divine than human, and one might deem it advisable for men, being men, to think of human things, and being mortal, of mortal things; viz., one might regard moral conduct to be more suitable to man than contemplation, and political affairs than science. Aristotle, however, insists upon the idealistic view of man against such a realistic view. According to him, man ought to make himself immortal as far as possible, and do every thing to live in accordance with the highest part in himself. "This would seem, too, to be each man himself, since it is the authoritative and better part of him."[242] In the same way, the pleasure that is suitable to man is that with which a wise man would be delighted,[243] viz., the pleasure of contemplation in the first place, and the pleasure that follows moral conduct in the second place.

Thus all animals feel their particular pleasure in the actions that arise from their own nature or habit, so that it is the mark of one's character in what thing he feels pleasure and in what pain. The pleasure that follows the satisfaction of desire by no means detracts from the moral merit of the act, rather proves it. One who does a good conduct with pain, is of inferior character, and one who does it with pleasure is a man of virtue. The end of education, is nothing but the rearing of a character that feels pleasure in a good conduct and pain in a bad one.[244]

Here is a remarkable peculiarity of Aristotle's eudaemonism as against the rigorism of Kant's. Kant might have correctly said that the conduct which aims at enjoyment is impure, instead of saying, as he actually did, that the conduct which has a material ground makes the pleasure its end. He misunderstood the fact that the realization of a desire is accompanied by pleasure, to signify that the pursuit of pleasure is itself the motive of such a desire.[245] In truth, however, to have a material ground for conduct is not the same as to pursue pleasure.[246]

[241] *Eth. Nic.* I. 6. 1098 a 7.

[242] *Eth. Nic.* X. 7. 1177 b 26; 1178 a 3; X. 5. 1176 a 24–29.

[243] *Eth. Nic.* X. 5. 1176 a 15; Pol. VIII. 3. 1338 a 4–9.

[244] *Met. VII.* 4. 1029 b 5–7; *Eth. Eud.* V. 2. 1237 a 1; 1236 b 39–1237 a 9; *Eth. Nic.* II. 2. 1104 b 3–13; I. 9. 1099 a 7–21.

[245] Kant, *K.d.p.V.I.1.* 2. *Lehrsatz* 1. *Cass. V.* 23; *ibid. Lehrsatz* II & *Folgerung.* V. 24 f.; Kant neglects the difference of values among material desires (cf. *ibid.* Anmerkung), but it is not right to assume that every material rule is related to an expected pleasure.

[246] Trendelenburg, *Beiträge III.* 184 f. Scheler, *Formalismus* I. 2.

Kant rejected all kinds of inclination, while Aristotle distinguished qualitative difference among them, and admitted moral value to the conduct which arises from an excellent inclination. Ethical virtue is just such a rationalized disposition and nothing else. Kant, by deeming obligation the essence of morality, radically rejected happiness or pleasure, and therefore encountered a difficulty in making the moral ideal accord with human nature. But, both an idealist and a man of common sense as he was, Kant could not advise man to sacrifice the general wish for happiness to moral purity. The only solution that he could present was to offer the old-fashioned religious consolations of the highest good and the immortality of the individual soul. [247]Obviously there is no essential reference between virtue and happiness. God alone can combine the two heterogeneous requirements by means of His benevolence and providence. Immortality of the soul is nothing but a promissory note that postpones the payment of fortune without any guarantee except the faith. Thus, life would, in the last analysis, amount to mere betting.

According to Aristotle, on the contrary, happiness is essential to morality from the outset. It is not the grace of God, but the end of conduct and, so to say, a part of oughtness. Not that a man of virtue should become happy, but that he ought to be happy because a man of virtue is such a man who feels happiness in good conduct. As aforesaid, Aristotle's concept of the highest happiness involves lower values like Kant's concept of the highest good, though the essential of ideal happiness is satisfaction that follows virtuous conduct. With respect to the relation between virtue and happiness, it is well known that old philosophical schools Epicurians and Stoics both assumed the harmony of virtue and happiness, only differing in the element they emphasized. According to Kant, "The Epicureans said that to be conscious of the maxim which leads to happiness, that is virtue, while the Stoics said that to be conscious of one's virtue, that is happiness. To the former cleverness is the same as morality, while to the latter, who preferred a higher name for virtue, only morality was the true wisdom." Kant remarks[248] thereupon that their sharp wit ... was unhappily applied to making out the identity of the two extremely unequal concepts of happiness and virtue. But through separating these concepts so strictly Kant was led to no more successful solution than a kind of *deus ex machina* theory. Taking this in consideration, we perfectly approve

[247] Trendelenburg, *op. cit.* 189 f.
[248] Kant, *K. d. p. V. I.* 2, 2. *Cass.* V. 121.

Trendelenburg,[249] wo finds the most complete solution of this problem in Aristotle's theory that assumes gradual development into the ideal harmony of virtue and happiness, as well as of reason and feeling; neither making virtue equal to happiness nor again appealing to *deus ex machina* to combine virtue and happiness as heterogeneously conceived.

On the other hand, however, even Kant,[250] who regarded duty as the essence of morality, could not deny the deep satisfaction that follows a moral conduct, and on the other hand, there is a problem whether Aristotle was right in identifying satisfaction of desire in general with pleasure. To avoid the suspicion of hedonism, he should have rather called it, e.g., joy, or merely happiness. Indeed, happiness was for him a very extensive concept covering sensitive pleasure, the satisfaction of possessive desire and desire for honour, as well as the bliss from moral conduct and pure contemplation.[251] What one would regard as happiness, or what one would feel happy about, expresses his character. Happiness is a value concept, while pleasure is a natural one. Pleasure may also have some value – only in so far as it is considered to be happiness.[252] And to think something to be happiness is to esteem it; the proof is that happiness is considered to be respectable and not praisable,[253] for to be praisable is to partake in a value, while to be respectable means to be the value itself. Happiness is almost synonymous with the good, so that everyone would agree in taking the good for happiness,[254] the only difference is that the one is the subjec-

---

[249] Trendelenburg, *op. cit.* 210 f.

[250] Kant, *K. d. p. V. I.* 2,2. *Cass.* V. 128; *K. d. U. K.* Einl. III. *Cass.* V. 247, 264.

[251] *Eth. Nic.* I. 3.

[252] *Eth. Nic.* I. 5. 1097 b 2–5; 3. 1095 b 16; III. 6. 1113 a 34 f.

[253] *Eth. Nic.* I. 12. 1101 b 12–14; 21–23; 1101 b 35–1102 a 1. τίμιον is different from Kant's *Achtung* which is accompanied by a kind of pain.

[254] *Eth. Nic.* I. 4. 1095 a 14–22. As to the indefiniteness of happiness, cf. Kant, *K. d. p. V. I.* 1. 3. *Lehrsatz* II. *Cass.* V. 28: *Glücklich zu sein, ist notwendig das Verlangen jedes Vernünftigen, aber endlichen Wesens und also ein unvermeidlicher Bestimmungsgrund eines Begehrungsvermögens. Denn obgleich der Begriff der Glückseligkeit der praktischen Beziehung der Objekte aufs Begehrungsvermögen allerwärts zum Grunde liegt, so ist er doch nur der allgemeine Titel der subjektiven Bestimmungsgründe und bestimmt nichts spezifisch, darum es doch in dieser praktischen Aufgabe allein zu tun ist, und ohne welche Bestimmung sie gar nicht aufgelöset werden kann. Worin nämlich jeder seine Glückseligkeit zu setzen habe, kommt auf jedes sein besonderes Gefühl der Lust und Unlust an, und selbst in einem und demselben Subjekt auf die Verschiedenheit der Bedürfnisse nach den Abänderungen dieses Gefühls, und ein subjektiv notwendiges Gesetz (als Natur-Gesetz) ist also objektiv ein gar sehr zufälliges praktisches Prinzip, das in verschiedenen Subjekten*

tive, and the other the objective, aspect of value. Why, then, was
Aristotle not content himself merely with calling the satisfaction of a
desire happiness? Perhaps this is not without reason. The satisfaction
of a desire has two aspects: the aspect of value and the aspect of nature.
From the first aspect, it is happiness, but from the second aspect, it is a
kind of pleasure. The experience of a moral conduct may be happiness,
as far as the subject is a moral person, but the same experience is
pleasure as far as he is an animal. The natural aspect cannot be neglected since morality is not a matter of pure spirit, but a matter of
concrete person. And the foundation of morality is life[255] *in concreto*.

But how can this eudaemonism stand against the criticism from
Kantian ethics? To make happiness the ultimate end of conduct might
amount to reducing morality to inclination. Is it not in the last analysis
a spiritual egoism, not different from Epicureanism? The thoroughgoing counter- argument will be made after the investigation as to
practice and production. But anticipating our conclusion for the
moment, we maintain that the end-concept in Aristotle should be
primarily understood in objective sense. It is the object or result, which
is aimed at, rather than the consciousness of purpose. That every act
aims at happiness means not that man makes this his conscious purpose, but that it acts as regulative principle of his conduct. The end in
this sense is virtually acting in the world without being noticed, and
the consciousness of purpose is a partial appearance of it. So a biologist may rightly recognize self-preservation to be the end of all living
activities, though animals and plants are not conscious of this end.

Even if happiness is the objective end and not the subjective purpose of a conduct, this detracts nothing from the moral value of
practice. The satisfaction of a desire will naturally result in happiness
though man does not always pursue satisfaction with consciousness.
Moreover, even when happiness should be made the subjective end, it
does not of necessity harm the dignity of morality. For happiness,
being, as aforesaid, the highest value, is not the same as the natural
feeling of satisfaction. To pursue happiness is after all to pursue the

sehr verschieden sein kann und muss, mithin niemals ein Gesetz abgeben kann,
welches bei der Begierde nach Glückseligkeit nicht auf die Form der Gesetzmässigkeit
sondern lediglich auf die Materie ankommt, nämlich ob und wieviel Vermögen ich in
der Befolgung des Gesetzes zu erwarten habe. A mere concept of happiness never
gives a moral rule, still a character which feels happiness in a good act has by
feeling so a moral value. It is not mere satisfaction, but the satisfaction in a
certain situation that constitutes the value of a man's character.
   [255] *Eth. Nic.* X. 1. 1172 a 20–26; cf. Trendelenburg, *op. cit.* 200 f., 209 ff.

highest good, or to intend to realize the highest value. Of course the desire for happiness is *per se* neither praisable nor blamable; it is praisable only when the desire is fulfilled by some virtuous conduct.

4. Voluntary act

Generally speaking, desire is the effort to acquire or realize the object which is recognized through sensation, imagination or intellect. Voluntariness simply means the causality of desire and an animal is called to have acted voluntarily when its movement is caused by a conscious desire. Though all living activities are in a sense movements, movement in respect of place, which is fundamental to conduct, is found only in animals[256] but the principle of this movement must be either body or soul, since body as such is passive and is moved, the active principle must be the soul.[257] It is evident moreover that it does not belong to the nutritive part, because this part involves only the function of accepting and assimilating external objects. This movement also aims at a certain end, and is accompanied by imagination and desire. All these functions do not belong to the nutritive part.[285] Besides, if nutrition were the principle of this kind of motion, even plants would move themselves.[259] Nor is sensation the principle of motion, for there are some animals that have sensations yet do not exhibit locomotion.[260] How then is it with reason or intellect? Aristotle distinguished three modes of reason. Firstly, theoretical reason is not the principle we are seeking, for it thinks nothing about practical matters, and cannot tell whether an object should be pursued or avoided, while motion is some kind of pursuit or avoidance.[261] Secondly, there are cases, when reason, even though thinking about practical affairs, does not command pursuit or avoidance, while the heart or some other part of the body acts as the direct moving principle.[262] How should this second kind of reason be called; is it theoretical or practical? It seems to be practical as far as it is concerned with practical affairs, but theoretical as far as this cognition does not determine the conduct. On this point, Aristotle himself gave no decision, but to most likelihood, it corresponds to the habit called σύνεσις or γνώμη i.e.,

---

256 *De An.* I. 5. 410 b 20; II. 3. 415 a 7; 415 b 22; III. 9. 432 b 19–21.
257 *De An.* I. 5. 410 b 19–21; II. 3. 415 b 21–22.
258 *De An.* III. 9. 432 b 14.
259 *De An.* III. 9. 432 b 17.
260 *Ibid.*
261 *De An.* III. 9. 432 b 26.
262 *Ibid.* 29 ff.

insight or judgement, which is somewhat inert knowledge of practice.[263]
An indifferent judgement about practical affairs might suggest a kind
of theoretical knowledge like the theory of ethics. This may appear to
serve as the ground for Zeller's interpretation to the effect that Aristotle admitted the theoretical knowledge about practice,[264] and for
Walter's opinion that ethics and politics consist in theoretical knowledge.[265] But this is far from being truth, for Aristotle attached no
importance to this kind of knowledge, which is nothing but a deviated
mode of intellect. Ethics, on the contrary, is the system of φρόνησις and
is practical through and through. It is by no means an inert intellect
that gives no command about practical affairs, but the very source of
power which fosters the virtues of man and brings both the individuals
and society the highest good.[266] It was the Greek view of ethics, and at
the same time Aristotle's belief thereof that ethics should be ἀρχιτεκτο-
νικὴ φρόνησις practical wisdom – of the most general and fundamental
sort – and that the moral philosopher should be a man of practical
wisdom *par excellence*.[267] This, however, does not amount to slighting
theoretical knowledge. To make the theoretical knowledge identical
with that inert practical knowledge would be a serious misunderstanding and an inadmissible debasement of it. If theoretical knowledge
were such a thing, it is quite incomprehensible why theoretical knowledge was esteemed so highly. In reality, theoretical knowledge was

---

263 *Eth. Nic.* VI. 11. 1142 b 34–1143 a 24; *ibid.* 12. 1143 a 25–35. σύνεσις and
γνώμη are concerned with practical objects, and are distinguished not only
from ἐπιστήμη but also from δόξα, for δέξα may sometimes be theoretical, though
it is concerned with individuals. That this reason is critical and not imperative,
does not imply its being theoretical. Rather, it is a faculty that judges rightly
another man's speech about practical affairs. Cf. *ibid.* 11. 1143 a 11–15. It is not
imperative, presumably because it is concerned with the affairs of another man
and not with one's own. Yet it is none the less a kind of practical knowledge,
and sometimes may become imperative. A sympathetic person who understands
another man's words, is practically wise. σύνεσις or γνώμη may become imperative, when one is obliged to act, and feels an inner desire; otherwise, he would
remain a mere observer of life. In *Eth. Nic.* X. 10. 1181 a 18, these words are
used to indicate something like a righteous judgement through experience.
Similarly, in the theoretical area we find a kind of non-professional knowledge called
παιδεία or culture, which belongs to an observer of professional works. Cf. *Part.
An.* I. 1. 639 a 1 ff.; *Eth. Nic.* I. 1. 1094 b 23; 1095 a 1. *Pol.* III. 11. 1282 a 6;
Pol. I. 5. 1254 b 20–24.
264 Zeller, *Ph. d. Gr.* II. 2. 77 n. 5.
265 Walter, *op. cit.* 157 ff., 537 ff. cf. Teichmüller, *Neue Studien zur Geschichte
der Begriffe*, III.: Die praktische Vernunft bei Aristoteles Ch. 1. This point shall
be studied later.
266 *Eth. Nic.* II. 2. 1103 b 26–30; I. 1. 1095 a 5 f.
267 Cf. Teichmüller, *Neue Studien* 24 ff.

admired because it is concerned with what is universal and necessary.[268] Thus theoretical intellect is concerned with such objects as God, nature or mathematical principles, the knowledge of which being metaphysics, physics, mathematics etc. They are higher than practical science such as ethics or politics.[269] But this is not our present concern. In this reference Aristotle is inquiring only about the *sine qua non* of conduct, and intending to prove that it is not reason. For this purpose he enumerates various forms of intellectual activity which are wanting in practical efficiency. Of the two above mentioned, viz., σύνεσις and γνώμη, the one is purely theoretical and the other is powerless, though it is in some way related to practical affairs. At any rate, neither of them is the efficient cause of conduct. But there is in the third place, another kind of intellectual activity that orders a man to pursue or avoid something, yet is wanting in practical efficiency.[270] This is the case with an incontinent person. Generally speaking, the fact that not all who know medical art are always successful at healing, is the proof that something else than knowledge has dominating power over conduct. It might appear therefore as if intellect cannot be the efficient cause of conduct.[271] But it does not follow of necessity that only appetite is the dominating power of conduct. In the case of a continent man, on the contrary, he obeys the command of his intellect in spite of his appetite.[272] Thus, either intellect or desire must be the agent of conduct.[273]

Aristotle admits that both of them can be the principle of motion or conduct. Of course, not intellect in general: at least theoretical intellect must be excluded. The intellect that acts as the principle of motion is that which calculates about some purpose,[274] viz., practical

---

[268] *Eth. Nic.* I. 1. 1094 b 11–27; VI. 7. 1141 a 20; *Met.* VI. 1. 1026 a 21; XI. 7. 1064 b 1; *Met.* I. 2. 981 b 17; 982 a 1; X. 9. 1074 b 27; VIII. 1. 157 a 9.

[269] *Met.* VI. 1. 1026 a 13; 1069 a 30; 6. 1071 b 3; *De An.* I. 1. 403 b 7; *Phys.* II. 2. 193 b 31; *An. Post.* I. 10. 76 b 3; 13. 79 a 7; *An. Pr.* I. 41. 49 b 35; *Met.* VII. 10. 1036 a 8; XIII. 2. 1077 a 9; III. 2. 997 b 20; 996 a 27; *De An.* III. 7.

[270] *De An.* III. 9. 433 a 1.

[271] *Cf. Met.* IX. 5. 1048 a 8; 8. 1050 b 30. cf. Ando, *Aristoteles no Sonzairon* 221.

[272] *De An.* III. 9. 433 a 8.

[273] *De An.* III. 10. 433 a 9.

[274] *De An.* III. 10. 433 a 14. There is a question how to translate the phrase: ἕνεκά του λογιζόμενος. If, following Trendelenburg, we take this as "calculating the end," the practical reason would be a thinking about the end, but if we follow Walter and others in translating this as "calculating the means to an end," the practical reason would be concerned with the means exclusively. We prefer the theory of Loening, who takes this as meaning calculation about conduct. cf. *Zurechnungslehre des Aristoteles* 30.

intellect. Desire also contributes something to motion by intending the end, for the object of desire is the beginning of conduct. Thus, both desire and practical intellect may be regarded as the principle of motion. At first, the object of desire moves, and through it the intellect: the intellect is moved through the object of desire. Even when not intellect, but imagination moves, it does not move by itself, but requires desire in addition.

Arguing thus, Aristotle concludes that a more radical and general agent, which precedes intellect and desire, is the object of desire. For, if both intellect and desire move a man, they move through a common principle. Whereas intellect does not move without desire, wish, though intellectual, is itself a kind of desire. And when some one moves through reasoning, he moves not only through reasoning but also through wish. On the other hand, desire may be an agent without being accompanied by intellect,[275] for there is a kind of desire which moves contrary to reasoning, viz., appetite. It follows therefore that what always moves is the object of desire.

Now, since reason is always right, but imagination and desire are sometimes right and sometimes not, the object of desire will be either the good or the apparent good.[276] That is to say, the object of desire is sometimes intended by mere imagination, and sometimes by practical intellect, and one may commit an error in the former case. Needless to say, the one is the case of passion and appetite, and the other that of wish.[277]

The object of desire is the good or the apparent good, it is not the good in general, but the practical good, viz., one which sometimes exists and sometimes does not exist.[278] The most fundamental principle of motion is thus the object of desire, and next to it, desire is more necessary than intellect,[279] the latter partaking only indirectly and incidentally in it. Thus, Aristotle, excepting at first the nutritive faculty, next supposing for a time intellect and desire to be the principle of conduct, then found the common principle in the object of desire, and finally decided that the desiring faculty is the direct efficient cause of conduct. Almost the same thought appears in the *De Motu Animalium*,[280] where intellect, imagination and sensation are

[275] *Part. An.* I. 1. 641 b 7.
[276] *De An.* III. 10. 433 a 26; *Met.* XI. 1. 1059 a 36–38.
[277] *Rhet.* I. 10. 1368 b 37–1369 a 7.
[278] *De An.* III. 10. 433 a 29.
[279] *De An.* III. 10. 433 b 11.
[280] *Motu An.* 6. 700 b 15–28.

all summed up in the concept of reason; appetite, passion and wish in that of desire; while will is analysed in reason and desire. Thus the two generic faculties of reason and desire being provisionally supposed as the principle of motion, the ultimate efficient cause is settled in the object of them, desire is regarded as the proximate agent. The final principle that makes the agent an agent, i.e., the *causa finalis* of the act was identified with the intellect, presumably because desire is related to its object in terms of reason in the generic sense, namely, sensation, imagination, and reason in the strict sense. In this respect, the object of desire is the same as the object of reason. It moves at first reason, and then through it, the desiring faculty.[281] The proximate agent of conduct may be desire, but the object of intellect viz., the object of sensation, of imagination, and of reason must precede it. Here is a remarkable implication as to the function of practical reason. Reason, or the faculty of knowing practical affairs, not only searches for the means to realize a given desire, but also determines the desire itself.

The process, in which the desiring part arouses movement is as follows: Motion contains three constituents: the first is that which moves, the second, the means through which it moves, and the third, that which is moved.[282] The first is subdivided into that which does not move itself, and that which moves itself and moves others. The unmoved mover is the valuable object which is the *causa finalis* of motion. In human conduct, it is the practical good and the object of desire as well as of reason or imagination.[283] The moved movent is the desiring part of the soul,[284] which is the *causa efficiens* of motion. It moves in so far as it desires, for desire is a kind of motion and action.[285] Only it belongs to the motion in a wider sense, as a qualitative change, yet compared with the act as a kind of locomotion, it is not the moved

---

[281] *Motu An.* 6. 701 a 2–6; 33–b 1.

[282] *De An.* III. 10. 433 b 13.

[283] *Met.* XII. 7. 1072 a 23–31. Teichmüller is not right in taking (*op. cit.* 207) the unmovable movent as practical reason in the wide sense. In truth, practical reason is a kind of efficient cause; it is moved by another and moves another, it is a medium which stands between the good as an unmoved movent and the desire as the last movent. Teichmüller's error seems to have arisen from the fact that Aristotle here mentions merely the appetitive part as an agent. But following the sequence more carefully, we find that the cognitive part of the soul comes between the object and the desire as explained in our text.

[284] *De An.* III. 10. 433 b 16; *Motu An.* 6. 701 a 1; 10. 703 a 5.

[285] *De An.* I. 4. 408 b 16; III. 10. 433 b 17; cf. Hicks's note *ad loc.* Desire itself is not a locomotion, but a mental action, as Plutarch holds.

but the movent.[286] We may easily see that the medium between the object and the soul, which makes *causa finalis* determine the *causa efficiens*, is the cognitive functions such as sensation, imagination and intellect, or the reason in a wider sense. In the third place, the moved is the animal and the instrument through which desire moves others is the body.[287]

Desire is no doubt a function of the soul; but since the soul is the form of the body, no function of the soul can exist apart from the body, except the active reason which, however, is something transcendent of the soul. Desire is more or less correlative with the body.[288] The central organ of sensation is the heart, to which belong *sensus communis* and imagination. This is also the seat of desire. Thus, the determination of desire through sensation or imagination corresponds to the process in which the stimuli from the nerve endings are carried to the heart and arouse there a delicate expansion and contraction through heating and cooling; those movements are further transmitted to the periphery and cause the motions and changes in limbs, skin, etc.[289] Not that pure mental function moves the body, but that desire moves the body with its physiological concomitants.[290] The heart is the crux to which concentrate the functions such as nutrition, sensation, imagination, desire and motion.

There are, however, various kinds of desire: appetite being the irrational desire, wish, the rational, and between them there is passion, which is partly rational, and partly irrational. The relation of these desires to the body naturally differs. Generally speaking, the more irrational the desire, the nearer is it to the body; the lowest of desires is appetite, which aims at sensual pleasure and immediately serves self-preservation and reproduction. Wish, on the contrary, is most free from the body, still it is not quite independent of the body.[291] For even the contemplation of theoretical intellect, which is the purest and most transcendent of all mental functions, is impossible without imagination, and therefore not independent of the body. Much more is it the case with desire, which is practical through and through. However rational it may be, it must needs be under bodily conditions.

[286] *Phys.* VIII. 2. 253 a 12.
[287] *De An.* III. 10. 433 b 19.
[288] *De An.* I. 1. 403 a 5–403 b 19.
[289] *Motu An.* 7. 701 b 13–32; 7. 701 b 33–702 a 19; 11. 703 b 26–36.
[290] *Part. An.* II. 1. 647 a 23–31; III. 4. 666 b 15.
[291] *De An.* I. 1. 403 a 9; III. 7. 431 a 16; 8. 432 a 8, 13; *De Memor.* 1. 449 b 31; *De Sensu* 6. 445 b 16.

Rational desire does not serve the immediate need of the body, but it aims in the last analysis at the highest happiness. The end of wish is imagined with the feeling of appraisal or aversion, and is considered as good or as bad, as beautiful or as ugly. Hence the object of wish is said to be good or beautiful, while that of appetite to be pleasant. But however beautiful and good the ideal may be, it is realized in terms of bodily movement or action, so that it must needs be mediated through the movement of the heart. Even a rational image acts upon the central organ of sensation and desire, the heart, in terms of pleasure and pain. Hence, as aforesaid, the good and beautiful does not exist independently as a mere spiritual value, but requires to be pleasant, and the absolute good is identified with the absolutely pleasant.[292] Unless thinking and imagination are accompanied by the feelings of pleasure and pain and produce a desire, they cannot move the body and can never act. The body is dominated, in this case, by another appetite that moves the heart with a stronger emotion.[293] This is a physiological explanation of the so-called incontinent act, or more generally, of unvirtuous character. Ethical virtue is nothing but the harmony of reason and sensibility, of soul and body. For the good and beautiful to remain a mere spiritual value is the mark of powerless intellect. In order that such an ideal may become actual, it must first be realized in a bodily habit. The spiritualization of the body is at the same time the embodiment of the spirit.

Whether it aims at a bodily value or a spiritual value, every desire is an efficient cause that moves the body through the physiological function of the heart, which, in its turn, is caused by an image accompanied by an emotion. Desire moves through itself being moved, it is affected by an object and moves a person by means of the body. Desire exhibits an actual form, in so far as it is the act of the desiring part; yet it remains potential in so far as it must be realized in the external world. It is an active potency, or more exactly, a ἕξις in the particular sense previously indicated.[294] Aristotle himself in fact calls it a habit in one place,[295] but in most cases "habit" is applied rather to virtue or vice, which underlies desire or conduct.[296] This is because desire is more

[292] *Eth. Eud.* VII. 2. 1235 b 32; 1236 b 26; 1237 a 27.
[293] *Eth. Nic.* VIII. 4. 1156 b 22, 15; (*Mag. Mor.* II. 11. 1209 a 7; b 32)
[294] Cf. ch. I. n. 8.
[295] *Pol.* VIII. 15. 1334 b 17–20.
[296] *Cat.* 8. 8 b 29; *Eth. Nic.* II. 4; *Eth. Eud.* II. 2; (*Mag. Mor.* III. 7); *Phys.* VIII. 3. 246 a 12, 30; *Pol.* I. 13. 1259 b 25; II. 6. 1362 b 13; II. 12. 1388 b 34;

casual than a character, and because the interest of ethics is concerned
not so much with the process from desire to act than to the process
from character to desire. Desire, originating from particular character
produces particular act. This internal origin of an outward-turning
action is the essence of voluntariness. As is often said by Aristotle, the
object of an act, or the practical affairs is contingent being or that
which may be otherwise as it is. This possibility of being otherwise
does not consist of contrary ἕξεις or δυνάμεις, but of contradictory
ἐνδεχόμενα, not of real potencies, but of ideal possibilities of being thus
and not being thus.[297] In this way, one member of the contradictory
opposition has no more reality than another. In order to give one
direction to this indefinite state, there must be some determinant. This
is true everywhere, in man, in animal as well as in nonliving beings.[298] But
when such a determinant exhibits as a conscious desire, the act which
is determined by it is called voluntary.[299] Things may occur either
from nature, from necessity, or from accident;[300] such things are all
outside of our responsibility. We are responsible only for what is caused
by us; on account of this causality we submit to praise or blame, and
have virtue or vice.[301] In short, voluntariness means the freedom of an
act, and this is the fundamental condition of moral estimation, either
positive or negative. Inquiring about voluntariness, the *Eudemian
Ethics* asks directly for the positive mark of it, while the *Nicomachean
Ethics* making a detour, tries to explain it through the characteristic
of involuntariness. In the former work, it is asked, which, among desire,
will and intellect, is most essential for making an act voluntary and
various difficulties are rendered thereof. In the first place, since desire
is divided into wish, passion and appetite, if some kind of desire makes
an act more voluntary than another kind, a difficulty will follow to the
effect that a single conduct would be at the same time voluntary and
involuntary, when there is a conflict of desires. In the second place, if
will is to be regarded as more essential to voluntariness, there occurs
another difficulty, for an act which arises from a wish would not be
voluntary unless it is accompanied by deliberation, and therefore does
not form a will. In the third place, if neither desire nor will can be the

III. 7. 1408 a 29; *Eth. Nic.* II. 6. 1106 b 36; VI. 4. 1140 a 4; *Eth. Nic.* II. 4.
1105 b 19—26.
  [297] Cf. ch. I. n. 8.
  [298] *Eth. Eud.* II. 10. 1226 a 22—25.
  [299] *Eth. Eud.* II. 6. 1223 a 1—9.
  [300] *Part. An.* I. 1. 639 b 20—640 a 12; 642 a 1—13; 30 b 2.
  [301] *Eth. Eud.* II. 6. 1223 a 10—20.

essence of voluntariness, there remains only intellect, viz. the intellect which is concerned with the object, the means, and the end of a conduct.[302] But Aristotle stops here and notice that the reason why that desire and will appeared not to be the essence of voluntariness, was that neither of them could not form the sole principle of voluntariness, whereas in lifeless things, the principle of movement is either in the thing itself, or outside it, and in the first case the thing is in a sense free, while in the second case, it is constrained. In the animal, the interior principle does not remain as mere nature, but becomes appetite, yet, the animal having in it no conflict between appetite and intellect, is akin to lifeless things. But this is not the case with man, who experiences a conflict of desires; in this case, every kind of desire, i.e., appetite, passion, wish and will, belongs to his essence and they are not differentiated in such a way as the one group of desires is interior and the other exterior. Therefore, as aforesaid, if we adopt only one kind and exclude the others, we cannot avoid a dilemma: viz., we are voluntary as far as we follow an appetite, yet involuntary as far as we oppose wish. Now that all belong to the man as a whole, we should consider that man is voluntary to whatever kind of desire he may follow.[303] Thus argues the *Ethica Eudemia*. In the *Ethica Nicomachea*,[304] too, Aristotle mentions the sophistry such that claims praise for good deeds because of their voluntariness, while refusing the blame for disgraceful conduct, on the pretext that it has been compelled by appetite and so is not voluntary. Against this argument Aristotle maintains that all the acts that arise from our desires are equally voluntary, and that if one regards a good conduct to be voluntary, a disgraceful act must be regarded to be voluntary none the less.

Generally speaking, all animals, including man, are moved movents. They exhibit locomotion, which, however, is generally originated from their circumstance.[305] But the exterior stimulus sometimes moves at first intellect and desire, and next through them the body of the animal, sometimes it moves the body directly without perception or desire, as e.g., in sleeping.[306] When the domination of circumstantial power is indirect, the act is voluntary, but when it is direct, it is involuntary. Whether the desire is rational or irrational, is irrelevant to the problem of voluntariness. Man is apt to complain of pleasure's

[302] *Eth. Eud.* II. 9. 1225 b 2.
[303] *Eth. Eud.* II. 7. 1223 a 21 ff.
[304] *Eth. Nic.* III. 3. 1111 a 22–b 3.
[305] *Phys.* 21. 252 b 17–28; 253 a 7–21; VIII. 6. 259 b 1–20.
[306] *Phys.* VIII. 2. 253 a 11–21.

compulsion when he yields to a lower appetite, but strictly speaking, compulsion is proper to the act which is accompanied by pain,[307] pleasure being rather the common motive of all human conducts. Even a noble wish does not become actual without being accompanied by a kind of pleasure. Man is neither rational nor irrational exclusively, but rational and irrational at the same time. Man acts voluntarily no matter whether he pursues sensitive pleasure or moral goodness. Any conduct performed through desire can be rightly called voluntary whether it be rational or irrational, morally good or bad.

In the *Nicomachean Ethics*, voluntariness is explained in terms of its opposition, involuntariness. It is stated that the act done from compulsion or by ignorance is involuntary. Compulsion means that the origin of an act is quite external, and that there is no activity of the agent: it is, e.g. the case when a storm blows a ship off its course to a land other than the intended destination.[308] In such a case namely the desire of the agent contributes nothing to the actual result; the one is quite accidental to the other. But not every phenomenon to which the agent contributes nothing is called involuntary: for instance, a pure natural phenomenon is neither voluntary nor involuntary, for example, growing old or dying.[309] What is involuntary is that which might be done by a person, but is not really done by him, his actual desire being overcome by an external force. On this account, a compulsory phenomenon is accompanied by pain, and a voluntary act is followed by pleasure.[310] Voluntariness is thus the character of a conduct originated from a desire of any kind, whether rational or irrational, and that involuntariness is not the privation of desire, but its disturbance.

Thus, compulsion or physical enforcement makes an act involuntary. Otherwise with mental enforcement, which takes place when e.g. a powerful man threatens one with such a serious injury as to compel one to do what he naturally never wants, or when a mighty power causes one to give up property that he usually values, in order to avoid a great danger. It might be doubted whether such conduct is voluntary or involuntary. Aristotle, first admitting in it a mixture of voluntariness and involuntariness, then decides its essential part to be voluntary. For, seen with all its conditions on the moment of action, it is voluntary in the final analysis. There are, at all events elements of voluntari-

---

[307] *Met.* V. 5. 1015 a 26–33. Here also ἀνάγκη and βία are not distinguished. *Rhet.* I. 11. 1370 a 10.
[308] *Eth. Nic.* III. 1. 1109 b 35–1110 a 4; 1110 b 15–17.
[309] *Eth. Nic.* V. 10. 1135 a 31–b 2.
[310] *Eth. Eud.* I. 8. 1224 a 30; *Eth. Nic.* III. 1. 110 b 11.

ness in so far as one is willing to submit to an enforcement to do something which is *per se* undesirable, through the consideration of injuries or pain that may arise from refusal. In such an act the movement of his organ is originated in himself, and it is in his power to decide whether to act or not, so that this act is surely voluntary. But considered in the abstract, it may be involuntary; for no one would like to do such an act for its own sake.[311]

This interpretation of enforcement proves that voluntariness consists not in the origin of desire, but in its process of realization. Through whatever enforcement or temptation a desire may arise, it does not fail to be the voluntary principle of an act, as far as it is one's own desire. The voluntariness of an act is irrelevant to the origin of desire.

Obviously, what is voluntary or involuntary is an act instead of a desire. To say some desire to be voluntary is redundant, and to say some desire to be involuntary is to commit a *contradictio in adjecto*. It is possible to do something without desiring it, but impossible to desire without desiring it. Therefore, Aristotle's implication in saying that the act with mental enforcement is the mixture of voluntary and involuntary is only that disregarding all concrete circumstances and observing the bare fact of an act, it is not desirable by itself. And since there is no such desire by nature, the corresponding act is regarded to be involuntary from an abstract point of view. Whatever cause or motive it may have, an act must be voluntary, as far as it is considered in reference to the motivating desire. What will not be desired without qualification, may be preferred in certain situations, the act which is caused by such a calculative desire is voluntary none the less.

In short, the first requisite of voluntariness is spontaneity, which is common to every kind of desire. Under whatever form a desire may arise, its undisturbed realization is equally voluntary. The second condition that makes an act involuntary is ignorance. But an act through ignorance is not of necessity involuntary, though it is not-voluntary. In order to be involuntary, the act must be followed by repentance moreover.[312] The explanation is found in the *De Motu Animalium*,

---

[311] *Eth. Nic.* I. 1110 a 4 ff. In the *Nicomachean Ethics*, βία is distinguished from ἀνάγκη, but in the *Eudemian Ethics*, there is no such distinction, and βία is treated generally as compulsion or enforcement. Though physical enforcement is distinguished from psychological compulsion, this distinction is reduced to a difference of degree, so that we can find no decision of the problem. cf. *Eth. Eud.* II. 8. 1225 a 1–34.

[312] *Eth. Nic.* III. 2. 1110 b 18–24. Scholars have found an extraordinary difficulty in the theory that repentance constitutes the difference between ἀκουσία

where Aristotle, dividing certain kinds of physiological phenomena into the involuntary and the not-voluntary, presents as an example of the former, the movement of the heart and the sexual organs, and of the latter, such acts as sleeping, awaking, and respiration. [313] The former are called involuntary, because such organs move through imagination without the command of reason. This does not however imply that all acts which follow imagination and oppose intellect are involuntary. The term "involuntary" is rather used on the negative ground that a higher wish is overcome by such an irrational affect. And the actions of the second class are called not-voluntary, because they are mere physiological movements and changes of the body,[314] and are not mediated by imagination or desire.

An act done through ignorance, yet is not followed by repentance or pain, is thus not-voluntary. On the contrary, even when accompanied by knowledge, a mere natural phenomenon, e.g., decay or death, is neither voluntary nor involuntary.[315] Similarly, heating and hunger,

and οὐκ ἑκουσία. According to Hildenbrandt (*Geschichte und System der Recht- und Staatsphilosophie* II. 275), and Siebeck (*Geschichte der Psychologie* I. 2. 102), Aristotle regarded the act in the past which is followed by repentance to be not voluntary, while Kastil (*Willensfreiheit* 4), counted the conduct without repentance voluntary. Stewart (*Notes on Aristotle's Nicomachean Ethics*) and Loening (*Zurechnungslehre des Aristoteles* 174), point out a discordance of this statement with the statement in *Eth. Nic.* III. 1. 1110 a 14 f., where it is argued that the difference between voluntary and involuntary consists in the moment of the act itself. Loening further argues that "voluntary" *versus* "involuntary" forms a contradictory opposition, and that there is no intermediate term between them. We cannot agree with Loening because the real implication of Aristotle's statement in 1110 a 14 f. is only that every act is voluntary as far as it is originated from a desire as most desirable in the concrete situation of the act, not that what was voluntary at the moment of conduct becomes afterwards involuntary on account of repentance. Repentance was rather admitted as a mark by which we discriminate whether an act is voluntary or not. An involuntary act produces repentance owing to the discrepancy of one's general purpose and the result of the act, while a non-voluntary act is not followed by repentance, because it has never aimed at a certain end. Further, the accompaniment of pleasure with a voluntary act, pain with an involuntary one, or apathy with a non-voluntary one is not accidental, because pleasure and pain are the emotional sides of success and failure and nothing else. Finally, the non-voluntary physiological phenomena cited in the *De Motu Animalium* are nothing but the "non-voluntary" here at issue.

[313] *Motu An.* 11. 703 b 5.

[314] *De An.* III. 9. 432 b 29 ff.

[315] *Eth. Nic.* 4. 10. 1135 a 31; b 1. According to Rassow, Spengel and Stewart, such a phenomenon is involuntary, and not οὐκ ἀκούσιον. So, Rassow alters ὧν οὐθ'ἑκούσιον οὔτ' ἀκούσιον ἐστιν to ὧν οὐθὲν οὔτ' ἐφ' ἡμῖν οὐθ' ἑκούσιόν ἐστιν, and Spengel to ὧν οὐθὲν ἑκούσιόν ἐστιν, Stewart also takes οὔτ' ἀκούσιον as an inter-

being neither conscious nor spontaneous, are not voluntary, but strictly speaking, they are not-voluntary instead of being involuntary.[316] This confirms our foregoing statement to the effect that involuntariness is not the privation, but the negation of spontaneity. What is naturally outside our spontaneous desire is not involuntary, though it is not-voluntary. What is involuntary is such an act which may be avoided by our efforts, and still in fact was compelled by an external force. In this case, we feel pain and repentance, because we are forced to do so against our own desire. This is evident in the case of physical compulsion, but the same analysis is also applicable to involuntariness through ignorance: the agent does not know the real meaning of what he is committing; when a result comes about which he would have prevented if he had had cognition of it, he regrets that his general wish was disturbed by it. There are many examples,[317] enumerated by Aristotle, of such involuntary acts through ignorance, viz. wishing to explain the construction of a catapult, one lets it go off through an error, or one kills one's own son, mistaking him for an enemy, or being ignorant of the fact that a spear is pointed, one unintentionally kills a man, or taking a stone for a pumice stone, harms a man with it, or giving a draught to save a man, one really kills him. In every instance, an unintended result happens, on account of one's ignorance of the individual states of affairs.

Further, proceeding with these considerations, Aristotle distinguishes δι' ἄγνοια, acting through ignorance, from ἀγνουντά, acting in ignorance.[318] The former is the case, when the agent is ignorant of individual facts, and a result comes about which is different from his desire and intention;[319] the latter is the case, when the knowledge that

polation. cf. Stewart's note *ad loc.* But these alterations would be unnecessary, because decay and death are neither ἑκούσια nor ἀκουσία but μὴ ἑκούσια.

[316] *Eth. Nic.* III. 7. 1113 b 26–30.

[317] *Eth. Nic.* III. 2. 1111 a 6–18; *Eth. Eud.* II. 8. 1225 b 1–6.

[318] *Eth. Nic.* III. 2. 110 b 24–27. In *Eth. Eud.*, this distinction about ignorance is not clear. Also, *Eth. Nic.* V. 10. 1135 a 23 f.; *ibid.* 32; *Eth. Nic.* V. 10. 1136 a 5–9. A fault from ignorance might well be called involuntary, but it is unconceivable why an act done in ignorance and arising from an unnatural and inhuman passion should be called involuntary. It is acknowledged that such an act is not free from responsibility, so it must be voluntary at all events. This seems to be the brutal habit which is distinguished from vice in the strict sense; cf. *Eth. Nic.* VII. 6. 1149 a 1 ff. But even if it is not vice, it is voluntary, for the acts of children and beasts are said to be voluntary. Therefore, such an act would be called involuntary by Aristotle, simply because it does not originate in one's will. cf. Stewart's note *ad loc.*

[319] *Eth. Nic.* V. 10. 1135 b 11–16.

one ought to have, is disturbed or wanting on account of an enduring character or temporary state of mind. Sometimes, one may be careless of his usual knowledge[320] through drunkenness or anger, sometimes he may be ignorant of the general norm of practice as to what one ought to do and not, viz., in the case of ignorance in the will, τῇ προαίρεσει ἄγνοια.[321] This distinction corresponds to that of incontinence and self-indulgence. The former is the case, when will itself, being good, is overcome by a stronger appetite, and a result takes place that is undesirable and disagreeable to reason. The latter is the case, when will itself is ignorant of the norm. The one is the disturbance, and the other the privation of reason. In both cases ignorance belongs to the very character of the agent, so that an act in ignorance is by no means involuntary. The kind of ignorance which is the real cause of an involuntary or not-voluntary act is that which is exterior and accidental to the character of the agent, and is not concerned with such a universal principle as morality or law, but is concerned with individual facts.

Ignorance in the will, by the way, might appear to make an act involuntary and irresponsible, when, as is usually the case, the rational activity in the will is considered to be the searching for the means to realize an end. But what Aristotle calls here *ignorance* in the will is, in truth, the character of a will which calmly calculates about the means for satisfying an appetite; therefore it might rather be called the will which is dominated by ignorance. The fact that such a state of mind is called ignorance in the will shows that the practical intellect is not only concerned with the means how to realize a given end but also with the end to be aimed at.[322] If ignorance is the cause of an involuntary act, a voluntary act on the contrary should be accompanied by knowledge.[323] On the other side, not only the act that arises from a rational desire, but also the act which arises from an irrational

---

[320] *Eth. Nic.* III. 2. 1110 b 24; VII. 4. 1147 a 10 ff.

[321] *Eth. Nic.* III. 2. 110 b 28–1111 a 2. Against our interpretation to regard the ignorance of the ἀκρατής, to be related to a value, Walsh maintains (*Aristotle's Conception of Moral Weakness* 116), that it may relate not only to value, but also to fact, taking as an example the case when one is drunken and is ignorant whether it is a pumice or a stone that he throws at people. But a drunkard is only used as an analogy to explain the state of incontinence, not as precise description of it. A real drunkard is not incontinent though he is voluntary none the less. What an incontinent man is ignorant of is, for example, that this is an excessive amount of wine or that this woman is another man's wife. Both of these judgements contain some evaluation or at least qualification, which are something more than mere facts.

[322] This is a point to be borne in mind for our consideration to come as to the formula of deliberation and practical syllogism. Cf. *ch. V.*

desire may be voluntary. Animals and children are regarded to act voluntarily as well as men.[324] Hence it is evident that the knowledge required for a voluntary act, is irrelevant to the quality of desire. What kind of knowledge is it then that accompanies all desires, including the appetites of animals and children? Now, desire is the conscious effort of animals to realize the potential forms which are apprehended by sensation, imagination, and intellect. Imagination is sometimes opposed to intellect, but it forms a kind of knowledge in a wider sense, and even sensation is ranked with intellect as a faculty of discriminating forms. But neither sensation nor imagination is the knowledge that makes an act voluntary. For not every act that arises from a desire is voluntary without exception. One may act involuntarily, though he has sensation or imagination about the object or contents of his desire, and he feels repentance when his expectation is betrayed by the result; such a feeling would not occur if he had no cognition about his desire.[325] For instance, a woman who, wishing to give a man medicine, gave him a poison by mistake, surely had a good wish to cure him of his illness; but she did not know the drink in question to be a poison, so that mistaking it for a remedy she gave it to the man, and killed him *involuntarily*. In such a sense, the cause of involuntariness is said to be the ignorance about individual facts. If this proves to be the case, conversely, the knowledge that makes an act voluntary, must also be the knowledge about individual facts which are necessary to realize the end. Such knowledge of means is no longer involved in desire itself, but is the contents of βούλευσις or deliberation.[326] The deliberation of means presupposes an end, and traces the series of means up to the proximate step, which can be managed immediately. The terminus of this deliberation is precisely the starting point of an act, and the desire thus integrated by the consideration of means is called προαίρεσις or will.[327] But a voluntary act is not always done through will or deliberation. Aristotle implicitly admits that conduct through will is voluntary in a superior grade,[328] but he never excludes other kinds of conduct as not voluntary. The acts of children and animals are none

[323] *Eth. Nic.* III. 3. 1111 a 22–24; *Eth. Eud.* II. 8. 1224 a 7; 9. 1225 b 1 ff.
[324] *Eth. Nic.* III. 3. 1111 a 26, 4. 1111 b 7.
[325] *Eth. Nic.* III. 2. 1110 b 18–23.
[326] *Eth. Nic.* III. 5. 1112 a 30; b 11; 2. 1139 a 13; (*Mag. Mor.* I. 35. 1196 b 29); *Rhet.* I. 2. 1337 a 4; 6. 1362 a 18; b 5; 1383 a 7.
[327] *Eth. Nic.* III. 5. 1113 a 9–12; VI. 2. 1139 a 23; *Eth. Eud.* II. 10. 1226 b 17; (*Mag. Mor.* I. 17. 1189 a 31).
[328] *Eth. Nic.* I. 8. 1168 b 34.

the less assumed to be voluntary,[329] though they do not follow deliberation or will.

According to Aristotle, the ignorance which results in involuntariness is concerned with what, how much, who, whom, through what, why, and how one should do, and above all it is concerned with the object and the end of an act.[330] Consequently, the knowledge which makes an act voluntary must be about the essence, the quality, the agent, the object, the means, the reason, and the method of conduct. It is also stated that the ignorance that results in involuntariness is concerned with the individual and not with the general. For instance, Merope,[331] who killed her son through ignorance, killed him not without knowing that she was killing an enemy, but she killed him without knowing that it happened to be her own son.

With regard to ignorance of ends, one might wonder how it is possible that a man should do something without knowing his own purpose. But what is really meant would be rather that a man may act without knowing what will really happen, though he knows his general end or purpose, e.g., when an act done for the purpose of explaining the function of a catapult happens to hurt a fellow, what remains unknown is the actual result of this conduct, viz., to hurt a man. Such a result is an effect rather than a purpose, to be sure, but the concept of end in Aristotle is not so much a conscious purpose as objective form, so that the effect of a conduct may be called an end in this particular sense. At any rate, the ignorance that makes an act involuntary is related to individual facts, and this kind of ignorance hinders one to attain the ultimate end. Now, individual facts are not the objects of deliberation, but of perception. We do not deliberate whether it is bread or not, whether it is baked well or not,[332] or taking the above examples, whether the drug is a remedy or a poison, whether the spear is pointed or round, and whether the object is an enemy or one's own son; these are all the matters of perception.

Thus considered, the knowledge which makes an act voluntary seems to be the intuition of individual facts, and not the reasoning as to cause and effect like the deliberation which constitutes the will. This is the difference between voluntary act and will. But more profound thinking will reveal that even if there should be the imagination of the

[329] *Eth. Nic.* III. 4. 1112 a 14–16; V. 10. 1134 a 19–21. This implies that the knowledge about individual affairs of conduct makes an act voluntary.
[330] *Eth. Nic.* VI. 1. 1235 a 25.
[331] *Eth. Nic.* III. 2. 1111 a 12; *Poet.* 14. 1454 a 5.
[332] *Eth. Nic.* III. 5. 1113 a 1.

object and the perception of the individual facts, unless the two are not combined, no act would occur. Hence there must be some reasoning which combines the two. Thus voluntary act again requires deliberation to some extent.[333] If voluntary act as well as the act done with a will requires delineation *sui generis* the only difference between the two lies in the degree of integration. In other words, deliberation is primordial in a mere voluntary act and not so developed as in will. This is the reason why will appears in a mature person, though even children and animals act voluntarily, and on this account, the morality in the strict sense is found in a conduct through will.[334] Will is the *sine qua non* of moral significance, if not the sufficient condition of moral excellence. Voluntary acts of children and animals are responsible in a certain sense, but they are neither good nor bad in the strict sense of morality. What is morally good or bad is only such an act[335] which is performed through will. The reason why will or deliberate desire has moral importance is that the act from deliberation expresses one's character more fully[336] than the act without deliberation. But this is not all that is concerned. Seeing that practical intellect administers the desiring part, and ethical virtue consists in the *ratio* or moderation of desire, there must needs be some function of practical intellect other than the aforesaid deliberation which constitutes the will. The deliberation in will is mere searching for the means, while the deliberation in wish is such an intellect as makes desire itself rational, viz., the evaluating intellect.

Theoretical intellect remains in pure contemplation, having no interest in practice.[337] Practical virtue serves it by making man ready for such contemplation, but theoretical intellect contributes nothing to practical virtue.[338] Practical intellect is divided into two species: one, presupposing a desire, is concerned only with the means, while the other makes desire itself rational and gives to it a positive value. In order, however, to inquire more minutely into these two forms of practical intellect, we must analyse the structure of conduct. Conduct

---

[333] *Eth. Nic.* IX. 8. 1169 a 1; cf. *Rhet.* II. 9. 1369 b 21.
[334] *Rhet.* I. 9. 1367 b 21–23.
[335] *Eth. Eud.* II. 11. 1228 a 11–15; *Rhet.* I. 13. 1374 a 11–13; 1374 b 14; *Top.* IV. 5. 126 a 36; *Eth. Nic.* VII. 11. 1152 a 17; VI. 13. 1144 a 20; VIII. 15. 1163 a 23; III. 4. 1111 b 34; 1111 b 6; *Rhet.* I. 10. 1368 b 6–14; cf. *Eth. Nic.* III. 4. 1111 b 7, 13.
[336] *Eth. Nic.* III. 4. 1111 b 5 f.
[337] *De An.* III. 9. 432 b 27.
[338] *Eth. Nic.* VI. 7. 1141 a 20; *Eth. Eud.* VII. 15. 1249 b 9 ff.

is a kind of animal behaviour guided by intellect, practice and production being its two main forms. Our next problem, then, should be the study of practice and production, i.e. πρᾶξις and ποίησις, and our inquiry about the soul will be thus combined with the investigation of conduct.

CHAPTER III

PRACTICE AND PRODUCTION

1. Practice and Production

The human soul is divided into two parts: the rational and the irrational, and both of these further have a two-parts structure. The rational part is subdivided nto the theoretical intellect and the practical, while the irrational part is subdivided into the vegetable soul, which is quite unconscious, and the animal soul, which either obeys or disobeys the practical intellect. Of this irrational soul in the secondary sense, the passive side is sensation and imagination, and the active side, desire. Sensation and imagination, being accompanied by pleasure and pain, give rise to pursuit and avoidance, i.e., to positive and negative desires. Strictly speaking, Aristotle's concept of αἴσθησις is not limited to elementary sensation, but contains more figural perception, the principle of its organization being the so-called *sensus communis* as a mode of imagination. Though perception is more concrete than sensation because of its organization, what is more proper to cause desire is imagination rather than perception, since desire requires the expectation of future state. It may be said that desire is the imagination taken in the dynamic aspect. But imagination is either sensitive or intellectual; the desire based upon the former is appetite, and that based upon the latter is wish, passion being situated between the two.

In reflex, where stimulus and reaction are in a close contact with each other, there may be an elementary sensation, but no perception that gives rise to a desire. It is only when there is a detour between stimulus and reaction that the cognitive form of desire takes place, called sensitive imagination. This is primitive form of imagination approximate to sensation. In such a simple case, there is hardly any intellectual activity, either in setting up the end or in its realization. Hence appetite and passion are called irrational desires, or desires without calculation. Whereas a complex act, which instead of pursuing an instantaneous pleasure, chooses a certain end among various possibilities and realizes its end through some means, must be mediated by intellect. Here there is a collaboration of the irrational part with the rational. Fundamentally desire is irrational, but it is sometimes accompanied by intellect.

Rational activity in man is either theoretical or practical. Theoretical intellect is concerned with eternal and necessary beings, and performs no act other than to know these objects.[1] In this case, though it may sound strange, human intellect is quite passive. It is true that the so-called active reason finds its proper stage in theoretical cognition, but as we have seen, it is the medium rather than the subject of cognition. It is a universal principle and an unconscious holder of eternal forms. It makes human thinking possible as far as it enters in our soul, but essentially it is rather separable from our soul. Being the medium of God and man, it is compared to light which conveys the forms to the eye. We have interpreted this reason to be something like science or objective mind.[2] Whether or not this interpretation be accepted, at least it is certain that the human reason which is combined with the body through imagination is passive, even when it engages in theoretical cognition. It receives the forms from outside and cannot create them. We only think about the forms as they exist, without being able or intending to change them. The object of theoretical cognition is a necessary being which cannot be otherwise as it is, μὴ ἐνδεχόμενον καὶ ἄλλως ἔχειν, while, on the contrary, that of practical cognition is what can be otherwise; it is transient and contingent,[3] so that the practical subject can afford free activity. And when practice does not remain an impulsive act, but is accompanied by intellect, rational desire as a whole is active, whether the direct agent is intellect or desire.[4]

The object of practical intellect is contingent or what can be otherwise. Not all things, but at least some of them are to be modified by our effort; we impress the forms of our volition upon them. This is rational conduct, or πρᾶξις in a wider sense, which is further divided into πρᾶξις in a narrower sense and ποίησις, i.e., practice and production.[5] In practice the end is the act itself, while production aims at some other result.[6] Contemplation is absolutely non-practical, practice

---

[1] *Eth. Nic.* X. 7. 1177 b 1–4; *De An.* III. 9. 432 b 26–28.
[2] Ch. I. 4.
[3] *Eth. Nic.* VI. 2. 1139 a 6–12.
[4] Ch. II. 4.
[5] *Eth. Nic.* VI. 4. 1140 a 1–6; VI. 5. 1140 b 3 f.
[6] *Eth. Nic.* VI. 5. 1140 b 6 f.; X. 6. 1176 b 6–9; *Eth. Nic.* VI. a. 1139 b 1–4; cf. *Mag. Mor.* I. 35. 1197 a 11.

makes conduct itself the end, and production aims at the result of conduct.[7]

We must notice, however, that in Aristotle's terminology, a word may be used both in a wider and in a narrower sense, and that daily usage is often confused with a scientific use of a term.[8] With regard to the word πρᾶξις, this word expresses in its wider sense the act of any living creature, and is applied not only to human conduct but also to the movements of animals, plants and heavenly bodies.[9] For they are all possessed of soul, which is the principle of life. Seeing that even the activities of nutrition and reproduction of lower living creatures are called πρᾶξις as far as they are the acts of the soul, it is no wonder that the sensation which appears in animals should be called πρᾶξις.[10] On the other hand, a superhuman rational being is also assumed to perform πρᾶξις as far as it is possessed of soul and is in a sense a living being. For instance, the essence of happiness is εὐπραξία while God lives in "happiness" though being employed only in the contemplation of Himself. Thus, mere contemplation is also πρᾶξις, and sometimes may even be called πρᾶξις in the most excellent sense.[11] This is of course the widest sense of the word. Next in a slightly narrower sense, contemplation is excluded from the notion, so that God would not share in "practice" in this sense.[12] At last, in the most strict sense, absolutely irrational functions such as sensation or nutrition are also excluded,[13] and πρᾶξις is restricted to human conduct alone.[14]

Being distinguished from sensation, πρᾶξις seems to be attributed to

[7] *Eth. Nic.* X. 7. 1177 b 1 ff.

[8] Cf. Nuyens, *op. cit.* 205 f.

[9] *De Cael.* II. 12. 292 b 1–8; 292 a 18–21.

[10] *Hist. An.* I. 1. 487 a 11–17; *Hist. An.* VIII. 1. 589 a 2–5; 596 b 20 f.; *Gen. An.* I. 23. 731 a 25 f.; *Pol.* VII. 14. 1333 a 34 f.

[11] *Pol.* VII. 3. 1325 b 14–23; *Phys.* II. 6. 197 b 5: ἡ δ' εὐδαιμονία πρᾶξις τις· εὐπραξία γάρ. Zeller is right in taking the ποίησις which is predicated of contemplation in a wider sense, but he is wrong in identifying it with πρᾶξις in opposition to the ποίησις in the strict sense. As the proof thereof he quotes: *Eth. Nic.* VI. 2. 1139 b 3; 3. 1140 b 6 etc. (*Ph. d. Gr.* II. 2. 368 n.l). The πρᾶξις which is thus predicated of happiness and contemplation should be taken as act in general.

[12] *Eth. Nic.* X. 8. 1178 b 8 22; cf. *Met.* XIII. 7. 1072 b 18; *Pol.* VII. 1. 1323 b 23; *Eth. Eud.* VII. 12. 1244 b 8; *De Cael.* II. 2. 292 b 5.

[13] *Eth. Nic.* VI. 2. 1139 a 19 f. It is quite another thing that sensation is said in *De An.* III. 9. 432 b 19, not to be the principle of locomotion. For in the first place, conduct is not a mere locomotion, and in the second place, the reason for this statement in the *De An.* is that there are some animals that do not exhibit locomotion.

[14] *Eth. Eud.* II. 6. 1222 b 18–20; 1224 a 28–30.

the part of the soul which governs locomotion.[15] Not only man, however, but also most animals move in space. To what part of the soul, then, belongs πρᾶξις in the strict sense? Nutrition, sensation, and imagination, as well as thinking, being excluded, the only remaining part is the desiring part. Yet desire does not act by itself, but presupposes sensation or intellect; and an animal acts through desire, which is preceded by sensation and imagination. Therefore the πρᾶξις proper to man must be a locomotion through intellectual desire. Thus we have arrived at πρᾶξις *qua* human practice. But in spite of this restriction, πρᾶξις in this meaning covers a realm which contains both practice in the strict sense and production. And while πρᾶξις or πράττειν is applied to production, ποίησις or ποιεῖν is applied to practice as well.

It is by no means an undue expansion of meaning to use the verb ποιεῖν not only for production but also for conduct in general including practice. It means moreover even the act in general of all things. This is not astonishing, because ποιεῖν in the primary sense is one of the most general concepts which forms a kind of category together with πάσχειν.[16] It is an aspect of movement, or its active side.[17] But the notions of active and passive are applicable exclusively to qualitative change, distinguished from the movements as to substance, quantity and place.[18] Active and passive are the aspects of movement that takes place between opposite qualities imposed upon the same substratum.[19] But in the widest and usual sense the term πρᾶξις even surpasses the limitation to qualitative change. It is applied not only to production, but also to sensation,[20] memory,[21] desire,[22] emotion,[23] and further to

[15] *De An.* III. 9. 432 a 17.
[16] *Cat.* 4. 2 a 3 f.; 9. 11 b 1; *Top.* I. 9. 103 b 23; *Met.* V. 7. 1017 a 28; *Gen. et Corr.* I. 7–9.
[17] *Gen. et Corr.* I. 7. 323 a 15 ff.
[18] *Phys.* II. 1. 192 b 14; V. 1. 225 b 7; 2. 226 a 25; VII. 2. 243 a 6; VIII. 7. 260 a 27; 261 a 32 ff.; *De Cael.* IV. 3. 310 a 23; *Met.* IX. 1. 1042 a 32; XI. 12. 1068 a 10; b 17; *De An.* I. 3. 406 a 12; *Long.* 3. 465 b 30; *Cat.* 14. 15 a 13.
[19] *Gen. et Corr.* I. 6. 322 b 18, 23; 7. 323 b 31; 324 a 2, 34; b 16; *De An.* III. 4. 429 b 26; *De Cael.* II. 3. 286 a 33; *Long.* 3. 465 b 16; cf. *Gen. An.* I. 21. 729 b 10.
[20] *De Sensu* 3. 440 a 17 *Met.* XI. 6. 1063 b 4; *Part. An.* II. 3. 650 b 4; 17. 661 a 9.
[21] *Pol.* II. 8. 1268 b 31; IV. 2 1289 b 23; 8. 1293 b 28.
[22] *Eth. Nic.* I. 1. 1095 a 10.
[23] *Eth. Eud.* III. 1. 1228 b 15.

every living activity[24] such as locomotion,[25] nutrition,[26] reproduction,[27] and even to the movements of lifeless bodies.[28] It is also applicable to theoretical cognition[29] in the same way as is πρᾶξις or πράττειν. Consequently, it may be regarded as even more comprehensive than πρᾶξις.

Seeing that πρᾶξις and ποίησις or πράττειν and ποιεῖν are used in such various meanings, we must treat them with extreme prudence and distinguish the scientific terminology from the ordinary usage. To those who read Aristotle without this prudence, the system of this father of logic would appear as a heap of confusion and paradox. Indeed for modern dialecticians, there would be no novel opinion that might not be constructed from Aristotle.

Let us then express the strict scientific sense of the terms πρᾶξις and ποίησις by the words "practice" and "production." They are distinguished in that the one has its end in itself, and the other its end outside itself. The end is usually taken as the contents of will or as the imagination which precedes the result and leads the act. But, taken the end thus as a conscious purpose, the difference between practice and production would amount to mere subjective distinction, and an act may be either practice or production in accordance with personal attitude. For instance, the accumulation of wealth would be practice to a miser who aims at money-making, but the same act would be production to a man who makes money for the purpose of education or some political end. Whereas it is at one's liberty whether to regard an act as

---

[24] E. g. an animal catches its prey (*Hist. An.* III. 20. 603 a 2; IX. 32. 619 a 31), digs a hole (*ibid.* 2. 590 b 23), hides itself (*ibid.* VIII. 17. 601 a 15; 13. 599 a 7; IX. 5. 611 a 20) bees make their combs (*ibid.* V. 22. 554 a 16), a spider bites a prey (*ibid.* I. 39. 623 a 1), hairs grow (*ibid.* VII. 4. 504 a 23), and milk is produced (*ibid.* III. 21. 522 b 32).

[25] *De Cael.* IV. 4. 312 a 5; *Inc. An.* 15. 713 a 13; *Hist. An.* IV. 4. 530 a 9; V. 6. 541 b 16; VIII. 12. 597 a 20; 13. 599 a 4; IX. 37 b 622 b 7; VI. 29. 579 a 13.

[26] *De Sensu* 10. 475 b 27; *Hist. An.* I. 1. 487 a 16 ff.; 24; IV. 8. 534 a 11; VIII. 2. 589 a 17; 591 a 9; 3. 593 a 27; 10. 596 a 14; IX. 1. 608 b 20; 19. 617 a 17.

[27] *Hist. An.* I. 1. 488 b 6; V. 2. 540 a 17; 4. 540 b 5; 5. 540 b 7; VI. 14. 568 a 17; 18. 573 a 29; 29. 578 b 6, 16; VII. 2. 583 a 2; 4. 584 a 34; X. 29. 618 a 28.

[28] Various phenomena are called ποιεῖν such as the confusion of colours (*Meteor.* I. 5. 342 b 7), the change of quantity and figure (*ibid.* I. 6. 343 b 35), qualitative change (*Gen. An.* II. 2. 735 b 18), the coming of night (*Meteor.* II. 1. 354 a 31), or the occurrence of noise (*ibid.* 8. 368 a 14; *Hist. An.* IV. 8. 533 b 16; IX. 37. 621 a 29), of burning and of fire (*Meteor.* II. 5. 361 b 19; IV. 9. 387 b 30; *Part. An.* II. 2. 649 b 5), etc.

[29] *An. Pr.* I. 8. 30 a 10; 15. 34 b 9; 25. 42 a 22; 27. 43 a 24; 28. 44 b 26; 6. 28 a 23; *Top.* V. 2. 130 a 7; *Poet.* 16. 1455 a 15, cf. *Pol.* VII. 17. 1336 a 5; *Eth. Nic.* I. 3. 1096 a 5; *Part. An.* I. 1. 640 a 11; *Hist. An.* V. 1. 539 a 5; I. 6. 491 a 12; *Top.* VI. 4. 142 a 2; 141 b 18; VII. 2. 129 b 18 etc.

the end or to regard it as the means. Further, practice would be impossible apart from production, and *vice versa*, especially when practice involves an external act as well as production does, for such an act is not attained at a stroke, but requires some means, whereas as far as an act is concerned with the means, *ex hypothesi* it is not practice, but production. If on the contrary, practice *par excellence* is not accompanied by any production, it must be restricted to a most simple and elemental act. E.g., seeing might be regarded as practice *par excellence*, inasmuch as it does not go through a process and aims at no other end than itself. In fact, Aristotle himself is hinting at such a view.

Even in these cases, however, if it be necessary to resort to a complicated means in order to see the object, this process, being not the end itself, must be production. An act which has no means and no external end, if anything, is nothing but simple sensation. But it is absurd to identify practice *par excellence* with simple sensation. Aristotle not only distinguished practice from sensation, but also regarded moral conduct to be something more than mere voluntary act. It was an act which comes from προαίρεσις or βουλευτικὴ ὄρεξις,[30] i.e., from will or a deliberate desire. On the other hand, βουλεύσις and προαίρεσις are related not to the end, but to the means.[31] Consequently, an act which bears moral significance must be a complex of practice and production. Hence one might conclude that practice and production presuppose each other. But this explanation is neither satisfactory in itself nor faithful to Aristotle's statement.

According to Aristotle, practice always aims at an end,[32] and a practice is made the means for another practice, which, in its turn, serves for another practice and so on. Similarly with regard to production. For instance, every conduct concerning war is subordinated to strategy.[33] But, if an act which has an end outside itself should be

---

[30] *Eth. Nic.* III. 4. 1112 a 14 f.

[31] *Eth. Nic.* III. 5. 1112 b 11; 1113 a 2; 4. 1111 b 27 *Eth. Eud.* II. 10. 1226 b 9; (*Mag. Mor.* I. 17. 1189 a 7); *Eth. Nic.* VII. 5. 1140 a 30.

[32] *Eth. Nic.* III. 3. 1112 b 3 αἱ δὲ πράεις ἄλλων ἕνεκα. Many interpreters felt difficulty in this statement. Walsh seems to take this for a slip (*op. cit.* 134). But Stewart explains that it is only εὐπραξία or a systematic life of καλαὶ πράξεις which is its own τέλος. Each individual πρᾶξις in the system is correctly described as ἄλλου ἕνεκα. *Eth. Nic.* III. 10. 1115 b 23: καλοῦ δὴ ἕνεκα ὁ ἀνδρεῖος ὑπομένει καὶ πράττει τὰ κατὰ τὴν ἀνδρείαν.

[33] *Top.* VI. 12. 149 b 31 f.; *Eth. Nic.* I. 1. 1094 a 14–18. The distinction between the act which has no end other than itself and that which has such an end (1094 a 5 f.), is of course the distinction between practice and production. Where-

production instead of practice, such subordinate conduct must be production rather than practice, whereas Aristotle considers that a conduct is not concerned with a universal end, but always with particular facts.[34] Further, admitting that both practice and production require instruments, he divides the instruments into two kinds, the instrument in the strict sense, which belongs to production, and the instrument of practice such as wealth. The productive instrument of practice is, e.g., a reed, which produces some other result, whereas the instrument of practice, e.g. clothes or beds, produce no result besides their use. The slave is also regarded to be a kind of wealth, and consequently to be an instrument of practice. For, life is not production but practice, and the slave is the means of life.[35] From what has been said, it is evident that Aristotle admitted that there are the means of practice as well as the means of production. Even Teichmüller seems to have stuck to the modern sense of practice and instrument, when he opposed Aristotle by saying that instrument belongs naturally to art and that there can be no instrument of practice.[36] But inasmuch as our task is interpretation instead of criticism, we must endeavour to find out a particular meaning of practice to understand Aristotle's statement. Aristotle surely admits that the instrument naturally belongs to art and production. Hence wealth or slave is called the instrument of practice only in an analogical way.

According to Teichmüller, the act of a slave is not measured by his intention, but by his performance of the master's order; that he opens the door or washes his master's clothes is a pure technical activity instead of a practice. It is true that the act of a slave is not in accordance with his own purpose, but is for the sake of his master's wish. But from this fact, it does not follow of necessity that the act of a slave should be a production. Teichmüller's criticism appears to be founded upon the misunderstanding of the end-concept, which he took

as there is a similar relation both inside practice and production. This might seem to be quite paradoxical, if we take the end which is realized in the act itself as a subjective purpose (cf. Loening, op. cit. 7. n. 13), and one might ask "How is it possible that a practice which is essentially the end itself, should be subordinate to another master practice?" This becomes comprehensible only when we take the end which is actual in practice, to be an objective form and a moral value. A practice which subordinates itself to another practice realizes its objective form always in complete actuality.

[34] Met. I. 1. 981 a 17; Eth. Nic. III. 1. 1110 a 13, b 6; VI. 8. 1141 b 16; Pol. II. 8. 1269 a 12.
[35] Pol. I. 4. 1254 a 1 ff.
[36] Teichmüller, op. cit. 53.

in the subjective meaning. According to our opinion, on the contrary, the act of a slave who opens a door or washes clothes for his master is a production rather than a practice, not because he obeys his master, but just because it is the opening of a door or washing of clothes. If we take the end as a subjective purpose, and distinguish practice and production through it, opening the door or washing clothes should be regarded as practice when the master himself does these things. This is, however, against Aristotle's real meaning. An act is practice for the master, if it is so for the slave. What is practice for the master is similarly practice for the slave, even if he performs it through his master's order. Hence it was said that the slave is the instrument of practice, but not that of production. What distinguishes practice from production is not whether the act is done from one's own will or from another man's order. Practice and production are distinguished in essence and need a means in either case. If a master uses a slave in his life, and if life be essentially practice,[37] it will follow that a slave is the instrument, not of production, but of practice. Consequently, the end through which practice is distinguished from production, must be an objective form rather than a subjective purpose.

It is usually admitted that Aristotle's philosophy is a teleological system. Teleology is of course a type of thought which regards the world as the realization of an end. And we moderns are apt to suppose a teleological world to be ruled by a conscious agent analogous to us, viz., a world which is dominated by Divine Providence. In fact, there are, in Aristotle, some remnants of Platonic myths which tend in this direction, for instance, the theory of cosmological souls.[38] Aristotle, however, was the greatest positivist and scientist in his period, even compared with Democritus and Epicurus, to say nothing of Plato and Plotinus. As to his hackneyed expression, "Nature makes nothing in vain,"[39] it is not unusual to find its like in the works of modern scientists. For all that, we are not so malicious as to interpret such expressions as acknowledgements of Divine Providence. Whereas it was just Aristotle's idea of God, that He thinks only Himself without having any interest in transient beings. He not only never meddles in

[37] *Met.* IX. 6. 1048 b 25.
[38] *Met.* XII cf. Ross's Introduction to Aristotle's . *Metaphysica.*
[39] *De Cael.* I. 4. 271 a 33; II. 8. 290 a 31; 11. 291 b 13; *De An.* III. 9. 432 b 21; *De Resp.* 10. 476 a 13; *Part. An.* II. 13. 658 a 8; III. 1. 661 b 24; IV. 6. 683 a 24; 11. 691 b 4; 12. 694 a 15; 13. 695 b 19; *Motu An.* 2. 704 b 15; 8. 708 a 9; 12. 711 a 18; *Gen. An.* II. 4. 739 b 19; 5. 741 b 4; 6. 744 a 37; V. 4. 788 b 20; *Pol.* I. 2. 1253 a 9; 8. 1256 b 21; *Fr.* 221. 1518 b 20.

human affairs, but also engages in no practice or production, having neither desire nor will.[40] So that, even if there be some anthropomorphic expressions in Aristotle, they must be taken as mere rhetorical expressions.

Aristotle's teleology admits no personal god who creates and dominates the world through his free will, [41]its principle is an objective end rather than a subjective purpose, intention or purpose being mere appearance of it. Everything in the world is regulated by this end, even when there is no deliberation.[42] This is the principle of nature as well as of art. Rather, nature is the main area of the end, and art is merely an incomplete imitation of it.[43] It is said that such an end is the essential form[44] of an appearance, viz., the form which becomes actual in the result of movement or change.[45] The tree is the end of the seed, in the sense that a tree grows out of a seed. Man's purpose is a kind of end, but not the end *par excellence*, since it is merely a presupposed end, i.e., an image supposed before the result. While τέλος is a πέρας[46] and perfection,[47] the purpose or the image of an end is mere preparation, and will become a real end only when it is realized through acts. In modern philosophers since Descartes there is a steadfast inclination to admit supremacy to consciousness, which was the main obstacle to understanding Aristotle's teleology as well as Plato's theory of ideas. In Aristotle's philosophy, an end is an objective form rather than an idea in psychological sense, which is only the undeveloped stage of an end like a seed. An end is somehow immanent in every process of move-

[40] *Eth. Nic.* X. 8. 1178 b 8.

[41] Brentano's theory that takes Aristotle's god as an almighty creator, is a Christian misinterpretation. cf. *Psych. d. Ar.* 234 ff.

[42] *Phys.* II. 8. 199 b 26.

[43] *Phys.* II. 8. 199 a 5–20. Nature is similar to art in its constitution: they are both teleological. Not that an incomplete idea produces a complete effect, but that a complete form regulates the realization of a potential form. What is mentioned here is only the analogy between natural growth and production, but the statement is also applicable to moral conduct. cf. *Pol.* VII. 13. 1331 b 28; *Eth. Nic.* I. 1. 1094 a 18; also *De An.* II. 4. 415 b 16 f. It is not always an anthropomorphic interpretation to explain nature by means of an analogy of human conduct. *Part. An.* I. 1. 639 b 19–21. The native land of the end is rather nature than production or practice, the latter is nothing but a special appearance of the former.

[44] *Met.* VIII. 4. 1044 b 1; V. 4. 1015 a 11; *Phys.* II. 8. 199 a 30; 9. 200 a 34; *Gen. et. Corr.* I. 7. 324 b 18; (*Meteor.* IV. 2. 379 b 25); *Gen. An.* I. 1. 715 a 8.

[45] *Part. An.* I. 1. 641 b 24.

[46] *Met.* II. 2. 994 b 16.

[47] *Met.* IX. 8. 1050 a 9, 21; *Eth. Eud.* II. 1. 1219 a 8; (*Mag. Mor.* II. 12. 1211 b 27).

ment: if there were in a seed no potential form of a tree, its germination would be impossible. But the tree is not yet actual in the seed, so that there is not yet the actual end of the tree.

Assuming that Aristotle's end is an objective form rather than a subjective purpose, the distinction between practice and production must be whether the form is always actual throughout the process of an act, or becomes actual only in the result, rather than whether this form is a direct or an indirect purpose. But such a distinction as to the objective form is just what Aristotle recognized as existing between movement and actuality.

According to Aristotle, κίνησις or "movement" is an incomplete process tending to realize an end-form,[48] while ἐνέργεια or "actuality" is the constant realization of this form.[49] Thus learning or walking is a movement, while seeing or thinking is an actuality. Man completes the form of learning and walking only when he has finished learning or walking; he has not learned at the same time that he is learning, nor has he walked when he is walking. Whereas in seeing and thinking, an actual form is always present and man sees and thinks throughout the whole process. He has seen and is seeing, has thought and is thinking at the same time, so that there is in reality no process.

Our next problem is then, how practice and production are related to actuality and movement. Aristotle calls practice sometimes an actuality,[50] sometimes a movement.[51] But such an ambiguity is not limited to this case: what properly should be called actuality is often called movement. Hence we may suppose that strictly speaking, practice is an actuality, though it is sometimes called movement. In fact, Aristotle says: "Since of the actions which have a limit none is an end but all are relative to the end, ... this is not a practice or at least not a complete one, for it is not an end, ... but that movement in which the end is present is a practice. E.g., at the same time we are seeing and have seen, are understanding and have understood, are thinking and have thought (while it is not true that at the same time we are learning and have learnt, or are being cured and have been cured) ... Of these processes, then, we must call the one set move-ments, and the other actualities.[52]

[48] *Met.* XI. 9. 1065 b 14–23, 33 f.; *Met.* XI. 9. 1066 a 17–24.
[49] *Eth. Nic.* X. 3. 1174 a 14 ff.; 1174 b 2–9; I. 4. 1096 b 16 ff.
[50] *Eth. Nic.* I. 1. 1094 a 5; 6. 1098 a 13; *Pol.* VII. 3. 1325 a 32; (*Mag. Mor.* I. 35. 1197 a 10).
[51] *Met.* II. 2. 996 a 22–27; *Eth. Eud.* II. 3. 1220 b 27.
[52] *Met.* VIII. 6. 1048 b 19–35; cf. *Met.* VIII. 9. 1050 a 21 ff.

The above statement seems in the first place to distinguish actuality as the complete reality of the end, and movement as the incomplete, and then to make practice *par excellence* an actuality. But, there is some discrepancy between the two parts of the above quotation, viz., while the first part deals with πρᾶξις, the examples in the second part are related immediately to ἐνέργεια and κίνησις. From this statement alone, it is not evident how practice and production are related to actuality and movement. Even if practice were actuality, production would not of necessity be movement. It is also probable that neither is every actuality practice, nor is every movement production.

In the first place, it is evident that not every movement is production, e.g., the movement of an automatic agent, nutrition and reproduction of living creatures, natural movements of lifeless things, such as the burning of fire or rain-fall, and so on. Production in the strict sense is something more than natural movement, it is an act of human being guided by art. As to the relation between actuality and practice, Aristotle mentions seeing and thinking as examples of actuality, but he does not regard such acts to be practice. We have learnt from Aristotle that practice is concerned with what can be otherwise. Whereas not all objects of sight and thought are variable things, e.g. heavenly bodies are eternal and yet seen, numbers are what cannot be otherwise and yet thought of. The objects of pure contemplation, which are actual beings *par excellence*, are necessary and cannot be otherwise. Since such constant and eternal things are not πρακτά, the acts that relate to them cannot be πρᾶξις. Seeing is an αἴσθησις and thinking is θεωρία, neither of them is πρᾶξις; the contemplation of God is not practice, though it is called εὐπραξία. It would be a hasty conclusion to make seeing and thinking practice, because of their being called actuality. Much more absurd is the opinion[53] that takes the practice distinguished from production as identical with contemplation, and neglects the peculiarity of practice against both production and contemplation. In such an interpretation, not only the division of intellect into the theoretical, the practical and the productive becomes vain, but also the situation of Aristotle's important works, such as the *Politics* and the *Ethics*, in his system becomes ambiguous. However highly appreciated contemplation may be, we cannot afford to neglect the importance of practice as the basis of culture. As for production, Aristotle admitted it to a rank lower than that of practice, so that it is a view quite contrary to correct to substitute production for practice.

[53] K. Miki, *Gizyutu no Tetugaku* (Philosophy of Art) 72.

Practice is similar to contemplation in that they are both without
process and are actual *eo ipso*. However, not every actuality is contemplation, for though sensation is also an actuality it is by no means identical with contemplation. Thus, practice is only *a kind* of actuality
along with sensation and contemplation.

Thus far, we have seen that practice in the strict sense is actuality,
but not every actuality is practice. There remains the question whether
every production is movement, or there be any form of production
which is actuality. No doubt, in most cases production is movement,
but it is doubtful whether a performance which produces no result
other than act itself, e.g. playing on the harp or dancing is actuality or
movement. In the *Magna Moralia*, such an act is regarded to be not
only actuality, but also practice in the strict sense,[54] but in the *Ethica
Nicomachea* it is made rather as production.[55] Obviously, such production is actuality rather than movement, for it realizes a constant
form like seeing or thinking, and does not approach the result by degrees. In spite of such exceptions, generally speaking, practice is
actuality and production is movement, but the reverse is not true.
Practice is a species of actuality and production is one of movement;
they belong to different genera, but both originate in the human soul,
especially in its rational part. They are different from contemplation
in that they act upon the outside world and bring about some change in
it.

In short, practice and production are distinguished from each other
in that the former actualizes a form in itself, while the latter does not.
What is then the kind of conduct, in which such an objective end or
form is actualized? Aristotle endeavoured to explain it through reducing practice to actuality, but the relation of practice and actuality
was not distinct enough. He avoided presenting an example of practice
and merely contented himself with presenting examples of a more
universal concept of act or actuality. But, seeing or thinking is not
practice in the strict sense. To play on the harp or to dance is essentially
an artificial act rather than a practice. Eating and drinking as well as
curing, which are mentioned as examples of practical syllogism, belong
rather to production than to practice.[56] What remains as that which

---

[54] (*Mag. Mor.* I. 34. 1197 a 9); *Eth. Nic.* I. 6. 1098 a 11. Here the playing of
a harp is cited as an analogy of rational act or practice, but it is not mentioned
whether the playing of a harp is a practice or a production.

[55] *Eth. Nic.* II. 1. 1103 a 34 b 8.

[56] *Met.* IX. 6. 1048 b 25.

would seem most likely to be accounted a practice, is simply "living."[57] But life is the most indefinite of all concepts. It comprises all living activities, viz., vegetable functions such as nutrition and reproduction, animal functions such as sensation, imagination, desire and movement, as well as partly human and partly superhuman functions such as production, practice and pure contemplation. Therefore, life would be unsuitable as an example of practice. That Aristotle could not mention a suitable example of practice, was presumably due to the difficulty essential to the concept of practice.

N.B.

The attempt to illustrate practice in terms of a factual form always fails to catch the essence. For instance, an act like murder or money-making is denominated in terms of its result, viz., killing a man or accumulating money. In such a denomination, every act is in a process towards an end. As is often repeated, practice in the strict sense, i.e., the act which holds its form always in actuality, is the realization, not of a subjective purpose, but of an objective form, whereas the actualization of a subjective purpose is a voluntary act which is the basis of both production and practice. When a form other than the purpose is realized, the act is accidental to the actor's desire and is involuntary, much less rational. What is then the objective end which constitutes the essence of practice; the form which is to be realized without being in a process. That, we say, is not a mere fact, but a form of moral significance.[58] The factual form of a practice is the subjective end which is realized in a process, while the moral significance of it is actual in eternity and forms the objective end. One might suspect our theory of a Neo-Kantian misconstruction which brings into Aristotle the dualism of value and fact. It is true that Aristotle's distinction between value and fact was not so clear and consistently held as to leave no ambiguity. This is the reason why he felt some difficulty in exemplifying the concept of practice. The mistake of the *Magna Moralia*, which makes performance a practice, might have to some degree originated in Aristotle himself. The explicit distinction of value and fact must be looked for in Kant, or rather in Neo-Kantians. For all that, we feel no great difficulty in finding some examples in favour of our supposition. In *Eth. Nic.* II. 1. 1103 a 32, playing on the harp is classed under production, while practice *par excellence* is exemplified by just or temperate conduct. Such virtuous conduct is nothing but the content

---

[57] *Ibid.*

[58] *Eth. Nic.* VI. 5. 1140 b 6 f.; 71 1168 a 15–17; *Pol.* VII. 14. 1333 a 9–11; *Eth. Nic.* X. 6. 1176 b 2–9.

of εὖ ζῆν or living well as previously mentioned.[59] Therefore, living, which we said to be the most indefinite of all concepts, should be taken not as mere physiological activity, but as moral practice. Practice *par excellence* would be bravery, cowardice, generosity, niggardliness etc., rather than fighting, escaping, giving or taking. From the aspect of fact, every instance of conduct is in process and incomplete, but from the aspect of value, it is actual throughout the whole process; it is rather complete in the will,[60] as declared by the Sermon on the Mount, and as adopted by Kantian Ethics. The germ of this thought is found in the foregoing statement of Aristotle's and it is not difficult to add other examples of this kind, for instance, *Eth. Nic.* X. 6. 1176 b 6: "Now those activities are desirable in themselves from which nothing is sought beyond the activity. And of this nature virtuous actions are thought to be, for to do noble and good deeds is a thing desirable for its own sake."[61] Also in *Eth. Nic.* II. 3. 1105 a 26: "Again, the case of the arts and that of the virtues are not similar; for the products of the arts have their goodness in themselves, so that it is enough that they should have a certain character, but if the acts that are in accordance with the virtues have themselves a certain character it does not follow that they are done justly or temperately."[62]

These passages all mean that production is the actualization of a certain fact, while practice is rather the expression of the moral character of an agent. The former is the realization of a subjective end, while the latter is the expression of an objective form.

2. Comparison with Kant's Theory

Thus, production is movement, and practice is actuality, the one is the realization of a fact and the other the expression of a value. That which distinguishes actuality from motion must be an objective end

[59] *Part. An.* II. 10. 656 a 6; *Pol.* III. 9. 1281 a 2; cf. *Eth.* Fil. I. 1. 1214 a 31; 2. 1214 b 8, 16, 17; 3. 1215 a 10, 13; *Pol.* III. 6. 1278 b 23; 9. 1281 a 2; *Eth. Nic.* I. 10. 1170 b 27; I. 8. 1098 b 21; VI. 5. 1140 a 28; cf. n. 56.

[60] *Top.* VI. 12. 149 b 29 f.; IV. 5. 126 a 36; *Rhet.* I. 13. 1374 a 11–17.

[61] Cf. *Eth. Nic.* VI. 2. 1139 b 1 ff.; 5. 1140 b 7 ff. This self-endness of πρᾶξις has some resemblance with the autarchy of θεωρία and caused some interpreters to take it as Aristotle's confusion. But this is not really the case. The end of practice is *per se* good, while contemplation aims at no end at all, and consequently needs no means. Both practice and production needs the means to realize their ends, but the end of production is not *per se* good like that of practice; it is only useful for some other end. cf. n. 32, 33.

[62] *Eth. Nic.* VI. 10. 1134 a 20; 10. 1135 b 25; VI. 13. 1144 a 20.

rather than a subjective purpose. Further, in production, the objective end agrees with the subjective purpose, but in practice they do not agree as a rule. We have seen that a fact may be a subjective purpose as far as it forms the principle of voluntary act, and that production is distinguished from mere movement in that it is performed through a subjective purpose. For instance, natural movement such as the growth or the reproduction of animals and plants are the process in which their natural forms, as the objective ends, are gradually realized, without forming the subjective ends or the purposes. Animals neither take nourishment with the intention to sustain life, nor perform sexual acts in order to preserve their species. Whereas in human production, the end is also the purpose that guides the conduct, and in this respect, production is distinguished from mere movement. The consciousness of this purpose is just the cognition which was assumed to be necessary for a voluntary act.[63] In practice, on the contrary, the value which ought to be realized is usually an objective end instead of a subjective purpose. For while a subjective purpose is realized in a process, practice is, from its definition, a realization without any process.

Talking of subjective end and objective end, we cannot avoid to compare them with Kant's usage of these concepts. According to Kant, a subjective end is the content of any will, while an objective end is the moral ideal at which everyone should aim.[64] The agent to which the objective end belongs is an idealized rational being, which in spite of this idealization keeps its consciousness. According to Kant, the end is generally an image of presupposed result,[65] it is possible and inperfect, while Aristotle's concept of end is the complete actuality of a form, which is rather extrinsic to consciousness. Thus the end was conceived by Kant in psychological meaning unlike in ancient teleology including Aristotle's. And this gave a subjective trait to Kantian ethics, according to which the good will, as the necessary and sufficient condition of morality, is a will, which is determined mainly through the consciousness of duty. Whenever a will has any material ground, it is always egoistic and unmoral, no matter what merit belongs to the result.

Thus, for instance, the conduct of a soldier who fights to help his fatherland may be courageous and beautiful, yet it falls short of moral

---

[63] Ch. II. 4.

[64] Kant, *Gr. z. Met. d. Sitt. Cass.* IV. 287.

[65] Kant, *K. d. U. K. Einl.* IV. Cass. V. 249; *Weil nun der Begriff von einem Objekt, sofern er zugleich den Grund der Wirklichkeit dieses Objekts enthält, der Zweck*; *ibid.* 505; *Met. d. Sitt. Cass.* VII. 194; *Rel.* 3. 1. A. 2 *Anm. Cass.* VI. 144.

approbation, as far as it originates from passion or attachment. In order to be morally good, one ought to act not from passion but only from the command of reason.[66] The moral value of an act is determined only through the subjective form of resolution. This idea of Kant's, respectable as it was as an attempt to preserve the purity of morality, aroused much discontentment owing to its rigorous formalism.[67]

A really moral mind, on the contrary, is not concerned with duty, as Max Scheler argues,[68] for the consciousness of duty is nothing but the phenomenon of inward struggle with an immoral desire. A moral will should rather devote itself to realizing an end without regarding it a duty. For instance, true charity should be done, not with the consciousness of duty, but with the emotion of love and sympathy. Kant failed to catch the essence of morality because he confused the objective end with the subjective end. It is true that to a being whose will is not determined solely through practical rules, these rules appear as imperatives, but the consciousness of duty appears only when there is a struggle between the order and the desire. In other words, the consciousness of duty is the negative aspect of law, to which there must correspond a positive aspect. Where there is no positive desire to obey the law, there cannot be any resistance against unlawful desires,[69] and a heteronomic will would come to pass.[70] Kant himself found in humanity a principle of establishing a law. Even if moral conduct which is entirely free from the consciousness of duty is, as Kant assumed, impossible for a finite rational being,[71] it would be an exaggeration to say that only the consciousness of duty makes moral conduct possible. This is as false as to substitute a body with its shadow, or as to assume fever to be a condition of health for the reason that it is a kind of antitoxic function of a living body. The consciousness of duty is an appearance of the conflict between a moral wish and a natural desire. It is an accident, not the essence, of the law.

It is well known that Kant distinguished the goodness of moral intention from that of conduct, calling the value of the former morality, that of the latter legality, and admitting the superiority to the former.[72] We do not confuse legality with moral goodness in saying

[66] Kant, *K. d. p. V. Cass.* IV. 145–158.
[67] Scheler, *Formalismus* etc. 233.
[68] Scheler, *op. cit.* 196 ff,; N. Hartmann, *Ethik* 234.
[69] Scheler, *op. cit.* 67; Trendelenburg, *Beiträge* III. 196 ff.
[70] Kant, *Gr. z. Met. d. Sitt. Cass.* IV. 290 ff.
[71] Kant, *K. d. p. V.* I. I. 1. *Cass.* V. 37.
[72] *Ibid.* I. 1. 3. *Cass.* V. 80 ff.

good conduct to be the realization of an objective end or a valuable form. We assert that a genuine moral conduct is possible without making duty the subjective end, and that this is real morality.[73] When Kant defined legality as the character of the conduct which is objectively in accordance with the law, he implied in reality what we now call the satisfaction of a factual form. This only means that the external fact of a conduct conforms to the law which is *per se* an external norm and lacks in profundity,[74] whereas we assume that the objective end is not confined to mere fact and that it may as well be a value, so that a conduct which realizes such a value attains moral value without being constrained by the consciousness of duty. In such an ideal state of character, the subjective end of conduct being e.g., to help the fatherland, its objective end, i.e. its moral significance, say, bravery, is fulfilled without any consciousness of duty.[75]

The most remarkable example which characterizes the difference between the ethical thought of Aristotle and that of Kant, is the relation of temperance and continence. Both of these virtues consist in the moderation of nutritive and sexual appetites, temperance being the character in which appetites themselves are in conformity with the norms, while in continence the appetites that are excessive are suppressed and regulated by reason. Now, for Aristotle, temperance is better than continence; the latter finds its ideal in the former, which is the state of a wise man, who conforms to the law without any effort. Kant, on the contrary, who considered that the moral value of a character consists in freedom, assigned moral goodness to temperance acquired through freedom – which is nothing but continence in Aristotle's terminology – rather than to temperance as a blessed disposition. The essence of morality was found, not in the harmony of reason and emotion, but in the domination of the former over the latter.[76] Even Kant did not deny that a holy will without the consciousness of duty has objectively a higher value than continence, only he would not admit to it the moral value in the strict sense. Kant emphasized the finiteness of human nature, while Aristotle set up the ideal of man. This fundamental disagreement is, no doubt, brought about mainly through the Christianity that lies between them. But the difference is not so antagonistic as it appears:[77] the one is due to the practical attitude that

[73] Cf. Scheler, *op. cit.* 19 ff.
[74] Kant, *K. d. p. V.* I. 1. 3. *Cass.* V. 91.
[75] Scheler, *op. cit.* 32; Hartmann, *op. cit.* 241.
[76] Trendelenburg, *op. cit.* 209 ff.
[77] *Ibid.* 212.

aims at the improvement of character, while the other to the intellectual attitude to contemplate the ideal state of mind. In this respect, Aristotle's conception might be regarded as more theoretical than Kant's.

According to Kant, moral value is attached to the agent rather than to the object of conduct. The utility of conduct for society never guarantees its moral value. Morality is found mainly in the form of resolution. But, Kant did not explain how the subjective function of conduct itself is valuable.[78] In reality, this value is due to the social utility of conduct. It differs from the objective value of the conduct only through the constant efficacy that is premissed by the enduring intention of the agent. Fitting conduct without any firm foundation is accidental and transient in its effect, whereas the good will of a person is the constant principle of social welfare. It would be nonsense to talk about the moral value of conduct apart from its effects upon society.[79] Continence may be estimated more highly than temperance as far as the latter is considered to be accidentally favourable disposition. But what Aristotle calls σωφροσύνη is something more than a natural disposition. It is an ethical virtue, the essence of which is constituted with practical wisdom.

What must be borne in mind in reference to this is that virtue for Aristotle is not confined to the value of an object. Though the objective end of conduct does not always agree with the subjective end, they are closely related to each other. The objective end or the value-form depends upon the subjective end or the fact-form of conduct. When a man obeys a law in order to avoid the pain of punishment, the objective end of his conduct is negative in its value, viz., his conduct has no moral merit. On the contrary, when he fights in order to help the fatherland, his objective end is positive and praisable. The value of acts depends upon the objective value attached to the subjective ends; altruism is superior to egoism, because the public welfare is more valuable than the individual welfare.[80] But since morality is essentially a social value, it is imposed as a duty upon the individual who is apt to

---

[78] Kant, *Gr. z. Met. d. Sitt. Cass.* IV. 249 ff.

[79] *Rhet.* I. 9. 1366 a 36-b 11; 1366 b 36–1367 a 6; cf. *ibid.* 1367 b 5 *Eth. Nic.* I. 1. 1094 b 7; IX. 8. 1168 b 31; *Pol.* VII. 2. 1324 a 5; 15. 1334 a 11. But, Aristotle's theory is not altruistic. In a virtuous man, the love of self and the love of others coincide, cf. *Eth. Nic.* IX. 8. This results from the fact that the state is essentially a community to realize a good life. *Pol.* III. 6. 1278 b 16; 9. 1280 a 31; b 30; II. 2. 1261 a 25.

[80] *Eth. Nic.* I. 1. 1094 b 7–10.

turn against society. The objective end or the value of an act depends not only upon the matter but also upon the form of the subjective end. For instance, to avoid punishment is a sensible motive, and to help the fatherland is a rational motive, the one is determined by special interest, while the other is determined by universal welfare. We opposed to the undue depreciation of passionate conduct, but, passion is not sufficient for morality; what is more important is of course reason or intellect; the reason viz., which is not opposed to passion, but which is in accord with passion. In other words, the consciousness of duty being a negative feeling which presupposes an evil desire, conduct which is determined by it falls short of the highest value, but there is a rational and moral will which is not accompanied by the consciousness of duty. Such a beautiful agreement of reason and passion was just the ideal of Aristotle's ethics.

We have also said that a conduct which aims at some material effect may agree with a norm even when one does not make duty one's subjective end. Such a conduct is the realization of ethical virtue. Ethical virtue is the ἕξις or the habitual character, which is fostered through lawful conduct and does not need the consciousness of duty. It is rather the proof of moral accomplishment that one becomes free from the consciousness of duty.[81] The complete reality of ethical virtue is practical wisdom. But as far as this practical wisdom is not perfectly assimilated to one's personality and remains somewhat extraneous, one's conduct is accompanied by the consciousness of duty. As moral improvement advances, this consciousness changes into a positive estimation of moral conduct. Practical wisdom becomes purely one's own, or rather one becomes himself pure practical intellect. Thus considered, Aristotle was by no means inferior to Kant in appreciating the moral consciousness.

A remarkable correspondence is found between Kant's distinction of legality and morality on the one hand, and Aristotle's distinction between κατὰ λόγον and μετὰ λόγου on the other. According to Aristotle, neither is Socrates right in identifying virtue with practical wisdom, nor is the common opinion of his contemporaries right in defining virtue as a habit in accordance with right reason. They are right in assuming practical wisdom or reason to be necessary for ethical virtues, only the former goes too far in making practical wisdom identical with virtue, while the latter is insufficient in saying it "to be in accordance with reason;" Aristotle himself characterizes it with the expression

[81] *Eth. Nic.* I. 1. 1099 a 7–21; II. 2. 1104 b 3–12.

"habit accompanied by reason."[82] κατὰ λόγον, "in accordance with reason," means conforming to law, while μετὰ λόγου, "accompanied by reason," applies to the expression of a rational character which is acquired completely.[83] This interpretation is supported by the following statement in *Eth. Nic.* VI. 12. 1144 a 13:[84] "As we say that some people who do just acts are not necessarily just, i.e., those wo do the acts ordained by the laws either unwillingly or owing to ignorance or for some other reason and not for the sake of the acts themselves (though, to be sure, they do what they should and all the things that the good man ought), so is it, it seems, that in order to be good one must be in a certain state when one does the several acts, i.e., one must do them as a result of will and for the sake of the acts themselves."

Thus, an act which is *per se* good was considered even by Aristotle to be an act which is done with moral consciousness, though not from the consciousness of duty. What makes an act good is a good will, and what makes a will good is a right desire and a right deliberation. But a right desire is fundamentally rational and may be acquired only through practical wisdom. Consequently, what makes a will good is after all reduced to right estimation. The only difference between the two

[82] *Eth. Nic.* VI. 13. 1144 b 17–27.
[83] *In Mag. Mor.* I. 35. 1198 a 15 ff. κατὰ λόγον is distinguished from μετὰ λόγου in that the one signifies mere external legitimateness, while the other means to be accompanied by a right purpose and the knowledge of the good. This seems to be a right interpretation made in reference to the present statement (1144 a 13–20). But Walter is opposed to this interpretation, because he wants to refer this distinction to Aristotle's criticism of Socrates who identified virtue with λόγος. According to Walter, the interpretation in the *Mag. Mor.* would lead to the supposition that Socrates identified mere external legitimateness with virtue, which, however, is contrary to reality. But it is evident from the context that the distinction of κατὰ λόγον from μετὰ λόγου has no direct reference to Socrates's identification of knowledge and virtue. Aristotle's theory to make virtue μετὰ λόγου is an attempt to reconcile the rigid opposition between the view of Socrates and the common opinion of his contemporaries which identified virtue with external legitimateness. Walter attaches much importance to the distinction of κατὰ and μετὰ spending a great part of his study on this point. (cf. *op. cit.* 84–138). Though this part comprises most successful arguments in his work, they cannot reject the interpretation of *Magna Moralia* after all. J. A. Smith (*Classical Quarterly* 1920) suggests to read the sentence as "It is not only the disposition which accords with (κατὰ) reason, but also the disposition which accompanies (μετὰ) reason that is virtue." His suggestion is unacceptable.
[84] *Eth. Nic.* VI. 13. 1144 a 13 ff. We treat λόγος and νόμος as synonymous on the basis of Aristotle's statement that law is reason without desire. cf. *Pol.* III. 16. 1287 a 32; 15. 1286 a 19; *Eth. Nic.* X. 10. 1180 a 20; V. 10. 1134 a 35; *Pol.* VII. 14. 1333 a 6 ff.

theories is that in Aristotle the estimation is accompanied by positive value-feeling, while in Kant, it is negative.

How much Aristotle attaches importance to rational will, we can see in what he says about courage. Conduct through mere anger he does not admit to be courageous, and real courage he assumes to consist in the will,[85] which aims at moral goodness and endures the pain of death.[86] Consequently, an act may be objectively useful to society, and have a positive value, yet it lacks in moral value if it is done through passion. To be morally good, one must act through practical consideration and resolution. Needless to say, this consideration is not the calculation of interest or the mere searching for a factual means, but the calculation of moral values – as N. Hartmann puts it: "The value of the fact which one endeavours to realize, is always selected through a moral value-feeling."[87]

It is true that the consciousness of duty presupposes apprehension of value along with a worthless desire, but apprehension of value is not identical with the consciousness of duty. One often understands law as a duty, to be sure, but this fact of human nature should be distinguished from ideal morality. However rare and difficult the will may be, which is determined through the positive apprehension of value, without this apprehension being accompanied by the consciousness of duty, it is none the less the ideal state of moral personality. And morality is obviously a system of ideals, not the mere facts, of human nature. The antagonism of reason and sensibility is a fact of human nature, not its ideal. To act through the consciousness of duty is not itself a duty. It is more desirable, if not a duty for man to get rid of the consciousness of duty, for this sort of consciousness is an appearance of morally inferior personality, and withdraws as moral improvement proceeds. The ideal of moral freedom is the harmonious state of reason and passion, it is the complete rationalization of one's desires. Moral system always imposes upon us a new duty, but moral accomplishment consists in changing this duty to a feeling of happiness. Not the antagonism between reason and feeling, but precisely their harmony, is the measure of moral progress.

How is it then possible to have apprehension of value without pre-

---

[85] *Eth. Nic.* II. 3. 1105 a 31–33; 4. 1106 a 3; V. 10. 1136 a 3 f.; VI. 13. 1144 a 19 f.; *Eth. Eud.* II. 7. 1223 a 21 ff.; III. 1. 1230 a 27 ff.; *Rhet.* I. 9. 1367 b 21.

[86] *Eth. Nic.* III. 10. 1115 b 11–13; 11. 1116 a 28; b 30; 15. 1119 b 16; IV. 2. 1120 a 23; 4. 1122 b 8; VI. 13. 1144 a 13 ff.; X. 10. 1180 a 6; cf. *ibid.* I. 4. 1166 a 14 ff.; *Pol.* VIII. 13. 1332 a 22.

supposing base desires? Reason or consciousness grows in order to regulate the conflict of motives, and apprehension of value seems to be impossible if there be no opposition between value and its opposite. No doubt, consciousness or reason grows from the necessity of choosing the most effective act out of many possibilities.[88] But the opposition which causes consciousness is not always the opposition between value and unvalue, but may be an opposition between positive values.[89] When we look back from the decision, the chosen value may seem to relate to the rejected one as positive to negative, still they may be both positive values in themselves. One might maintain that if practical reason presupposes the opposition of values, the norm must appear as a duty; for the lower value will exhibit itself as an irrational attachment, against which the higher value will claim itself as a duty; there will not be in truth an absolute value or unvalue, but every value will appear either positive or negative in each reference. Even if we admit these arguments, moral value needs not be founded upon the consciousness of duty. For, even if the conflict between value and unvalue be inevitable, it does not follow of necessity that the agent takes the part of the latter. Our conscious experience may not exhibit a complete harmony but requires effort and self-restraint; yet there is all the difference in the world between obeying duty with pain and following law with pleasure. Moral accomplishment is the transition from the state of mind in which moral value commands as a duty to that in which one positively desires the value. The rigid opposition between reason and desire passes into harmony; such a harmony is found in the character of wise men, the ideal state of morality.

The moral value of a conduct is sustained by the calculation of values. This is the reason why an act motivated by passion is inferior to one which is accompanied by rational insight into value. Passionate conduct may conform to the norm, but only by good luck and neither constantly nor universally. What ensures constant morality is a steady character regulated by reason.[90] In order to sail a rough sea we need an exact compass instead of impetuous sailors. One who acts with passion, may succeed through a lucky chance, but he cannot end well. There are too many tragedies of passionate persons who erred from righteousness through personal feeling. Solon said that man's fortune cannot be

[87] N. Hartmann, *op. cit.* II. 1. *Kap.* 27.
[88] Cf. Bergson, *L'évolution créatrice* 115 ff.
[89] Cf. Hartmann, *op. cit.* 339 ff.
[90] *Eth. Nic.* III. 10. 1115 b 19 ff.; 11. 1116 b 23 ff.; 1117 a 4–9.

known until his death. But Aristotle does not agree with him, seeing in this view a confusion of happiness and fortune. He rather assumes a happy man to be one who has a constant character such that he can endure even an unfortunate fate with confidence.[91] It is a wise man whose faculties are all regulated by reason and keep a complete harmony.

3. The Relation Between Practice and Production

Practice and production were distinguished in that the former is the realization of a moral value as an objective end, and the latter that of a factual form as a subjective end. But the objective end is not quite irrelevant to the subjective end, for even in Aristotle, good will is *sine qua non* of moral excellence, though what is required for good will is not consciousness of duty, but insight into value. According to Aristotle, what the will aims at, is not an abstract good, but a good thing. He repeatedly rejects Plato's theory of ideas, which admits the idea of the good as abstract goodness and explains thereby not only moral conduct, but also the whole universe. The end of conduct is regarded by Aristotle to be happiness as the highest valuable object instead of value itself, but it does not rule out the possibility of making moral value itself the subjective end.[92] It is possible to wish to be a good man or to do a virtuous act. Aristotle himself uses the word προαίρεσις not only in the sense of a concrete particular will, but sometimes also in the sense of a general intention.[93] Still, the value as the subjective end of an act, is not identical with the value as its objective end. To intend a moral value is the beginning of practice, not its finale. Just as a youth who sets his mind on learning is not yet a scholar, so also a man who wishes to be good is not yet accomplished as a good man. A continent man, for instance, is not yet temperate in spite of his good intention. As for an incontinent man, he is far from being virtuous for all his good intention.[94] Morality as a subjective end may be realized only in process. By making moral accomplishment our subjective end, we become students of virtue who proceed to the end by degrees. As an objective end, moral significance is given at once in its perfect form, but as a subjective end, it is the ideal which should be pursued and realized

[91] *Eth. Nic.* I. 11. 1100 a 10– b 11.
[92] Cf. Hartmann, *op. cit.* 237 f.
[93] Cf. Teichmüller, *op. cit.* 96 f.
[94] *Eth. Nic.* VII. 2. 1145 b 12–14; 4. 1146 b 22 VII. 9. 1151 a 20–24; *Eth. Nic.* III. 7. 1114 a 13–15.

gradually. Hence morality is incarnate in the ideal image of a wise man. The progress towards this idea is, strictly speaking, not practice, but production, the art that leads one to this end being education or politics. Of course, the process of moral exercise consists in individual practices, and the activities of teachers and statesmen are also in a sense practices. For all that, as far as they aim at the formation of character or the accomplishment of personality, their end is attained only in the result, and according to our previous definition, the process must be called production rather than practice.

We must admit that our explanation as to the distinction between πρᾶξις and ποίησις is somewhat excessively clean-cut. But in truth, Aristotle is not clear enough about the distinction of these concepts. Hence it is not of necessity the fault of historians, that they failed to explain the essence of these concepts and merely repeated the formal distinction between them. This is a limit unavoidable for those who are determined to remain perfectly faithful to Aristotle's text. But our wish of clarification did not allow us to stop on the same level. We only hope that our interpretation did not commit a very serious distortion of Aristotle's implication.

What remains for us to consider is the relation between practice and production. But, regrettable as it is, Aristotle's reference to this point is extremely scanty. As Teichmüller noticed,[95] here is an example of Aristotle's fault to be detailed in analysis and rough in synthesis. From whatever reasons this might have resulted, all we can do is to make some conjecture as modestly as possible.[96] In the first place, practice as well as production brings about some change in the objects which are variable in many points. Now that production is the realization of an effect, and practice that of moral value, practice must be accompanied by production, for the realization of a value presupposes the actualization of a fact. We have admired the Sermon on the Mount as showing the essential of practice. But taking practice *in concreto*, we must point out the exaggeration contained in the Sermon, for a mere desire or will is not yet a real practice. As far as desire involves the effort towards realization, it must needs be distinguished from theoretical thinking or imagination, but production or ποίησις *par excellence* is not any act whatever which produces some change in the outside world. Instinctive or reflexive act in man and animal must be excluded from

---

[95] Teichmüller, *op. cit.* 337.
[96] Some suggestion may be found in *Pol.* III. 4. 1278 a 9 18. 1288 a 38; VII. 14 1333 a 11; *Eth. Nic.* V. 5. 1130 b 29 etc. cf. also ch. V.

production in the strict sense, which is the realization of art, i.e. productive habit accompanied by reason.[97] If, therefore, there be no practice which is not accompanied by production, it will follow that every act which has moral significance must be performed through art. But this is not really the case, because there may be some conduct which is important from a moral point of view, though it is not performed through art. Similarly, it is not the case that every production would be practice or should be accompanied by practice, for example, when a solitary artist is absorbed in his work. Even in such a case, his way of living may have some moral significance, but at least it is certain that the moral significance of his act does not proportionate to the technical significance of the same act.

Let this suffice for the explanation of the essence and the interrelation of practice and production. In short, they are both acts guided by practical intellect in a wider sense; the construction of which will be investigated in the next chapter. Now, the last but not the least important question is how practice and production are related to theoretical thinking. Aristotle admitted on the one hand, that practice aims at nothing but the act itself, and has value in itself, stated on the other hand that ethical virtues and political activities are the foundations of pure theoretical thinking or contemplation, the latter of which is the highest activity of man, and that politics is like the service of a steward, who guarantees the leisure of his master to enable him to be occupied with more noble engagements.[98] Seeing thus, ethical virtue and practice would be the means for contemplation. It is not unreasonable therefore that some one should find an apparent discrepancy between the two statements. Teichmüller actually pointed it out as the fatal contradiction of Aristotle's dualism.[99]

But, is it really so fatal a contradiction? Does it really amount to reducing practice into production, if it refers to contemplation in this manner? This supposition implies the same conclusion that we rejected above, viz., the assumption that practice without production is mere contemplation. But what must be borne in mind is that the end which divided practice and production was an objective end instead of a subjective purpose. Consequently, both practice and production may be regarded either as end or as means. It is not a contradiction either to find the objective end of production in the result and to aim at the

[97] *Eth. Nic.* VI. 4. 1140 a 7.
[98] *Pol.* I. 7. 1255 b 20–37; *Eth. Nic.* VI. 13. 1145 a 6–11.
[99] Teichmüller, *op. cit.* 331 f.

process of production subjectively, or to find the objective end of practice in itself and to make the practice subjectively the means for another practice. For instance, the act of a sculptor, who makes a statue for its own sake, is a pure production, while the act of a statesman who makes a public establishment for a far-reaching aim, is a practice *par excellence*. A practice, though being in a sense a self-end, may be none the less a means for another practice or contemplation.

However, the above suspicion does not dissolve, even if we take the end in the objective sense. Practice will not be the end itself, if the value of it depends upon that of contemplation, and if it is valuable as far as it makes contemplation possible. Still, practice and ethical virtues may subserve theoretical virtues without losing their own merits;[100] in other words, their means-value is compatible with their self-value, every value has its place in a scale without losing its independency. In this respect, the *highest value* should be distinguished from the *most universal value*. Contemplation is the highest value instead of the most universal; the most universal value of human life is happiness, rather than contemplation. Aristotle neither identified happiness with contemplation, as is often mistakenly supposed, nor did he refuse other activities the claim to constitute the most complete happiness. Happiness is what everyone desires, so it is indefinite in its contents and varies for each man. Moral characters differentiate themselves through this variety;[101] some feel happiness in bodily pleasure, some in the accumulation of wealth, and some in social fame; none of these is wrong *a priori*. But it was the character which finds happiness in contemplation, that was admitted to be the highest by Aristotle, and he really considered that this action affords us the most excellent happiness, both in quality and in quantity. Happiness is not found exclusively in contemplation, but may be found either in moral practice, in social fame, bodily pleasure or in wealth. Hence it is praisable to find happiness in contemplation. If on the contrary, every value subsists only as the means for contemplation, there would be no real difference among the values, except the difference of direct and indirect. Aristotle not only admitted various types of happiness, but also required for complete happiness to be composed of various kinds of satisfaction more or less valuable,[102] since even a saint, being man and animal,

---

[100] *Top.* VI. 12. 149 b 35 f.

[101] Cf. n. 81.

[102] Cf. *Eth. Nic.* X. 8. 1178 a 32; *Rhet.* I. 5. 1360 b 20 ff. This relation between contemplation as the highest happiness and the synthesis of values as complete

cannot live without social or natural goods. These lower ways of living and their concomitant values are subordinate to contemplation as the highest value, to be sure. Yet, contemplation does not rule out inferior ways of living. It is not like a tyrant who makes everyone a slave, but like a philosopher-king who allows every one his liberty and allows him a life suitable to his worth.

Contemplation, practice and production are different in their value; contemplation is the most self-sufficient, next comes practice, and production is the last. To be self-sufficient does not mean, as it might seem to do, not to presuppose the others, but to be desirable by itself. Its realization surely requires other lower conditions to be fulfilled. Practice and production are the activities of the irrational part of the soul, which is dominated by the rational part. They are irrational on the one hand, but rational on the other. In our inquiry into the correspondence of the rational and irrational parts of the soul in practice, the next problem must be the analysis of the rational part in general.

happiness is similar to the relation between *das oberste Gut* and *das höchste Gut* in Kant. cf. *K. d. p. V.* I. II. 2. *Cass.* V. 120. cf. n. 32, 33, 61.

CHAPTER IV

THE STRUCTURE OF INTELLECT

1. The classification of intellect

The rational part of the soul as well as the irrational part, is subdivided into two parts respectively. The rational part in the strict
sense engages in pure self-sufficient thinking, while that in the secondary sense administers the irrational part. The former act is theoretical knowledge, and the latter practical. They are distinguished
either from the metaphysical or the ethical point of view. But, the
denomination of the whole rational part or its function in general is not
definite. None of the concepts such as νοῦς, διάνοια, λογισμός, ἐπιστήμη,
or βούλευσις is the strictly generic term; they are only occasionally
used more or less in a representative sense, either in the form of noun
or of adjective.[1] Among them, νοῦς, διάνοια and ἐπιστήμη are more
comprehensive than others, while λογισμός and βούλευσις are usually
confined to practical thinking. νοῦς is esteemed not only as the highest
part of the human soul, but also as the essence of divine being, which is
the divine reason or the so-called *intellectus agens*. This is a traditional
concept that can be traced back to Thales, Anaxagoras, or even more
remote ages. But remarkable as it is, Aristotle sometimes means by it
a faculty of theoretical intellect, or presumably, even a faculty of
practical intellect. We must therefore be careful not to confuse these
different usages.

διάνοια is sometimes synonymous with νοῦς in a wider sense, for
instance, the virtues of the desiring part is called ἠθικαὶ ἀρεταί and

---

[1] Places where these concepts are used in the general sense are as follows:
νοῦς: *De An.* II. 2. 413 a 24; 3. 414 b 18; III. 10. 433 a 13; b 4; *Eth. Nic.* X. 7.
1177 a 12, 18; *Phys.* VII. 3. 247 a 28; (*Mag. Mor.* I. 1. 1182 a 18, 20); *Eth. Nic.*
I. 4. 1166 a 17. λογισμός: *De An.* II. 3. 415 a 8; III. 9. 432 a 26. ἐπιστήμη: *Eth.
Nic.* VI. 2. 1139 a 12; (*Mag. Mor.* I. 35. 1196 b 17); *De An.* III. 8. 431 b 27; 11.
434 a 16; II. 2. 414 a 10. δόξα: *De An.* II. 2. 413 b 30. cf. *Eth. Nic.* VI. 5. 1140 b
26. Walter. βούλευσις: *De An.* III. 10. 433 b 4.

those of the rational part, comprehending both the theoretical and the practical, are generally called διανοητικαὶ ἀρεταί.[2] These two kinds of rational part are provisionally distinguished in the *Nicomachean Ethics* as the ἐπιστημονική and the λογιστική.[3] The ἐπιστημονική is also called the θεωρητική,[4] to which belong ἐπιστήμη and νοῦς, both in a narrower sense, as well as σοφία, which is the synthesis of the two.[5] On the other hand, the λογιστική or βουλευτική [6] means the practical intellect in a wider sense, which involves φρόνησις and τέχνη.[7] Hence it is said that the function of intellect is generally the cognition of the truth, and that the chief kinds of this cognition are τέχνη, ἐπιστήμη, φρόνησις, σοφία and νοῦς.[8]

But ἐπιστήμη, which is just mentioned as a kind of theoretical intellect, is not seldom used as a generic concept in place of διάνοια or νοῦς. In the *Metaphysics*, for instance, it is divided into the θεωρητική, the πρακτική and the ποιητική.[9]

[2] *Eth. Nic.* I. 13. 1103 a 5, 6. II. 1. 1103 a 14; *Eth. Eud.* II. 1. 1220 a 5; 4. 1221 b 29.

[3] *Eth. Nic.* VI. 2. 1139 a 12.

[4] *Met.* VI. 1. 1025 b 25.

[5] *Eth. Nic.* VI. 3, 6, 7.

[6] *Eth. Nic.* VI. 2. 1139 a 12; *Eth. Eud.* II. 10. 1226 a 26; (*Mag. Mor.* I. 35. 1196 b 16).

[7] *Met.* VI. 1. 1025 b 21 ff.; *Top.* VI. 6. 145 a 16; *Met.* IX. 2. 1046 b 3; XI. 7. 1064 a 1; *Eth. Eud.* I. 5. 1216 b 17; I. 1. 982 a 1; b 11; *Eth. Nic.* VI. 2. 1139 b 1; a 27.

[8] *Eth. Nic.* VI. 3. 1139 b 15. Of course, cognition is not confined to these five kinds; in *De An.* III. 3. 428 a 4, αἴσθησις, δόξα, ἐπιστήμη and νοῦς are enumerated as faculties which discriminate true and false. Amongst them, ἐπιστήμη and νοῦς never commit a fault. Walter considers that intellect is not only the faculty of cognition, but also the principle of conduct as well. (*op. cit.* 242 f.) But intellect does recognize even when it acts as the principle of practice. Aristotle affirms distinctly that true and false are homogeneous with good and bad (*De An.* III. 7), and that affirmation and denial correspond to pursuit and avoidance (*Eth. Nic.* VI. 2. 1139 a 21 ff.). But this does not amount to saying that practical intellect performs another act than cognition. Practical intellect determines conduct and will in terms of cognition.

[9] *Eth. Nic.* VI. 2. 1130 a 27; *Part. An.* I. 1. 640 a 2; *Met.* IX. 7. 1064 a 17; I. 1. 982 a 1. cf. *Top.* VI. 6. 145 a 15: *De An.* III. 4. 430 a 4. Reason is also divided into the theoretical, the practical, and the productive. But while the phrases νοῦς θεωρητικός and νοῦς πρακτικός are used, though not frequently, νοῦς ποιητικός is never used, presumably because νοῦς is restricted to intellectual intuition. Walter's opinion about this point is probably right. According to him, it is merely accidental that the concept νοῦς ποιητικός does not appear in the *Ethics*, while Aristotle seems to have intentionally avoided this expression in the *De Anima* and substituted for it such a negative one as impassive or unmixed reason, presumably to avoid confusion with the νοῦς ποιητικός or productive reason that is coordinate with practical reason. Alexander of Aphrodisias's

The object of theoretical knowledge is what is eternal and immovable, or what is movable, yet possessing the principle of motion in itself.
The knowledge which is concerned with the former is metaphysics,
that which is concerned with the latter, natural sciences.[10] The object
of practical or productive knowledge is movable, but does not possess
the principle of motion in itself, so that it may be moved and changed
by human intellect.[11]

Since Aristotle does not go into detail about practical or productive
knowledge, it is not evident whether they include the practical sciences
such as the *Politics*, the *Ethics*, the *Poetics*, and the *Rhetoric*, which
compose his works, or are confined to somewhat more serviceable
thinking. We must, at any rate, distinguish this generic sense of ἐπιστήμη
from the above mentioned special one, in which it is coordinate with
reason and wisdom. ἐπιστήμη as the generic concept implies knowledge
in general rather than science. If we take it for a species of theoretical
knowledge, we should also admit, in accordance with the foregoing
statement of Aristotle's that ἐπιστήμη πρακτική is practical theoretical
knowledge. But it would be quite absurd for practical knowledge and
productive knowledge to be theoretical, because knowledge is practical
or productive just as far as it is not theoretical.

For all that, we must be confronted with a powerful objection to the
effect that practical knowledge or productive knowledge should mean
the theory of practical or productive affairs, such as the *Ethics*, or the
Poetics, rather than a direct principle of action. These kinds of knowledge are considered to be theoretical as far as they are reflective and
universal, though their objects are practical. Zeller,[12] for example, on
the ground that Aristotle calls theoretical philosophy what he should
have called theoretical knowledge,[13] takes the ἐπιστήμη, which is
divided into the theoretical the practical, and the productive, to be
science rather than knowledge. Such sciences are, he argues, different
from φρόνησις and τέχνη, which are merely immediate faculties of
practice and production. We can find no such concept as practical
philosophy or productive philosophy,[14] yet Aristotle really means

usage of the words νοῦς ποιητικός in this sense appears to be faithful to Aristotle's thought; for Aristotle νοῦς ποιητικός is synonymous with art. (Walter,
op. cit. 276–282).
10 *Met.* XI. 7. 1064 a 16 ff.
11 *Ibid.*
12 Zeller, *op. cit.* 177 n. 5.
13 *Met.* VI. 1. 1026 a 18.
14 In Bonitz's *Index Arist.* 821 a 36 ff., φιλοσοφία is divided into theoretical,

by the concept of "philosophy concerning human affairs"[15] or
"political philosophy,"[16] ethics and politics, and defines φιλοσοφία as a
theoretical knowledge or a knowledge which aims at truth.[17] Still, if
philosophy is a kind of theoretical knowledge, θεωρητική φιλοσοφία
would no longer be equal to θεωρητική ἐπιστήμη. If, on the contrary, we
identify such ἐπιστήμη with φιλοσοφία, it would follow that philosophy
is not necessarily theoretical, but merely synonymous with knowledge.
The verb φιλοσοφεῖν is not only confined to the strict sense of philosophical contemplation,[18] but is also sometimes used in a wider sense
to express thinking in general [19] in the same way as ἐπιστήμη, and still
holds a somewhat universal character as compared with practice.[20]
This is much more the case with the noun φιλοσοφία, which seems to
indicate universal thinking rather than thinking without qualification.
At any rate, ἐπιστήμη and φιλοσοφία, being theoretical knowledge, are
concerned only with necessary being or with nature.

Julius Walter, though he does not, like Zeller, identify the classification of knowledge with that of science or philosophy, regards the
contents of the *Ethics*, the *Politics* and the *Poetics*, which constitute
the system of Aristotle, as theoretical knowledge. He admits that
ἐπιστήμη and φιλοσοφία, as generic terms, implied in antiquity, including Aristotle, all faculties of intellect, their range not being limited
to science and philosophy in the strict sense[21], and he notes that what
Aristotle himself gives as exemplifying theoretical ἐπιστήμη is confined
to physics, mathematics and metaphysics, – excluding ethics and
poetics.[22] He assumes, nevertheless, that ethics is obviously different
from practical wisdom, and poetics from art, the former in each case
being theoretical, the latter practical.[23] Thus, according to Walter,
Aristotle's *Ethics* and *Poetics* were, in their contents, the product of

practical and productive, whereas in fact, the division in the statement there
mentioned is either that of διάνοια (e.g. *Met*. VI. 1. 1025 b 25) or of ἐπιστήμη (e.g.
Met. XI. 7. 1064 b 1–14).

[15] *Eth. Nic*. X. 10. 1181 b 15.
[16] *Pol*. III. 12. 1282 b 23.
[17] *Met*. II. 1. 993 b 20.
[18] *Met*. I. 2. 982 b 13; IV. 2. 1004 b 9; 5. 1009 b 37; *Eth. Nic*. II. 3. 1105 b 13,
19; *Pol*. I. 7. 1255 b 37; *De Cael*. III. 1. 298 b 12.
[19] *Pol*. VII. 11. 1331 a 14–17; *De Divin*. I. 463 a 4–7; *Met*. I. 3. 983 a 33–b 3;
Pol. II. 10. 1272 a 22–24; *Pol*. VII. 10. 1329 a 40–b 2; *Pol*. VIII. 5. 1340 b 5 f.;
Eth. Nic. VII 12. 1152 b 1 f.
[20] *Pol*. III. 8. 1279 b 12–15.
[21] Walter, *op. cit*. 538, 542.
[22] *Ibid*. 543.
[23] *Ibid*. 540 f.

theoretical intellect, yet in their form, were lacking in independency
and attributed rather to practical or productive faculty such as practical wisdom or art.[24] These interpretations of Zeller's and Walter's
which reduced the *Ethics* and the *Poetics* to theoretical knowledge, were
fiercely attacked by Teichmüller.[25]

Teichmüller proves the homogeneity of practical philosophy and
practical wisdom from the following four grounds. In the first place,
ethics and politics are concerned with the same objects as practical
wisdom is; and likewise with poetics and art. Though ethics and politics are different in that the one is concerned with the happiness and
virtues of individuals, and the other with those of nations or states,[26]
they are similarly concerned with human conduct, and both are the
knowledge which regulates conduct with rules, bringing about human
good.[27] Ethical and political knowledge contributes much to life, just
as the archer who aims at a mark may hit upon what is right.[28] But
practical wisdom is also concerned with human good and evil,[29] aims
at the good of human conduct,[30] and regulates or employs other practical faculties for this end.[31] In other words, practical wisdom recognizes the worth in general of life, and is not a mere subordinate faculty
of practice. Ethical and political knowledges are intellectual as well as
practical and their end is to serve the conduct[32], so that the universal
knowledge relevant to them must be applied to individual cases. Thus,
besides the universal knowledge as to what is the best constitution and
what is the best legislation for each nation, there must be special
knowledge, how a state can be governed.[33] Practical wisdom too must
involve universal knowledge and its application. If it is lacking in
universal knowledge, it will be unable to indicate an infallible direction for our life, though it may be a practical power of lower grade.

In the second place, politics and ethics have the same content as
practical wisdom. Since practical wisdom exhibits itself in consideration, each decision forms a practical inference. But, the minor premise of this practical inference being indefinite in each case, its essen-

[24] *Ibid.* 548 f.
[25] Teichmüller, *Neue Studien zur Geschichte der Begriffe* III. 12–35.
[26] *Eth. Nic.* I. 1. 1094 b 7.
[27] *Ibid.* b 4.
[28] *Ibid.* a 22.
[29] *Eth. Nic.* IV. 5. 1140 b 4.
[30] *Eth. Nic.* IV. 10. 1142 b 22.
[31] *Eth. Nic.* IV. 5. 1140 a 25.
[32] *Eth. Nic.* IV. 7. 1141 b 3.
[33] *Pol.* IV. 1. 1288 b 25; 1288 b 35.

tial contents must be determined by the major premise. This major premiss exhibits the constant state of practical wisdom, and characterizes a man of wisdom as distinguished from a clever man or a mediocrity. Practical wisdom shows us the highest good. Now the practical good exists not in actuality, but only in potentiality, as the end which is aimed at. For this end, a man of practical wisdom must recognize every means. This is the same knowledge as forms the contents of ethics, so the contents of ethics and politics are contained in the activity of practical wisdom. One would exhibit a gross ignorance concerning Aristotle's thought, by reducing ethics and politics to some knowledge other than practical wisdom. It is because moderns mistakenly suppose knowledge and insight to be objectively found in books, that they are led to assume such a science of practice. Being a man of antiquity, Aristotle did not know any ἠθική or πολιτική that were not at once the virtue of φρόνησις. Thus, practical wisdom must needs involve knowledge of the individual as well as of the universal.[34]

In the third place, ethics and politics have the same method as practical wisdom. Unlike theoretical science, these practical sciences are wanting in exact necessity and must be content with mere probability. Richness and courage may sometimes result in harm, hence the belief arises that moral law is merely conventional and not by nature.[35] Further, since ethics and politics are not self-sufficient, but aim at some sort of conduct, it would be vain only to know. This is also the reason why these sciences cannot attain a strict exactitude.[36] For, the good as the object of practical knowledge is not so definite as the object of theoretical sciences; it must be determined in accordance with the given case and with the given individual. To determine the right resolution requires not only a major premiss, but also a minor one. Hence even the major premiss itself is not constant, but suffers modifications in each case.[37] Consequently, ethics and politics have no more exactitude than practical wisdom has. In order to gain universal knowledge, one must have sufficient experience, moral will, continence, and virtue. Only under these conditions are political and ethical theories really appreciated. The word σωφροσυνή means to σῳζεῖν the φρόνησις, i.e., to preserve practical wisdom. Self-indulgence does not corrupt mathematical insight, but ruins moral assurance,[38] because we

[34] *Eth. Nic.* VI. 5. 1140 a 27.
[35] *Eth. Nic.* I. 1. 1094 b 12.
[36] *Eth. Nic.* II. 2. 1103 b 26.
[37] *Eth. Nic.* II. 2. 1103 b 34.
[38] *Eth. Nic.* VI. 5. 1140 b 11.

may preserve or lose practical wisdom owing to pleasure or pain. Young men have only little experience, so they can neither appreciate and use the ideas in a book, nor have moral wisdom. A boy may be a mathematician, but not a wise man:[39] he may speak about morality but is unable to have a firm belief in what is right.

In the fourth place, and finally, Aristotle himself uses πολιτική and φρόνησις in the same meaning. He says in the *Ethica Nicomachea*:[40] "Politics and practical wisdom are the same state of mind, but their essence is not the same. Of the wisdom concerned with the city, the practical wisdom which plays a controlling part is legislative wisdom, while that which is related to this as particular to their universal is known by the general name politics; this has to do with action and deliberation, for a decree is a thing to be carried out in the form of an individual act. This is why the exponents of this art are alone said to "take part in politics," for these alone 'do things" as manual labourers "do things." Practical wisdom also is identified especially with that form of it, which is concerned with a man himself – with the individual: and this is known by the general name of "practical wisdom;" of the other kinds, one is called household management, another legislation, the third politics, and of the latter, one part is called deliberative and the other judicial." This may be illustrated as follows:

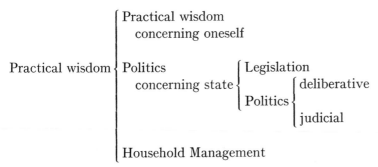

Aristotle adopting this usual terminology as technical terms, calls attention to the fact that they are all founded upon the same habit, and censures the man who pretends to practical wisdom without the knowledge of politics and household management. He calls ethical theory politics, in so far as practical wisdom requires political wisdom.[41] There is no principle of politics and ethics other than πολιτική or φρόνησις

[39] *Eth. Nic.* I. 1. 1095 a 2; VI. 9. 1142 a 11.
[40] *Eth. Nic.* VI. 8. 1141 b 23.
[41] *Ibid.* 1141 b 25.

as Walter presumed; these two kinds of science are regarded by Aristotle as to be studied just for the sake of conduct.[42] If, as Walter holds, ethics is a theoretical science, and πολιτική, as the virtue of the statesmen, aims at individual act, Aristotle would never have identified the problems and requirements of ethics with those of a practical statesman. In reality, Aristotle says that a true statesman is thought to endeavour especially for virtue, because he wants to make citizens good and obedient to laws.[43] Further, he says, the study of ethics is the work of πολιτική[44] and the problem of ethics requires more knowledge of the soul than medical science does; accordingly, a statesman also requires the study of the soul for practical purposes. Further precision, he adds, may be attained by strict theoretical psychology, but exceeds the area of ethical research. In the first half of this statement, Aristotle states the necessity of psychological study for a statesman, and in the second half, he states that precise psychological study is beyond ethical research.[45] There exists therefore no essential differrence between the knowledge of a statesman and the knowledge of ethics. Of course, a real statesman does not always possess ethical knowledge, Aristotle only indicates the ideal of the statesman. Just as there is no medical science without the art of a physician, so there is no politics apart from the soul of a statesman. Aristotle says that every artist should, like a statesman, first, recognize the best form, secondly, consider what form is suitable for a man or a society, and thirdly, how one should produce this form and preserve it; and he observes that a practical statesman can dispense with political science as little as with practical talent.[46] These conditions, however, are not satisfied by any man, or a man of practice, but require the philosophical scholarship which has been credited since Socrates and Plato. In order to live well as a citizen or a private person, one requires philosophical contemplation about morality and politics, instead of the rhetorical art of a sophist or the mere experience of a practical statesman. It would, however, be a paradox, if it were a theoretical philosophy that is required for life. What is required must be the practical philosophy which aims at conduct or life rather than mere knowledge. Aristotle's *Ethics* and *Politics* present it; hence it is called philosophical wisdom (φιλοσοφία

---

[42] *Eth. Nic.* II. 2. 1103 b 26.
[43] *Eth. Nic.* I. 13. 1102 a 6.
[44] *Ibid.* a 12.
[45] *Ibid,* a 18.
[46] *Pol.* IV. 1. 1288 b 16; b 25.

φρόνησις) or political philosophy.[47] He maintains, none the less, that
men, if they would master these sciences, also require natural endow-
ments just as does practical wisdom or prudence.[48] For, man can neither
rightly love and hate, nor recognize and choose what is good, without
ethical virtues. So that, in order to be good, it is not enough to obey
the words of a wise man, just as one may only obey the words of a
physician in order to be healthy. In moral virtue, knowledge and intention are more important than obedience. Moral intention is given
through ethical virtues and makes the end of conduct right, while
practical wisdom indicates the means for this end. This cognition, being
philosophical, is displayed in the form of syllogism, which is found in
the *Ethics*. The rightness of the principle or the major premiss depends
upon the ethical virtue, for we know what habit is the end and the
highest good, only through our virtues. The principle is recognized
only through moral intellect or practical wisdom, and this syllogism is
practical rather than theoretical, for its conclusion results in conduct
and in one's way of life, instead of mere knowledge.[49]

These arguments of Teichmüller's for the identification of the cognitive function in ethics and politics with practical wisdom seems to be
nearly perfect and satisfactory. In short, the classification of ἐπιστήμη
by Aristotle is, both in its form and matter, the classification of
knowledge in general and not of science. Practical or productive
ἐπιστήμη is by no means theoretical knowledge, but practical and productive through and through. They are different from experience only
in that they are master-arts, i.e. architectonic. Now, the essence of
knowledge is correlative with its object; just as knowledge about
number and heavenly bodies cannot be practical, so the cognition of
virtues and constitutions cannot be theoretical. Thus the analysis of
knowledge agrees with that of intellect, and will be summarized as
follows:[50]

---

[47] *Top.* VIII. 14. 163 b 9.
[48] *Eth. Nic.* III. 7. 1114 b 6; VI. 5. 1140 b 17; VI. 13. But these references of
Teichmüller's seem to be insufficient for proving the point.
[49] *Eth. Nic.* VI. 13. 1144 a 31.
[50] Cf. the classification in Régis's *L'opinion selon Aristote* 62. The determinations of λογιστικόν and δοξαστικόν are different from *ours*. This point will be
examined later.

```
                              ⎧ νοῦς    ⎫ ⎧ πρώτη φιλοσοφία
            ⎧ ἐπιστημονική ⎨ ἐπιστήμη ⎬ ⎨ μαθηματική
            ⎪ (θεωρητική)    ⎩ σοφία    ⎭ ⎩ φυσική
  νοῦς      ⎪
  διάνοια ⎨                  ⎧ πρακτική   ⎧ ἠθική
  ἐπιστήμη ⎪                 ⎪ – φρόνησις ⎨ πολιτική
            ⎪                 ⎪            ⎩ οἰκονομική
            ⎪ λογιστική     ⎨
            ⎪ (βουλευτική)   ⎪
            ⎩ (δοξαστική)    ⎪
                             ⎪            ⎧ ποιητική
                             ⎪ ποιητική  ⎨
                             ⎩ – τέχνη    ⎩ ῥητορική
```

2. Doxa and Doxastikon Part

The cognitive faculty is generally called either νοῦς, ἐπιστήμη or διάνοια in a wider sense, and is divided into the theoretical and the practical; the one being called ἐπιστημονική or θεωρητική, and the other λογιστική or βουλευτική. The latter seems to be sometimes called δοξαστική. But as for the δοξαστική, it is doubtful whether we should understand by it practical intellect or not. The division of intellect into the ἐπιστημονική and the δοξαστική being most emphasized by Socrates and Plato, it is quite natural that the classification of intellect into the ἐπιστημονική and the δοξαστική should have been adopted by Aristotle at first. But we must refrain from the hasty conclusion that this is a distinction between theoretical and practical knowledge. Rather we should go back to Plato and investigate the concept of δόξα in opposition to ἐπιστήμη.

This pair of concepts was a favourite subject of discussion for Socrates,[51] and it is argued that in Plato's dialogues the interpretation of these terms differed according to the date of the dialogue.[52] In the works of Plato's early or middle period, such as the *Phaedo* and the *Republic*, ἐπιστήμη and δόξα are clearly distinguished both in their objects and in their value. Besides ideas, which are real being, and perfect not-being, there are also changeable phenomena or the world of generation. The knowledge of ideas is ἐπιστήμη, and not-being is quite unknowable while the changeable world of phenomena is the object of αἴσθησις and δόξα, i.e., sensation and opinion. Opinion is a kind of cognition which comes from sensation. Consequently, sensa-

[51] *Phaed.* 96.
[52] Burnet, *Greek Philosophy* I. 248. Taylor, *Plato* 339.

tion and opinion stand, in respect of cognitive value, between knowledge and ignorance. "They are darker than knowledge, but clearer
than ignorance."[53] Considered in reference to their agent, sensation
and opinion are inferior, because they are not the pure function of the
soul, but come from the impinging of bodily elements upon it.[54] In the
Republic, ἐπιστήμη and διάνοια form νόησις as the cognition of being,
while πίστις and εἰκασία form δόξα as the cognition of generation.[55]

This thought of Plato's, however, is said to have been remarkably
changed after the *Theaetetus*. Sensation, being regarded as a function
of the soul, is esteemed rather higher,[56] though it is not independent of
the body. On the other hand, opinion is assimilated to knowledge,[57]
which is cognition through the independent soul, and its characteristic
is to be seen in talking with oneself.[58] In the *Sophist*, which belongs to
the same period as the *Theaetetus*, monologue is assigned to the intellect in general, while opinion is regarded as the accomplishment of
intellect since it involves moreover affirmation and denial.[59] The expression of opinion is a sentence which is either true or false.[60] Opinion
seems here to imply almost the same thing as judgment in general.

How, then, should right opinion be distinguished from knowledge?
We cannot find a precise answer in the *Theaetetus*,[61] except in the
hypothesis[62] that "the true opinion accompanied by λόγος is knowledge,
but what is without λόγος is outside knowledge. What has no λόγος is
not known, but what has λόγος is knowable." This line of thinking is,
however, already seen in the early works such as *Meno* and the *Symposium*. According to the *Meno*, true opinion and knowledge are essentially different, though they are equivalent from a practical point of
view.[63] Opinion makes everything good and beautiful as far as it remains in us, but it is apt to escape from our mind; it is only when

---

[53] *Rep.* 477, 478.
[54] *Phaed.* 53.
[55] *Rep.* 533 f.
[56] *Theaet.* 184. In the Republic, sensation belongs to the body, while in the
Theaeteus and the *Sophist*, it belongs to the soul which acts through various
kinds of sense organs.
[57] *Theaet.* 187.
[58] *Ibid.* 189 E.
[59] *Soph.* 263 E.
[60] *Ibid.* 264 A.
[61] *Theaet.* 201 ff.
[62] *Ibid.* 201 C, D.
[63] *Meno* 79 C.

secured by reasoning as to cause[64] that it becomes knowledge.[65] In the
Symposium too, right opinion for which the holder cannot give a
reason is not qualified as knowledge. Opinion "is awakened into knowledge by putting questions."[66] In the *Theaetetus*, there is no explicit
definition of the word λόγος, but the foregoing passage suggests that it
means the process of inference.

Though it is said that Plato's concept of δόξα has suffered a remarkable modification after his middle period, we can find no conspicuous
change except that opinion has come to be regarded as a function of
independent soul. It is true that in the *Theaetetus*, the thought in the
Phaedo and the *Republic* that characterizes opinion as concerned with
unreal objects does not come in front. No doubt, this may be taken as
suggesting the decay of Plato's ἀνάμνησις-theory in contrast to his
newly adopted view which attaches more importance to the pheno-
menal world. But presumably it is not so much due to the change of
thought as to the difference of viewpoints. In the *Phaedo*, opinion and
knowledge were distinguished in that the one is concerned with provisional phenomena, and the other with eternal ideas. Whereas in the
Theaetetus, the distinction turns to the form of cognition rather than
to the object. This fact perhaps implies an increased estimation of
phenomena and opinion. But this does not amount to saying that
the distinction of δόξα and ἐπιστήμη by means of their objects was
abandoned by Plato in his later period. The formal distinction of
opinion and knowledge by means of λόγος is not limited to the later
period, but appears more distinctly in the early works such as the *Meno*
and the *Symposium*. It is true that in those early works, opinion is
regarded to be potential knowledge, while in the *Theaetetus* and the
Sophists, it is called the completion of thinking. But the discrepancy
here is a mere appearance and there is no real change of thought.
Opinion is potential and less complete than knowledge, inasmuch as
it lacks in corroboration by reason, but it is the completion of the thinking as far as it is presumed to be true. It may commit a fault because it
is not accompanied by the reflection on the procedure of reasoning,
so that, though in a sense it is the completion of thinking, it may
form a supposition when combined with sensation.[67]

Plato's thought of knowledge and opinion considered above will be

[64] *Ibid.* 98 A.
[65] *Symp.* 202 A.
[66] *Meno* 86 E.
[67] *Soph.* 264 B.

serviceable to clarify Aristotle's thought on the same concepts. In Aristotle too, opinion is opposed to knowledge: as the cognition of contingent facts[68] to the cognition of eternal things.[69] This is obviously a continuation of Plato's thought related in the *Phaedo*. Here, opinion and knowledge are also distinguished not through their objects but through the modes of thinking. There is knowledge whenever we recognize that something belongs of necessity to something else through its essence, but there is only opinion whenever we recognize that it belongs accidentally to the same thing.[70] Thus the distinction between opinion and knowledge is analogous to that between false and true opinions, so that true opinion is assimilated to knowledge. This concept of opinion is the same as what is found in the *Theaetetus*. The first distinction, viz., the distinction through the objects is compatible with the second, viz., the distinction through the modes of thinking. Aristotle himself admits that the object of knowledge is in a sense the same as that of opinion, just as the object of true opinion is the same as that of false opinion; e.g., the diagonal of a triangle may be either the object of knowledge, i.e., when it is studied essentially, or the object of opinion, when studied as an accidental fact. In the same way, animal is the object of knowledge when considered as the essence of man, but the object of opinion when considered as the accidental attribute of him.[71] In other words, the object of knowledge is, strictly speaking, the necessary being that cannot be otherwise than it is, and the object of opinion is the contingent or what can be otherwise than it is; but in respect of appearance, the same thing can be either the object of knowledge or the object of opinion.

Opinion, being thus the cognition of things which can be otherwise, or of things considered as capable of being otherwise, may be sometimes true and sometime false,[72] but from a subjective point of view, it is a judgement accompanied by conviction.[73] It may presuppose an inference,[74] only lacking in the real ground of its conviction or in the

[68] *An. Post.* I. 33. 88 b 30–89 a 4; cf. *Met.* VII. 15. 1039 b 34; IX. 10. 1051 b 14; *Eth. Nic.* VI. 5. 1140 b 27.
[69] *An. Post.* I. 2. 71 b 9–12, 15; *Eth. Nic.* IV. 3. 1139 b 20–24; cf. *An. Post.* I. 4. 73 a 21; I. 6. 74 b 5; I. 8. 75 b 21.
[70] *An. Post.* I. 33. 89 a 17–23.
[71] *An. Post.* I. 33. 89 a 33 ff.
[72] *An. Post.* I. 33. 89 a 5; IV. 19. 100 b 7; *De An.* III. 3. 428 a 19; *Eth. Nic.* VI. 3. 1139 b 17; *Met.* X. 6. 1062 b 33; *De Int.* 14. 23 a 38.
[73] *De An.* III. 3. 428 a 20, 22; *Eth. Eud.* VII. 2. 1235 b 29.
[74] *De An.* III. 3. 428 a 22 f.

actual procedure of inference;[75] in this sense, it is nothing more than a dogmatic conclusion.[76] From a theoretical point of view, it is inferior to knowledge, but from a practical point of view, it is as effective as knowledge,[77] because practice is concerned with the individual and what can be otherwise.[78] This however does not amount to saying that opinion is the cognition of individual things, or is concerned only with practical affairs.

It is true that the object of knowledge is the universal,[79] while what moves us is an opinion concerning individual things.[80] But opinion is concerned not only with the individual, but also with the universal as well. For instance, in *Eth. Nic.* VII. 5,[81] both the major and the minor premises of theoretical and practical inferences are called opinions: the one being universal, and the other individual, opinion. The universal is such as "All sweet food should not be tasted," while the individual is such a perceptive judgement as "This is sweet." In *De An.* III. 11,[82] it is said that not a universal opinion but an individual one moves animals. This shows evidently that [opinion should not be limited to individual judgement, but that there is also universal opinion.[83] On the other side, knowledge is taken as the cognition of the universal, and applied not only to theoretical but also to practical objects. The practical cognition which was called universal opinion is in this terminology called knowledge. For instance, in *Eth. Nic.* X. 9,[84] it is said: "But the details can be best looked after, one by one, by a doctor or gymnastic instructor or any one else who has the general knowledge of what is good for everyone or for people of a certain kind (for the sciences both are said to be and are, concerned with what is universal); . . . it will perhaps be agreed that if a man does wish to become master of an art or science he must go to the universal, and come to know it as well as possible; for, as we have said, it is with this that

[75] *Eth. Nic.* VI. 12. 1143 b 11.
[76] *Ibid.* 10. 1142 b 13.
[77] *Ibid.* 12. 1143 b 11–14; vf. n. 64.
[78] *Met.* I. 1. 981 a 17; *Eth. Nic.* III. 1. 1110 a 13; b 6; VI. 8. 1141 b 16; *Pol.* II. 8. 1269 a 12.
[79] *Met.* XI. 1. 1059 b 25; 2. 1060 b 19; III. 6. 1003 a 15, XIII. 9. 1089 b 5; 10. 1086 b 33; *An. Post.* I. 31. 87 b 38; *De An.* II. 5. 417 b 23; *Eth. Nic.* VI. 6. 1146 b 31; X. 10. 1180 b 15.
[80] *De An.* III. 11. 434 b 16.
[81] *Eth. Nic.* VIII. 5. 1147 a 25.
[82] *De An.* III. 11. 434 a 19.
[83] Cf. Régis, *op. cit.* 134.
[84] *Eth. Nic.* XI. 10. 1180 b 13; cf. *Eth. Nic.* II. 5. 1106 b 5.

the sciences are concerned. And surely he who wants to make men, whether many or few, better, by his care must try to become capable of legislating, if it is through laws that we can become good. For to get any one whatever – any one who is put before us – into the right condition is not for the first chance comer; if any one can do it, it is the man who knows, just as in medicine and all other matters which give scope for care and prudence."

We can see from the above quotation that though knowledge is the cognition of the universal, it may also be applied to productive activities such as healing and gymnastics, as well as to practical activities such as politics and education. Although the things which can be otherwise than they are may be individuals, it is possible to have universal cognition about the genus of such things, and such cognition is called either knowledge or opinion.

That the cognition of productive and practical affairs may be universal as well as individual, was already explained by Teichmüller. As he put it: practical wisdom is not a mere experience that meets individual circumstances, but also reaches a universal and master cognition;[85] a practically wise man *par excellence* is the man who knows the essence of virtue and the highest end of life,[86] and lives a harmonious life.[87] A good disposition without practical wisdom, is merely a natural virtue and even not ethical.[88] Practical wisdom, being the principle of ethical virtues, or that which gives λόγος to the irrational soul,[89] contains, of course, a universal cognition.[90] The *Ethics* and the *Politics* of Aristotle are nothing but the realization of this masterprudence.[91]

---

[85] *Eth. Nic.* IV. 8. 1141 b 21–23; *Met.* I. 2. 982 a 14 ff.; 30 ff.; *Eth. Nic.* VI. 12. 1143 b 4; cf. Teichmüller, *Studien* etc. 224 f.; *Pol.* VI. 3. 1325 b 14; Newman's note on Arist. *Pol. ad loc.*; Plato. *Pol.* 259 C, E.

[86] *Eth. Nic.* VI. 13. 1144 a 31 ff.; VI. 5. 1140 b 16 ff.; a 25 ff.

[87] *Eth. Nic.* VI. 2. 1139 a 26 ff,; VI. 13. 1144 b 24, 31; *Rhet.* III. 16. 1417 a 26; X. 8. 1178 a 16 ff.; Trendelenburg, *op. cit.* II. 384; Hartenstein, *Historisch-Philosophische Abhandlungen*, 279.

[88] *Eth. Nic.* VI. 13. 1144 b 1 ff.

[89] Practical wisdom is the right reason which makes desire moderate (*Eth. Nic.* VI. 13. 1144 b 28). It is a kind of intellectual virtue, which is in conformity with ethical virtues. *Rhet.* I. 9. 1366 b 29; 7. 1364 b 18; 1363 b 14; *De Sensu* I. 437 a 1; *Top.* V. 7. 137 a 14; *Eth. Nic.* VI. 12. 1143 b 15; 5. 1140 b 26; 13. 1144 a 1; *Top.* V. 6. 136 b 11; VI. 6. 145 a 29.

[90] Though practical wisdom is said to be concerned with particulars, (*Eth. Nic.* VI. 12. 1143 a 34), it does not rule out the possibility of being concerned with the universal, for it is mentioned that it is not only concerned with the universal, but also with the particular (*Eth. Nic.* VI. 8. 1141 b 14).

[91] *Eth. Nic.* I. 1. 1094 a 24–b11.

Similarly with art: it is the principle of production; and production, being concerned with what can be otherwise, contains various kinds of cognition from the individual and immediate faculty of production up to the most general knowledge of master-art.[92] This last mentioned is essentially universal cognition.[93]

Although there are, as above argued, universal knowledge about production and practice, as well as a particular one, these kinds of knowledge are all concerned with what can be otherwise. Compared with particular knowledge they have of course much higher cognitive value, but compared with the knowledge of necessary being such as metaphysics, they are much inferior.[94] Hence it might rather be called general opinion than knowledge. But the genus of what can be otherwise, is more constant than individual facts. It is just on this account that cognition of such genera is called knowledge in a derivative sense.

Nor is opinion distinguishable from knowledge as practical from theoretical. Opinion is concerned with what can be otherwise, in which the affairs of practice are also contained. Yet it does not follow from this that opinion is practical cognition. Such an inference would commit the fallacy of undistributed middle. What can be otherwise is not always practical; natural phenomena are surely what can be otherwise and not necessary, yet they are not the object of practice or production. Production and practice are concerned with what is in our power, whereas in nature, the principle of movement and change is contained in things in themselves.[95] And nature is the object of theoretical rather than of practical knowledge.[96] For example, it is generally the case that the sum of the inner angles of a triangle is two right angles, and this is the object of universal and theoretical knowledge, whereas the fact that the particular angle of this triangle is a right angle is the object of a theoretical one, though it is particular none the less. In the same way, rainfall is a phenomenon neither eternal nor constant, it is temporary and what can be otherwise, nevertheless it is a matter of nature that it will rain tomorrow, because we cannot voluntarily make rainfall. Consequently cognition about rainfall is surely an opinion, but theoretical rather than practical.

Aristotle really distinguishes προαίρεσις and δόξα in that whereas will is concerned with action, "opinion is thought to relate to all kinds of

---

[92] *Eth. Nic.* I. 1. 1094 a 6–15.
[93] *Met.* I. 1. 981 a 5–12; 981 a 12–17.
[94] *Eth. Nic.* I. 3. 1094 b 11–27; *Eth. Nic.* II. 2. 1103 b 34 ff.
[95] *Eth. Nic.* VI. 4. 1140 a 10–16; *Met.* VI. 1. 1025 b 18–24.
[96] *Met.* VI. 1. 1025 b 25–28; 1026 a 10–12.

things, no less to eternal things and impossible things than to the things in our own power, and it is distinguished by its falsity or truth, not by its badness or goodness, while will is distinguished rather by the latter."[97] Here opinion is explained as if it were a kind of theoretical knowledge. It is not once that we find it so explained: in making the distinction between the excellence of deliberation and that of opinion, he says, "The correctness of opinion is truth; and at the same time everything that is an object of opinion is already determined."[98] Now the first sentence involves more than what we need. It will be enough for our present purpose to look at the words "No less ... than to things in our own power." For it is enough to make clear that the opinion is not only related to practical affairs which are in our own power, but also related to the things beyond our power. We feel rather a little embarrassed when we find Aristotle referring to these objects as "eternal things and impossible things," for, if these words mean "what are necessary and cannot be otherwise," cognition about these objects should be according to the definition, knowledge rather than opinion. There is an alternative: either this clause is a redundant one or it must be interpreted somewhat differently. In the latter case, "impossible things" would mean what are beyond our power and cannot be realized by us, and what are paradoxical and cannot exist by their nature. These are nothing but the impossible things he speaks of when he says, "For will cannot relate to impossibles, ... but there may be a wish even for impossibles, i.e. for immortality."[99] Now if immortality as the object of wish be an example of the "impossible," the "eternal things" which were mentioned along with the impossibles, would be natural phenomena which appear independent of us, e.g., weather, or the angle of a particular triangle. We also learn from Aristotle that the demonstration or knowledge about the eclipse of the moon is the knowledge of the eternal, as far as it often happens, but of the particular, as far as it does not happen usually.[100] This kind of phenomenon might be regarded as an example of the eternal thing to which theoretical opinion is related.

Though opinion is often counted by Aristotle theoretical cognition, we cannot agree with Walter who wants to restrict it to theoretical knowledge.[101] For opinion is related to what can be otherwise, which

---

[97] *Eth. Nic.* III. 4. 1111 b 30.
[98] *Eth. Nic.* VI. 10. 1142 b 11; cf. 1142 b 34.
[99] *Eth. Nic.* II. 4. 1111 b 22.
[100] *An. Post.* I. 8. 75 b 33; cf. *ibid.* 21 ff.
[101] Walter, *op. cit.* 437 ff.

however forms the region where practice has its being, and there is no ground for excluding practical affairs from the objects of opinion. Plato regarded the function of opinion to be leading practice where knowledge is lacking,[102] while Aristotle also describes opinion as practical.[103] Though opinion *per se* is a kind of cognition and is measured by truth and falsehood, not by goodness and badness, just as sensation *per se* is a mere discrimination and not the immediate agent of action,[104] it does not exclude opinion and sensation from the region of practical affairs.

Opinion is the cognition that is concerned with what can be otherwise, but it may be related to the universal as well as to the particular, to the theoretical as well as to the practical. Does it follow then that the intellect which is determined by the adjective δοξαστικόν is not assumed to be practical? Walter actually thought so. He refused namely any practical function whatever to the δοξαστικόν part, and limited opinion to theoretical knowledge, against the common view that identifies the δοξαστικόν part with the practical cognition called deliberation. Therefore, he takes the δοξαστικόν as the rational part in the primary sense, i.e., the rational part which involves both theoretical knowledge and practical knowledge.[105] But unlike Walter, we would

---

[102] *Meno* 99.

[103] *Eth. Nic.* VI. 11. 1143 a 12–15; *Eth. Nic.* VII. 5. 1147 a 25–28; 9. 1151 a 16 f.; 10. 1151 b 3 f.; *Eth. Eud.* II. 10. 1226 a 4–15; *De An.* III. 3. 427 b 21–24; *Eth. Nic.* III. 4. 1112 a 4; a 9–11; I. 12. 1101 a 24; 15. 1128 b 24; VI. 9. 1142 a 8.

[104] *De An.* III. 7. 431 a 8; 9. 432 a 15–17; cf. *An. Post.* II. 19. 99 b 35; *Motu An.* 6. 700 b 20.

[105] There are but few examples where the concept δοξαστικὸν μέρος seems to indicate practical intellect in the same way as βουλευτική or λογιστική. The remarkable example is found in the end of *Eth. Nic.* VI. 5, where making a distinction between practical wisdom and art, it is said that there is the virtue of art, but not of practical wisdom, which is itself a kind of virtue, and further, *Eth. Nic.* VI. 5. 1140 b 25–30: δυοῖν δ' ὄντοιν μεροῖν τῆς ψυχῆς τῶν λόγον ἐχόντων, θατέρου ἂν εἴη ἀρετή, τοῦ δοξαστικοῦ· ἥ τε γὰρ δόξα περὶ τὸ ἐνδεχόμενον ἄλλως ἔχειν καὶ ἡ φρόνησις. ἀλλὰ μὴν οὐδ' ἕξις μετὰ λόγου μόνον σημεῖον δ' ἐστι λήθη τῆς τοιαύτης ἕξεως ἐστι, φρονήσεως δ' οὐκ ἔστιν. The δοξαστικόν is usually taken as the practical and calculative part which is opposed to the theoretical and scientific. This is reasonable in reference to the fact that the sixth book which treats practical wisdom enumerates the five cardinal virtues of intellect, among which art and practical wisdom are contained as kinds of practical cognition. This is also congruent with the following statement in *Eth. Nic.* IV. 13. 1144 b 14–17: ὥστε καθάπερ ἐπὶ τοῦ δοξαστικοῦ δύο ἐστὶν εἴδη, δεινότης καὶ φρόνησις, οὕτω καὶ ἐπὶ τοῦ ἠθικοῦ δύο ἐστί, τὸ μὲν ἀρετὴ φυσικὴ τὸ δ' ἡ κυρία, καὶ τούτων ἡ κυρία οὐ γίνεται ἄνευ φρονήσεως. It seems that ἠθικόν implies the irrational part in the secondary sense, or the desiring part, and τὸ δοξαστικόν implies the rational part in the secondary sense, which is nothing but another side of the desiring part.

To Rassow and Walter, however, who attach importance to the determination

not restrict δόξα to theoretical cognition, and even if it should involve theoretical knowledge as well as practical, we must investigate more carefully whether the word δοξαστικόν may not be the determinant of practical knowledge.

3. Practical Cognition and Theoretical Cognition

This investigation must be extended to the relation between ἐπιστήμη and ἐπιστημονική, θεωρία and θεωρητική, βουλεύσις and βουλευτική, etc. When these adjectives derived from special cognitive faculties are applied to determine the intellect, the determination refers either to the end or the activity of thinking, θεωρητική ἐπιστήμη

of opinion as assertion rather than inquiry (cf. 1142 b 13), and take opinion as theoretical cognition, it appears to be incongruent to make the δοξαστικόν part as practical intellect. They attempt therefore to solve the difficulty either through making the statement in 1144 b 14 an interpolation by a later hand (Rassow, *Arist. Forsch.*3 4–45, 30 f.), or by taking the δοξαστικόν as the rational part in general (Walter, *op. cit.* 437–450). According to Walter, although opinion and practical wisdom are both concerned with what can be otherwise, they are not identified by Aristotle with each other. Walter considers that "the two kinds of the rational part of the soul" does not imply the ἐπιστημονικόν and the λογιστικόν but the ἠθικόν and the δοξαστικόν; the δοξαστικόν in this context being synonymous with the διανοητικόν.

Walter admits that intellect is divided in *Eth. Nic.* VI. 2 into two parts: the ἐπιστημονικόν and the λογιστικόν. But he distinguishes this division of intellect from that duopartite division of the soul, viz., the ἠθικόν and the δοξαστικόν; the two parts told in *Eth. Nic.* VI. 13. 1144 a 5 are also of this kind. Thus, according to Walter, the δοξαστικόν part should be identified with the διανοητικόν part instead of with the βουλευτικόν, while the βουλευτικόν and the ἐπιστημονικόν constitute the parts of intellect. In determining practical wisdom (VI. 5. 1140 b 25), it is to be distinguished from ethical virtues and other intellectual virtues, not to be counted in calculative virtue, for it presupposes the distinction of act and practical wisdom, the one being ἕξις μετὰ λόγου ἀληθοῦς ποιητική, and the other ἕξις ἀληθής μετὰ λόγου πρακτική – the adjective "true" refers in the one case to "reason," in the other, directly to "habit." A true habit means the habit which involves a true end. Art does not involve such a good end, while practical wisdom does; hence it is said that there is the virtue of art, but not the virtue of practical wisdom. Walter continues arguing: since the subject matters of investigation hitherto were restricted to ethical virtues, Aristotle here calls practical wisdom merely virtue in contrast to art, of which the latter is rather intellectual than ethical. (VI. 5. 1140 b 24). In the next stage, however, practical wisdom must be distinguished from ethical virtue, being itself none the less an intellectual virtue, hence practical wisdom is assigned to the δοξαστικόν part, which is opposed to the ἠθικόν rather than to the ἐπιστημονικόν: it is intellectual and not practical. Thus, according to Walter, practical wisdom is an intellectual habit, and still inseparable from ethical virtues. Walter finds a proof for his interpretation in the sentence "It (φρόνησις) is not a mere habit which is accompanied by reason" (1140 b 26), saying that this statement would amount to

is the first case, λογιστική (διάνοια)[106] is the second case; the former implied the intellect which aims at thinking itself, the latter the intellect
which calculates something. Fundamentally θεωρία is thinking in
general, not only theoretical, but also practical, for practice and
production contain θεωρία *sui generis*.[107] But when the adjective
derived from this is applied to determine the thinking, the resulting
compounds, e.g. θεωρητικὴ ἐπιστήμη signifies the thinking for the sake
of thinking itself.[108] Whereas in the case of ἐπιστήμη, it is *per se* theoretical thinking, and the derivative ἐπιστημονική determines διάνοια,
not in respect to the end, but in respect to the activity of the intellect,
so that ἐπιστημονικὴ διάνοια means the intellect of scientific character,
rather than the intellect which aims at scientific knowledge.

As to βουλεύσις and λογισμός, these are the types of *per se* practical
thinking, and the derivative βουλευτική and λογιστική determine the
intellect into practical in respect to activity, whereas δόξα is as aforesaid, either practical or theoretical, and the adjective δοξαστική

nonsense, unless one considers the δοξαστικόν part, which contains practical
wisdom, to be the intellectual as opposed to the ethical. Another ground is
sought in ch. 13, 1144 a 5 ff., and explained as follows: – In the preceding
chapter, φρόνησις and σοφία are attributed to different parts of the soul, ethical
virtue constituting the third part, whereas in this chapter, the nutritive part is
counted as the fourth. This shows that in the consideration of practical wisdom
and ethical virtue, the opposition of theoretical and practical intellects is de-
emphasized and replaced by the opposition of the intellectual and the ethical.
Aristotle did not enumerate any intellectual virtue other than δεινότης and φρόνησις as belonging to the δοξαστικόν part. This fact seems to be favourable to the
opinion that takes the δοξαστικόν part as practical intellect. But Walter avoids
the difficulty by regarding this enumeration as mere analogical exemplification
instead of a complete enumeration of intellectual virtues.

As to Rassow's attempt to regard the statement about the δοξαστικόν part to
be an interpolation, Walter opposes to the effect that it cannot explain why that
part was called δοξαστικόν against Aristotle's usual terminology. It might be
answered that it is because that δόξα is concerned with what can be otherwise;
but this is not sufficient for making practical wisdom the virtue of the δοξαστικόν
part. Thus, Walter, rejecting Rassow's opinion, restricts the interpolation to the
sentence 1140 b 27: ἥ τε γὰρ δόξα περὶ τὸ ἐνδεχόμενον ἄλλως ἔχειν καὶ ἡ φρόνησις,
and conjectures that this is a note of a later scholar who misunderstood the real
meaning. Walter acknowledges that he himself in the first half of his work has
mistaken the δοξαστικόν for βουλευτικόν. (cf. *op. cit.* 438 n. 2. and 174).

[106] In *Eth. Nic.* VI. 2. 1139 a 12, ἐπιστημονικόν, λογιστικόν or βουλευτικόν is
applied to the μέρος τῆς ψύχης, but it is evident from the immediately preceding
statement (1139 a 1) that it is the subdivision of διάνοια.

[107] *Eth. Nic.* VI. 7. 1141 a 25 f.; IV. 4. 1122 a 34 f.; b 8–10; X. 10. 1181 b
6–9; VI. 2. 1139 a 6–12.

[108] *De An.* III. 9. 433 a 14 f.; *Eth. Eud.* I. 5. 1216 b 9–25; *Eth. Nic.* I. 3. 1095 a
5 f.; II. 2. 1103 b 26–30; X. 10. 1179 a 35–b2.

determines the intellect into practical none the less. The δοξαστικὴ (διάνοια) is the intellect which operates as opinion-making activity. But as far as δόξα may be theoretical as well as practical, opinion-making intellect is not synonymous with practical thinking. It is only by detour that δοξαστικὴ (διάνοια) gets the meaning of practical thinking, namely, δοξαστικὴ (διάνοια) is practical, because δόξα is concerned with what can be otherwise, which is essentially the domain of practical affairs.

To return, Aristotle divided the cognitive faculty into the theoretical and the practical, calling the one ἐπιστημονικὴ (διάνοια), scientific (intellect), or θεωρητικὴ ἐπιστήμη theoretical knowledge, the other βουλευτική, λογιστική, or δοξαστικὴ διάνοια, i.e., deliberative, calculative, or opinion-making intellect. The practical thinking is subdivided into the practical *par excellence* and the productive. This division seems to presuppose Plato's classification. Plato set knowledge in opposition to opinion, taking the former as the cognition of eternal, necessary and universal truth, and the latter that of temporary, accidental and particular facts.[109] But Plato tried another classification from another point of view; viz., in the *Statesman* 258, he divided knowledge into the ἐπιστημονική, i.e. the cognitive, and the πρακτική, i.e. the practical, and subdivided the former into the κριτική, the discriminating, and the ἐπιτακτική, the imperative. At first glance, this subdivision appears to be the same as the distinction between theoretical knowledge and practical. But in fact, the ἐπιτακτική is tantamount to ἀρχιτεκτονική, and means rather universal knowledge which comprizes both practical cognition and theoretical, so that the πρακτικὴ ἐπιστήμη, which is opposed to this, has not so wide a meaning as common usage gives to it, but is rather the habitual and empirical cognition which immediately dictates individual acts. The ἐπιστημονική and the πρακτική are opposed to each other as the theoretical is to the practical, while the κριτική and the ἐπιτακτική being the species of the former, exhibit the opposition of the universal to the particular.

Thus, according to the classification in the *Statesman*, universal knowledge about practice appears to be theoretical. This is correspondent to Aristotle's oscillation in calling this kind of cognition sometimes opinion, and sometimes knowledge. What we find here is a disharmony of thought brought about through the complexity of classification into practice and theory on the one hand, and into the universal and the particular on the other. Aristotle seems to have inherited Plato's

109 *Pol.* 258 f., 267.

thought with some modification, when he divided knowledge into the theoretical and the practical, and subdivided the latter into the productive and the practical in the strict sense, so that he finally admitted three kinds of knowledge, viz., theoretical, practical and productive. In other words, he summed up Plato's imperative knowledge and practical knowledge into practical knowledge, in a wider sense, and set discriminating knowledge in opposition to it, calling the latter theoretical knowledge. Besides, Aristotle assigned the knowledge about individual phenomena of nature to theoretical knowledge,[110] whereas in Plato there was ambiguity as to how this kind of knowledge should be characterized. When Aristotle states that opinion and sensation are discriminating, he seems to imply that, they may at least in part, if not entirely, be theoretical cognition.

We have stated in detail the growth and development of cognitive functions in Chapter II. To resume this briefly, the development of the soul is conditioned by the way of life, and the qualitative differences of these functions depend upon the quantitative differences of the latter. The evolution of functions is proportionate to the complexity of animal life, to the temporal and spacial expansion of the environment. The cognitive function is a development from unconscious functions of nutrition and generation, and there rules among the cognitive functions the law of continuity and accumulation. Thus, at first appear the sensations necessary for life, such as touch and taste, then higher sensations such as smell, hearing and sight. As abstraction and synthesis proceed, φαντασία or imagination emerges, which more or less, is independent of the outward world. This grows, combined with the consciousness of time, itself being a mode of imagination, to imaginations of higher grade such as memory, remembrance and expectation; and these are organized into experience. When this becomes conceptual and is elaborated by means of analysis and symbolization, we possess art, which is classified into master-art and lower skill, the one tending to science, while the other is contiguous to experience. Art already involves science implicitly, but science acquires independence by degrees till it is accomplished as pure science, the knowledge for the sake of knowledge itself, apart from any practical interest. Science is a kind of theoretical knowledge.[111] It does not rule out the knowledge of the particular, but what is most essential to science is the knowledge of the universal, especially the knowledge of the ultimate principles.

[110] Cf. n. 10, n. 96.
[111] *An. Post.* II. 19. 100 a 3; *Met.* I. 1. 980 a 28; 981 b 13; cf. ch. II. n. 95.

In this sense, the highest theoretical knowledge is σοφία as the synthesis of νοῦς and ἐπιστήμη; more concretely speaking, it is metaphysics or theology. Thus, theoretical cognition is the last in the process of development, but in respect to value, it is the first[112] whereas practical and productive cognitions, being the prerequisites of theoretical knowledge, are inferior in their value.

The virtues of the theoretical and the practical intellects are enumerated: they are τέχνη, i.e. art, ἐπιστήμη, i.e. knowledge, φρόνησις, i.e. practical wisdom, σοφία, i.e. wisdom, and νοῦς, i.e. reason. There is a question as to whether all of these are to be called virtues, or some of them should be excluded. In *Eth. Nic.* VI. 3,[113] Aristotle states: "Let it be assumed that the states by virtue of which the soul possesses truth by way of affirmation or denial are five in number, i.e. art, knowledge, practical wisdom, wisdom and reason; we do not include judgment and opinion, because in these we may be mistaken." Of these five concepts, Prantl[114] assumes only practical wisdom and wisdom to be virtues, excluding the others as mere faculties, viz., knowledge and reason are the constituents of theoretical intellect, the one being reasoning, and the other the intuition of principles; while wisdom is the virtue of these theoretical faculties. On the other hand, he denies art to be a virtue, and finds its virtue also in wisdom, making reference to Aristotle's statement to the effect that there may be the virtue of art, but not of practical wisdom, and to the fact that art was not counted in the kinds of knowing the truth. Thus, according to Prantl, the only legitimate virtue of practical intellect is practical wisdom, and it involves εὐβουλία, σύνεσις, γνώμη, δεινότης, etc. Against this interpretation Prantl's Zeller[115] points out that the subject matter of the sixth volume is declared to be the intellectual virtues, whereas virtues are regarded as excellent habits. Though Zeller's argument is not satisfactory to prove the point, there is no doubt that Prantl's view is not right.

In the first place, the text which precedes the quotation states as follows: "The work of both the intellectual parts, then, is truth. Therefore the states that are most strictly those, in respect of which each of these parts will reach the truth are the virtues of the two parts." In succession to this, the third chapter in question continues, "Let us

---

[112] *Met.* I. 1. 981 b 30–982 a 1; f. *An. Post.* I. 31. 88 a 4.
[113] *Eth. Nic.* VI. 3. 1139 b 14.
[114] Prantl, *Ueber die dianoetischen Tugenden der nikomachischen Ethik.* cf. Rassow, *Forschungen* 124 b. Stewart's note on 1139 b 14.
[115] Zeller, *op. cit.* II. 2. 649 n. 2.

begin, then, from the beginning, and discuss these states once more."
From this context alone, it is quite natural to take the five states
enumerated as intellectual virtues. Besides, the remark that "We do
not include judgement and opinion because we may be mistaken,"
seems precisely to mean that, while judgement and opinion are mere
faculties, the other five habits are virtues. For if three of the above
enumerated habits were mere faculties without value, there is no reason
why judgement and opinion should be particularly excluded from the
virtues, since both judgement and opinion may be true as well as false.
With regard to art, we may solve the difficulty by assuming two usages: the one as meaning a faculty, and the other as meaning a virtue.
Aristotle really uses these concepts more frequently as virtues than as
mere faculties. To see the virtue of art in wisdom is, without doubt,
the worst solution;[116] for then the classification of intellect into the
theoretical, the practical, and the productive, would be utterly over-
thrown. It might rather more suitably reduced to practical wisdom;
but strictly speaking, art is an independent virtue different from practical wisdom. In short, we assume the above five concepts as the representative virtues of intellect. We say representative, because there
are also other subordinate virtues. Among the cardinal virtues, reason,
knowledge and wisdom are the virtues of theoretical intellect, practical wisdom that of practical intellect in the strict sense, and art is the
virtue of productive intellect. Inasmuch as our chief interest is in the
cognitive functions, and not in the virtues, the above arguments have
no great importance. Moreover in order to solve the problems of
practice, it is not necessary to go in detail through all of these virtues,
but it will be enough, if we survey the theoretical intellect in such a
degree that we may thereby understand the structure of practical
intellect.

We have seen above that the theoretical intellect is divided into
reason, knowledge and wisdom. The function of reason is the intuition
of principles, that of knowledge the reasoning about the universal and
the particular, that of wisdom, the incorporation of the two, hence
wisdom is regarded as the most complete actuality of the theoretical
intellect. The chief function of intellect is inference by scientific
knowledge, but the highest principle of inference cannot be attained
by inference;[117] it must be apprehended intuitively by reason or

[116] In *Eth. Nic.* VI. 7. 1141 a 9, the excellence of art is called σοφία, but this is
merely an example of vulgar usage.

[117] *Eth. Nic.* VI. 3. 1139 b 29–31; cf. *An. Post.* I. 31. 72 b 6, 18; *Met.* IV. 4.
1006 a 10; III. 21. 997 a 7; *Am. Post.* I. 19. 82 a 7; 84 a 31; *Eth. Nic.* VI. 6.

νοῦς.[118] It is similar to sensation as far as it is intuitive, but is opposed to sensation as fas as it is the cognition of the universal. Wisdom is the synthesis of reason and knowledge;[119] it realizes itself in philosophy as the most complete system of theoretical cognition.[120]

There are two types of scientific inference. The one is deduction, which depends, from the universal to the particular, and it is called ἀποδείξις,[121] i.e. demonstration. The other is induction,[122] which ascends from the particular to the universal. Of the universal principles, which form the major premise of demonstration, some are apprehended *a priori*, but others are to be induced from experience.[123] Though metaphysics and physics are counted in theoretical science along with mathematics, the cognitions of their principles are fundamentally different from each other. The principles of mathematics being purely abstract, are apprehended *a priori*, while those of metaphysics and physics require experience. Hence a young man cannot be a physicist or a philosopher, though he may master mathematics.[124] Since deduction and induction are correlative and form a system of scientific knowledge, science requires the intuition of the universal as well as the intuition of the particular. We have assumed opinion and sensation to be the cognition of individuals. But, opinion is something more than mere sensation; it is related not only with present sense data, but also

---

[118] *An. Post.* I. 23. 84 b 39–85 a 1; IV. 19. 100 b 8–12; *Eth. Nic.* VI. 6. 1141 a 7; 12. 1143 a 35–bl.

[119] *Eth. Nic.* VI. 7. 1141 a 18–20; *Met.* I. 1. 981 b 21.

[120] We have stated at the beginning of this chapter that φιλοσοφία does not always mean philosophy in the strict sense.

[121] Not all inferences that come down from general principles to particulars are demonstration: demonstration is the true cognition which starts from a necessary premise, while dialectic starts from either one of two contradictory propositions. cf. *An. Pr.* I. 1. 24 a 30, 20, 23; b 13; *An. Post.* II. 2. 72 a 10; II. 23. 68 b 10; *Met.* V. 5. 1015 b 7; VI. 15. 1039 b 31; *An. Post.* I. 4. 73 a 24; *Eth. Nic.* VI. 5. 1140 a 34.

[122] *An. Post.* I. 13. 81 a 40–b 1; IV. 7. 92 a 35; *Phys.* VIII. 1. 252 a 24; *Met.* I. 9. 992 b 33; VI. 1. 1025 b 15; XI. 7. 1064 a 9; *Top.* I. 12. 105 a 11–14; *An. Pr.* 42 a 3; *An. Post.* I. 1. 71 a 5; II. 7. 92 a 35; I. 31. 88 a 2.

[123] *Eth. Nic.* VI. 3. 1139 b 28 f.; cf. *Eth. Nic.* I. 7. 1098 b 3; *Rhet.* II. 20. 1393 a 27.

[124] *Eth. Nic.* VI. 8. 1142 a 11–20. Here the relation between knowledge and age is considered in three stages. In the first place, pure abstract theory such as mathematics needs no experience and is comprehensible even to youths. In the second place, the principles of physics and metaphysics are induced from experience, but requiring no ethical virtue, are comprehensible to them. In the third place, ethics and politics presuppose ethical virtue, which are fostered through long habituation, so that they are incomprehensible until one grows to a mature age. cf. *Eth. Nic.* I. 7. 1098 b 3.

with possible objects in the past and in the future, and contains more-over implicit inference. Consequently, the starting point of induction must be sensation rather than opinion.[125] In some respect, sensation is akin to practical cognition, and actualizes itself in a volition when it is accompanied by pleasure and pain. But sometimes sensation acts as an element of theoretical cognition. In the case of intuition, the distinction between practice and theory is not explicit, so that it may be an element of practical as well as of theoretical cogniton. But sen-sation is not a species of theoretical cognition, for it may either develop in the theoretical or in the practical, whereas the end of theoretical knowledge is the universal, while that of practical knowledge is the particular. Sensation may be the beginning of theoretical knowledge, but not the end.[126] The cognition of the individual is not highly esti-mated in the theoretical, because it is most remote from the end of cognition, whereas in the practical the contrary is the case.

As to the present subject of consideration, practical intellect, it is divided into the practical in the narrow sense, and the productive; their virtues being represented by practical wisdom and art. But what must be borne in mind is that "art" is sometimes used as almost synony-mous with "knowledge,"[127] and is estimated more highly by Aristotle than experience, which is concerned with individuals. This presupposes Plato's thought which takes ἐπιστήμη as the knowledge of the universal, and this terminology is more frequent in the early works of Aristotle. When ἐπιστήμη is restricted to theoretical knowledge, art is opposed to it as a kind of cognition related to another sort of object; namely, while the former is related to what is necessary and cannot be other-wise, the latter is related to what is contingent and can be otherwise.[128] Knowledge is self-sufficient, but art serves to production, and its ulti-mate end is the individual. Still art requires the knowledge of the universal no less than that of the individual. In this respect there is no essential difference between knowledge and art. The only difference lies on which side is the end, whether on the universal or on the individual.

---

[125] *Eth. Nic.* I. 7. 1098 a 33–b 4; *An. Post.* II. 19. 100 b 3–5; cf. *ibid.* 2. 90 a 28; I. 31. 88 a 3.

[126] *An. Post.* I. 31. 88 a 5; 2. 71 b 33–72 a 5.

[127] *An. Pr.* I. 30. 46 a 22; *Met.* I. 1. 981 a 3; b 8; XII. 8. 1074 b 11; *Eth. Nic.* I. 1. 1094 a 7, 18; *Pol.* III. 12. 1282 b 14; IV. 1. 1288 b 10; VII. 13. 1331 b 37; *Rhet.* II. 19. 1392 a 26; cf. *Met.* I. 1. 981 b 28; III. 2. 997 a 5; *An. Post.* I. 1. 71 a 4; *Top.* I. 9. 170 a 30; 11. 172 a 28.

[128] *An. Post.* II. 19. 100 a 8; *Met.* I. 1. 981 b 26; *Eth. Nic.* VI. 4. 1140 a 1; 12, 22; 5. 1140 b 2.

The universal cognition in art is not theoretical knowledge, but the so-called ἀρχιτεκτονική or master-art.[129] Being universal, it gives an instruction as to how to manage individuals.

With respect to art, there is, as stated above, the question whether to regard it as a mere faculty[130] or a virtue as well. One hypothesis takes it as a faculty on the ground that Aristotle says: "While there is such a thing as excellence in art, there is no such thing as excellence in practical wisdom"[131] and that while practical wisdom is defined as "a true practical habit with reason[132]," art is called "a productive habit with true reason."[133] This view assumes that art becomes virtue only when it serves for a good end, which in fact, seems to be endorsed by a statement in the *Magna Moralia*.[134] For all that, since virtue is not confined to ethical or moral virtues, but means the excellence of any kind of faculty,[135] and art is certainly a kind of cognitive faculty, the virtue of this faculty must consist in the rightness of cognition. Consequently, even if the same concept may sometimes be used in the sense of a mere faculty, it does not rule out the possibility of sometimes indicating an intellectual virtue. In the proof thereof we find that the concept ἀτεχνία[136] is used as meaning the lack of this virtue. If ἀτεχνία is the habit of potential production with false reason, τέχνη must be the habit of potential production with true reason, and therefore art must be a kind of intellectual virtue.

Another kind of practical cognition is practical wisdom. According to Jaeger, Plato used this concept φρόνησις as tantamount to ἐπιστήμη, without the distinction of practical and theoretical. The same usage was succeeded by Aristotle in his early works such as the *Protreptikos*, but later he distinguished φρόνησις from ἐπιστήμη as practical *versus* theoretical knowledge. It is well known that Jaeger adopted this change of terminology as a key to determine the period of the *Ethica Nicomachea* and the *Ethica Eudemia*. Jaeger's theory is so familiar to the present readers of Aristotle as to make any elucidation unnecessary.[137] The only point to be noticed is that though Plato did not

[129] *Eth. Nic.* I. 4. 1094 a 14; *Phys.* II. 2. 194 b 1; *Met.* V. 1. 1013 a 13.
[130] Walter, *op. cit.* 512; cf. 464 f.
[131] *Eth. Nic.* VI. 5. 1140 b 22.
[132] *Eth. Nic.* VI. 5. 1140 b 20.
[133] *Ibid.* 4. 1140 a 10, 21.
[134] *Mag. Mor.* I. 9. 1190 a 30.
[135] *Met.* V. 16. 1021 b 20–23.
[136] *Eth. Nic.* VI. 4. 1140 a 21.
[137] Jaeger, *Aristoteles* 241 ff.

distinguish φρόνησις from ἐπιστήμη, it does not follow of necessity that he made no distinction between theoretical and practical intellect. In fact, this distinction is found in the classification in the *Statesman*, as we have already referred to. Plato also argued in his early works such as the *Meno*, that knowledge is instructible while virtue is not, and further that as far as virtue is useful and good for man, what manages it must be in a sense knowledge – thus, the leading cognition in practical affairs must be true opinion or good opinion.[138] This is obviously the specialization of practical intellect common to Aristotle. Consequently, it is not Aristotle's original thought to use the concept φρόνησις as specifically practical knowledge, only that the distinction became more explicit in Aristotle than in Plato.[139] As to the constituents of productive knowledge, we have already answered that it involves both the universal and the particular. Similarly with practical wisdom and practical cognition. The end of practical cognition is the particular, but the knowledge of the universal is indispensable none the less. Thus, practical wisdom or practical cognition in general contains as Teichmüller maintains, universal knowledge such as ethics and politics, as well as the most immediate and particular cognition of practical affairs.

Practical cognition is distinguished from theoretical knowledge in that it aims at an individual act. It is also distinguished from art in that it has no end other than act itself. It contains nevertheless both the universal and the particular knowledge. Now in theoretical knowledge, the particular limit is known intuitively by sensation, the universal end by reason, and the two are combined by scientific knowledge. How then is it with the act of practical intellect? On this point, Aristotle's statement is inadequate and there is no authoritative interpretation. The representative virtue of practical intellect is φρόνησις without doubt. But as practical cognition involves many constituents, φρόνησις must bear a generic sense, and cannot be restricted to the intuition of principles or reasoning exclusively. The functions or virtues of practical intellect are βούλευσις,[140] εὐβουλία,[141] σύνεσις,[142] δεινότης,[143] πανου-

---

[138] *Meno* 98.

[139] Even in early works such as the *Topica*, we find the special usage of φρόνησις *Top.* VII. 7. 137 a 12–14; IV. 21. 121 b 33.

[140] *Eth. Nic.* III. 5. 1112 a 30; b 11; VI. 2. 1139 a 13; (*Mag. Mor.* I. 35. 1196 b 29); *Rhet.* I. 2. 1357 a 4, 6; 1362 a 18; II. 5. 1383 a 7.

[141] *Eth. Nic.* VI. 10, 1142 b 22, 27.

[142] *Eth. Nic.* VI. 11. 1143 a 4–10; cf. (*Mag. Mor.* I. 35. 1197 b 11); *Pol.* IV. 4. 1291 a 28.

[143] *Eth. Nic.* VI. 13. 1144 a 24–27; cf. 1144 b 2; VII. 11. 1152 a 11 ff.; (*Mag.*

ργία,[144] etc. Among them, the most important is βούλευσις or deliberation, and its kindred εὐβουλία or good deliberation, all the rest being something derivative of slight importance. What is then universal cognition of principles, and what is the intuition of the individual? It would seem most probable that they are the ethical virtues and the so-called practical reason respectively. For Aristotle states that ethical virtues are the necessary condition of practical wisdom, and that they form the premises of practical syllogism[145] or set up the end which acts as the beginning of practical thinking.[146]

4. Practical Reason

Remarkable as it is, we find at the particular limit of practical thinking, the concept of the reason, which knows individual facts intuitively. Before taking up the problem of the relation between ethical virtues and practical wisdom, let us first study this interesting concept, νοῦς πρακτικός. Hitherto, two meanings of reason were recognized; the one is intellect in general, which is divided into the theoretical and the practical, the other, a kind of theoretical intellect which knows universal principles intuitively. Reason in the latter sense was one of the intellectual virtues above mentioned. Now we encounter a new concept, practical reason, which being a kind of practical intellect, seems to constitute a part of practical wisdom. Since it is a kind of practical intellect, it must be different from practical reason in the generic sense. No doubt, this is one of the most difficult concepts in Aristotle's philosophy, along with the active reason, which was already investigated.[147] Just as the concept of "active reason" appears only once in the De Anima among the whole works of Aristotle, and strictly speaking there is no such set phrase as νοῦς ποιητικός (although it is often discussed by this name) the concept of "practical reason" in a specific sense also appears only once in the Ethica Nicomachea, and here again the word νοῦς πρακτικός as such does not appear. Consequently, just as the difficulty about the "active reason" was in whether Aristotle really admitted such a special reason, here also, the first question to be asked is

Mor. I. 35. 1197 b 17 ff.; II. 6. 1204 a 13 ff.); Pol. V. 5. 1305 a 12; Eth. Nic. VIII. 7. 1158 a 23.

[144] Eth. Nic. VI. 13. 1144 a 27; cf. n. 143; Eth. Eud. II. 3. 1221 a 12.
[145] Eth. Nic. VI. 13. 1144 a 29–b 1; 1144 b 30.
[146] Eth. Nic. VI. 13. 1145 a 4–6.
[147] Cf. Robin, La pensée grecque 365.

whether it is Aristotle's real intention to admit such a special concept as "practical reason." The statement in question is as follows: *Eth. Nic.* VI. 12. 1143 a 36:[148] "And (intuitive) reason is concerned with the ultimates in both directions; for both the first terms and the last are objects of (intuitive) reason and not of argument, and the (intuitive) reason, which is presupposed by demonstrations grasps the unchangeable and first terms, while the (intuitive) reason involved in practical reasonings grasps the last and variable fact, i.e. another premise. For these variable facts are the starting points for the apprehension of the end, since the universal is reached from the particulars; of these therefore we must have perception, and this perception is (intuitive) reason."

There are three interpretations about the reason here mentioned. The first is that of Ritter[149] and Trendelenburg[150], which takes the "reason in demonstration" as the intuition of universal principles in theoretical cognition, and the "reason in practical reasonings" as the intuition of special facts which forms the minor premise of practical syllogism. The second is that of Teichmüller,[151] who takes "demonstrations" in the sense of practical syllogism, and regards the present statement as a whole to be related to practical reason, so that the above statement would amount to admitting two kinds of practical intuition – both of the universal and of the particular limits of practical cognition. The third interpretation is that of Julius Walter,[152] who on the contrary, considers that the reason is to be theoretical whether it functions in practical cognition or in demonstration, and admits no special faculty like "practical reason."

As far as "demonstration" and "the practical" are concerned, the first interpretation seems to be most plausible. What "demonstration" here means is that form of theoretical syllogism which starts from necessary principles, and the reason which is concerned with its first

---

[148] *Nic.* VI. 12. 1143 a 35: καὶ ὁ νοῦς τῶν ἐσχάτων ἐπ' ἀμφότερα· καὶ γὰρ τῶν πρώτων ὅρων καὶ τῶν ἐσχάτων νοῦς ἐστὶ καὶ οὐ λόγος, καὶ ὁ μὲν κατὰ τὰς ἀποδείξεις τῶν ἀκινήτων ὅρων καὶ πρώτων, ὁ δ' ἐν ταῖς πρακτικαῖς τοῦ ἐσχάτου καὶ ἐνδεχομένου καὶ τῆς ἑτέρας προτάσεως· ἀρχαὶ γὰρ τοῦ οὗ ἕνεκα αὗται. ἐκ τῶν καθ' ἕκαστα γὰρ τὰ καθόλου· τούτων οὖν ἔχειν δεῖ αἴσθησιν, αὕτη δ' ἐστὶ νοῦς.

[149] Ritter, *Gesch. d. Ph.* III.

[150] Trendelenburg, *Historische Beiträge zur Philosophie* III; Brandis *Handbuch der Geschichte der griechisch-römischen Philosophie* II. a. ii.; Zeller first followed this theory, but afterwards turned to Walter's.

[151] Teichmüller, *Neue Studien zur Geschichte der Begriffe* II.

[152] Walter, *Die Lehre von der praktischen Vernunft in der griechischen Philosophie.*

premise is nothing but the reason which forms a constituent of wisdom. Therefore, the reason, which, in contrast, is concerned with the other premise is, no doubt, a kind of practical intellect. Neither is it theoretical knowledge, nor practical knowledge in the wide sense, instead, it must be a special function of practical intellect. Why then, are these faculties called after the same name "reason," though they are concerned with opposite limits in the case of theoretical cognition, and in the case of practical cognition? It is indeed a strange thing as Hartenstein[153] wondered at.

Among the three interpretations above mentioned, only that of Teichmüller is free from this difficulty. He maintains[154] that "demonstration" means practical syllogism, and that the reason here spoken of is to be taken exclusively as the practical reason, which is quite different from theoretical reason. For the proof thereof, Teichmüller quotes *Eth. Nic.* VII. 5.[155], where Aristotle states of those who under the influence of passions utter demonstration and the verses of Empedocles without really using practical wisdom. Demonstration, in this context, means, according to Teichmüller, practical syllogism. It follows, according to him, that Aristotle took practical reason as the intellectual intuition both of the highest major premise and of the lowest minor one. This interpretation is fairly plausible, because the statement in question is made in reference to the structure of practical intellect. Still to recite Empedocles's words and to make "demonstration" are not identical, for it is possible that the man who is under the influence of passion is not disturbed in his theoretical cognition.[156] Moreover, a demonstration consists in the combination of the universal knowledge with the particular one. This is surely incongruent with the above statement to the effect that in demonstration reason is concerned with the most universal, but in practice, with the lowest particular. To avoid this difficulty Teichmüller restricts practice to a direct action. But, since he makes both reason and demonstration to be practical, the statement "in demonstration, the reason is concerned with the universal" could scarcely have any significance except that practical syllogism can exist only through the highest universal principle. Of course, theoretical syllogism also contains both universal and particular knowledges. Therefore, strictly speaking, it would be nonsense to say

[153] Hartenstein, *Ueber den wissenschaftlichen Werth der Ethik des Aristoteles.* The following quotations from this book are all through Walter's *op. cit.*
[154] Teichmüller, *op. cit.* 210.
[155] *Eth. Nic.* VII. 5. 1147 a 19; VI. 5. 1140 b 14.
[156] *Eth. Nic.* VI. 5. 1140 b 11.

that in demonstration reason is concerned with the universal. Aristotle's statement would have some meaning only when we take "demonstration" as the theoretical cognition which aims at demonstration itself. The word demonstration appears sometimes to be applied even to practical syllogism,[157] but in its strict sense, it is confined to the syllogism which has necessary premises, and any demonstration about variable facts was rejected decisively.[158] In order to keep a balance with theoretical reason, he might rather admit a universal cognition of principles to practical reason than to call sensation of individuals reason *sui generis*. Theoretical reason is not concerned with such individual matters, but is concerned with the universal extremity. Therefore, it would be more consistent to make practical reason concern the individual than both extremities, and inquire why the universal principle of practice cannot be apprehended by intuitive reason.

Walter's attempt[159] to deny the practical and intuitive intellect, restricting the word practical reason to the generic sense, is due to his assumption that the only function of the practical intellect is the cognition of means. Our full criticism on this point is to be given when deliberation will be considered. But Walter's is, no doubt, the least satisfactory interpretation of the sentence in question. It is too abrupt to take up pure theoretical cognition and assert that one part of it is the intuitive intellect concerned with the individual, in a context where practical intellect is considered. Further, it is more inconceivable that this intuition of the individual is called the beginning or the principle of the end. Walter maintains that there is no ground for taking demonstration as theoretical and "the practical" as practical reason. For, according to him,[160] practical wisdom is distinguished from σύνεσις in that it is epitactic and practical, while σύνεσις is only discrimination, whereas the reason which is concerned with the indivi-

---

[157] *Eth. Nic.* VI. 12. 1143 b 11–13: "Therefore we ought to attend to the undemonstrated sayings and opinions of experienced and older people or of people of practical wisdom no less than to demonstrations," *Part. An.* I. 1. 640 a 1 f.: "The mode of necessity, however, and the mode of ratiocination are different in natural science from what they are in the theoretical sciences." From this statement alone, it might appear as if demonstration were concerned with natural sciences and theoretical sciences and not with practical intellect. But the physical demonstration mentioned in the following is a medical syllogism to realize health, which, however, is usually assumed to be an example of deliberation.

[158] *An. Post.* I. 2. 71 b 18 f.; *Eth. Nic.* VI. 3. 1139 b 31 f.; 5. 1140 a 33–35; *Met.* V. 1015 b 7; VII. 15. 1039 b 31; *An. Post.* I 4. 73 a 24; *Eth. Nic.* VI. 5. 1140 a 34; *An. Post.* I. 8. 75 b 24.

[159] Walter, *op. cit.* 5–81.

[160] *Ibid.* 43.

dual is not specifically determined as practical. But what Aristotle
really states is not that the reason which is concerned with the individual is practical, but that in practical affairs reason is concerned with
the individual. The practical character of this reason, therefore, cannot be denied by Walter's argument. In other words, Aristotle did not
assert that the reason is practical when it is concerned with the individual, but rather regarded the object of reason which acts practically
to be individual. Consequently, we cannot refuse practical reason
even if not every kind of knowledge which is concerned with the individual should be practical. Another inconsistency for Walter is to divide,
on the one hand, the syllogism into the practical and the theoretical,
to deny on the other hand, any practical character to the reason. Since
he takes every universal knowledge to be theoretical, the major premise of practical syllogism is theoretical as well as the major premise of
theoretical syllogism. But, according to Walter, even the minor premise of practical syllogism is not practical, and it differs from that of a
theoretical syllogism only as far as it is a perceptive judgement about
the individual.[161] Thus, the practical syllogism is distinguished from
the theoretical only in that the former reaches the individual, while
the latter remains in the sphere of the universal. Although Walter
reduces the minor premise of the practical syllogism to reason, he
refuses a practical character to it on the ground that it is not calculative but intuitive.[162] But why is it necessary for reason to be calculative
in order to be practical? Seeing that practice is concerned with the
individual, and the end of the syllogism is the beginning of conduct,
it seems more probable that the minor premise of this syllogism
should be practical. Walter failed to recognize this, because he was ob-
sessed with Aristotle's classification of intellect into the scientific and
the calculative or deliberative. But, if the function of practical intellect
should be confined to calculation, because of its being called calculative, on this same ground, theoretical knowledge or scientific intellect
might not have engaged in anything but scientific reasoning, because
ἐπιστήμη or scientific knowledge *par excellence* is, as aforesaid, syllogistic thinking instead of the intuition of principles, which is rather the
function of νοῦς. But, it is evident that scientific knowledge is impossible without this kind of intuition. Consequently, we should not
reject the intuition of the individual in practical thinking, because of
the practical knowledge being called calculative, just as we should not

161 *Ibid.* 230, 242.
162 *Ibid.* 32 f.; 46, 60 f., 322.

infer that theoretical knowledge cannot involve the intuition of principles because of its being called scientific.

Every syllogistic cognition presupposes the intuition of the principle whether practical or theoretical. Such a principle is neither to be restricted to theoretical knowledge, nor be sought outside intellect, as Walter attempted. According to Walter, reason is theoretical exclusively and grasps both the universal and the particular extremities. Therefore, reason is either the intuition of the individual or that of the universal, and the intuition of the individual is nothing but the perception in the ordinary sense.[163] But how is it possible for theoretical reason to be concerned with the object of perception, which is contingent and what can be otherwise?[164] If we take "reason" everywhere in the same meaning, to admit that reason is concerned with what can be otherwise would directly contradict Aristotle's statement[165] to the effect that practical wisdom is concerned with what can be otherwise, while reason is with necessary beings. Walter's answer on this point grows more strange.[166] His argument runs as following: Calculation is the only intellectual act that is concerned with the ἐνδεχόμενον,[167] whereas reason is not calculation, and the act of reason

163 *Ibid.* 314 f.; 335.
164 There is a question how to take the last ἐνδεχόμενον in the statement in *Eth. Nic.* VI. 12. 1133 b 3. According to Walter, it is identical with the minor premise, but according to Zeller, (*op. cit.* II. 2. 651 n. 2), it must imply the conclusion, because the second premise "This is sweet" is not sufficient to lead one to actual conduct, and the immediate motive of an act is rather the conclusion: "This should be tasted." Zeller refers to *Eth. Nic.* VI. 8, and 9, where πρακτόν is shown as the last term. But, this is because Zeller takes the ἐνδεχόμενον as potential or future being. The same interpretation is also adopted by Walter, *op. cit.* 332. This interpretation is not impossible when we take into account such a statement *Eth. Nic.* VI. 2. 1139 b 7–9: οὐδὲ γὰρ βουλεύεται περὶ τοῦ γεγονότος ἀλλὰ περὶ τοῦ ἐσομένου καὶ ἐνδεχομένου, τὸ δὲ γεγονὸς οὐκ ἐνδέχεται μὴ γενέσθαι· or *Motu An.* 7. 701 a 23–25: αἱ δὲ προτάσις αἱ ποιητικαὶ διὰ δύο εἰδῶν γίνονται, διά τε τοῦ ἀγαθοῦ καὶ διὰ τοῦ δυνατοῦ, and ἐνδεχόμενον means in fact logical potentiality or possibility, when it is used independently. But in the statement in question (1143 b 3), we should rather add καὶ ἄλλως ἔχειν and read as "may be otherwise." Cf. Rassow, *Forsch.* 77, Stewart, note *ad. loc.* Even without the addition, this would be the real meaning. For the phrase in 1139 b 9: οὐκ ἐνδέχεται καὶ μὴ γενέσθαι is to be rendered as "it is not capable of not having taken place," and this is a case of what cannot be otherwise, so that its contrary would be "what can be otherwise" instead of "what is possible." Consequently, if one should take it as do Walter and Zeller, it would lead to the conclusion that theoretical reason is concerned with what is impossible, i.e. a contradictory concept or a past event, but this is absurd.
165 *Eth. Nic.* VI. 6. 1141 a 4.
166 Walter, *op. cit.* 319 ff.
167 As mentioned above, Walter seems to take the ἐνδεχόμενον as a mere

concerning the ἐνδεχόμενον, is not an intellectual act, but perception in the literal sense. Though perception sometimes is opposed to reason, they are combined as stages of development.[168] Since perception is potentially reason, it is said to be reason; thus the first function of reason in the wide sense is universal knowledge, and the second function is perception of the ἐνδεχόμενον. When Aristotle states that practical wisdom is concerned with the ἐνδεχόμενον, while reason is concerned with the μὴ ἐνδεχόμενον, he is restricting the first function of reason to the μὴ ἐνδεχόμενον without ruling out the possibility of its second function being concerned with the ἐνδεχόμενον. The perception of individual things is called reason because it is the *sine qua non* of every cognition. Both practical wisdom and reason are concerned with the ἐνδεχόμενον, only differing in that the one is concerned with remote existences, but the other with present beings. Reason is a constituent of practical wisdom as well as of wisdom. And since reason is a virtue of theoretical intellect, it follows that practical wisdom involves a virtue of theoretical intellect, though itself is another kind of virtue. So argues Walter.

In short, according to Walter, both reason and perception are essential and common to every kind of cognition, so that no significance can be found in setting up a rigid opposition between the sensitive and the intelligible, as well as between theoretical knowledge and practical knowledge. This is indeed a creation of Walter's rather than an interpretation of Aristotle's theory. We shall take up only one difficulty in particular, viz., how is it possible for practical wisdom to be practical, if it is constituted of pure theoretical knowledge. According to Walter, the process of practical inference is not practical, but it is composed of theoretical knowledge through and through, only it results in a epitactic conclusion.[169] But whence in the world comes the imperative so suddenly to this conclusion? Obviously, it is not an intellectual function at all, but merely an immediate volition.[170] Thus for Walter, there is no real practical intellect; reason or intellect, itself being theoretical, becomes practical owing to its combination

possible being or potentiality. Then μὴ ἐνδεχόμενον would mean what is impossible. Whereas in *Eth. Nic.* VI. 2. 1139 a 6, the statement which Walter refers to in his work p. 322, runs: ὑποκείσθω δύο τὰ λόγον ἔχοντα, ἓν μὲν ᾧ θεωροῦμεν τὰ τοιαῦτα τῶν ὄντων ὅσων αἱ ἀρχαὶ μὴ ἐνδέχονται ἄλλως ἔχειν, ἓν δὲ ᾧ τὰ ἐνδεχόμενα κτλ. Walter quotes *Eth. Nic.* VI. 6. 1141 a 1, omitting, either with or without intention, ἄλλως ἔχειν which occurs in the text. This μὴ ἐνδεχόμενον would be nonsense without the addition of ἄλλως ἔχειν. cf. n. 163.

[168] Walter, *op. cit.* 321.

with a volition, and there is no genuine practical cognition at all. To avoid this utter bankruptcy, we must take the reason in question, which recognizes the individual intuitively, as practical, and investigate its essence.

The reason in question was said to be the ἀρχή of the end. Now, ἀρχή means principle, cause or beginning in general. What then does it imply that the individual intuition of practical reason is the ἀρχή of the end? There are many different interpretations. According to Trendelenburg,[171] it means that the essential act of practical reason is to determine the end. In proof thereof he quotes *De An.* III. 10. 433 a 13 ff.[172] Trendelenburg seems to have read it as follows: "What I speak of is the reason that calculates about an end, namely, practical reason. It is different from the theoretical in its end. And desire is generally for the sake of an end. For what a desire is concerned with is the principle of practical reason, and the last is the principle of conduct." According to Trendelenburg, the object which is aimed at is the principle which moves practical reason, whereas inasmuch as every end leads to an act, and every act is individual, the individual end which ought to be realized moves intellect without being itself moved – thus what is individual acts as the principle of practical reason.

Walter criticizes this interpretation so severely as to call it an utter misunderstanding. But now that we know Walter's own theory, we cannot give hasty credit to his criticism, for it is quite doubtful which of the two opinions is utterly wrong. At any rate, Trendelenburg's interpretation has two main characteristics: the one is that he takes ἕνεκά του λογιζόμενος to mean "to calculate about the end," the other is that he takes ἔσχατον as "the ultimate," i.e., as "individual affairs." Hartenstein's[173] attack was directed to these points. He points out firstly that ἕνεκά του means not "about the end," but refers to the search for the means. Trendelenburg, considering on the one hand, that the essence of practical reason is the determination of the end, states on the other hand, that the end-object is the principle that moves practical reason. But Hartenstein argues that the first view neither belongs to Aristotle nor is it in accord with the second. In the first sentence, reason determines the end, while in the second, the end determines the reason. in the first, the determination of the end

---

[169] Walter, *op. cit.* 483, 499 f.
[170] Cf. Teichmüller, *op. cit.* 42 ff.
[171] Trendelenburg, *op. cit.* II. 378; cf. Walter, *op. cit.* 44.
[172] *De An.* III. 10. 433 a 13.
[173] Hartenstein, *op. cit.* cf. Walter, *op. cit.* 35.

depends upon reason, but in the second, the act of reason depends upon the end which is already determined. This criticism of Hartenstein's however, is due to a misunderstanding of Trendelenburg's real meaning. The first sentence in question really means that reason determines the image of an end, while the second means that the object which is aimed at acts upon the reason. There is no contradiction between the two statements as Hartenstein suspects.[174] Reason determines the image of an end, in so far as the end-object moves reason: reason is an efficient cause, and the object a final cause; the causality of an efficient cause involves that of the final cause. Unlike Hartenstein, Walter rightly conceived that in Trendelenburg's view the cause of reason was found not in the purpose, but in the object. But being unable to understand the real meaning of this distinction, he accuses Trendelenburg's theory as a sophism.[175] This only betrays his ignorance about the distinction between efficient cause and final cause, as well as that between the image of an end and the end-object.

We must however admit that Walter rightly pointed out the fault of Trendelenburg, who identified the practical reason as an intuitive faculty which appears in *Eth. Nic.* VI. 12, with the practical reason that calculates about the end, which is described in *De An.* III. 10. In fact, the practical reason in the *De Anima* is the generic concept, not a special part of practical wisdom. Since Walter takes practical reason in generic sense and identifies it with the deliberation about the means, it follows that what occasions thinking is desire, and the end of deliberative thinking is the starting point of conduct. ἕνεκά του λογιζόμενος is the cognition of the means, οὗ ἡ ὄρεξις is the ἀρχή of practical reason – indicating that desire forms the motive of searching for the means – and τὸ ἔσχατον is the end of deliberation which constitutes the beginning of the act. Reasoning thus, Walter concludes that Trendelenburg confused this ἔσχατον with ἔσχατα in the *Ethics*, and mistook it for individual affairs to which conduct is related.

In short, the opposition between these interpretations is due to a fundamental difference of opinion as to whether to restrict the function of practical reason to the searching for the means, or to admit a practical reason which is concerned with an end. The decision between these views must wait a scrutiny of deliberation. Now it is very probable that τὸ ἔσχατον means the last term of practical reasoning. But even

---

[174] Cf. Loening, Die Zurechnungslehre des Aristoteles 30.
[175] Walter, *op. cit.* 52.

if we follow this assertion of Walter's and reject Trendelenburg's theory on this point, it does not exclude the possibility that the cognition of "the last" in the *Ethics* should be the principle of the end. The last term of practical reason in the generic sense is an individual fact, which is the first step of conduct and a concrete end determined somehow by reason. The practical reason in the special sense, which is found in the *Ethics*, may form a part of this generic intellect. Even Walter admits that the practical reason in the generic sense is a mediating thinking. But, if this is once admitted, it is evident that reason must involve many constituents, among which we should find the intuitive intellect which apprehends the individual. In just the same way, the theoretical reason in the wide sense involves not only knowledge, but also reason in the narrow sense, viz., an intuitive intellect. Besides, we have previously observed that the practical intellect in the *De Anima* determines the end.[176] From the grounds we then stated, we can by no means submit to the theory which restricts it to the cognition of the means.

Moreover, Walter is not right in taking the sentence "οὗ ἡ ὄρεξις is the ἀρχή of practical reason" to mean that desire determines reason. οὗ ἡ ὄρεξις is what a desire is concerned with, viz., an objective end, and not the idea of an end or a desire itself. That the end-object becomes the principle of practical reason must only mean that the object acts upon the desiring faculty in terms of reason and results in a desire. Aristotle clearly divided desire into the rational and the irrational, and identified the object of desire with the object of reason. Then he noticed that a rational purpose presupposed the estimation of an object and not the reverse. There is in practical reason the function of searching for a means, to be sure, but there is also a practical reason that determines a desire itself for an end. It is very probable that the practical reason in the narrow sense should have such a faculty.

Since Walter confines practical reason to the cognition of means, the setting up of an end is, according to him, assigned entirely to an immediate desire. The end is set up by the desire, and the practical reason contributes only to its realization. Combined with the desire, it produces a rational act towards what is originally desired.[177] Walter does not, however, absolutely refuse rationality to the desire, but argues as follows: "It can do this, however, only through rational representation, which being logically mediated, has a power of conviction that deter-

---

[176] Ch. II. 4.
[177] Walter, *op. cit.* 207 ff.

mines the desire. But to this representation belongs in the first place the end as a rational concept of a universal end ... the universal end, e.g. that man ought to keep moderation, cannot be created by the practical reason. The universal end is, generally speaking, not something determinable, but it stands definitely, once for all, and can only be recognized. This cognition, however, is like all the universals, the object of scientific insight, as the principle of which Aristotle just introduced the νοῦς or intellect."[178]

But this argument is so confused that we can hardly understand its real meaning. If the function of practical reason is mere searching for the means, how can its determination of the end depend upon the rational image which determines the desire? How is it possible to say "Rational representation, logically mediated, has a power of conviction to determine the desire," after saying "The end is established by the desire," and "The practical reason is here unable to change anything"? Further, it is no less unintelligible to say that "the end as rational concept, i.e. the universal end, belongs to those representations," since the end is said to be nothing but the object of desire. It is also said that the judgement that we should be moderate is not the product of practical reason, but being itself a theoretical cognition, is borrowed from outside. Not only Teichmüller, but anyone would be astonished to hear that the fundamental judgement of φρόνησις does not belong to practical intellect. All these absurdities follow from Walter's attempt to restrict the function of practical intellect to the searching for the means, without contributing anything to the end.

We have taken the practical reason in the *Ethics* as the intellectual intuition of the individual. What then does it mean to say that "from the individual comes the universal"? According to Hartenstein,[179] the individual is the means, while the universal is the end. Thus understood, the above statement would amount to saying that the end comes from the means, or that the first and the highest end is realized through the nearest means. But even if ἕνεκά του λογιζόμενος may be the cognition of the means, ἀρχαὶ γὰρ τοῦ οὗ ἕνεκα αὗται cannot be rendered as "it is the principle of the end." Consequently, the individual cannot be taken as the means to an end. But we do not maintain against Hartenstein that the universal is the means while the individual is an end. Rather, we understand the statement as meaning that the universal end comes from the individual one, that is to say, the universal end or

<hr>

[178] *Ibid.* 53; cf. 208 ff.; 215 ff.; 230.
[179] *Ibid.* 47 ff.

the so-called moral intention which characterizes personality, results from individual ends and their realization.[180]

There remains finally the fact that this cognition of individuals is said to be a perception, and that this perception is identified with reason. No doubt, from its context this reason must be taken to be practical. What then does it mean to say that practical reason which intuitively comprehends the last minor premise of practical cognition is a perception? Neither Walter nor Trendelenburg are successful in the interpretation of this point. Walter, who admits nothing but the theoretical reason, thinks that the perception of individuals here mentioned is perception in the literal sense, and that it is called reason only because universal and theoretical knowledge is induced from perception of particular things.[181] We hardly find it necessary to disprove such a theory. Trendelenburg[182] also explains the designation of perception as mere metaphor employed on account of the intuitive character applicable to both of them, though perception is concerned with present things, and the object of purpose with future beings. But there is no sufficient reason for taking it as a metaphor, and we can by no means recognize the essence of practical reason through such an interpretation. In this respect, the theory of Ritter is more plausible; it identifies the practical reason with *sensus communis*, a kind of intellectual intuition, which determines what is good and what is bad for oneself. This interpretation is probably based upon the following statement in the *Ethics* a little preceding the statement in question, viz., *Eth. Nic.* VI. 8. 1142 a 25: "It (practical wisdom) is opposed, then, to reason, for reason is of the limiting premise, for which no reason can be given, while practical wisdom is concerned with the ultimate particular, which is the object not of scientific knowledge but of perception[183] – not the perception of qualities peculiar to one sense but a perception akin to that by which we perceive that the particular figure before us

---

[180] Walter regards both premises of a practical syllogism to be essentially theoretical, and the minor premise to be perception in the ordinary sense. So that for him the phrase in question would imply that general knowledge is induced from perception (*op. cit.* 324 f.). But, since he takes, on the other hand, deliberation as a cognition that searches for the means to a given end, it follows that this induction would proceed from the knowledge of a particular means to that of a universal end; thus the order of practical syllogism would be turned around, which is unreasonable.

[181] Walter, *op. cit.* 323 ff.

[182] Trendelenburg, *op. cit.* II. 378.

[183] It is not seldom that moral valuation is called perception: e.g. *Pol.* I. 2. 1253 a 14 f.; *Eth. Nic.* II. 9. 1109 b 14–23.

is a triangle;[184] for in that direction as well as in that of the major premise there will be a limit."[185]

If we compare this with the first quotation from *Eth. Nic.* VI. 11., the correspondence is remarkable enough; hence there is hardly any doubt that the "reason in the practical," in the earlier quotation is the same as the practical wisdom here mentioned,[186] and there is no room for the reason in question to be theoretical. Walter's objections to this are not worthy of serious attention; he argues for instance, that common sensation is not of necessity practical reason, or that it is a specially defined concept in the psychology and cannot be the same as this

[184] *Eth. Nic.* VI. 9. 1142 a 28 f.: ἀλλ᾽ οἵα αἰσθανόμεθα ὅτι τὸ (ἐν τοῖς μαθηματικοῖς) ἔσχατον τρίγωνον. – following Bywater and Ross. Michelet reads this: "the sensation that perceives that the last term of the mathematical analysis is the triangle," implying namely that the triangle is the most simple of all figures. But this reading is untenable, because as pointed out by Stewart, such a qualification is to be assigned to the point rather than to the triangle. Walter, who followed Michelet, cannot understand the reason why it is a common sensation. cf. Walter, *op. cit.* 389 ff.

[185] Walter takes this στήσεται κα᾽κεῖ also as the end of pursuit and deliberation. But this only indicates the individual as the ultimate member of the conceptual series. cf. Walter, *op. cit.* 392.

[186] Trendelenburg's interpretation on this point is quite different from ours. According to him, the intuitive practical reason is different from practical wisdom, the former bearing quite another sort of resemblance to perception than the latter. Practical reason resembles perception in that they are both immediate cognition; while practical wisdom resembles perception in that they are concerned with the last term of research. Trendelenburg seems to have arrived at this view, because he, like Walter, following the statement in *Eth. Nic.* III. 5. 1112 b 12, finds the function of practical wisdom mainly in deliberation, and makes the essence of deliberation lie in the searching for the means. He finds an example in *De Motu An.* 7. 701 a 20: "And the action goes back to the beginning or first step. If there is to be a coat, one must first have B, and if B then A, and so one gets A to begin with." Further, reading the text in 1142 a 28, like Walter, to mean that the perceptive judgement that assumes the triangle to be the ultimate element of geometrical analysis, he finds the ground for the function of φρόνησις being compared to the perception of the ultimate individual in geometry in *Eth. Nic.* III. 5. 1112 b 20–24: "For the person who deliberates seems to investigate and analyse in the way described as though he were analysing a geometrical construction ... and what is last in the order of analysis seems to be first in the order of becoming." (cf. Trendelenburg, *Beiträge* II. 381 f). But, to take the minor premise of a practical syllogism for a perceptive judgement is incompatible with taking the relation of practical reason and perception for a mere metaphor. Besides, geometrical analysis is by no means the function of perception; what are perceived are only particular figures, which are the termini of the analysis, thus the similitude between practical wisdom as analytical deliberation and perception is untenable. Much the more implausible is Trendelenburg's theory to assign sensitive imagination to a geometrician, and deliberative imagination to a man of practical wisdom.

perception which is here identified with reason, or that this perception may teach us the good, yet does not teach us what is good for us, and the like. Even if common sensation is not always practical, it is none the less possible for practical reason to be a function or a form of common sensation. And if one says that the common sensation in the *De Anima* is not the same as the perception here mentioned, one ought to state in detail the difference between them. Further, though common sensation is sometimes not followed by pleasure and pain, e.g. in the case of mathematical figures, it does not follow that it is always theoretical and does not teach us the good for us. Perception is naturally concerned with individuals, and teaches us particular modes of being. As a rule, it is followed by pleasure and pain, and teaches us the subjective and relative good.[187] Of course, there must be some reservation with regard to this comparison; practical reason and *sensus communis* are not identical through and through. As Aristotle puts it after the above quotation: "But this is rather perception than practical wisdom, while the former belongs to another form."[188] The interpretations of this sentence are not in agreement, and even the text is not perfectly settled. It means presumably that the perception of individual figures in geometry is sensitive, while the practical reason should be intellectual. Though practical wisdom is assimilated to common sensation in respect to the intuitive character, some other name was required for strictness' sake. This short notice suggests the generic concept of practical wisdom not to be perfectly suited to this particular function, and that Aristotle adopted such ambiguous concept as "the reason in the practical," with some hesitation. Presumably, Teichmüller's special denomination "phronetische Wahrnehmung"[189] is not far from the mark.

Through the foregoing examination of various interpretations, we

---

187 Cf. ch. II. 2.

188 Ross translates ἀλλ' αὕτη μᾶλλον αἴσθησις ἢ φρόνησις, ἐκείνης δ' ἄλλο εἶδος as "But this is rather perception than practical wisdom, though it is another kind of perception than that of the qualities peculiar to each sense." Following this version, the statement is only related to the perception of a triangle without any relevance to practical wisdom. But the real implication of the sentence is rather that practical wisdom is not strictly identical with *sensus communis*. Rolfes's version seems to be better, it runs namely: *Jenes Vermögen für die eigentümlichen Sinnesqualitäten ist mehr Sinn als Klugheit, das hier gemeinte Vermögen aber ist von anderer Art.* On this point, we cannot agree with Walter's opinion either.

189 Teichmüller, *Aristotelische Forschungen* I. 262. *Neue Studien zur Geschichte der Begriffe* III. 297; cf. Walter, *op. cit.* 396, 383, 554.

have reached the conclusion that the intellectual intuition of the minor premise which is mentioned in *Eth. Nic.* VI. 13, is practical reason in a special sense. It is a kind of practical intellect, which recognizes particular facts in a practical way and intuitively, and in this respect is assimilated to common sensation. This cognition of practical reason constitutes the minor premise of practical inference, or the principle of the end, while a moral habit or character grows from the setting up of individual ends, and forms the major premise of a practical syllogism.

To return, why the same word "reason" is applied to theoretical as well as to practical cognition, indicating on the one hand the intuition of the universal, and on the other, that of the particular? It may be that the universal proposition of theoretical cognition is essentially different from that of practical cognition; the one being *a priori*, and the other *a posteriori*. For instance, the principle of identity or that of contradiction is universally applicable and *a priori*, while the general laws of morality and politics are probable and *a posteriori*. It is true that even in the theoretical, some general knowledge is attained by induction. Still in theoretical knowledge, the universal has greater importance than the particular, and is prior in itself though it is posterior for us. Otherwise with practical intellect. Moral principle is *a posteriori* and empirical, not only for us, but also in itself. The universal principle of practical cognition has no such strictness as that of theoretical cognition.[190] Aristotle maintains that it is here that we find the very characteristic of the method of practical philosophy. According to him, to require the same strictness in all departments of cognition is a mark of ignorance as to the method or the lack of culture. Aristotle admits only *a posteriori* and probable morality. Nevertheless, as far as there is a syllogism, the particular must be associated with the universal. Their universal principles grow from sensation and experience, but once obtained through induction, they may be applied deductively to each individual case. One may wonder how is it possible to characterize the practical principle in opposition to the theoretical. For it may seem as if in either case the principle is perceived as self-evident; but this is not really the case. From a logical or essential point of view, theoretical

[190] *Eth. Nic.* II. 7. 1107 a 28–31; X. 10. 1179 a 35–b 10. Further, an incontinent character is assumed to be one which has only a general judgement and a good intention, yet is unable to practice it in a particular case, while on the contrary, a continent man can suppress an excessive desire, yet is lacking in perfect harmony between desire and reason, it is, in this respect, inferior to temperance as a perfect harmonious character. Herein we may confirm the inferior significance of general knowledge in practice; cf. ch. V.

principle is self-evident, but practical rule is not. Hence, the universal rules of practice cannot be the object of intellectual intuition. On the other hand, sensation as the lowest limit of theoretical cognition is hardly rational; it contains only the minimum potentiality of conceptual form in itself, which however, will be finally realized in a universal knowledge. Therefore, the end of theoretical cognition is not the individual, but the universal. In the realm of practice, on the contrary, the individual is the end, wherein practical principle is realized. The universal knowledge of practice is nothing but the summary of practical experience.[191] In theoretical knowledge, the universal is more important, in the practical, on the contrary, the individual is predominant.[192] This, presumably, is the reason why Aristotle remarks that reason in the theoretical is concerned with the universal limit, while in the practical, it is rather concerned with the individual limit.

5. *Practical Wisdom*

Practical reason is closely related to *sensus communis* though they are not quite identical. *Sensus communis* is a function of imagination based upon the heart,[193] and practical reason or practical wisdom is the principle which regulates desire and yields moderation,[194] whereas imagination and desire are, so to say, two aspects of the same activity, the one being static and cognitive, and the other dynamic and active.[195] Hence it may be said that practical wisdom or practical reason is another side of *sensus communis*, the former being exclusively practical, while the other extends to the theoretical as well. Thus, practical reason or practical wisdom is also based upon the body, especially upon the heart as the organ of *sensus communis*.[196] It can manage and control

---

191 *Eth. Nic.* I. 2. 1095 a 30–b 7; cf. Stewart's and Grant's note *ad loc.*; *Eth. Nic.* VI. 12. 1143 b 4; I. 7. 1098 b 3 f.
192 *Eth. Nic.* VI. 8. 1141 b 14–22.
193 Cf. ch. II. 2. p. 94
194 *Ibid.* p. 108.
195 *Ibid.* p. 96.
196 Cf. Teichmüller, *op. cit.* 138 ff. Practical wisdom is not directly attributed to heart, but it is regarded as the highest principle of ethical virtues. Now ethical virtue depends upon our body (*Eth. Nic.* X. 8. 1178 a 15), being excellence of character with regard to pleasure and pain (*Phys.* VII. 3. 247 a 7, 24; *Eth. Nic.* II. 2. 1104 b 9; VII. 12. 1152 b 9), whereas pleasure and pain depend upon the heart (*Part. An.* III. 4. 666 a 11), in other words, the physiological state of the heart determines the character (*ibid.* 667 a 11). Hence we may conclude that practical wisdom depends upon the physiological state of the heart.

desire, which is derived from the body, by being itself a form of this same body. On this account, practical wisdom cannot be taught, but must be habituated.[197] However, as far as it is a kind of intellect, it is not a mere function of the body, but bears some transcendent character. We have interpreted the active reason in general to be something transcendent, like the objective mind in Hegel. Though there is no elucidation of its activity, we may suppose that this so-called active reason acts in practical thinking as well as in theoretical thinking. Whether theoretical or practical, human intellect, which is by nature passive, can act in virtue of the cooperation of active reason and imagination. The only difference between theoretical cognition and practical cognition consists in that the former aims at thinking itself, while the latter aims at another end, i.e. practice. Hence it may be inferred moreover that active reason is predominant in theoretical thinking rather than in practical thinking.

Since practical wisdom is the right measure of desire, and desire depends upon the heart, practical wisdom is founded, though indirectly, upon the heart. The heart is the factory and depository of the blood,[198] and the nature of the blood determines not only the desire, but also the intelligence,[199] of an animal. Generally speaking, an animal of cold and thin blood is more intelligent than one of warm and dense blood. The heart is also the central organ of sensation, and its physiological changes are experienced by the mind as pleasure and pain,[200] while its expansion and contraction cause the reaction of the limbs. Not that conduct comes from the mind independent of the body, but that mental phenomena such as emotion, image, or desire are always accompanied by physiological phenomena, especially those of the heart.[201] Consequently, though practical wisdom *par excellence* is appropriate to man, animals of all kinds are considered to possess it in a lower degree.[202] All living beings want to preserve themselves, and as practical wisdom is the complete actuality of self-preservation instinct, all animal behaviors such as nutrition, love, or intercourse among the same species, are guided by practical wisdom in a wider sense.[203]

---

[197] *Eth. Nic.* X. 10. 1179 b 21; *Pol.* VIII. 3. 1338 b 4.
[198] *Part. An.* III. 4. 666 a 7.
[199] *Part. An.* II. 2. 648 a 3–12; II. 4. 650 b 18–26.
[200] *Part. An.* III. 4. 666 a 11.
[201] *Ibid.* 666 a 31, b 13.
[202] *Eth. Nic.* VI. 7. 1141 a 25 f.
[203] *Gen. An.* III. 2. 753 a 7–11; *Eth. Nic.* VI. 7. 1141 a 26–28.

That practical wisdom depends upon the heart, implies the domination of nature over morality. Does it not then amount to the negation
of freedom? Does it not follow that neither is virtue a merit, nor vice a
sin, if our moral character is determined by the natural constitution of
our heart?[204] It is well known that in Aristotle, and generally in all
ancient philosophers, there was no problem of freedom in the sense of
liberum arbitrium indifferentium. The only concept of freedom to be
found is ἐχουσία which implies the voluntariness of an act, viz., that
an act is originated from one's own desire. Though προαίρεσις or will is
regarded as something more than a desire, the only superiority of this
consists in its being accompanied by deliberation as to the means and
there is no special concept of freedom associated to this. The origin of
the desire or the will is irrelevant to the question of freedom.[205] The
so-called *liberum arbitrium indifferentium* in later ages, which implies
an accidental decision of a will without any sufficient reason either in
nature or in spirit, by no means constitutes the principle of responsibility of a person. We are responsible only for what is done by ourselves in virtue of our own characters. The characters which are
determined or modified by our circumstances do not discharge us from
responsibility. A transcendent character quite irrelevant to nature or
society has no place in the realistic mind of Aristotle's. Thus, human
freedom is not ruled out by the fact that ethical virtues and practical
wisdom depend upon bodily conditions.[206]

Further, because practical wisdom exists of necessity, its functions,
advice as well as prohibition, are also necessary for us. In other words,
nature controls us in terms of practical wisdom. "Nature without
practical wisdom" must be distinguished from "nature through practical wisdom;" the one is the mode through which nature commands the
animal and the plant, while the other is that through which it commands
the human being. Nature appears in various modes and there is no
nature itself apart from its appearances, for such a nature would be
quite inactive, and inactive nature is mere nonsense.

Now practical wisdom is related to desire as form to matter, and the
same relation is found between desire and heart. Further, though it
may be said on the one hand that practical wisdom gives the right
measure to desire, it may also be said on the other hand that practical

204 *Eth. Nic.* III. 7. 1114 a 31–b8.
205 *Eth. Nic.* III. 7. 1114 b 12 ff.; III. 3. 1111 a 29 ff.; *Eth. Eud.* II. 7. 1223 a
21 ff.; cf. ch. II. 4.
206 Cf. *Phys.* VIII. 21. 253 a 8 ff.; II. 8. 199 a 5 ff.

wisdom is the complete actuality of moderate disposition which depends upon a certain state of heart. The good disposition which does not yet reach ethical virtue is called natural virtue.[207] Practical wisdom presupposes it, but its development requires other conditions as well, viz, education,[208] the education, which is carried out methodically by a wise man who has accomplished his moral personality.[209] Nature aims at intellect as its completion, while intellect acts upon nature. Intellect grows and sows its seed in the good soil – the good soil being a young man of good disposition, and the seeds the virtues. Thus in theory as well as in practice, intellect maintains itself through being revived in new generation and new personality.[210] This is the only immortality sanctioned to the mortal.

What, then, does it mean to say that practical wisdom is the complete actuality of natural virtue? Natural virtue is different from ethical virtue in that the one is partial and lacks unity, while the other is entire and harmonious.[211] For instance, courage is surely founded upon a natural disposition, but that alone is not sufficient to make one behave well; one who relies only upon natural virtue is apt to be rash and unjust. Natural virtue is a disposition to obey the command of practical wisdom; it is the most primitive virtue of the irrational soul in the secondary sense, so to say, the minimum of ethical virtue. As to practical wisdom, it is the gift of seniors as well as the development of natural virtue. In practical wisdom, what is interior is inseparably united with what is exterior, the rational with the irrational, the passive with the active. Natural virtue realizes its end completely when it has developed itself into practical wisdom.

Moreover, natural virtue is one-sided. For instance, one may have a courageous disposition, but not the disposition of temperance, whereas practical wisdom does not allow such separation of virtues. A man of practical wisdom is at the same time courageous and practically wise; he is always in conformity with reason. This is because natural virtue is a mere fact, while ethical virtue or practical wisdom is the ideal of morality. Practical wisdom brings about a complete harmony among virtues, and affords man to adapt himself to his circumstances. In this sense practical wisdom is the perfection of the ethical virtues and

---

[207] *Eth. Nic.* VI. 13. 1144 b 1–17.
[208] *Eth. Nic.* X. 10. 1179 b 31–1180 a 12; *Pol.* III. 4. 1277 a 14.
[209] *Eth. Nic.* X. 10. 1180 b 25–28; 10. 1180 a 14–22; 1180 a 32 ff.
[210] *Eth. Nic.* X. 10. 1179 b 23 ff.
[211] *Eth. Nic.* VI. 13. 1144 b 34–1145 a 2.

ethical virtues are the completion of natural dispositions. Practical wisdom, striking its root deep into the nature, rises high up in the spiritual world, originating in the same source as the animal and the plant, it affords the human mind to participate in divine thinking. Practical wisdom itself is just a kind of human intellect, and is concerned with human affairs, but man ought to keep the health of body and the calmness of mind in order to communicate with eternal ideas and to partake in the divine activity of God. Just as a state ought to be well governed and to be rich in order to be prosperous in its culture and civilization, so it is with the individual man. Practical wisdom is necessary for the attainment of theoretical knowledge which is *per se* the most valuable of all things. It is as much the medium of the eternal intelligible world and the human beings, as the process from the irrational to the theoretical intellect.[212]

Practical wisdom is based upon the heart and is correlative with ethical virtue which originates from natural virtue. So, in its strict sense, practical wisdom is proper to man, in its wider sense it may be found in animals as well. Man and animal were not so strictly separated in Aristotle as in Christianity. However, it would be a great mistake if one should imagine that Aristotle's theory of ethics is merely biological and lacks in social significance. It would be rather astonishing if the Greek who found the essence of man in political activity should have neglected the social character of morality. The naturalistic basis of morality does not rule out the social significance of it. This is congruent with Aristotle's determination of the state to the effect that it originates in the bare needs of life, and continues in existence for the sake of good life.[213]

Thus far, we have studied the practical wisdom which is synonymous with practical reason in the narrow sense. But there must be, beside this, a kind of universal knowledge of practical affairs, though there is no special concept for this faculty. Practical wisdom is related both to the individual and to the universal; in the latter case, it may be called architectonic wisdom of practice. The end of practice is an individual act, yet we need a universal knowledge to act rightly in a particular case. A man of practice is not yet a practically wise man, unless he has attained a universal cognition about the essence of practice. Without

---

[212] *Eth. Nic.* VI. 13. 1145 a 6–11; cf. *ibid.* 7. 1141 a 20; *Pol.* VII. 15. 1334 a 14–20.

[213] *Pol.* I. 2. 1252 b 29.

this kind of knowledge, moral conduct would be impossible except accidentally. Now these two kinds of practical wisdom, i.e. the universal and the particular are to be combined with each other and form a kind of inference analogous to scientific knowledge. This would be the so-called practical syllogism.

CHAPTER V

THE PRACTICAL SYLLOGISM

1. Deliberation

The end of practical cognition is a particular act, but its directing principle must be something universal. Therefore, practical wisdom in the wide sense would contain both universal and particular knowledge and form a syllogism. How, then, is it related to the kinds of practical intellect? Is it that every kind of practical intellect should conjoin to a syllogism, or is it rather that they are independent from each other and that practical syllogism is a partial phenomenon of practical intellect? Now that among the functions of practical intellect, deliberation is the most important and is analogous to scientific knowledge in pertaining to inference, it is reasonable first to investigate how it is related to practical syllogism.

Deliberation is explained as follows.[1] It is not concerned with eternal beings such as heavenly bodies or geometrical figures, nor natural phenomena which always happen in the same way, such as the solstices or the rising of the stars. Neither is it concerned with the things which happen now in one way, now in another, e.g., draughts or rains; nor chance events like the finding of treasures. We deliberate about what we can manage, and not always in the same way, e.g., the healing of sickness or the accumulating of wealth, and especially what involves indefiniteness. Besides, we deliberate not about ends, but about means. For a physician does not deliberate whether he shall heal, nor an orator whether he shall persuade, nor a statesman whether he shall produce law and order, nor does anyone else deliberate about his end. They assume the end and consider how and by what means it is to be attained; and if it seems to be produced by several means, they

---

[1] *Eth. Nic.* III. 5. 1112 a 18–1113 a 2.

consider by what it is most easily and best produced, while if it is
achieved by one only, they consider how it will be achieved by this and
by what means this will be achieved, till they come to the first cause,
which in the order of discovery is the last. And if we come on an im-
possibility, we give up the search. Thus deliberation is the search for
the series of possible means within our power. Just by this special
character is deliberation distinguished from wish. In summarizing the
above statements, Aristotle says[2]: "It seems, then, as has been said,
that man is a moving principle of actions; now deliberation is about
the things to be done by the agent himself, and actions are for the sake
of things other than themselves. For the end cannot be an object of
deliberation, but only the means; nor indeed can the particular facts
be an object of it, ... If we are to be always deliberating, we shall have
to go on to infinity." This object of βούλευσις is also the object of will
only differing in that the object of will is determined but the object of
deliberation is not. "Since the object of will is one of the things in our
own power which is desired after deliberation, will must be deliberate
desire of things in our own power; for when we have decided as a result
of deliberation, we desire in accordance with our deliberation." The
end is said to be what we wish for, and the means what we deliberate
about and will.[3]

Thus it is repeated that the object of deliberation and will is not the
end, but the means.[4] Therefore, deliberation presupposes a desire as
its motive,[5] and searches for the means[6] to realize this original desire.
By this procedure the original desire is elaborated and determined into
a concrete will. On the other hand, however, as we have argued before,
deliberation may be the efficient cause of desire as well, and the desire
which presupposes such deliberation was called not προαίρεσις, but
βούλευσις, i.e. wish .This wish, being a calculated desire, was more highly
estimated than ἐπιθυμία or θύμος. Deliberation in will was the cognition
of means, but deliberation in desire was, according to our interpretation,
the estimative calculation of ends.[7]

Thus deliberation is divided into two kinds, the one being the esti-

[2] Eth. Nic. III. 5. 1113 a 2–14.
[3] Eth. Nic. III. 7. 1113 b 3.
[4] Eth. Nic. III. 4. 1111 b 26; 5. 1112 b 32; VI. 2. 1139 a 13; Eth. Eud. II. 10.
1226 b 10; (Mag. Mor. I. 35. 1196 b 29); Rhet. I. 2. 1357 a 4; 6. 1362 a 18; III.
5. 1383 a 7; cf. Eth. Eud. II. 11. 1227 b 20 ff.
[5] Eth. Nic. III. 5. 1113 a 10 f. Eth. Eud. II. 10. 1662 b 16 f.
[6] Eth. Nic. III. 13. 1112 b 15; Eth. Eud. II. 10. 1226 b29.
[7] Ch. II. 2.

mation of the ends, and the other the searching for the means. Though Aristotle does not mention the matter explicitly, these two kinds of deliberation may have some reference to the distinction between practice and production. For according to our investigation, production is the realization of a fact, and practice that of a moral value, and the one realizes the form in a process, while the other realizes it at once.[8] May we not infer then that the βούλευσις which is here qualified as estimative calculation, is practical cognition or φρόνησις, while the βούλευσις, which was qualified as the searching for the means is productive cognition or τέχνη. In fact, the objects of βούλευσις are what can be otherwise – not natural phenomena of which the determinative principles exist in the phenomena themselves, but what are in our power, and can be brought about by our efforts. And since conduct is either practice or production, there would be deliberation of practice as well as deliberation of production.[9]

But, as a matter of fact, the distinction between practice and production was not explicit enough in Aristotle, and a mere actualization of a factual form was often presented as an instance of practice. Deliberation surely contains practical intellect, but it is in most cases explained as being a technical intellect – just as in the above quotation, where it is illustrated by healing, oration, or administration, and in other places, by navigation, gymnastics, and accumulation of wealth.[10] Those conducts are all productions, so that deliberation about them would be technical.

Deliberation is generally said to be the searching for the means, whereas the end of production lies in the results, and that of practice in the act itself.[11] Therefore, deliberation in production is the thinking of the process which will lead to the end, i.e., the thinking of the means in the strict sense. But practice is not a movement that realizes its factual end

[8] Ch. III. 3.

[9] Eth. Nic. III. 5. 1112 b 6–8. But, Phys. II. 8. 199 b 28; καίτοι καὶ ἡ τέχνη οὐ βουλεύεται seems to suggest that deliberation does not involve art. According to Teichmüller, it means that art is concerned with the universal, whereas deliberation applies it to the particular (Arist. Forsch. II. 398). According to Zeller, this is a statement about an expert, who performs art without deliberation. Ross, quoting Eth. Nic. III. 5. 1112 a 34, interprets it to mean that strict and self-sufficient knowledge involves no deliberation. These are all probable interpretations, but what is stated in the text is the analogy between nature and art, so it would rather mean: "In the minimum consciousness of art, there is only minimum deliberation." Though deliberation is an essential element of production, it goes down as art approaches either to science or to nature.

[10] Eth. Nic. III. 5. 1112 b 4 f.

[11] Eth. Nic. VI. 2. 1139 b 5; 5. 1140 b 6 f.

ally, it is an actuality without process. Consequently, the con-
:ion for reaching a practical end cannot be the thinking as to
nd effect in the ordinary sense, but the thinking as to the sub-
on or subsumption of practical values or at least the application of a rule on an individual case. But to what extent can we confirm
our supposition with Aristotle's statements? To answer this question,
let us study his statements about the virtues of deliberation.

The concept which indicates the virtue of deliberation most literally
is εὐβουλία. According to Aristotle, εὐβουλία or excellence in deliberation
is a certain correctness of deliberation, but since there is more than
one kind of correctness, excellence in deliberation plainly is not any
and every kind; for an incontinent man or a bad man, if he is clever,
will reach as a result of his calculation what he sets before himself, so
that he will have deliberated correctly, but will get for himself a great
evil.[12] Consequently, not every correctness is a good thing. Now excellence of deliberation is thought to be a good thing. In what sense,
then, is it correct?

Since it is a good thing, and brings about happiness, it must be the
correctness of deliberation which tends to attain what is good,[13] for
however correctly the means to a bad end may be deliberated, it will
only lead to an evil. When the value of an end is left out of account,
and the deliberation concentrates itself upon the means, excellence in it
is called δεινότης, i.e., cleverness. When it subordinates itself to a good
end, it may be practical wisdom, but if, on the contrary, to a bad end,
it will be πανουργία or craftiness.[14]

If we should distinguish εὐβουλία from πανουργία by attributing the
goodness of the end to the former, excellence of deliberation must contain both cognition about the means and the virtue of desire, whereas
deliberation was defined as the thinking about the means, and to indicate the virtue both of desire and thinking, there is the concept of
practical wisdom. How, then, is φρόνησις related to εὐβουλία? Considering practical wisdom independently, Aristotle attributes to it 1) both
the good end and the excellent calculation,[15] but comparing it with
the ethical virtue, he says as if 2) practical wisdom were confined to the

---

12 *Eth. Nic.* VI. 10. 1142 b 16–20. *Prima facie*, εὐβουλία appears to be some
deviated natural gift like σύνεσις or γνώμη (cf. Joachim 215), but thorough
examination will reveal it to be the virtue of deliberation in general. Perhaps
l. 18 ἀκρατής is an slip for ἀκόχαστος, i.e., a self-indulgent man. cf. Grant and
Stewart *ad loc.*
13 *Eth. Nic.* VI. 10. 1142 b 20 ff.
14 *Eth. Nic.* VI. 13. 1144 a 23–28.
15 *Eth. Nic.* VI. 5. 1140 a 29.

thinking of the means.[16] Finally, when he distinguishes practical wisdom from δεινότης, he states that 3) practical wisdom is the apprehension of a good end.[17]

3) No doubt, it is not accurate to take practical wisdom merely as apprehension of a good end. For to establish a purpose is the function of desire rather than that of intellect, and the virtue of desire is an ethical virtue, while practical wisdom is regarded as a kind of intellectual virtue.[18] 2) But if practical wisdom is confined to the thinking of the means, it is hardly distinguishable from deliberation or even from cleverness. 1) Therefore, practical wisdom must contain both the good end and the excellent calculation.[19] Thus we are confronted with the original difficulty how to distinguish excellence of deliberation from practical wisdom. At all events, εὐβουλία is tantamount to φρόνησις, and the difference, if any, only consists in whether the end or the means is emphasized.

To resume, it was said that εὐβουλία does not mean the excellence in general of deliberation, but the excellence of deliberation which serves a good end.[20] But as far as the combination of deliberation and the good end is accidental, and the same faculty may become either good or evil in accordance to the end which it serves, excellence of deliberation is not different in its essence from cleverness or smartness. There would be one identical virtue of deliberation, which may serve either to a good end or to the evil. But this is nothing but the δεινότης or cleverness. As Aristotle puts it[21]: "There is such as to be able to do the things that tends towards the mark we have set before ourselves, and to hit it. Now if the mark be noble, the cleverness is laudable, but if the mark be bad, the cleverness is mere smartness; hence we call even men of practical wisdom clever or smart." This shows that in usual language practical wisdom and cleverness are often confused. But what is the real difference between them, and how is the one related to the other? Aristotle continues saying[22]: "Practical wisdom is not this faculty, but it does not exist without this faculty." Is it then that cleverness is a constituent of practical wisdom, and that cleverness combined with something will become practical wisdom? What is then that which

---

[16] *Eth. Nic.* VI. 13. 1144 a 8 f.; 1145 a 4–6.
[17] *Eth. Nic.* VI. 10. 1142 b 31–33.
[18] *Eth. Nic.* I. 13. 1102 b 28–1103 a 10; VI. 5. 1140 b 26; 13. 1144 b 14.
[19] *Eth. Nic.* VI. 8. 1141 b 14 f.; *ibid.* 21–23. cf. Grant, *Eth.* II. 176 note.
[20] *Eth. Nic.* VI. 8. 1141 b 8–10.
[21] *Eth. Nic.* VI. 13. 1144 a 23.
[22] *Eth. Nic.* VI. 13. 1144 a 28.

constitutes another part of practical wisdom? What is most likely to be the case is natural virtue. For in succession to the statement above mentioned, Aristotle states[23] that both cleverness and practical wisdom belong to the opinion-making part, and they are related to each other just as natural virtue is to ethical virtue. Cleverness and natural virtue are both natural dispositions which are devoid of moral value in the strict sense. A mere natural virtue is possible even to children and animals, and is not under the control of reason. "But without reason these are evidently hurtful. While one may be led astray by them, as a strong body which moves without sight may stumble badly because of its lack of sight, still, if a man once acquires reason, that makes a difference in action; and his state, while still like what it was, will then be virtue in the strict sense."[24]

Obviously, cleverness and natural virtue are the foundations of practical wisdom and ethical virtue, and it may appear as if once these two kinds of natural disposition be combined, they will be elevated to practical wisdom and ethical virtue. But the matter is not so simple[25]; mere mixture of cleverness and natural virtue does not produce practical wisdom or ethical virtue. Cleverness does not teach us what is good, but only presupposes an end, which may be either good or bad. Similarly, natural virtue combined with cleverness is short of ethical virtue, for cleverness cannot give a right rule to natural virtue. What is then the meaning of the statement, "if a man once acquires reason, that makes a difference in action; and his state, while still like what it was, will then be virtue in the strict sense?" This reason cannot be the mere cleverness, for cleverness presupposes the end and cannot establish it. The reason which determines a good end must be essentially laudable. Aristotle suggests that εὐβουλία is such a faculty. As he puts it[26]: "The man who is without qualification good at deliberating is the man who is capable of aiming in accordance with calculation at the best for man of things attainable by action." Here εὐβουλία is regarded something more than a mere searching for the means to realize any arbitrary end. "What is best for man" is not given by immediate intuition or by natural virtue, but it must be prepared by λογίσμος or calculation, and this calculation must be the proper function of εὐβουλία.

---

[23] *Ibid.* 1144 b 1 ff.
[24] *Ibid.* 10–14.
[25] On this point we admit the ambiguousness noticed by Walsh (*op. cit.* 145 n.). But we cannot follow him in admitting practical cleverness besides productive cleverness.
[26] *Eth. Nic.* VI. 13. 1144 b 9–32; X. 8. 1178 a 16–19.

One may assert that the end is immediately desired in accordance with one's own character, and that it was that which was maintained by Aristotle himself. As far as the ultimate end is concerned, it is true. But it is not sufficient for action, because action is concerned with the particular. Therefore there must be some faculty which mediates the universal with the particular. But this is the function not of volition, but of intellect; the intellect which is concerned with the contingent and what can be realized by action, viz. the intellect which deals with the practical. This is why Aristotle stated in succession to the statement quoted above: "Nor is practical wisdom concerned with universals only – it must also recognize the particulars; for it is practical, and practice is concerned with particulars."[27]

The reason why natural virtue cannot be ethical virtue, even if it be combined with cleverness is, according to Aristotle, "without reason these (natural virtues) are evidently hurtful." and "one may be led astray by them, as a strong body which moves without sight may stumble badly because of its lack of sight." The λόγος or reason which changes natural virtue into virtue in the strict sense is identified with practical wisdom. If on the contrary, practical wisdom were nothing but the thinking of the means in a factual sense, it can neither be the prerequisite of moral wish nor be identical with ethical virtues taken as a whole, as Aristotle puts it: [28] "This is why some say that all the virtues are forms of practical wisdom, and why Socrates in one respect was on the right track while in another he went astray; in thinking that all the virtues were forms of practical wisdom he was wrong, but in saying they implied practical wisdom he was right. This is confirmed by the fact that even now all men, when they define virtue, after naming the state of character and its objects, add 'that (state) which is in accordance with the right rule'; now the right rule is that which is in accordance with practical wisdom, all men, then, seem somehow to divine that this kind of state is virtue, viz. that which is in accordance with practical wisdom. But we must go a little further. For it is not merely the state in accordance with the right rule, but the state that implies the presence of the right rule, that is virtue; and practical wisdom is a right rule about such matters ... It is clear, then, from what has been said, that it is not possible to be good in the strict sense without practical wisdom, nor practically wise without ethical virtue." Thus it is evident that the λόγος which determines a good end is the practical

[27] *Eth. Nic.* VI. 8. 1141 b 15.
[28] *Ibid.* 13. 1144 b 17–32.

wisdom, other than cleverness or deliberation concerning factual means. It must be the estimation of what is good and what is bad, or of what is the mean[29] between too much and too little; in other words, the practical deliberation distinguished from the productive one. It is just because the cognition by practical wisdom is essentially ethical that one may say, "with the presence of practical wisdom, will be given all the virtues."[30] Otherwise, each of the ethical virtues would have to be acquired independently.

2. Practical Syllogism and Productive Syllogism

So far we have assumed that deliberation as the chief constituent of practical wisdom should be divided into what is concerned with practice or moral value, and what is concerned with production of mere fact. Next we must confirm it through the study of the practical syllogism as the form of deliberation. Deliberation is the main function of

---

[29] Eth. Nic. VI. 5. 1140 b 8–10; 1140 a 25; II. 6. 1106 b 36–1107 a 2: ἔστιν ἄρα ἡ ἀρετὴ ἕξις προαιρετική, ἐν μεσότητι οὖσα τῇ πρὸς ἡμᾶς, ὡρισμένη λόγῳ καὶ ᾧ ὁ φρόνιμος ὁρίσειεν. The ὀρθὸς λόγος which is the measure of moderation, is precisely the intellectual element of φρόνησις. It is not mere cognition of causality, which serves us to realize any end whatever, but the faculty of discriminating what is suitable in respect of time, matter, person, and other situations in reference to passion and conduct. Similarly, calculation as the element of continence is not the cognition how to attain enjoyment, but the estimating of what is suitable enjoyment. Cf. Eth. Nic. VII. 2. 1145 b 10; Eth. Nic. VI 2. 1139 a 21–31: "What affirmation and negation are in thinking, pursuit and avoidance are in desire; so that since moral virtue is a state of character concerned with choice (will), and choice is deliberate desire, therefore both the reasoning must be true and the desire right, if the choice is to be good, and the latter must pursue just what the former asserts. Now this kind of intellect and of truth is practical; of the intellect which is contemplative, not practical nor productive, the good and the bad state are truth and falsity respectively (for this is the work of everything intellectual); while of the part which is practical and intellectual the good state is truth in agreement with right desire." How is it possible for such an intellect to be the cognition of factual means employed only incidentally by a good desire? Further it is said Eth. Nic. VI. 5. 1140 b 20–24: "Practical wisdom, then, must be a reasoned and true state of capacity to act with regard to human good. But, further, while there is such a thing as excellence in art, there is no such thing as excellence in practical wisdom; and in art he who errs willingly is preferable, but in practical wisdom, as in the virtue, he is the reverse." This is because art is concerned merely with the means, while practical wisdom is concerned with the end as well as the means. By the virtue of art, Walter understands, presumably not rightly, the art which serves a good end. The foregoing passage rather suggests that art may sometimes signify a mere faculty instead of a virtue. Virtue is not confined to the ethical; the virtue of art is an intellectual virtue without doubt. Cf. Eth. Nic. X. 8. 1178 a 16.

[30] Eth. Nic. VI. 13. 1145 a 2.

practical intellect, just as scientific knowledge is of theoretical intellect. Just as scientific knowledge, being the composition of the universal and the particular in the theoretical area, forms a syllogism, deliberation, being the composition of the universal and the particular in the practical area, realizes itself in the so-called practica syllogism. But the concept "practical syllogism", does not appear in Aristotle's works except in an incomplete expression in *Eth. Nic.* VI. 13. 1144 a 31. This is a strange fact for a philosopher who analysed the forms of the syllogism in his logical works so elaborately. Hence it might be supposed that Aristotle assumed the syllogism in general to be theoretical and only applicable accidentally to practice. On the other hand, however, in the *Analytica* and the *Topica*, the syllogism is divided into the demonstrative and the dialectic. This presumably suggests the distinction between the theoretical and the practical syllogism. According to the statement in the *Topica*, the demonstrative syllogism starts from asserting one of the contradictory opposites, whereas the dialectic depends upon the adversary's choice between two contradictories, which are both probable.[31] Also, according to the *Analytica*, the one starts from a true and fundamental principle, while the other starts from a general opinion.[32] Now the principle of the demonstrative syllogism is evidently the object of theoretical reason, but the so-called general opinion which is considered to be the principle of the dialectic syllogism, is according to the explanation in the *Topica*, "'the opinions which are accepted by every one or by the majority, or by philosophers – i.e. by all, or by the majority, or by the most notable and illustrious of them."[33] We know that theoretical knowledge was concerned with what is necessary and cannot be otherwise, and practical cognition was concerned with what is accidental and may be otherwise than it is. Further the principle of the former is grasped *a priori*, without experience or skill, while that of the latter presupposes the ethical virtues which are acquired through habituation. Taking this into account, we cannot overlook an affinity between the demonstrative syllogism and the theoretical syllogism on the one hand, and between the dialectic syllogism and the practical syllogism on the other. It is true that demonstration and dialectic are distinguished with respect to form and

---

[31] *An. Pr.* I. 1. 24 a 22–26; *ibid.* a 30–b12; *An. Post.* I. 2. 72 a 8.
[32] *Top.* I. 1. 100 a 27 ff. Here Aristotle enumerates ἐριστικὸς συλλογισμός and παραλογισμός.
[33] *Top.* I. 1. 100 b 21.

intention rather than to object.[34] The one aims at the truth, while the other aims at persuasion. But the form and certainty of cognition differ in accordance with its object, and the certainty which is possible with regard to eternal and necessary beings, is not looked for in the area of changeable and accidental appearances. It is no less a methodical fallacy to demand a demonstration in the area of practice than to argue dialectically in the area of theoretical knowledge.[35] Plato was lacking in this reflection on methodology, and even Aristotle was not sure enough about the correspondence of method and object in his early age as represented by the *Organon*. But we may regard this distinction between demonstration and dialectic to be equivalent to Aristotle's later distinction between theoretical knowledge and practical knowledge. In fact, practical affairs were a hotbed for the quibbles of the Sophists, and both Socrates and Plato devoted themselves to establishing a science about these matters. Whereas the merit of Aristotle consists in his early age, in the organization of logical formulae as the weapon of this science, and, in his later age, in the acknowledgement of the peculiarity of practical cognition. The principle of the dialectic syllogism, which was not determined *a priori* is now determined through the habitual character of desire. This is the practical determination through ethical virtues, without which a theory would result in nothing.[36] In spite of this remarkable resemblance between the dialectic syllogism and the practical syllogism, a detailed treatment of the practical syllogism is found only in the later works.

The most fundamental mark of the practical syllogism is that the conclusion causes a practice directly. The distinction between the theoretical syllogism and the practical was not, as aforesaid, that the one is concerned with the universal and the other only with the particular, but in whether the cognition is self-sufficient or subserves practice. Therefore, the theoretical syllogism should be distinguished from the practical in respect to the end, viz., the former results in nothing but knowledge, while the latter produces conduct. It is said[37] in *Eth. Nic.* "The one opinion is universal, and the other is concerned with the particular facts, and here we come to something within the sphere of perception; when a single opinion results from the two, the soul must in one type of case affirm the conclusion, while in the case of opinions

[34] *Met.* IV. 2. 1004 b 22–26.
[35] *Eth. Nic.* I. 1. 1094 b 19–27; *Eth. Nic.* II. 2. 1103 b 34 ff.
[36] *Eth. Nic.* I. 1. 1095 a 2; 2. 1095 b 4; II. 3. 1105 b 11; VI. 12. 1143 b 6; VII. 5. 1147 a 10.
[37] *Eth. Nic.* VII. 5. 1147 a 25.

concerned with production, it must immediately act." Similarly in the
De Motu Animalium,[38] following the statement that the animal acts
through imagination, sensation or reason, it is argued: "But how is it
that reason (viz. sense, imagination and reason proper) is sometimes
followed by action, sometimes not; sometimes by movement, sometimes not? What happens seems parallel to the case of thinking and
inferring about the immovable objects of science. There in the end is the
truth seen ... but here the two premises result in a conclusion which is
an action ..." But whence comes this practical conclusion? If the
principle comes from outside the inference, the inference itself can no
longer be essentially practical, but at most only accidentally so. In
order that a cognition itself may be essentially practical, the inference
itself must involve a practical element. Now the inference is constituted
of two elements, viz. the major premise and the minor. Therefore in
order that the practical syllogism may be essentially practical, either
both or at least one of these judgements must be an expression of
some volition.[39] And the object of volition is generally a value or a
valuable thing, so the judgement which expresses a volition is concerned with a value. There are two possible ways of such concernment.
The one orders one to pursue a general value, and the other recognizes
a particular object as bearing the value in question. In a wider sense,
both may be called estimation, but estimation in the strict sense is
confined to the second kind of judgement which recognizes a particular
thing to be valuable. If the practical syllogism is constituted of these
two sorts of estimation, the major premise should be the former, and
the minor the latter. Now, there are various kinds of value, and
Aristotle divides them into three, viz., virtue, pleasure and utility.[40]
The former two are themselves valuable, while the third is valuable
only as a means to an end.[41] Consequently, we will expect estimation
and syllogism to be divided into three kinds. The one is that which
involves the cognition of virtue and the command of its pursuit, the
second involves the desire for pleasure, and the third the pursuit of

[38] *Motu An.* 7. 701 a 7–13.

[39] Cf. Teichmüller, *Neue Studien* III. 42 ff.

[40] *Eth. Nic.* VIII. 2. 1155 b 18–21. A similar division of value is also given
corresponding to the three modes of life; e.g. *Eth. Nic.* I. 3. 1095 b 14–19; *ibid.*
1096 a 5–7. Also in *Eth. Eud.* I. 1. 1214 a 32, and 4. 1215 a 32, virtue, practical
wisdom, and pleasure are enumerated as the contents of the good or of happiness.
Since φρόνησις or θεωρία is a kind of intellectual virtue, what is here called merely
virtue is to be understood as ethical virtue, which is essential to political life. A
more detailed explanation of value is found in *Rhet.* I. 6.

[41] Cf. *Pol.* VII. 13. 1332 a 7.

utility. Virtue and pleasure are themselves valuable and order us to pursue them without qualification, but the advice of utility subserves an indefinite end, the decision of which is left to our volition. The one is the so-called categorical imperative, and the other the hypothetical. As to the infinite pursuit of wealth, Aristotle takes it as the pursuit of the means to satisfy bodily pleasure.[42] But it might rather be more suitably regarded as pleasure in the acquisition of wealth. At any rate, if the syllogism is thus divided according to three corresponding kinds of value, the practical intellect also should be divided into three; viz., practical wisdom which determines the moral value of a practice, cleverness which advises for the enjoyment of pleasure, and technical calculation about the means which leads to virtue or pleasure. But the second, which is concerned with enjoyment, has slight importance to the practical syllogism. For a mere pursuit of pleasure scarcely takes a syllogistic form, and is by nature impulsive and irrational.[43] Only when an appetite asserts itself against the moral wish under the cloak of rationality, does it appear in the form of the sophistic syllogism.[44] We must suppose the practical syllogism in the strict sense to be the type of the first and the third. Thus according to our investigation, the practical syllogism is constituted of two premises, the major premise, which orders one to purpose a value in general, and the minor premise, which recognizes the presence of a value in a particular case.[45] This value is sometimes the virtue, which is *per se* valuable, sometimes a utility for an end. Therefore, the practical syllogism would be divided into that which infers about the moral value of a practice and that which infers about the factual means for an end. We must investigate whether our supposition be confirmed by the statements of Aristotle himself.

To begin with, let us examine the *Organon*. For, logic, being the science of the formulae of thinking, precedes the distinction between theoretical and practical thinking. Judgement as the element of inference, is here divided in respect of modality, as well as in respect of

[42] *Pol.* I. 9. 1258 a 4; cf. *ibid.* 1257 a 1–1258 a 19; 10. 1258 a 38 ff.; *Eth. Nic.* I. 3. 1096 a 5.

[43] *Eth. Nic.* VII. 7. 1149 a 34; *Eth. Eud.* II. 8. 1224 b 2.

[44] *Eth. Nic.* VII. 5. 1147 a 24; cf. Teichmüller, *Neue Studien* III. 43f .

[45] Hardie argues that our contention is not justified by Aristotle's own statement (*Aristotle's Ethical Theory* 288). We admit that the justification is not complete, but our present concern is to present an ideal formula of practical syllogism, which was suggested by Aristotle, not to assert that Aristotle himself formulated it explicitly, and we believe that our supposition is confirmed to a considerable extent. Cf. n. 142.

quality and quantity. Aristotle's "modality" is not, like that of Kant, the degree of certainty, but is the ontological relation between a subject and its attributes. Possible judgement, pure judgement and necessary judgement are the judgements in which the predicate is attributed to the subject either possibly, purely or necessarily. Now, there is a certain correspondence between modality of the premises and that of the conclusion. Generally speaking, a pure conclusion is inferred only from pure premises, and if at least one premise is possible or necessary, the conclusion must also be possible or necessary.[46] In other words, to get a possible or a necessary judgement, at least one of the premises must be possible or necessary.

The rule that the inference which leads to a possible or necessary conclusion must have possible or necessary premises is analogous to the supposed rule that the judgement which gives a practical conclusion must be practical. If a practical syllogism may be constituted of mere theoretical judgements, an inference which is constituted of pure judgements might also lead to a necessary or to a possible conclusion. This, however, is, as aforesaid, incompatible with the statement in the *Analytica*. So much is what we can deduce from the argument concerning the forms of thinking in the *Organon*.

Among the statements about the practical syllogism, the most complete description of its form is that in *De An*. III. 11.[47] Its major premise is "Such and such a man should do such and such a thing," and its minor premise is "I am such and such a man," and "This is such and such a thing." From these two premises, we conclude: "I should do this." And this conclusion immediately leads to a conduct. Now, this is a combination of two inferences: an inference about the agent and an inference about the object. It will be analysed into one pair of syllogisms, namely: "Such and such a man should do such and such a thing," and "I am such and such a man," therefore, "I should do such and such a thing." These judgements form the first group; and making this conclusion of the first inference the major premise, we add a minor premise "This is such and such a thing" and get the second conclusion: "So I should do this." From this formula, we may see that the major premise of the practical syllogism expresses that a certain act is practically necessary to a certain agent, or in other words, that

[46] *An. Pr.* I. 12. 32 a 6–12.
[47] *De An.* III. 11. 434 a 16.

a certain value demands to be realized through a certain agent.[48] Whereas the two minor premises express that a certain agent (or an act) satisfies the requirement. Hence it is inferred that a certain act is practically necessary for a certain agent. But from such a mere formal determination we cannot recognize what value these acts or beings have, or what kind of practical necessity there is. The middle term of the major premise, "such and such a thing" expresses a certain value for an agent. But, is it self-value or utility? And what is the ground of the practical necessity to realize the value? If it is a virtue as self-value, the demand would be without qualification. But if it is utility, the ground which makes it necessary would be a volition to some particular self-value. To explain the point, we must study the contents of the practical syllogism.

Regrettable as it is, of the practical syllogism, examples are not sufficient. The most remarkable of which is the statement in *Eth. Nic.* VII. 3.[49] Its major premise being "Dry food is useful for every man," the minor premises are of two kinds, the one dealing with the agent, the other with the object, viz., "I am a man" and "This is dry food." Thence we conclude: "This is useful for me." It is obvious from the fact that the predicate of this major premise is "useful" that this premise is not the necessary judgement which immediately commands the pursuit of a moral value, but so-to-say, a possible judgement, which only advices the adoption of a means for an end. The taking of dry food is necessary for a man only hypothetically. This usefulness is, of course, usefulness for health. It is only necessary for man to take dry food, in so far as he wants health: the necessity cannot be applied to a man who prefers pleasure to health.

Health is surely *per se* valuable, but its value demands further ground. It may be useful either for pleasure, for virtuous conduct, or for scientific and philosophical contemplation; its necessity must be proved by another inference. Therefore, this major premise is a mere hypothetical imperative, or an advice such as "If one desires health, he should take dry food," or "If one ought to be healthy, he should take dry food." Further, the minor premises of these examples are not estimative, but mere judgement of facts. Not only that I am a man,

[48] Cf. Teichmüller, *op. cit.* 43. In *Eth. Nic.* VI. 12. 1144 a 31 ff. the major premise of practical syllogism is given as: ἐπειδὴ τοιόνδε τὸ τέλος καὶ τὸ ἄριστον, and there is no particular determination such as δεῖ. This is, as Teichmüller conjectures, because such a concept as τέλος or ἄριστον implies in itself oughtness or value.

[49] *Eth. Nic.* VII. 5. 1147 a 5.

but also that this is dry food, is a cognition of fact. Consequently, the minor premise of this practical syllogism is not concerned with a special value. Everything that is useful is not *per se* valuable, it is valuable only indirectly through being the means to an end which is *per se* valuable. Since the predicate of this major premise is utility, it is natural enough that the particular object which bears this utility should be *per se* a mere fact without value. The dry food as a mere fact becomes valuable only through the causality which was stated in the major premise. It seems to be natural from the above distinction of practice and production, that this kind of inference should be called ποιητικὸς συλλογισμός i.e. the productive syllogism. It cannot be subsumed to practical intellect or practical wisdom in the strict sense, since it is concerned not with the moral value of an act, but with the particular means to a subjective end. This inference is essentially the same as the considering of means, which is usually called deliberation and assumed to be a constituent of will. The deliberation of means is the tracing back of causal relation, it traces the series of means from a given end to the fact immediately at hand. Thus, e.g. in *Met*. VII. 7. 1032 b 6[50], it is said: "Since this is health, if the subject is to be

50 Teichmüller inquires the essence of practical syllogism along the statement in *Eth. Nic.* VI. 8. 1141 b 18–21: "For if a man knew that light meats are digestible and healthy, but did not know which sorts of meat are light, he would not produce health, but the man who knows that chicken is healthy is more likely to produce health." This is obviously the comment by Aristotle that particular knowledge is more useful to practical life than universal knowledge.

Now Teichmüller remarks that if we arrange this as a theoretical syllogism, the minor concept would be the meat of birds, the middle concept, light, and the major concepts, both digestible and healthy, and that it is incomprehensible why Aristotle dealt with the concept "healthy" as the middle concept instead of the major.

From what has been said Teichmüller seems to have arranged the statement as follows:

Major premise: "Light meat is digestible and healthy."

Minor premise: "The meat of birds is light and healthy." And the conclusion which is to be produced from these premises would be either "I want the meat of birds." or "Choose the meat of birds." But Teichmüller regards it to be impossible to attain such a practical conclusion from such pure theoretical premises, for it is incomprehensible whence comes such a determination as 'I want" or "Choose."

The alternative offered by Teichmüller is to take the statement as implying a practical syllogism, which recognizes the object in reference to our volition. And this volitional element is, in this case, implied in the concept "healthy." Further, Teichmüller points out that Aristotle omitted here to mention two propositions, i.e. "Such and such a man should do such and such a thing," and "I am such and such a man, viz. weak in digestion." Both of these propositions are concerned with the agent. Thus, the statement is to be arranged as follows:

healthy, this must first be present, e.g. a uniform state of body, and if this is to be present, there must be heat, and the physician goes on thinking thus until he reduces the matter to something final which he himself can produce. Then the process from this point onward, i.e. the process towards health, is called a production."[51] The means to produce heat is elsewhere[52] stated to be rubbing, which is the first step of healing.

Thus technical thinking as the principle of production or making, viz. productive deliberation in our terminology, would be as follows: If health is to exist, there must be a uniform condition of the body, and if heat, then rubbing. Therefore, if health is to exist, there must be rubbing.[53] Compared with the foregoing syllogism about food,

(1) "I want health." or "One ought to desire health."
(2) "Digestible food is good for health."
(3) "Light meat is digestible."
(4) "The meat of birds is light."
(5) "So, I want the meat of birds." or "One ought to desire the meat of birds."

Aristotle, however, was not concerned with the references among propositions, and only maintained that the minor premise orders the same thing as that which is indicated by the major premise, in a special way, through experience. Hence he supplied the determinant "healthy" as what is to be desired. On this account, Teichmüller accuses Trendelenburg of overlooking the essence of practical syllogism by striking out the "light" from the proposition "The meat of birds is light and healthy," and making it "The meat of birds is healthy." Whereas in truth, the minor premise must, according to Teichmüller, contain both the middle and the major concepts." (Teichmüller, *op. cit.* 226–229).

Teichmüller's arguments are very persuasive, but we offer another alternative which seems to be more natural an arrangement, viz.

Major premise: "Light meat is digestible and healthy."
Minor premise: "The meat of birds is light."
Conclusion: "The meat of birds is healthy."

Now, even if one knows the major premise, he cannot get the conclusion and consequently cannot act, unless he knows the minor premise. But even if he does not know the major premise, he can act as far as he knows through experience both the minor premise and the conclusion, or at least when he knows the conclusion. Obviously, the major premise of this formula is an epicheirema attained from the second and the third propositions of Teichmüller's scheme described above.

Though Teichmüller regards that the concept "healthy" implies volition or imperative, it is not sufficient to make one actual choice. The conclusion "It is healthy" implies only a hypothetical imperative, not a categorical. The reasoning which leads to this conclusion is not of a theoretical nature, to be sure, but it is a productive inference as distinguished from the practical in the strict sense.

[51] *Met.* VII. 7. 1032 b 6.
[52] *Met.* VII. 7. 1032 b 15–26.
[53] Walter gives a strange interpretation as to the formula of practical syllogism. He distinguishes namely end and end-concept, and makes the former the transcendent and individual end, which precedes deliberation, and the latter the universal end which is immanent in deliberation. The individual end is, e.g.

wherein the two minor premises were co-ordinate to the same major premise, stating the factual qualities of an object, in this case all premises are hypothetical judgements, and form a sorites. This is, however, not an essential difference, but only a difference of degree between two homogeneous instances of thinking. Productive deliberation is not different from the productive syllogism, and the two examples differ only in that the one expresses the whole process of productive deliberation, while the other expresses only the last stage of it. If one objects that there is wanting the affirmation of a fact in the last stage of deliberation about healing, we may easily supply with the most immediate technical knowledge viz., "This is rubbing." And if one requires us to distinguish deliberation from syllogism, we shall say that deliberation is the searching for the means, while syllogism is the justification of it. The order of thinking is reversed. We might also say that deliberation is constructive, while syllogism is reflective.

3. Practical Cognition of Ends

Granted the above mentioned forms of practical syllogism to be of productive nature, we must further inquire whether there be another formula of practical syllogism which is practical in the strict sense. Productive syllogism presupposes an end and finds a means to serve this end, so that its conclusion is a hypothetical imperative or an in-

"This should be cured," the universal end-concept is, e.g. "Health is so and so." Walter compares the formula in *Met.* VII. 7. 1032 b 6: ἐπειδὴ τοδὶ ὑγίεια, ἀνάγκη, εἰ ὑγιὲς ἔσται, τοδὶ ὑπάρξαι with the formula in *Eth. Eud.* II. 11. 1227 b 30: ἐπειδὴ δεῖ τοδέ ὑγιαίνειν, ἀνάγκη τοδὶ ὑπάρξαι, and maintains that the latter is incomplete because it lacks the πρότασις: health is so and so. Deliberation is, according to Walter, the application of knowledge to the individual, and the knowledge comes either from mathematics or from perception, its origin being a matter of no importance. The most important element of deliberation is the end-concept, which determines the whole process of deliberation. (*op. cit.* 208 ff.)

Walter's theory cannot be accepted. The essential of this practical syllogism is not the analysis of a concept, but the investigation of causal relation. What is in question is not what health is, but how we can produce it. The πρότασις is not "Health is so and so," but "This should be cured." That the *Eudemian Ethics* is not essentially different from the *Nicomachean Ethics* on this point, is evident from the following statement, though Walter believes this type of thought to be peculiar to the *Nicomachean Ethics*. *Eth. Eud.* I. 8. 1218 b 16–20: "And that the end is the cause of all that comes under it the method of teaching shows; for the teacher first defines the end and thence shows of each of the other things that it is good; for the end aimed at is the cause. E.g. since to be in health is so and so, so and so must needs be what conduces to it; the wholesome is the efficient cause of health and yet only of its actual existence; it is not the cause of health being good."

stance of what Kant calls the advice of cleverness.[54] The taking of dry food is necessary only as the means, which one should adopt if one wants health. But there is no command that one should be healthy. Practical intellect, however, is not confined to the cognition of means, it must be employed none the less in the estimation of the end itself. The most important function of practical wisdom is the moral estimation of conduct rather than a technical consideration how to realize an end; its fundamental proposition is the universal imperative of morality. This imperative will be specialized through virtues and commands the performance of good acts, and when it commands a particular act, there must needs be the moral estimation of that particular act. The major premise demands that a certain moral value should be realized, while the minor premise assumes that a certain act bears that value, and thus a particular act is ordered to be realized as morally valuable. If there be such a form of practical syllogism, this is precisely the practical syllogism in the strict sense which we are now looking for.

The productive syllogism formulates itself, as aforesaid, in hypothetical necessity as distinguished from absolute necessity.[55] Hypothetical necessity consists in the causality among things which are ontologically accidental and can be otherwise, viz. if A should exist, B must exist, if B then C, and so on. This is the same pattern which the productive syllogism or deliberation follows to realize an end. The example given is also a medical deliberation for realizing health. On such a hypothetical necessity, the fundamental premise itself is not grounded. For instance, it is left to one's choice whether he aims at health or not, the inference does not refer to this decision. Production is determined by the "desire or will" which was mentioned in the *Metaphysica*[56] as the determinant of rational potency. Generally speaking, desire may be either direct or indirect[57]; it may be either instinctive appetite or rational wish. What employs the productive syllogism is in many cases a wish, which being a rational desire presupposes some kind of practical cognition. But this is not the cognition of absolute necessity. For absolute necessity is found only in eternal beings such as mathematical

---

[54] Kant, *K. d. p. V.* I. 1. 1. 8 *Lehrs.* IV. *Anm.* 2. *Cass.* V. 42.

[55] *Part. An.* I. 1. 639 b 21–640 a 8; *Part. An.* I. 1. 642 a 1 ff.; *Phys.* II. 9. 199 b 34 ff.; *Met.* V. 5. 1015 a 20 ff.

[56] *Met.* IX. 5. 1048 a 8; 8. 1050 b 30.

[57] Walter, *op. cit.* 214. We never confuse the rationality of desire with that of will. We only maintain that the former is the condition of the latter, for it is especially rational desire that demands the cognition of the means.

images or logical concepts. Practical affairs are contingent as well as the affairs of production and natural generation,[58] therefore practical cognition lacks in absolute necessity.

The highest major premise of practical syllogism depends upon one's character, which varies in accordance with one's way of life. But, man's character is somewhat fixed *a posteriori*, and this particular character gives determination to productive syllogism. Character determines a desire, and the desire employs productive deliberation as an instrument. But the major premise of practical syllogism is not left to one's choice like that of productive syllogism. In the beginning of its formation, character is comparatively indefinite and free, but in an adult individual, it becomes an established disposition.[59] The wish which results from a character determines the hypothetical syllogism and makes it categorical. The major premise of such a practical syllogism may be explained by the following proposition: *Eth. Nic.* VI. 13. 1144 a 31[60]: "For the syllogisms which deal with acts to be done are things which involve a starting point, viz. (it will begin) 'since the end, i.e. what is best, is of such and such a nature,' ... and this is not evident except to the good man; for wickedness perverts us and causes us to be deceived about the starting-point of action. Therefore, it is evident that it is impossible to be practically wise without being good." No doubt, this statement refers to the major premise of practical syllogism, which is the highest principle of morality. This is the same as the highest principle of rational or calculative imagination discussed in the *De Anima*.[61]

Practical estimation not only gives determination to productive syllogism, but also must itself form a syllogism. For even if one knows the highest good and the ultimate end of life, his practical intellect does not accomplish its function unless he knows the particular conduct which bears this universal value. This kind of cognition is distinguished from the knowledge of causality. We find a more specific example of moral estimation in the following case. To make the context distinct, let us venture a somewhat longer quotation.

Eth. Nic. VI. 5. 1140 b 7–20; "It is for this reason that we think

---

[58] *Part. An.* I. 1. 640 a 2. It seems to exhibit Aristotle's early thought which sets changeable phenomena in opposition to the unchangeable essence, that he here makes physics oppose to be theoretical sciences and reduces it to the same genus as practical intellect.

[59] *Eth. Nic.* III. 7. 1114 a 12–21.

[60] Cf. *Eth. Nic.* VI. 5. 1140 b 16–20.

[61] *De An.* III. 11. 434 a 8 f.

Pericles and men like him have practical wisdom, viz. because they can see what is good for themselves and what is good for men in general; we consider that those can do this who are good at managing household or states; – this is what we call temperance (σωφροσύνη). By this name, we imply that it preserves one's practical wisdom (σῷζουσα τὴν φρόνησιν). Now what it preserves is a judgement of the kind we have described. For it is not any and every judgement that pleasant and painful objects destroy and pervert, e.g. the judgement that the triangle has or has not its angles equal to two right angles, but only judgements about what is to be done. For the originating causes of the things that are done consist in the end at which they are aimed; but the man who has been ruined by pleasure or pain forthwith fails to see any such originating cause – to see that for the sake of this or because of this he ought to choose and do whatever he chooses and does; for vice is destructive of originating cause of action."

The concepts such as θεωρεῖν, ὑπόληψις, and φαίνεται imply moral estimations of the end, especially φαίνεται is the appearance of φαντασία λογιστική.[62] And the context shows that they are concerned with the practical particulars no less than universal rules. A similar statement can be found in *Eth. Nic.* III. 6. 1113 a 30: "... since the good man judges each class of things rightly, and in each the truth appears to him. For each state of character has its own ideas of the noble and the pleasant, and perhaps the good man differs from others most by seeing the truth in each class of things, being as it were the norm and measure to them. In most things error seems to be due to pleasure; for it appears a good when it is not. We therefore take the pleasant as a good, and avoid pain as an evil." In this quotation also the moral estimation of practice is expressed by κρινεῖν, φαίνεται, or ὁρᾶν, just in the same way as in the previous quotation. The cognition of what is good for oneself, in which one is apt to be misled by pleasure and pain, is neither theoretical nor the searching for the means. For such cognition is never misled by pleasure and pain. So, Teichmüller was right in spite of Walter's opposition when he recognized a *phronetische Wahrnehmung* in the first quotation.[63]

The premises of practical syllogism, the universal as well as the particular, are the expression of ethical virtue. The cognition of the ultimate end or the highest good which presupposes ethical virtue, is

---

[62] *De An.* III. 10. 433 b 29; 11. 434 a 5; cf. ch. II. 3.
[63] Teichmüller, *Arist. Forsch..* II; *Neue Stud.* III. 294 f.; Walter, *op. cit.* 382 f.

evidently most universal and forms the highest major premise of practical syllogism. But since conduct is really concerned with the particular, it requires not only universal, but also particular cognition, viz. the judgement as to what is good. This judgement requires in its turn ethical virtues and appears as practical reason in the strict sense or as perceptive prudence. The foregoing two quotations imply the existence of such a cognition especially, such an expression as "seeing the truth in each class of things" cannot be interpreted otherwise. That ethical virtue is necessary for practical intellect, does not mean, as Walter interprets, that the function of practical intellect or practical syllogism is merely the searching for the means, the end itself being left to immediate desire. It is true that the statement "virtue makes us aim at the right mark, and practical wisdom makes us take the right means,"[64] etc. might seem to support this interpretation of Walter's. But it is said on the other hand, that ethical virtue pre-supposes practical wisdom,[65] and that wish is based upon calculation.[66] Further, it is said that every desire follows imagination, and in the case of rational desire, imagination itself is deliberative or calculative,[67] or that desire is consequent on opinion rather than opinion on desire.[68] From what has been said, it seems to be undeniable that Aristotle assumed some intellect which determines desire itself.[69]

[64] Cf. *Eth. Nic.* III. 7. 1113 b 3.
[65] Cf. n. 26.
[66] *Rhet.* I. 10. 1369 a 1; *Eth. Eud.* VII. 2. 1235 b 22.
[67] *De An.* III. 11. 434 a 5; cf. II. n. 157.
[68] *Met.* XII. 7. 1072 a 29.
[69] *Eth. Nic.* VII. 7. 1072 a 25–b 3: "Anger seems to listen to argument to some extent, but to mishear it, . . . so anger by reason of the warmth and hastiness of its nature, though it obeys, does not hear an order, and springs to take revenge. For argument or imagination informs us that we have been insulted, and anger, reasoning as it were that anything like this must be fought against, boils up straightway, while appetite, if argument or perception merely says that an object is pleasant, springs to the enjoyment of it. Therefore anger obeys the argument in a sense, but appetite does not. It is therefore more disgraceful; for the man who is incontinent in respect of anger is in a sense conquered by argument, while the other is conquered by appetite and not by argument." The argument to which anger listens is no doubt something more than a mere searching for the means. It must be a deliberation or practical wisdom how to conduct oneself. Similarly with calculation (λογισμός) in *De An.* III. 10. 433 b 6, and a 25. This becomes more evident when we compare the statement about appetites in *Eth. Nic.* VII. 7. 1149 b 13–20: "Further, those who are more given to plotting against others are more criminal. Now a passionate man is not given to plotting, nor is anger itself – it is open; but the nature of appetite is illustrated by what the poets call Aphrodite, 'guile-weaving daughter of Cyprus,' and by Homer's words about her 'embroidered girdle': And the whisper of wooing is there, whose subtlety stealeth the wits of the wise how prudent soe'er. Therefore if this form

We cannot keep ourselves from associating again the reason which determines desire with the practical reason in Kant's theory. The fundamental proposition of Kant's ethics is that the reason becomes by itself practical. If we admit such a reason in Aristotle, it would seem that the thought cannot be ascribed to Kant's originality. Along with the problem of active reason, this is the most crucial concept in Aristotle's philosophy.[70] We have previously postulated the reason which determines desire itself in opposition to Walter's interpretation to the effect that the function of practical reason is to be restricted to the searching for the means.

According to Walter, the function of practical reason is deliberation, and its ideal is the so-called ὀρθὸς λόγος. Therefore, the essence of deliberation ought to be explained through the investigation of ὀρθὸς λόγος. This does not mean a right concept as Brandis supposed[71] to be, but a right reason, which is the principle of moderation and that which constitutes a virtue as such. But, strictly speaking, right reason is not sufficient for ethical virtue, and moderation is confined to the area of practice and production, so argues Walter.[72] But to make right reason the principle of ethical virtue runs counter to Walter's previous interpretation of practical reason. If practical

of incontinence is more criminal and disgraceful than that in respect of anger, it is both incontinence without qualification and in a sense vice.''

The incontinent man is previously said not to listen to reason, but anger does in a certain sense, whereas here on the contrary, the former is said to be plotting and the latter not. The only way to avoid contradiction is to take the λόγος in the first statement for valuation, and the ἐπιβουλή in the second statement for the searching of the means. ἐπιβουλή being a kind of βούλευσις acts in this case as productive deliberation; cf. *ibid.* 1150 a 4 f.: "For the badness of that which has no originative source of movement is always less hurtful and reason is an originative source.'' This νοῦς is also productive deliberation instead of practical. The vicious man may have productive deliberation, but he has not the practical deliberation in the strict sense.

[70] Walter, *op. cit.* 31 ff.; cf. Trendelenburg, *Hist. Beiträge* III. Herbarts praktische Philosophie und die Ethik der Athen; VI Der Widerstreit zwischen Kant und Aristoteles in der Ethik.

[71] Brandis, *Handbuch* II. 2. ii. 1441; Walter, *op. cit.* 65. The text in question is as follows: *Eth. Nic.* VI. 2. 1139 a 21 –31: ἔστι δ' ὕπερ ἐν διανοίᾳ κατάφασις καὶ ἀπόφασις, τοῦτ' ἐν ὀρέξει δίωξις καὶ φυγή· ὥστ' ἐπειδὴ ἡ ἠθικὴ ἀρετὴ ἕξις προαιρετική, 1) ἡ δὲ προαίρεσις ὄρεξις βουλευτική, δεῖ διὰ ταῦτα μὲν τόν τε λόγον 2) ἀληθῆ εἶναι καὶ τὴν ὄρεξιν ὀρθήν, εἴπερ ἡ προαίρεσις σπουδαία, καὶ τὰ αὐτὰ τὸν μὲν φάναι 3) τὴν δὲ διώκειν. αὕτη μὲν οὖν ἡ διάνοια καὶ ἡ ἀλήθεια πρακτική· τῆς δὲ θεωρητικῆς διανοίας καὶ μὴ πρακτικῆς μηδὲ ποιητικῆς τὸ εὖ καὶ κακῶς τἀληθές ἐστι καὶ ψεῦδος. τοῦτο γάρ ἐστι παντὸς διανοητικοῦ ἔργον· τοῦ δὲ πρακτικοῦ καὶ διανοητικοῦ ἡ ἀλήθεια ὁμολόγως ἔχουσα τῇ ὀρθῇ. Brandis translates 1) ἕξις προαιρετική as Fertigkeit des Vorsatzes, 2) λόγος as Begriff, and 3) φάναι as bestimmt.

[72] Walter, *op. cit.* 232 ff.

reason be restricted to the deliberation about means, how may its equivalent ὀρθὸς λόγος be the principle of moderation? If virtue consists of good desire and deliberation, the rationality of good desire should be not the searching for the means, but the calculation to estimate the end.

Walter, who misunderstood the rationality of the end, is led to neglect the practical character of reason itself. He says that the reason of Kant may become practical by itself, whereas the reason of Aristotle requires will in addition[73] in order to be practical. Seeing that will or προαίρεσις is defined as deliberate desire, it is not only superfluous but also unreasonable to say that practical reason requires will besides, and Walter mentions no successful proof of this assertion. What is more strange is that he argues in continuation that Aristotle's classification of reason is not that of cognition but of faculty. According to him, in dividing reason into the theoretical and the practical, Aristotle does not imply a distinction between the science of variable phenomena (presumably ethics, politics etc.) and necessary sciences, e.g. theology or mathematics, but rather a distinction between acts and cognition, because reason is concerned with the possible and the necessary, whereas the possible cannot be the object of knowledge.[74] This explanation of Walter's is extremely unsatisfactory. It is a sheer contradiction to say on the one hand that reason cannot be practical by itself but requires will, and on the other hand that Aristotle's classification of reason is the classification of faculty and not of cognition.[75]

A reason which does not recognize is surely a paradoxical concept, but if practical reason were such a faculty, isn't it just the reason which is *per se* practical and which Walter himself is longing for? Whether or not it may be called reason, at least it is from his theory necessary that it is practical. What else would he call such a reason but *practical*

[73] Walter, *op. cit.* 242 f.

[74] *Ibid.* Walter saying *"Das Zukünftige ist aber überhaupt nicht Gegenstand der Erkenntnis. Die Vernunfttätigkeit deren Objekt das Mögliche als Zukünftiges ist, kann keine erkennende sondern muss eine bestimmende, eine beratschlagende Tätigkeit sein,"* quotes *Eth. Nic.* VI. 3. 1139 b 7. Thus he confused ἐνδεχόμενον ἄλλως ἔχειν with mere ἐνδεχόμενον and misunderstood the well-known proposition of Aristotle's, that ἐνδχόμενον ἄλλως ἔχειν is not the proper object of ἐπιστήμη for the potential or future being cannot be recognized. But this is neither the fact, nor is the real meaning of Aristotle's statement.

[75] *Eth. Nic.* VI. 2. 1139 b 12 f; *Eth. Nic.* VI. 2. 1139 a 29–31; *Met.* IX. 2. 1046 b 2–4. This last mentioned place shows explicitly that art is knowledge as well as power to act. It is not Aristotle's way of thinking to consider that cognition is not practical at all.

reason? To our surprise, Walter says that the reason which is practical is only deliberation or the searching for the means. Thus, Walter, assuming, on the one hand, that deliberation forms practical syllogism, asserts, on the other hand, that both of its premises are theoretical cognition. This amounts to saying that a practical conclusion will result from theoretical premises, that is to say, the practical character of the conclusion would result from outside the inference, i.e. from a desire or a will. In other words, the process of inference is rational but never practical, while the will is practical but never rational. Thus, according to Walter's interpretation, the concept "practical reason" would become nonsense,[76] for it would turn out that practical reason is either not practical or not reason. Walter maintains moreover that Aristotle, in dividing reason into the calculative and the scientific, implied not that reason by itself performs these two kinds of function, but that it recognizes, when combined with sensation, and acts, when combined with desire.[77] It will follow, then, that neither is the former theoretical reason, nor the latter practical reason, but that a single reason becomes sometimes theoretical and sometimes practical only accidentally, so that reason *per se* would neither recognize nor act.

Deliberation was conceived by Walter to be the searching for the means, and the major premise of practical syllogism is theoretical knowledge, while the minor premise is perceptive judgement, which does not belong to practical reason, but to the reason *qua* perception. Thus, it seems as if he admitted no practical element at all in practical reason. Still, to our bewilderment, he does not agree with Prantl who takes deliberation for theoretical cognition.[78] If there be any meaning in Walter's contention, it would amount to saying that deliberation is neither theoretical nor practical but merely cognition without qualification. But in truth, Aristotle admitted practical cognition or practical truth, as is evident from the statement to which Walter himself refers a little later.[79] From such confused arguments of Walter's we can by no means expect any consistent interpretation. Anyhow, the only difference between theoretical reason and productive reason is, according to Walter, not in the contents, but in the forms of cognition. In respect to form, productive cognition belongs to the practical, but in respect to contents, it belongs to the theoretical. So argues Walter.[80] But is it

---

[76] Teichmüller, *Neue Studien* III. 42 ff. cf. ch. IV. 4.
[77] Walter, *op. cit.* 245.
[78] *Ibid.* 249. cf. Prantl, Ueber die dianoetischen Tugenden nach Aristoteles 11.
[79] Walter, *op. cit.* 252; *Eth. Nic.* VI. 2. 1139 a 30.
[80] Walter, *op. cit.* 255.

not an obvious distinction of contents that practical intellect is concerned with what can be otherwise, while theoretical intellect is concerned with necessary beings? On what ground does Walter neglect
this manifest distinction of contents? By the difference of forms, he
might imply that theoretical intellect has by itself no practical power.
Now, what Aristotle really states on this point is as follows: "No
animal which is not either seeking or avoiding something, moves except under compulsion."[81] "Similarly, it is not the sensitive faculty."[82]
"Nor, again, is it the reasoning faculty or what is called intellect that
is the cause of motion."[83] "For theoretical intellect thinks nothing
practical and makes no assertion about what is to be avoided or pursued, ... But, even if the mind has something of the kind before it, it
does not forthwith prompt avoidance or pursuit. For example, it often
thinks of something alarming or pleasant without prompting to fear;
the only effect is the beating of the heart, or when the thought is
pleasant, some other bodily movement."[84]

The peculiarity in Walter's interpretation consists in taking the
reason which fails to determine desire, as theoretical. He considers that
if it were practical reason, as other interpreters have mistaken, it will
follow that there is a practical reason which is indifferent to practice,
and that the theoretical reason cannot think anything which may
arouse emotion. It will follow, further, that practical reason would be
distinguished from theoretical reason through the object, whereas in
reality, the difference is that the one is cognition while the other is
determination. Such a false distinction, he says, would result in the
misinterpretation to the effect that practical reason recognizes moral
concepts.[85] In short, according to Walter, theoretical reason is distinguished from practical reason only from the point of view whether the
reason has practical power or not.

Granted that theoretical reason lacks practical power, while practical
reason has it, this does not, however, conform to Walter's foregoing
theory to the effect that the only function of practical reason is deliberation as the searching for the means. Therefore, it must follow of
necessity that what has really practical ability is not practical reason –
which is considered by Walter as practical only accidentally – but

---

[81] *De An.* III. 9. 432 b 16.
[82] *Ibid.* 19.
[83] *Ibid.* 26.
[84] *De An.* III. 9. 432 b 27; cf. ch. II. 2.
[85] Walter, *op. cit.* 256 f.

volition. As for practical knowledge which does not command, there is no need to repeat our foregoing statement.

On the other hand, as to the commanding reason, Walter refers to the following statement: *De An.* III. 10. 433 a 9[86]: "The motive causes are apparently at any rate these two, either appetency or intelligence, ... Both these, then, are causes of locomotion, intelligence and appetency. By intelligence we mean that which calculates the means to an end, that is the practical intellect, which differs from the speculative intellect in the end at which it aims. Appetency, too is directed to some end in every case; for that which is the end of desire is the starting point of the practical intellect, and the last state in this process of thought is the starting point of action." But Walter is not right in translating νοῦς δὲ ὁ ἕνεκά του λογιζόμενος καὶ πρακτικός, as *die eines Zweckes Willen betrachtende oder praktische Vernunft*, i.e. "the reason which deliberates for an end, or practical reason." By Trendelenburg,[87] to whom Walter is opposed, this is to be taken rather as the reason which determines the end. If Walter's interpretation were right, we cannot understand how it is possible to command or to bring about harmony with desire,[88] instead of itself obeying desire. Nevertheless, what requires the command must be just the desiring faculty. If what receives the command were mere body, the act would have no moral significance whether it obeys the command of reason or the command of desire. Walter himself without noticing his inconsistency, repeatedly quotes the statement of Aristotle's which undeniably implies the function of reason that determines the desire. As Aristotle puts it,[89] the primary movement is the object of desire, which is aimed at both by desire and thinking. It is the object of desire, in so far as it is desired, but it is also the object of thinking, as far as it is an end-concept. It moves other things, itself being unmoved. But we desire what we

---

[86] Walter, *op. cit.* 260.

[87] Trendelenburg, *Hist. Beiträge* II. 378; Walter, *op. cit.* 44.

[88] Cf. Walter, *op. cit.* 495 f. Walter, like Hartenstein (*Hist. Phil. Abhandl.*) accuses Aristotle of entirely failing to supply any ground for harmony between will and reason. The fact is quite contrary. We have shown in previous chapters how Aristotle's concepts of will, desire and practical wisdom are founded upon a physiological basis. The alleged fault is rather to be attributed to Kant's theory according to which the fact that reason becomes by itself practical is proclaimed to be quite inexplicable. This forms a fatal difficulty of Kant's theory along with the postulate of the *summun bonum.* cf. Trendelenburg, *Hist. Beiträge* III. 189 ff.; 195 ff.; 209 ff.

[89] Walter, *op. cit.* 264 f.; *Part. An.* 6. 700 b 28; 701 b 1; *Met.* XII. 7. 1072 a 30.

think to be good, rather than think to be good what we desire. And a good will is said to be the will which desires a thing on account of its goodness. This statement of Aristotle's means evidently that the desire for an end presupposes the estimation of that end, and that the reason determines the desire. The ultimate determinant is the end itself and not the end-concept, to be sure.[90] But we can by no means deny that there is admitted some reason which precedes and determines the desire. It is obviously different from the deliberation which presupposes desire and subserves it.

Without admitting any specific difference of practical reason, Walter identifies it with deliberation, which however, presupposes some desire. Thus, the end, being the unmovable movent, moves at first desire, which in its turn, moves practical reason. Practical reason presupposes an end as the direct object of desire, but accepting the latter in itself, forms an end-concept. This accepted concept constitutes the major premise, and in combination with a particular judgement as minor premise, forms the practical syllogism, which is nothing but the function of deliberation or practical reason. Desire mediates the object of desire (as the end) with conduct, and reason mediates the end-concept with conduct. From the combination of reason and desire grows the will, which is constituted of ὄρεξις and λόγος ὁ ἕνεκα τινός. The latter is deliberation instead of an end-concept; it is concerned with the means, not with the end. Thus argues Walter.[91]

In short, according to Walter, practical reason is concerned only with practice, and does not enter into scientific speculation. A man of practice is concerned with practice, but a philosopher is concerned with ethics; their tasks are regarded quite different. Walter nevertheless admits that Aristotle was an ideal Greek[92] in attributing truth to art and morality, notwithstanding the division of reason into the practical and the theoretical similar to that of Kant's. But once we admit that Aristotle really attributed truth to art and morality, we can by no means consider that he denied cognition to practical reason. Besides, if practical reason is related only to practice, it is rather a matter of course that it should be practical. Whereas Walter in fact allowed to it only the cognition of cause and effect, and regarded their premises to be purely theoretical. This is a sheer contradiction, without doubt.

What makes it difficult for us to admit practical cognition or practical

90 Walter, *op. cit.* 275.
91 *Ibid.* 265 ff.
92 *Ibid.* 269 f.

syllogism about the end, is Aristotle's explicit statement to the effect that we deliberate not about ends but about means. In *Eth. Nic.* III. 3. 1112 b 12,[93] it is said: "We deliberate not about ends but about means. For a doctor does not deliberate whether he shall heal, nor an orator whether he shall persuade, nor a statesman whether he shall produce law and order, nor does any one else deliberate about his end. They assume the end and consider how and by what it is to be attained." Similarly, in *Eth. Nic.* III. 5. 1113 b, it is stated: "The end, then, being what we wish for, the means what we deliberate about and choose." The same relation is found between virtue and practical wisdom, viz. in *Eth. Nic.* VI. 13. 1144 a 8: "For virtue makes us aim at the right mark, and practical wisdom makes us take the right means." In this last case, practical wisdom is identified with deliberation and seems to be restricted to technical deliberation as to the means how to bring about the end, which was directly set up by ethical virtue.[94] But does it amount to saying that there is no practical thinking about the end? Is it really possible for the author of *Ethics* and *Politics* to have repudiated the practical thinking which is realized in his lectures? This is a supposition quite implausible. Of course it is not the art that makes the end right. We have also no objection to the view that the good end is founded upon the ethical virtue engendered from good conduct. Still Aristotle asserts on the other hand that ethical virtue is impossible without practical wisdom.[95] What makes an end good is its rationality.[96] The end which is set up by ethical virtue is also founded upon estimation.[97] Ethical virtue, being the principle of estimation, realizes itself in this estimation.[98] The essence of ethical virtue is moderation, which is right reason or practical wisdom.[99] Consequently, rational desire arising from virtue, viz. wish, must be in accordance with, and accompanied by practical wisdom.[100] In other words, it must pursue the object of intellect, and this object becomes the object of desire through being thought of.[101] Wish gains its rationality only through this mediation by intellect.[102] Aristotle

---

[93] Cf. *Eth. Eud.* II. 11. 1227 b 23.
[94] Cf. *Eth. Nic.* VII. 9. 1151 a 17.
[95] *Eth. Nic.* VI. 13. 1144 b 17, 27; X. 8. 1178 a 16.
[96] *Eth. Nic.* II. 6. 1106 b 36; 1107 a 2.
[97] *De An.* III. 11. 434 a 5–10.
[98] *De An.* III. 11. 434 a 16–21.
[99] *Eth. Nic.* II. 6. 1106 b 36–1107 a 2.
[100] *Eth. Nic.* VI. 13. 1144 b 21–23.
[101] *Eth. Nic.* VI. 2. 1139 a 21–30; VI. 10. 1142 b 31–33.
[102] *De An.* III. 9. 432 b 5; 10. 433 a 24.

admits these points one by one. So, what he wishes to say is not that all desires are irrational and immediate, or that practical cognition is purely technical and aims at utility, but that the end grows rather from character than from technical deliberation. To emphasize this point, Aristotle characterized art to be concerned with the means and in-different to the end. This however does not make it impossible for ethical virtue to appear in intellectual form, and even in the form of a syllogism. It is merely that this matter is dealt with by Aristotle elsewhere.

It appears, at a glance, to be incompatible to say on the one hand that deliberation or practical syllogism does not determine the end but searches for the means, and on the other hand that rational desire or wish presupposes deliberative or calculative imagination.[103] This difficulty, however, may be solved by clarifying the notions of end and means. The means is the method or the starting point to realize an end, whereas the end is either the result of an act or the act itself.[104] Therefore the means also serves either the result or the act itself. In the former case, the means is concerned with a mere fact, and its form is different from the result, while in the latter case, it is concerned with a value to be realized on the act. In modern usage, "means" is mainly restricted to the former sense in accordance with the restriction of causality to the efficient cause. But this is not the case with Aristotle. The cause in modern usage is only an efficient cause, but, as is well known, Aristotle assumed besides this, the formal cause, the final cause, and the material cause.[105] Therefore ἕνεκά του or the means in Aristotle's usage may be differentiated to these forms of causality. Thus, besides the means that produces a fact, there may be another means which realizes a certain value. In this latter case, the means should be taken as a lower or special form and the end a higher or general form to realize a moral value.

Therefore, there is, besides the searching for the efficient means, the searching for the formal means.[106] The former is seen in productive

[103] *De An.* III. 11. 434 a 5–10.

[104] *Eth. Nic.* VI. 2. 1139 b 1; 5. 1140 b 6; (*Mag. Mor.* I. 36. 1197 a 11).

[105] *Phys.* II. 3. 194 b 23 ff.; 7. 198 a 16; III. 7. 207 b 34; IV. 1. 209 a 20; *De Somno* 2. 455 b 14; *Gen. An.* I. 1. 715 a 4; V. 1. 778 b 8; *An. Post.* II. 11. 94 a 21; *Met.* I. 3. 983 a 26; V. 1. 1013 a 24 ff.; 1013 b 16; VIII. 4. 1044 a 33 ff.; XII. 4. 1070 a 26.

[106] Cf. Walsh *op. cit.* 135. It is very interesting that Gauthier adopts the same position as we.

deliberation, but if the latter is possible, it must be the practical deliberation in the strict sense.[107] In practical deliberation, what is searched for is the particular practice which represents a universal value. The end thus attained, is not yet really actual, but must needs be realized in terms of productive operations. Starting from this point, art continues searching for the means to realize this particular value. What we have previously supposed as the practical cognition which determines the end itself, is just the thinking of this first type. In this kind of thinking too, the highest universal end is immediately given and cannot be inferred. That the practical intellect does not infer this highest universal end is one thing, that it does not determine a particular end is another. The highest universal end is set up immediately by ethical virtue,[108] only it is quite indefinite in its contents, for instance, a wish for a good and beautiful life is an important principle of conduct, but, since an act must be individual, a mere universal end is not sufficient for actual conduct. A particular end which represents the universal value must be set up. Here is the necessity of the so-called practical syllogism or practical deliberation which deals with the subsumption of values. It is different from the productive syllogism which deals with the causal relation of facts. The practical syllogism does not create the end, but only determines and specializes it.[109]

The productive syllogism which deals with causal relation forms a hypothetical syllogism, while the practical syllogism which is concerned with the subsumption of values forms a categorical syllogism. The conclusion of the latter determines the former and makes it categorical. The practical syllogism which has categorical form is analogous to subsumptive inference. This is evident from *An. Post.* I. 24. 85 b 23: "Demonstration is the syllogism that proves the cause, i.e. the reasoned fact, and it is rather the commensurate universal than the particular which is causative (as may be shown thus: that which possesses an attribute through its own essential nature is itself the cause of the inherence, and the commensurate universal is primary; hence the commensurate universal is the cause). Consequently, commensurately universal demonstration is superior as more especially proving the

---

[107] *Eth. Eud.* I. 8. 1218 b 20–22; *An. Post.* I. 24. 85 b 23–27.

[108] *Eth. Nic.* VII. 8. 1151 a 17. This highest universal end will be given to an individual through his character, but this character itself is formed through the habit which is nurtured by parents, teachers and statesmen, so that from the genetic point of view, it presupposes deliberation and calculation of a higher grade, i.e. politics and ethics.

[109] Cf. Loening, *Die Zurechnungslehre des Aristoteles* 29.

cause, that is, the reasoned fact." Thus the cause is found in the universal. This is explained in the following example: *Ibid.* 27: "Our search for the reason ceases, and we think that we know, when the coming to be or existing of the fact before us is not due to the coming to be or existence of some other fact, for the last step of a search thus conducted is *eo ipso* the end and limit of the problem. Thus: 'Why did he come? To get the money – wherewith to pay a debt – that he might thereby do what was right.' When in this regress we can no longer find an efficient or final cause, we regard the last step of it as the end of the coming – or being or coming to be – and we regard ourselves as then only having full knowledge of the reason why he came."

Aristotle suggests the cause in this example to be either efficient or final cause, but strictly speaking, it is rather to be regarded as formal cause. But this does not matter much, for soon after this he argues that all causes and reasons are alike in this respect. Hence at least it is evident that demonstration or syllogism is not confined to any single form of cause, but is common to any and every kind of cause. It is true that there is no specialization of demonstration as to whether it be theoretical or practical, but the example lastly mentioned is obviously concerned with practical affairs and is tantamount to the explanation of deliberation and practical wisdom in the *Ethica Nicomachea* and the *De Anima*.

As is evident from the above statements, inference, being the search for the means, not, however, in the ordinary sense of modern terminology, but in the sense of the specifically Aristotelian use of the word, may vary in accordance with the variety of causes. That deliberation or the practical syllogism is not concerned with the end, would in all probability mean that it does not set up the ultimate end. It does not rule out the possibility of practical intellect which deliberates about the intermediate ends both practical and productive. Generally speaking, productive deliberation is complementary with practical deliberation. In the above quotation, to return the money is the end for which one came there and gained the money, yet it is the means for doing justice. Whereas it is not a mere production to return the money in order to be just. Returning the money has itself the moral value of justice. Though the end to do justice and not to commit a fault is not the result of inference, but the realization of ethical value, deliberation about the moral value of a particular act is needed in order to realize that final end. The theoretical syllogism about a triangle is categorical, and is ruled by eternal or absolute necessity, but a productive syllogism is ruled by hypothetical necessity, viz., "If one is to return the money he must gain it. And if one is to gain the money, he must come here. So that, if one is to return the money, he must come here." What makes this hypothetical syllogism categorical, is the judgement that one should return the money, or the wish to return it. This wish further presupposes the inference: "One should not commit an injustice. It is an injustice not to return the money. So he must return the money." This is what we call practical syllogism in the categorical form. Thus, a complete practical cognition must be a compound of a productive hypothetical syllogism and a practical-categorical syllogism.[110]

4. Continence and Temperance

The most manifest and terse formulation of practical syllogism as opposed to the productive is seen in *De An.* III. 11. 434 a 16; "The major premise is universal, whether judgement or proposition, while the minor has to do with a particular fact: for, while the former asserts that such and such a person ought to do such and such an act, the latter asserts that a particular act is one of the sort and that I am such a person. Now it is the latter judgement which at once moves to action, not the universal." This is evidently a consideration not of cause and effect, but of rule and example. An instance of application may be found in *Eth. Nic.* III. 7., where Aristotle states that "the man, who faces and who fears the right things and from the right motive, in the right way and at the right time, and who feels confidence under the corresponding conditions, is brave; for the brave man feels and acts according to the merits of the case and in whatever way the rule directs. Now the end of every activity is conformity to the corresponding state of character. This is true, therefore, of the brave man as well as of others. But courage is noble. Therefore the end is noble; for each thing is defined by this end." This might, according to Teichmüller, be formulated as follows:

Major premise: The man is brave who fears the right things and from the right motive, in the right way and at the right time, and who feels confidence under the corresponding conditions.

---

[110] Greenwood's distinction (described by Hardie 255) between external means and component means seems to be analogous to our distinction between efficient means and formal means. Greenwood should have expounded his theory in reference to Aristotle's theory of four causes. Cf. Joachim's note on E. N. p. 218.

Minor premise: This is the right thing, the right motive, the right way and the right time one should fear.

Conclusion: He is brave, who fears this thing, for this motive, in this way, and at this time.

This conclusion directly determines our conduct and feeling. It presupposes the highest universal practical knowledge, and without it one would fall into vice. What is then the character which lacks the particular cognition? It is a pity that Teichmüller overlooked the characteristic of this syllogism which he himself presented as an example of practical syllogism, for he says that the ignorance of this minor premise is the cause of involuntariness, which is repented of by the doer and forgiven by the criticizer.[111] But the judgement, "This is the thing that should be feared," is not a mere judgement of facts, but a moral estimation.[112] Just for this reason, this kind of judgement was assumed by Aristotle to be particularly difficult, whereas the cognition of individual facts is not so difficult,[113] he is a complete fool who cannot judge whether this is bread or water, whether he is a king or a slave, but the estimation[114] of individual affairs depends upon desire and character, hence in order to be right in this judgement, one must have a good character.[115] Teichmüller on the other hand took the ignorance of the minor premise of the aforesaid inference which advises the taking of dry food to be the cause of incontinence. He considered namely that the ignorance that this is dry food, is the cause of incontinence which leads one not to take some food useful to health.[116] This is not without reason, because Aristotle himself mentions (1147 a 4) this kind of ignorance as the cause of incontinence. But as is often the case with Aristotle's statement, this is an unsuitable example for explaining incontinence, though it is not quite impossible to count it into the case of incontinence as far as we suppose that this kind of knowledge is disturbed by some appetite against it – viz. if the agent strongly desires some wet food, e.g. wine. In truth the ignorance of this minor premise is rather to be taken as the cause of involuntariness than of incontinence.

Ignorance about individual facts is usually enumerated as a cause of involuntariness, and in most cases the example shows that lack or

---

111 Teichmüller, *op. cit.* 76 f.; *Eth. Nic.* III. 7. 1115 b 17 ff.
112 Teichmüller, *op. cit.* 78.
113 *Eth. Nic.* V. 13. 1137 a 9–17; *Eth. Nic.* IV. 11. 1126 a 32–b 4.
114 *Met.* I. 2. 982 a 11 f.
115 *Eth. Nic.* I. 2. 1095 b 4.
116 Teichmüller, *op. cit.* 75.

error of the judgement about the fact, viz., when one kills an enemy being ignorant of the fact that he is one's son, when one poisons some-body mistaking a poison for a remedy and so on.[117] The minor premise of the first example, "This is dry food," belongs to this class. The lack of this knowledge is not the cause of incontinence, but rather the cause of involuntariness, whereas the minor premise of the second example is a kind of estimation about individual affairs. It is not involuntari-ness wrongly to fear or not to fear something because one does not know whether it should be feared or not. Let us focus the problem on temperance, since incontinence is related not to fearing but to pleasure. Now he who does wrong being ignorant of the proper quantity of wine that one may drink, is not so involuntary in his act as one who drinks spirits being ignorant of whether it is wine or water. The former kind of ignorance should be censured as incontinence, but in the case of the latter, the doer is not responsible. For, man is ignorant of the proper quantity of wine, because he is tempted by the appetite of drinking, or ignorant of the wickedness of having intercourse with another man's wife, because of his attachment.[118] When the ignorance of this kind be-comes complete, it is self-indulgence rather than mere incontinence.[119]

Incontinence is a character intermediate between virtue and vice, worse than virtue, but better than vice. In its strict sense, it is confined to nutritive and sexual appetites, but in a wider sense, it is also found in reference to other kinds of desire.[120] Now, a man is incontinent, if he is not quite ignorant of what moderation is, but knowing it in a sense, yet carries its enjoyment to excess owing to a disharmony of desire and intellect. A continent man, on the contrary, dominates his desire by intellect and keeps moderation, yet the harmony is not so complete as in temperance and desire is enforced by intellect. Thus the fault of

[117] *Eth. Nic.* III. 2.
[118] *Eth. Nic.* VI. 5. 1140 b 11–16; VII. 2. 1145 b 10–14; VII. 8. 1150 b 20 f.; V. 10. 1134 a 20 f.; "For a man might even lie with a woman knowing who she was, but the origin of his act might be not will but passion." This is a statement which distinguishes incontinence from self-indulgence, but we may also find in it the distinction between the knowledge of facts and that of value. If one had intercourse with a woman being ignorant who she was, this ignorance was related to the fact and was the cause of involuntariness, whereas in the above example, though there was the cognition of facts, the valuation was not actual enough (not wanting completely, for if so, the act will be voluntary and self-indulgent) so that one was incontinent. This is perhaps the case of ἀγνοοῦντες as distinguished from δι ἄγνοιαν (Cf. ch. II. n. 318) An incontinent man commits a fault, not from ignorance, but in ignorance.
[119] *Eth. Nic.* VII. 9. 1150 b 36; 1151 a 11; III. 2. 1110 b 31–1111 a 1.
[120] *Rhet.* I. 12. 1372 b 12 f.

incontinence consists in the disharmony of desire and intellect or in the comparative weakness of the power of intellect as compared with desire. What is then the weakness of the practical intellect? If the function of intellect is confined to theoretical judgement and inference, intellect would be neither strong nor weak, but only right or wrong. Now that it is said that intellect may be weak though it is right, we must admit that intellect is a source of power, and its act is the origin of conduct. When it acts as an inference, its conclusion must possess practical power. And in fact, practical syllogism was considered to produce such a power. If the power of conduct thus belongs to the essence of practical syllogism, the corresponding impotency must also originate in the act of intellect itself. The impotency of intellect which is the cause of incontinence must arise from the fault of intellectual activity itself. Otherwise, the practical power would be something exterior and accidental to the inference, so that it would result in the negation of practical intellect in the strict sense.

An incontinent man commits a fault in one sense knowing, and in another sense not knowing. For "to know" has two meanings: it is either to have the ἕξις of knowledge, or to know actually. Though it is strange to act against knowledge while one is exercising this knowledge, it is not strange if one has the knowledge only as a habit.[121] Is it then in this manner, that the incontinent man commits a fault though he knows it to be bad? Then, what does it mean to have the habit of knowledge and not to exercise it? If practical cognition forms a syllogism, a habitual cognition would be a state, in which all or part of its elements are present, except that they are not yet combined and integrated. Since the syllogism is constituted of the major and the minor premises, and it combines the universal with the particular by means of the intermediate term. Therefore, in an incomplete inference,

---

[121] *Eth. Nic.* VII. 5. 1146 b 31; cf. *Cat.* 8. 8 b 29; *Pol.* VI. 1. 1288 b 17; *Eth. Nic.* VI. 3. 1139 b 31; ch. I. n. 8. Similar usage of the term 'knowledge' is found in Plato's *Theaet.* 197. It is stated namely that knowledge is either in the state of ἕξις or of κτῆσις, the one is like the wearing of a garment, and the other its possession. In another metaphor, the one is like using a dove one has caught, and the other like possessing it in an aviary. Now, one who has an opinion, is possessed of knowledge, as far as he has memory, but not always using it and there is the possibility of committing a fault. The opposition of ἕξις and κτῆσις by Plato corresponds to the opposition of χρῆσις and κτῆσις by Aristotle, while the term ἕξις is used somewhat differently by the two philosophers: in Plato, it implies, as is evident from the above example, actuality, but in Aristotle, it is a kind of potentiality, though most active and contiguous to actuality. The ἕξις of knowledge in Aristotle is, to use the above metaphor, the possessing of a dove in the aviary.

at least one of the two premises would remain in mere potentiality. As Aristotle puts it in *Eth. Nic.* VII. 3. 1147 a 1: "Further, since there are two kinds of premises, there is nothing to prevent a man's having both premises and acting against his knowledge, provided that he is using only the universal premise and not the particular; for it is particular acts that have to be done. And there are also two kinds of universal term, one is predicable of the agent, the other of the object; for example, 'dry food is good for every man,' and 'I am a man,' or 'such and such food is dry'; but whether this food is such and such, of this the incontinent man either has not or is not exercising the knowledge. There will, then be firstly, an enormous difference between these manners of knowing, so that to know in one way when we act incontinently would not seem anything strange, while to know in the other way would be extraordinary."[122]

Thus the incontinent man has the universal knowledge but cannot apply it to the particular, so that his cognition does not realize itself in a syllogism. But, Aristotle, continuing the statement, pointed out that there is another way of possessing knowledge, as in the case of a man who is asleep, mad or drunk. Such a man may utter the words that follow from knowledge, but this is no more than an utterance by actors on the stage. The knowledge of the man who is under the influence of passion, as is the case with an incontinent man, is such an inert one.[123] It is worthy of special attention that Aristotle mentions here the somnambulistic states of mind beside the ignorance of particular facts, for it is more suitable for explaining the state of incontinence than the former, which is rather the cause of involuntariness. Incontinence and involuntariness should be distinguished not by the degree of ignorance, but in the respect whether this ignorance is concerned with facts or with value, and estimation or the judgement of value is disturbed not by accidents, but by emotion. For the state in which the disturbance of knowledge in incontinence becomes extreme, is as aforesaid, not involuntariness but self-indulgence. Aristotle explains this more in detail in *Eth. Nic.* VII. 4. 1147 a 25: "Again, we may also view the case as follows with reference to the facts of human nature. The one opinion is universal, the other is concerned with the particular facts, and here we come to something within the sphere of perception; when a single opinion results from the two, the soul must in one case affirm the conclusion, while in the case of opinions concerned with

122 *Eth. Nic.* VII. 5. 1147 a 1 ff.
123 *Ibid.* 10 ff.

production, it must immediately act (e.g. if 'every thing sweet ought to be tasted' and 'this is sweet', in the sense of being one of the particular sweet things, the man who can act and is not prevented must at the same time actually act accordingly). When, then, the universal opinion is present in us forbidding us to taste, and there is also the opinion that 'everything sweet is pleasant,' and that 'this is sweet,' (now this is the opinion that is active,) and when appetite happens to be present in us, the one opinion bids us avoid the object, but appetite leads us towards it.''[124]

This statement implies that the conduct of an incontinent man is determined by the maxim of enjoyment, which dominates particular cognition against the advice of practical wisdom. The cause of incontinence is that the particular knowledge of practice is not made actually practical. Hence Aristotle concludes: "Now, the last premise both being an opinion about a perceptible object, and being what determines our actions, this a man either has not when he is in the state of passion, or has it in the sense in which having knowledge did not mean knowing but only talking, as a drunken man may utter the verses of Empedocles.''[125] The opinion about a perceptible object here means, no doubt, the practical reason which apprehends particular facts to be good or bad. Therefore, the above statement would imply that the defect of intuitive reason about the moral significance of an individual act results in the state of incontinence.

If the impotency of rational desire, which results in incontinence, is founded upon a defect in practical syllogism, this kind of syllogism must needs be practical instead of productive, for it is said: "Nothing prevents a clever man from being incontinent.''[126] Since, however, an incontinent man is not unable to distinguish between good and bad, but only unable to realize the good which he wishes, it may appear as if he were lacking in productive or technical knowledge. Yet, ignorance of causality is the cause of involuntariness rather than that of incontinence; the want of such a productive deliberation is ἀτεχνία i.e. lack of art, not incontinence. An incontinent man harms his health not because of his ignorance of medical art, but because of his ignorance of

124 *Eth. Nic.* VII. 5. 1147 a 25 ff.
125 *Eth. Nic.* VII. 5. 1147 a 9 ff. According to Teichmüller (46f.), the knowledge which Walter assumes to be deliberation, viz., the knowledge which is constituted of theoretical premises and results in a categorical imperative, is rather a sophistic syllogism of an incontinent man than practical wisdom or practical syllogism.
126 *Eth. Nic.* VII. 11. 1152 a 10.

practical wisdom; he is indulging in an excessive enjoyment, though he knows generally that excessive enjoyment is harmful. We have explained that what disturbs this particular estimation is an irrational desire or an appetite. How is it then with practical intellect in a continent man? Seeing that continence is the contrary of incontinence, and incontinence results from the lack of particular estimation, a continent man ought to be regarded as performing a complete practical deliberation. But, then, we shall feel a difficulty in distinguishing a continent man from a temperate man. Complete practical deliberation is complete practical wisdom, which however is the complete domination of intellect over desires, the appearance of this dominance in appetites being temperance. Compared with temperance, continence is an inferior virtue, or a character intermediate between virtue and vice. A difference of degree similar to that which is found between the practical cognition of a continent man and that of an incontinent man, is also found between the cognition of a temperate man and that of a continent man. Since practical weakness of an incontinent man is due to the defect of the minor premise, we may suppose that a continent man is able in the same premise. Whereas a continent man is different from a temperate man in that he must suppress his excessive appetite because he is not blessed with a complete harmony of desire and intellect, that is to say, because his intellect is not practical enough, and is apt to fall into incontinence.

So, a continent man and a temperate one have the same kind of practical cognition, the former only being inferior to the latter in that his syllogism is not practical enough on account of poor experience and lack of training. The practical cognition of an incontinent man as well as of a continent man is not heterogeneous with that of a temperate man; it is the same practical wisdom, only differing in its practical power. The essence of practical wisdom may be explained through the character of a practically wise man. Yet this requires some precaution.[127] The complete actuality of practical wisdom is found only in a practically wise man to be sure, but since there is no perfect wise man in reality, there is no complete practical wisdom either. We may admit incomplete practical wisdom as well as complete one. Such an incomplete wisdom is found in a continent man, but in the minimum even in an incontinent man. Now, φρόνησις is related to φρονιμός just as ἐπιστήμη is to ἐπιστημονικός or θεωρία to θεωρητικός. Knowledge or

<hr>

127 Walter, op. cit. 492; Eth. Nic. VII. 11. 1152 a 6.

thinking is not always scientific or theoretical, but may be practical as well, still the corresponding adjective form (ἐπιστημονικός or θεωρητικός) expresses a special attitude of intellect that aims at knowledge or thinking itself as an end or as an ideal; just so, practical wisdom too is not confined to the ideal wise man, but may act in an inferior character to some extent. Temperance is the most complete actuality of practical wisdom concerning nutritive or sexual appetite, but a continent man or even an incontinent man may somehow partake in it, and may advance to temperance through effort and training. A character which is quite unimprovable is self-indulgence, in this character both premises are utterly corrupted, and cannot perform any practical syllogism in the strict sense.[128] But even in this case, there is a kind of practical deliberation, which may be called productive syllogism. A man of such a character does not know whether what he wishes to do is good or bad. His desires are not regulated by intellect at all. Nevertheless he knows the means to realize his desire, and is intellectual as far as he acts according to such a technical deliberation. On such a man Aristotle states that he is a clever man, only his cleverness brings him a great evil.[129]

As aforesaid, temperance and self-indulgence, as well as continence and incontinence are confined in the strict sense to nutritive and sexual appetites, but speaking more generally, one who lacks in the universal knowledge of moral estimation, or who has a bad intention is an evil man or a vicious one. What is called "ignorance in will" or "ignorance of the advantages of life" is such a character. Such a man may be clever,

---

[128] *Eth. Nic.* VII. 9. 1151 a 20–27; 11. 1152 a 4–6.

[129] *Eth. Nic.* VI. 10. 1142 b 20; VII. 11. 1152 a 10. Walsh maintains (154 ff.) that there is a kind of practical syllogism in the case of a self-indulgent man. For such a man has both the major premise and the minor premise, the one saying that "All sweet things are pleasant." the other that "This is a sweet thing." This can be affirmed provided that we allow a wider sense to practical syllogism. This is however not a sound syllogism, but a mere sophistry. As far as it lacks moral oughtness, it cannot be called practical in a positive sense. Aristotle calls such a character τῇ προαίρεσει ἄγνοια i.e. the ignorance in will, implying no doubt, that such a man wills an evil without knowing it to be an evil, though he knows that it is pleasant. It is true that the syllogism in a self-indulgent man, *prima facie*, appears to be practical as against productive. But in reality it is a disguised form of productive syllogism. For it teaches us in the last analysis only how to secure enjoyment. The formula of the sophistical (practical) syllogism is analogous to the productive syllogism to the effect: Light meat is good for health. The meat of birds is light. So the meat of birds is good for health. This conclusion will be activated if there is a desire for health. The δεῖ in the major premise of this pseudo-practical syllogism does not contain moral obligation as Anscombe noticed. (Intention 63 f.)

and knows well in what way he can satisfy his vicious desires. Such a knowledge is surely a kind of practical syllogism, of deliberation or of calculation. Therefore, a vicious man is in a sense possessed of practical knowledge, only he is either quite ignorant of moral value[130] or is confident of false opinion.[131] Whereas an incontinent man has, though incompletely, the right estimation of moral values, and is better than a self-indulgent and vicious man. His practical syllogism is incomplete in the minor premise that denotes the particular estimation, though it contains the major premise or the universal estimation, and retains the knowledge of obligation or "oughtness" to realize virtue in general.[132] This universal oughtness is originally alien to the agent; it is, e.g., an ideal, which was imposed upon him as the advice of old saints. Man ought to regulate his individual conduct through such a universal precept.[133] The precepts and commands that come from outside are accepted gradually till at last they become his constant character and form an ethical virtue. The completion of ethical virtue is at the same time the accomplishment of practical wisdom, i.e. the complete harmony of passion and intellect. The lowest stage of this moral progress is incontinence, next comes continence, and it reaches at last to temperance. This process is congruent with the state of affairs that was observed concerning active reason. According to our previous interpretation, active reason was an objective mind or so-to-say the "culture" that gives form to passive reason and actualizes real cognition. This is equally applicable both to theoretical and to practical intellect. The moral cultivation of man is a formation taking place gradually upon the basis of natural disposition by the implanting of principles which were designed by wise men. The principle of this formation is λόγος or reason, and universal practical knowledge, and this cultivation is performed in terms of natural feelings of pleasure and pain, viz., starting from the good for each man, gradually makes one feel good what is good without qualification for everybody.[134] Moral cultivation lies not in the categorical imperative of reason, but in the harmonization of feeling and reason.[135]

Principle is important both for practical and theoretical reasons, and

---

[130] *Eth. Nic.* III. 2. 1110 b 28–1111 a 1; cf. Loening, *op. cit.* 177, 179, 115.
[131] *Eth. Nic.* VII. 4. 1146 b 22; 11. 1152 a 5.
[132] *Eth. Nic.* VII. 9. 1151 a 20 ff.
[133] Cf. ch. IV. 4, 5.
[134] *Met.* VII. 3. 1029 b 5–7; *Eth. Nic.* V. 2. 1129 b 5.
[135] Cf. Trendelenburg, *Beiträge* III. 209 ff.; *Eth. Nic.* VI. 3. 1139 a 26 ff.; cf. *ch.* III. 2.

if it once be destroyed, the whole of thinking would be done away with. Therefore, a self-indulgent man or a vicious man who is deprived of the highest principle of practical cognition is the worst.[136] Next comes incontinence, which is divided into ἀσθενεία i.e. weakness and προπέτεια i.e. impetuosity.[137] The first is the character which fails after deliberation to stand by the conclusion of one's deliberation owing to his emotion, the other consists in being led by emotion because one has not deliberated.[138] In the former case virtue is defeated by violence, in the latter by the quickness of passion. Of these two characters, weakness is said to be inferior to impetuosity, because it involves the weakness of intellect. One might suppose the contrary to be the case, as there is in impetuosity no room for intellect, but Aristotle rather considered that such a man potentially has intellect and would be able to control his emotion if he recovers his composure, while weakness is beyond remedy.[139] This is the same line of thought as Aristotle depreciated the self-indulgence and vice which are corrupted in the intellectual principle, rather than brutishness, which entirely lacks in intelligence.[140] It was Aristotle's conviction that man is morally improvable as far as he preserves universal knowledge, of practice, the respect to reason and law, the good will and steadfastness.[141]

In short, incontinence, self-indulgence, or vice is a character in which either the minor or the major premise of the practical syllogism is lacking. We may find in the foregoing inquiry of these types of character a key for discriminating the two forms of the practical syllogism, viz. the productive and the practical *par excellence*.

5. The Relation Between Practical Syllogism and Productive Syllogism

We distinguished the practical syllogism from the productive syllogism. The one traces the causal series and searches for the means to

---

[136] *Eth. Nic.* VII. 9. 1151 a 15, 26.

[137] There was in the previous editions a slip of order as to προπέτεια and ἀσθένεια.

[138] *Eth. Nic.* VII. 8. 1150 b 19 ff.

[139] *Eth. Nic.* VII. 9. 1151 a 1–5.

[140] *Eth. Nic.* VII. 7. 1150 a 1–8. The end-congruent functions are unconscious in plants, subconscious or at least not reflective in animals, but reflective-conscious in mankind. So that a man who has lost this directing principle is unable to perform these functions, which are possible for plants and animals. Hence the perversion of reason becomes a positive vice. cf. ch. II. 4.

[141] *Eth. Nic.* VII. 8. 1150 a 19–22; 9. 1150 b 29–35; 1151 a 11–16.

realize an end; this is the function of deliberation that forms an element of προαίρεσις or will, the other is the thinking which makes desire itself rational, the desire thus being made rational is βούλησις or wish. This latter kind of syllogism is concerned with the end rather than the means; it considers about the moral significance of a conduct and estimates a particular act measuring it with moral rules. The productive syllogism consists of hypothetical judgements, or sometimes with one perceptive judgement as the last minor premise, and concludes that particular act should be performed to realize a given end, while in the practical syllogism, the major premise orders moral conduct in general or some kind of virtuous conduct, the minor premise apprehends that a particular conduct bears this moral value;[142] this is the so-called *phronetische Anschauung* or moral perception – and hence it is concluded that a particular act ought to be done. The productive deliberation or syllogism is hypothetical and presupposes some end, the end which is established either by an irrational desire or by a wish, which the latter presupposes another kind of practical syllogism. This has some reference to the theory of two-sided rational potency, which we have studied previously. The potentiality was then divided into the irrational and the rational, the

---

[142] Against our interpretation Walsh points out that the text of Book VII offers no clear examples of a minor premise which is itself moral and not factual (*op. cit.* 109), and Hardie argues that this comment of Walsh's is an underestimation of the difficulty, for the text does offer examples of minor premises which are factual (*op. cit.* 288). We admit Walsh's notice; the examples in Book VII were chosen unhappily from productive syllogism. But there is no reason that the examples of practical syllogism must be sought in Book VII exclusively, when there is undeniable evidence in other parts. It was another unfortunate factor that the example chosen is related to incontinence as to eating. For this is a case where social significance is at the minimum. But if an example were chosen from sexual affairs, the moral character of the minor premise would be unconcealable. The advice of moderate eating might be confused with a medical precept, which is nothing but a productive deliberation, but the advice of moderate sexual life would display a social norm more explicitly. Returning to the example in *Eth. Nic.* VII. 3: "Dry food is healthy. This is dry food. So this is healthy." This is not however an appropriate example of practical syllogism *par excellence*, for without the desire or wish for health this reasoning alone cannot result in an act, whereas it is said that the conclusion of practical syllogism is the act. Hence there must be another syllogism to the effect: "One should wish to be healthy. Dry food is healthy. So, one should wish (take) dry food." With the cooperation of the two syllogisms it will follow: "One should take this food." The practical reason which perceives moral goodness in each class of things, is just the same wisdom which constitutes the minor premise of the second class. Aristotle did not offer a clear-cut formulation of practical syllogism. This is a matter of great regret. But the consequence of his thought is so evident as to make us supply the lacking formula without much hesitation.

one, being one-sided, either realizes itself or not; the other, being two-sided, may produce contrary results. What gives decision to this indefinite potentiality was προαίρεσις or ὄρεξις, i.e., will or desire.[143] We also considered that δύναμις was properly speaking, one-sided power, which inclines so as to break the equilibrium of the opposites, and this analysis was applied both to rational and irrational potencies. It was also presumed that the original dynamism of potency in Aristotle's theory faded away,[144] when Aristotle found the determinant of rational potency outside it, and the dynamic element passed gradually into the concept of ἕξις or habit. But, considering more profoundly, just as matter is relative to form, and what is form to one thing may be matter to another, so there might be a difference of degree in the one-sidedness of potency or potentiality. What is active in one stage might be passive in another. Thus, rational potency would be active and one-sided as far as it is potent, passive and indefinite as far as it is rational. In fact, art is sometimes treated as a mere potency, sometimes as a habit,[145] whereas habit being one-sided, art *qua* habit is inclined to one side. Consequently, even rational potency is not indifferent to opposite actualities, but refers to one *per se* or naturally, to another accidentally,[146] e.g. medical art refers to health naturally and to illness accidentally; grammar is naturally the principle of right speaking, only accidentally that of wrong speaking, this is much more evident with the arts of navigation and building. Yet art cannot act alone, but needs some principle that moves it, it is only an instrument of volition. Hence it is said that medical art is the potency which may both heal and make illness, and it depends upon will or desire to decide which direction it takes. Now, will, being a deliberate desire, consists of deliberation and desire, so that, what determines rational potency in one direction must

[143] *Met.* IX. 2. 1046 b 15–24; 5. 1048 a 10 f.; 8. 1050 b 30.
[144] Cf. ch. I. n. 8.
[145] *Met.* IX. 2. 1046 b 2–4; 3. 1046 b 34–36; cf. *ibid.* 2. 1046 b 4–24; 8. 1050 b 31; *Eth. Nic.* V. 1. 1129 a 12. What is implied in these places under rational potency is art. Art is also treated as something similar to potency, e.g., *Met.* VII. 8. 1033 b 8; VI. 1. 1025 b 22; *Eth. Nic.* VII. 13. 1153 a 25; *Pol.* II. 8. 1268 b 26; VIII. 1. 1337 a 19; *Rhet.* I. 2. 1358 a 6; *Top.* IX. 9. 170 a 36 etc. On the other hand, art is as aforesaid, defined as a productive habit accompanied by true reason. Cf. *Eth. Nic.* VI. 4. 1140 a 7, 10, 22. (*Mag. Mor.* I. 35. 1197 b 22). Similarly with knowledge. ἕξις is not much different from active potency, they are intermediate between possibility and actuality. The development in art is accompanied by the acquisition of habitual potency through the repetition of acts. A mere possibility becomes thereby an acquired habit. Thus, habit mediated between potentiality and actuality, while actuality mediates between potentiality and habit.

be either deliberation or desire. And if deliberation be the searching for the means and constitutes the art, this would lead to a *regressus ad infinitum*. Consequently, either this deliberation is different from art, or else desire, as another constituent of will, must be the determinant. The deliberation which is other than art, is, as aforesaid, the estimative calculation of moral values, and this calculation is adopted in wish, so that the determinant must be, in either case, a kind of desire. Art, being hypothetical, presupposes a desire outside itself, and what makes the productive syllogism categorical is a desire, which is an expression of a habit or a character. Art is, as it were, the passive and material principle, and desire, the active and formal principle of a will. And thus determined, will forms the starting point of production. Compared with the material of production, art is active and is a form, but in relation to a concrete act, it is passive and material. Art commands only in a hypothetical form, and requires desire outside itself. The productive syllogism becomes categorical being determined by a desire; what makes an end good is desire, rather than art. Now, desire may be either rational or irrational; rational desire or wish seeks the good and avoids the evil, and irrational desire or appetite seeks pleasure and avoids pain. Art is in a sense a formal principle of production, but in relation to volition, it is merely matter. There is practical cognition of a higher grade, which conditions this dominating desire. This intellect determines the desire for happiness into the wish for virtuous conduct. This is, of course, not art, but practical wisdom; not the productive thinking, but the practical thinking *par excellence*. It deliberates not about the means for an end, but about the value of a concrete end. Though deliberation or calculation is more frequently used in the productive meaning, it is sometimes applied also to the estimating inference of practice, and what gives determination to a rational potency will be the wish which in its turn is determined by practical cognition. The desire that determines art is not of necessity rational, but may be irrational, i.e. an appetite. Art is employed either by a virtuous or a vicious man. When employed by a good man, it promotes goodness, but employed by a bad man, it aggravates evil. We may perceive here a relation between productive and practical cognition.

Conduct is the realization of desire, which may appear either as instinctive appetite or as wish founded upon deliberation. The former is determined by pleasure and pain which follow sensitive imagination, the latter by moral estimation. This moral estimation, however, forms a kind of practical syllogism, i.e. the syllogism which is practical in the strict sense, and forms the rational principle of desire itself instead of serving desire. Its major premise is the (architectonic) practical wisdom of a wise man that orders virtuous conduct, and the minor premise is the practical intuition that a particular act bears this moral value. Moral estimation is an expression of character, and in order to grasp the objective value, we need an education through practical wisdom. On the other hand, virtuous conducts which are guided by such an excellent education, gradually foster practical wisdom in everybody. The complete harmony of emotion and intellect is just the ideal of morality.

Now the realization of desire requires a right art. Whether rational or irrational, desire requires the deliberation of factual means. Here is the necessity of the productive syllogism. The productive syllogism presupposes an end to serve, and the practical syllogism demands the means to realize the end. Complete conduct is accomplished only through the combination of both kinds of cognition. As Aristotle puts it: *Eth. Nic.* VI. 2. 1139 a 35: "Intellect itself, however, moves nothing, but only the intellect which aims at an end and is practical; for this rules the productive intellect as well, since every one who makes for an end, and that which is made is not an end in the unqualified sense (but only an end in a particular operation) – only that which is done is that; for good action is an end, and desire aims at this."

The first expression of ethical virtue was, as aforesaid, a universal practical judgement, 'The highest good and the ultimate end of human life is happiness.'[147] This is a categorical judgement founded upon ethical virtue, its minor premise being e.g. 'Health is happiness' and the conclusion, 'Health is the end'; or 'You should heal.' This practical syllogism gives an end to medical deliberation and through its conclusion the doctor undertakes healing. What makes his act a production is productive deliberation or the practical syllogism in the secondary sense, while what makes the same act a practice must be rather practical deliberation or the practical syllogism in the primary sense.

[146] *Eth. Eud.* II. 11. 1227 a 25–28; *Pol.* I. 2. 1253 a 31–37.

[147] Hardie maintains (255) that ethical virtue does not entail the presence of practical wisdom in its architectonic form. Hence the idea that the definition of happiness is an ultimate major premiss cannot be what Aristotle has in mind. It is true that ethical virtue is not always accompanied by the definition of happiness. But it is none the less true that ethical virtue presupposes at least implicitly practical wisdom as to what conduces most essentially to happiness.

To explain the matter fully, we may be allowed to devise a formula from Aristotle's thoughts.

Happiness is the highest good.[148]

Virtuous conduct is happiness.[149]

Justice is a virtue.

One ought to do justice.

Justice is the right distribution of wealth, more to a wise man, less to a slave.[150]

A is a wise man, and B is a slave.

One ought to give more wealth to A, and less to B.[151]

This is a practical syllogism in the form of a sorites. In order, then, to make such a distribution without struggle, we should act e.g. through law and authority instead of private discretion,[152] and the ways are such and such.[153] This is the productive syllogism that realizes the conclusion of the practical syllogism. Thus, the practical syllogism produces a wish, which is realized in the will in terms of productive syllogism. Will is the principle of conduct along with other immediate desires, in other words, an act may result either from a will or from an immediate desire. Every instance of conduct which grows from a desire and is accompanied by the consciousness of individual circumstances is voluntary, but the will requires moreover the productive syllogism, without which we cannot act successfully. Every realization of a will is, in effect, a production, but it is a practice as far as it is accompanied by a practical syllogism. In complete intellectual conduct, the practical syllogism is followed by the productive syllogism, and the conclusion of the latter passes into conduct. Practical syllogism alone does not guarantee the possibility of conduct; not every good wish is realized unless it be sustained by a will and a productive syllogism how to produce the end. A man of good wish without productive knowledge is a mere phantastic idealist. If we may say, following Kant, "You can

---

[148] *Eth. Nic.* I. 2. 1095 a 16; 9. 1099 a 24; X. 6. 1176 a 31; b 31; *Eth. Eud.* I. 1. 1214 a 7; 1217 a 40; II. 1. 1219 a 28; *Pol.* VII. 8 . 1328 a 37; 13. 1331 b 39; *Rhet.* I. 6. 1362 b 10.

[149] *Eth. Nic.* I. 6. 1098 a 16; X. 6. 1177 a 10; *Eth. Eud.* II. 1. 1219 a 39; 35; (*Mag. Mor.* II. 7. 1204 a 28); *Pol.* VII. 1. 1323 b 21; 8. 1328 a 37; 13. 1332 a 9; *Poet.* 6. 1450 a 18; *Phys.* II. 6. 197 b 4.

[150] *Eth. Nic.* V. 1. 1129 b 6.

[151] *Eth. Nic.* V. 5. 1130 b 30 ff.; 9. 1134 a 1 ff.

[152] *Pol.* III. 15. 1286 a 9; 16. 1287 a 19, 29; IV. 4. 1292 a 2, 4, 32; 1292 b 6; 6. 1293 a 16, 32; cf. *Eth. Nic.* V. 10. 1134 b 1; X. 10. 1180 a 21; *Pol.* III. 16. 1287 a 32; 15. 1286 a 19.

[153] Cf. *Pol.* III. 9.

do because you ought to do," it is only when we restrict the meaning of "can do" or "ought to do" in a special sense. In their usual meaning, possibility and oughtness are not related to each other in this way. The same thing is predicable of Socrates' identification of knowledge and virtue. Just as Socrates could identify knowledge with virtue as far as he had stolen virtue into knowledge, and knowledge into virtue, so we may identify possibility with oughtness only when we use the words in a particular modified sense.

Needless to say, the productive syllogism alone is not sufficient to produce conduct, for it shows the means, but does not give an end. The imperative of an art is merely hypothetical, and what makes it categorical, i.e. its active and formal principle is desire, and the rationality which rules desire is the deliberation of moral values. These series of mental activities should have their own virtues: the virtue of the practical syllogism is practical wisdom, and that of good wish is the ethical virtues. Similarly, there are two kinds of defect with regard to the practical syllogism; that of the major premise is self-indulgence, or more generally, vice, and that of the minor premise, incontinence or the want of virtue. On the other hand, the virtue of the productive syllogism is cleverness or art (art being a virtue as well as a faculty), the defect of the major premise is ἀτεχνία[154] or the want of art, and that of the last minor premise is involuntariness, which is outside human responsibility. The lack of mere perception is a natural fault and does not constitute responsibility for a moral agent, were it not reduced to a careless way of living, for responsibility should belong to some constant personal being.

The combination of the virtues of productive and practical deliberation is φρόνησις in the most excellent sense, he who is possessed of this virtue is a φρόνιμος or a practically wise man, his wish is good, and his art is right; he can do a great good: Pericles[155] would be an appropriate example of this type. Of course, this is not the highest character, for practice is not the highest of human activities. What is the highest is the philosophical character like Anaxagoras or Thales.[156] The combination of the virtue of productive deliberation and the vice of the practical syllogism is the worst. From the intellectual side, it is πανουργία, and from the emotional side, μοχθηρία[157]; Archibiades might

154 *Eth. Nic.* VII. 4. 1140 a 21.
155 *Eth. Nic.* VII. 5. 1140 b 8.
156 *Eth. Nic.* VII. 7. 1141 b 7. φρονιμός is not distinguished from σοφός and exemplified by Hector. cf. *Eth. Nic.* VII. 1. 1145 a 20.
157 *Eth. Nic.* VII. 1. 1145 a 30.

be an example of it. He who lacks in both virtues is brutal, Palalis[158] being an example, but this is frequent rather in a savage race.[159] It is surely the lowest character from an objective point of view, but less dangerous for social life.[160] There is no name for the character which possesses the virtue of practical deliberation and is lacking in productive deliberation. Such a one is a gentle ordinary person, who has good will and good judgement, but lacks in the ability for great conduct[161]; from the active side, he is a man of good understanding, from the negative side, an incompetent fellow.

6. Comparison with Kant

Let this suffice for the explanation as to Aristotle's idea of practice and of practical intellect. Now, to divide thus the practical syllogism from the productive, making the one categorical, and the other hypothetical might suggest Kant's theory of practical reason. Therefore, it would hardly be a pointless attempt to compare the two theories. It is well known that Kant divided the use of reason into the theoretical and the practical; in the first case, reason becomes the things, and in the second case it determines the will.[162] According to Kant, practical reason orders an act as the means for an end which is aimed at, and this practical order either determines the causality of rational being so as to produce a result, or they determine only the will, regardless whether or not it is sufficient to produce the result. The one is a hypothetical imperative and an advice consisting of mere skill, the other a categorical imperative, and only this latter is a practical law.[163] A hypothetical imperative is necessary only in order to realize a certain desire, but a categorical imperative commands one to will something without presupposing any arbitrary desire. Every practical principle which is determined by the object of desire, being empirical and relative, has no necessity; a universal and necessary law is given only when reason directly gives the law itself, the determinative principle of which is not the object of desire but a pure form.[164]

[158] *Eth. Nic.* VII. 6. 1149 a 14.
[157] *Eth. Nic.* VII. 6. 1149 a 11; I. 1145 a 31.
[160] *Eth. Nic.* VII. 7. 1150 a 1–8.
[161] *Eth. Nic.* VI, 11. 1143 a 21. The ἀτεχνία in *Eth. Nic.* VI. 4. 1140 a 21; or ὀκνήσις in *Eth. Nic.* IV. 9. 1125 a 24 appears to be akin to the character in question, excepting the feeling of self-depreciation.
[162] Kant, *K. d. p. V. Einl. Cass.* V. 16.
[163] *Ibid.* I. l. i. 1. *Erk. Anm. Cass.* V. 22.
[164] *Ibid.* I. 1. i. Kap. 3. *Lehrs.* 2. *Anm.* II. *Cass.* V. 29. Kant regards the pro-

It is evident that the hypothetical imperative corresponds to productive deliberation, and the categorical imperative to practical deliberation. Productive deliberation is applied only by presupposing a desire, while practical deliberation sets up a desire itself. But what is the real meaning of saying that reason gives laws by itself? Is it that the law-giving practical reason orders a particular act without syllogistic deliberation? And does this agree with the view of Aristotle's that makes reason an intellectual intuition? By no means; what Kant's remark really implies is that practical reason commands one to have a desire directly without presupposing another desire; it never prohibits the reason to take a syllogistic form. Moreover, by demanding to investigate whether the contents of a particular will may be confirmed by a universal law, Kant implicitly acknowledged for practical reason to act in the form of inference. He admitted the practical syllogism, the major premise of which being moral principle, the minor premise, the subsumption of a particular act under the moral principle, and the conclusion the determination of a will.[165]

Then, what does it mean that reason produces a desire without presupposing any other desire, and how is it related to Aristotle's theory? This is the case, when a will is determined exclusively by reason as against the case when the rule of reason is employed by a sensitive desire. Similar distinction may be found in Aristotle, viz., productive deliberation searches for the means to realize an end which is established by a desire, so that the application of its advice is ruled by that original desire, which is not of necessity rational. Besides that, Aristotle admitted the case in which desire itself is fundamentally dominated by reason. In such a case, will presupposes a deliberation, which calculates the values of ends or of desires. This is what we called

ductive syllogism in the form of the hypothetical imperative, to be theoretical. He states namely: "*Prinzipien der Selbstliebe können zwar allgemeine Regeln der Geschicklichkeit (Mittel zu Absichten anzufinden) enthalten, alsdann sind es aber bloss theoretische Prinzipien (z.B. wie derjenige, der gerne Brot essen möchte, sich eine Mühle auszudenken habe.)*" Theoretical principle is explained as follows: "*Sätze, welche in der Mathematik oder Naturlehre praktische genannt werden, sollten eigentlich technisch heissen. Denn um die Willensbestimmung ist es diesen Lehren gar nicht zu tun; sie zeigen nur das Mannigfaltige der möglichen Handlung an, welches als alle Sätze, welche die Verknüpfung der Ursache mit einer Wirkung aussagen. Wenn nun die letztere beliebt, der muss auch gefallen lassen, die erstere zu sein.*" This might be the origin of Walter's misinterpretation of the practical syllogism to the effect that the premises being purely theoretical, while the conclusion is made categorical through the act of will or desire that comes from outside the syllogism.

[165] Kant, *K. d. p. V.* I. l. iii. *Kritische Beleuchtung d. An. p. v. V. Cass.* V. 99.

practical deliberation in distinction from productive deliberation. A will, which is thus dependent upon deliberation or syllogism, is neither an immediate sensitive desire, nor a purpose that depends upon such a desire. This desire is itself made rational, though it is not originated from pure reason as in Kant. According to Kant, such a will is by no means empirical or material, whereas Aristotle considered it to be derived from a character which is in the last analysis fostered by experience.[166] There is, however, not such a decisive divergence between the two philosophers as Kant considered. That practical reason determines a will merely through the form of law-giving, means in plain words, that one wills something not because it is pleasant to him, but only because it is good. Whereas according to Kant, what is absolutely good is not a good thing, but a good will, which is nothing else than the will determined by consciousness of duty. But as we have considered before, the consciousness of duty is a mere secondary and subjective appearance of the moral goodness. According to Aristotle, for a thing to be good is not different from its being an object of desire, and the highest good is the object of desire for every one or for an ideal person; man desires it because it is good, and there is no goodness apart from being the object of desire. Though the good is prior to duty, it is nonsense to ask which is prior, good or desire.[167] To wish something on account of its goodness, is the same as having a fundamental desire for it, and the satisfaction of a desire is happiness in a wider sense. Subjectively, one desires something not for the sake of satisfaction or pleasure, but for the sake of its realization.

Since, however, pleasure is the necessary concomitant of satisfaction,[168] every desire may objectively be said to aim at some pleasure, though the end ought not to be taken as a subjective purpose.[169]

As for the sense of duty, it is rather an experience for an inferior character, and is not essential to morality. An ideal character, Aristotle supposes, would rather feel pleasure in the realization of a rational wish. The training of character must be guided by a rational design, but it is

[166] Cf. ch. III. n. 82.
[167] *Eth. Nic.* I. 1. 1094 a 2 f.; 5. 1097 a 18, 20; V. 6. 1131 b 23; (*Mag. Mor.* II. 7. 1205 b 35); *Eth. Eud.* I. 8. 1218 b 6; *Rhet.* I. 6. 1362 a 22; 1363 a 9; 7. 1363 b 13; 1364 b 17, 25; *Pol.* I. 2. 1252 b 34; II. 8. 1269 a 4; III. 12. 1282 b 15; *Met.* I. 3. 983 a 32; 7. 988 b 9; III. 2. 996 a 24; XI. 1. 1050a 36; XII. 10. 1075 a 37; *Top.* III. 1. 116 a 19; *De An.* III. 10. 433 a 27–29; *Pol.* I. 1. 1252 a 3; *Eth. Eud.* VII. 2. 1235 b 26; *Met.* V. 2. 1031 b 26.
[168] *Eth. Nic.* VII. 13. 1153 a 14; 144. 1153 b 9 ff.; X. 5. 1175 b 27; 1175 a 19.
[169] *Eth. Nic.* VII. 14. 1153 b 31 f.; *Rhet.* I. 6. 1362 b 23; *Eth. Nic.* X. 1. 1172 a 20. (*Mag. Mor.* II. 7. 1205 b 36).

not accomplished at once through mere persuasion, rather, it must be fostered gradually, and becomes a semi-instinctive habit.[170]

Further, to Kant, moral law must be applicable to everybody as if it were a natural law. To Aristotle on the contrary, moral principles vary in accordance with the difference of the agents. For neither may everyone act in the same manner, nor ought he to act in the same way. A lord has his own morality and a slave another.[171] One ought not to act as though his own maxim were the universal law; he should rather make it the ideal to know himself, and act in his appropriate manner. There is indeed some ideal type of moral character, and one should endeavour for the harmonious progress of intellect and sensibility aiming at this ideal state.[172] It would contribute nothing to moral improvement to neglect the exercise of sensibility and give a formal law as duty. In order to accept the order or reason and obey it with pleasure, one must exercise his sensibility. The command of reason itself is the expression of the character which is fostered in such a way.

But how far may we follow the correspondence of the practical syllogism with the categorical imperative on the one hand, and the productive syllogism with the hypothetical imperative on the other? To Kant, the categorical imperative was a pure duty free from all attachment, a pure formal law-giving without material determination. To Aristotle on the contrary, the ground of morality was the universal desire for happiness, i.e. the tendency of self-love. Thus, even if the practical syllogism be categorical, it will subordinate to a hypothetical imperative as far as every man desires happiness, since the desire for happiness is a mere fact of human nature, and cannot be ordered as a duty or an ideal. Besides, happiness is, as Aristotle assumed, a formal notion with infinitely various contents, and it is left to everybody in what thing he will find his own happiness. But it does not follow of necessity as Kant considered, that the moral imperative in such a theory would turn to a mere advice for utility. Practice is good because it gives satisfaction to human feelings, but this does not amount to saying that such practice is nothing else than a means to happiness or self-contentment. Means has in itself no value, it is valuable only through the result which it produces, whereas virtuous conduct affords

[170] *Eth. Nic.* I. 2. 1095 b 4; X. 10. 1179 b 24; cf. *Rhet.* II. 12. 1389 a 36; 13. 1390 a 18.

[171] *Pol.* I. 13. 1259 b 21; 1260 a 15, 31, 33; cf. *Pol.* I. 13. 1259 b 33; 1260 a 3; 3; III. 4. 1277 b 19, 27.

[172] Cf. n. 134, 135.

us happiness apart from the result. If one yields a profit through a conduct, that conduct would be a mere means to the profit. But the happiness which accompanies just conduct, is an essential attribute of this conduct rather than its result.[173]

On the contrary, if we refuse, like Kant, any connection between moral law and attachment, we cannot understand how morality may be realized, form an naturally wishes happiness, and without this nature, human conduct would be impossible. If moral rule is nothing but the denial of attachment, how is it possible that man obeys such an unpleasant order? How is it possible that the moral rule becomes a motive of will, and reason becomes practical? There is no other way but to admit it as an inexplicable fact. The fact that the moral law arouses at least a feeling of respect, even Kant could not deny.[174] It was Kant's fundamental mistake that he assumed all material objects of desire to be sensible. Otherwise with Aristotle, who founded his ethical theory upon the human nature that desires happiness.[175] And it is just here that the condition of moral improvement is really found. Just as in the theoretical area we should proceed from what is knowable for us to what is knowable by itself, so in the practical area, we must start from what is good for us and proceed to what is good by itself. This is Aristotle's way of moral elevation:[176] neither to reject nature, nor to fall into it, but to follow and to accomplish it – to establish culture and virtue upon nature, it was just this that was the method of Aristotle.

[173] Cf. ch. III. 3.
[174] Kant, *K. d. p. V.* Cass. V. 128.
[175] Cf. Scherer, *Formalismus 56*; Hartmann, *Ethik* 88 ff.
[176] *Met.* VII. 3. 1029 b 2; *Eth. Nic.* V. 2. 1129 b 5.

GENERAL INDEX

Artist 172, 188
Asceticicism 111
ἀσθένεια weakness 254
Asleep 3, 249, v. sleeping
ἀτεχνία want of art 191, 260
Attribute
 accidenta
Automatic
 agent 186
Averroes 15, 23
Avicenna 14, 22
Awaking 3, 131
Axe 4
Bad v. good
Beautiful 126
Bed 144
Behavior 69
Being 174
 cognition of 175
Belief (πίστις) 175
Bergson 70, 90ff.
Biology, biological 11
 division 8, 74
 evolution 84f.
 teleological 85
Bliss 118
Blood 80f., 209
Bodily element 175
Body 1, 2, 5, 139, 207 v. soul
 the central organ of 80f.
 & desire 125f.
 form of 1, 73, 79, 209
 natural 4
 the substratum of soul 82
 the tool of soul 4
βουλεύσις deliberation 143, 165, 193,
 214ff.
βουλευτική deliberative 143, 183f.
 β, διάνοια 185
 β. ὄρεξις 102, 143
βούλησις wish 7, 215
Boy 53, 171
Brain 56, 16
Brandis 121, 151, 235
Bravery 151, 245
Brazen sphere 9
Brentano 8, 14, 19, 20, 21, 23, 26, 51,
 69, 70, 78
Brutal 254, 261
Calculation λογισμός 102, 197f., 215,
 253
 of moral value 158
 technical 225

Calmness 212
Category 1, 60, 241
 categorical imperative 225, 261,
 264, v. hypothetical
Causality 231
 causal relation 228
Cause 25, 41, 50f., 201, 242f.
 v. end, form
 c. or agent 13
 four causes, material, efficient,
 formal, final 50, 54, 98, 201, 242,
 244
 v. divine reason
 the modern usage of 58
 secondary 19
 c. in the universal 244
Certainty 226
Chance events 214
Change
 changeable phenomena 174
 v. otherwise, contiginent
Character 112, 113, 116, 161, 232, 246
 formation of 161 v. education
 habitual 223
 ideal 263
 rearing of 116
Charity 153
Child 16, 219
Christianity 154, 212
 v. separate, soul
Circumstance 128, 130
Citizen 172
Cleverness δεινότης 217ff., 225, 250,
 252
Clothes 144
Cognition 16, 61, 88, 91, 177 v.
 knowledge
 actual 20
 habitual 148
 intellectual 88
 particular 246
 practical 130, 192, 207, 209, 214ff.,
 240, 245, 248, v. practical wisdom
 productive 216 v. art
 productive c. conj. practical c. 257
 pure 109
 spiritual 16
 theoretical 139, 207, 209
 universal 179f.
 universal c. of practical affairs 212
Cognitive faculties of soul 44, 66, 174,
 186
Colour 13, 17, 27, 51, 54

BIBLIOGRAPHY

* limited to the books actually referred to

Ando, T.; Aristoteles no Sonzairon Tokyo. 1958.
Arnim, H. v.; Das Ethische im Aristotelischen Topik. Vienna 1927.
Baeumker, C.; Das Problem der Materie in der griechischen Philosophie. Münster 1890.
Bergson, H.; L'évolution créatrice. Paris 1926.
Matière et Mémoire. Paris 1929.
Biehl, G.; Aristoteles, De Anima. Leipzig 1884.
Bonitz, H.; Index Aristotelicus. Berlin 1870.
Brandis, C.; Die Entwicklung der griechischen Philosophie und ihrer Nachwirkungen im römischen Reiche. Berlin 1862.
Handbuch der Geschichte der griechisch-römischen Philosophie. Berlin 1857.
Brentano, F.; Aristoteles Lehre vom Ursprung des menschlichen Geistes. Leipzig 1911.
Die Psychologie des Aristoteles insbesondere seine Lehre vom Nous Poietikos. Mayens 1867.
Burnet, J.; Greek Philosophy: Thales to Plato. London 1914.
Bywater, J.; Aristotelis Ethica Nicomachea. Oxford 1890.
Cornford, F. M.; Plato's Cosmology. London 1937.
Corte, M. de; La doctrine de l'intelligence chez Aristote. Paris 1934.
Coulange, F. de; La cité antique. Paris 1890.
Dilthey, W.; Beiträge zur Lösung der Frage vom Ursprung unseres Glaubens an der Realität der Aussenwelt. Ges. Sch. V.
Grant, A.; The Ethics of Aristotle. 4 ed. London 1885.
Grote, G.; Plato and the other Companions of Socrates. 2 ed. London 1885.
Häcker, F.; Das Eintheilungs- und Anordnungsprinzip der moralischen Tugendlehre in der nikomachischen Ethik, Berlin 1863.
Hardie, W. F. R.; Aristotle's Ethical Theory. Oxford 1968.
Hartenstein, G.; Historisch-philosophische Abhandlungen Leipzig 1879.
Über den wissenschaftlichen Wert der aristotelischen Ethik. Berlin Abh. d. Kgl. Sachs. Ges. d. Wiss. Leipzig 1859.
Hartmann, N.; Ethik. Berlin 1935.
Hicks, R. D.; Aristotle, De Anima. Cambridge 1907.
Hildenbrandt, K.; Geschichte und System der Recht- und Staatsphilosophie. Leipzig 1860.
Huzii, Y.; Aristoteles Kenkyu. Tokyo 1940.
Ide, T.; Aristoteles no Rekonron to Nodo Rise. Tetugakuzassi No. 622.
Jaeger, W.; Aristoteles, Grundlegung einer Geschichte seiner Entwicklung. Berlin 1923.

NO

Studien zur Entstehungsgeschichte der Aristotelischen Metaphysilk. Berlin 1931.

Joachim, H. H.; Aristotle, Nicomachean Ethics, Oxford 1951.

Joivet, R.; Essai sur les rapports entre la pensée grecque et la pensée chrétienne. Paris 1931.

Kampe, F.; Erkenntnistheorie des Aristoteles. Leipzig 1870.

Kant, I.; Grundlegung zur Metaphysik der Sitten. (Werke, Hrsg. v. Cassirer IV).
Religion innerhalb der Grenzen der blossen Vernunft (WW. VI).
Metaphysik der Sitten. (WW. VII).
Kritik der reinen Vernunft. (WW. III).
Kritik der praktischen Vernunft. (WW. V).
Kritik der Urteilskraft. (WW. V).

Kastil, Zur Lehre von der Willensfreiheit in der nikomachischen Ethik. Prag 1901.

Loening, R.; Die Zurechnungslehre des Aristoteles. Jena 1903.

Michelet, C.; Aristoteles, Ethica Nicomachea. Berlin 1929–48.

Miki, K.; Gizyutu no Tetugaku. Tokyo.

Newmann, W. L.; The Politics of Aristotle. Oxford 1887–1902.

Nisitani, K.; Aristoteles no Kosoron. Tetugakukenkyu 1935.
Aristoteles Ronko. Tokyo 1948.

Nuyens, F.; L'évolution de la psychologie d'Aristote. Louvain 1948.

Prantl, C.; Über die dianoetischen Tugenden der nikomachischen Ethik des Aristoteles. München 1852.

Rassow, H.; Aristotelische Forschungen (tr. Stewart).

Ravaisson, F.; Essai sur la métaphysique d'Aristote. Paris 1837.

Renan, J. E.; Averroès et l'Averroisme, 1852.

Régis, L.-M.; L'opinion selon Aristote. Paris 1935.

Ritter, H.; Die Geschichte der Philosophie. 1829–53.

Robin, L.; La pensée grecque. Paris 1928.

Ross, W. D.; Aristotelis Metaphysica. Oxford 1924.
Nicomachean Ethics (The Works of Aristotle IX). Oxford 1925.
Aristotle, De Anima. Oxford 1961.

Scheler, M.; Der Formalismus in der Ethik und die materiale Wertethik. 3 ed. Halle 1927.

Siebeck, H.; Geschichte der Psychologie. Gotha 1880–84.

Stewart, J. A.; Notes on the Nicomachean Ethics of Aristotle. Oxford, 1892.

Taylor, A. E.; Plato, the man and his Work. 4 ed. London 1937.
Commentary on Plato's Timaeus. Oxford 1928.

Teichmüller, G.; Neue Studien zur Geschichte der Begriffe. 3. Heft, Die praktische Vernunft bei Aristoteles. Gotha 1879.
Studien zur Geschichte der Begriffe. Berlin 1874.
Aristotelische Forschungen. Halle 1867–73.

St. Thomas Aquinas; Summa Theologiae.
Opuscula XV De unitate intellectus contra Averroes.
In Aristotelis Librum de Anima Commentarium. Turin 1925.

Trendelenburg, A.; Aristotelis De Anima. Berlin 1877.
Historische Beiträge zur Philosophie. Berlin 1877.

Walsh, J. J.; Aristotle's Conception of Moral Weakness. N.Y. & London 1963.

Walter, J.; Die Lehre von der praktischen Vernunft in der griechischen Philosophie. Jena 1874.

Zeller, E.; Die Philosophie der Griechen in ihrer geschichtlichen Entwicklung. 4–6 ed. Berlin 1920–23.